City of Fortune

Roger Crowley read English at Cambridge. He has had a varied career as a teacher and publisher and is the author of three books on the history of the Mediterranean. He lives in Gloucestershire and now writes full time. His website can be found at www.rogercrowley.co.uk.

Praise for *City of Fortune*:

'A fast-flowing history of [Venice's] maritime empire . . . Splendid history . . . Crowley lends his swift narrative an extra gear thanks to well-selected quotations from eyewitness chroniclers.' Boyd Tonkin, *Independent*

'The memory of its power is everywhere palpable in Venice today and thrillingly evoked in its savageries and splendours by Roger Crowley.' Vera Ryan, *Irish Times* Books of the Year

'Crowley is a wonderfully lucid and enchanting writer who shines at siege warfare and combat operations but he is equally skilled in expressing the essence of Venetian economic power.' Christopher Silvester, *Daily Express*

'[Crowley's previous books] were notable for their lucidity and assurance and proved Crowley to be one of the best narrative historians currently writing. *City of Fortune* is of the same standard . . . Crowley's accounts are spare but thrilling.' Michael Prodger, *Financial Times*

'Both readable and informative . . . Compelling reading.' Alex Saril, *Irish Examiner*

'Roger Crowley chronicles the peak of Venice's past glory with Wordsworthian sympathy, supplemented by impressive learning and infectious enthusiasm.' William McNeill, *Wall Street Journal*

'A highly readable account of the city . . . it entertains as much as it informs – ideal holiday reading on a Mediterranean cruise.' John Ure, *Country Life*

'Venice receives a stirring account from British historian Crowley . . . An action-packed political and military history.' *Kirkus Reviews*

'A rousing, traditional account that emphasizes politics, war, and great men.' *Publishers Weekly*

---

by the same author

CONSTANTINOPLE: THE LAST GREAT SIEGE
EMPIRES OF THE SEA

ROGER CROWLEY

CITY OF FORTUNE

*How Venice Won and Lost
a Naval Empire*

N. ERICHSEN

ff

faber and faber

First published in 2011
by Faber and Faber Limited
Bloomsbury House
74–77 Great Russell Street
London WC1B 3DA
This paperback edition published in 2012

Typeset by Faber and Faber Limited
Printed in the UK by CPI Group (UK) Ltd, Croydon, CR0 4YY

A CIP record for this book
is available from the British Library

ISBN 978-0-571-24595-6

4 6 8 10 9 7 5

For Una

'The people of Venice neither have any foothold on the mainland nor can they cultivate the earth. They are compelled to import everything they need by sea. It's through trade that they have accumulated such great wealth.'

LAONICUS CHALCONDYLES, fifteenth-century Byzantine historian

Contents

CONTENTS

List of Illustrations

Illustrations in the plate section are reproduced by kind permission of the following: Roger Crowley (1, 7 and 12), Palazzo Ducale, Venice, Italy/The Bridgeman Art Library (2), Galleria

Maps

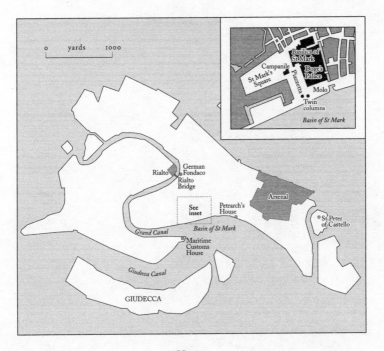

Venice

Italy and the Eastern Mediterranean 1000–1500

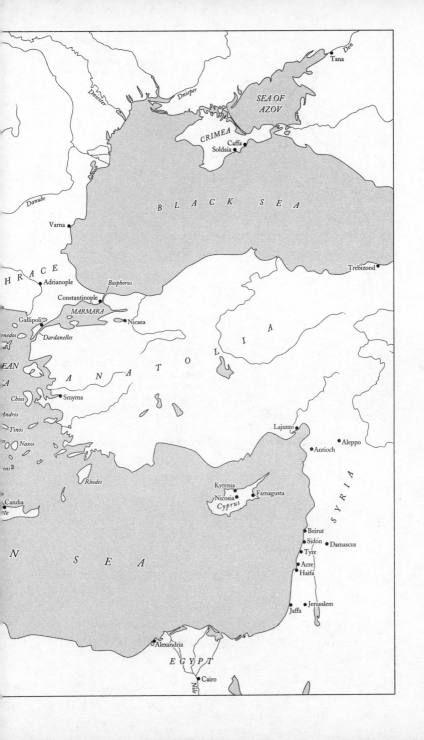

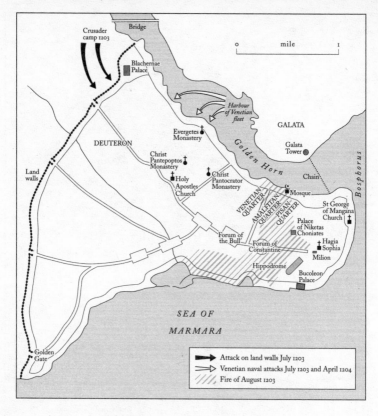

Constantinople during the Fourth Crusade 1203–1204

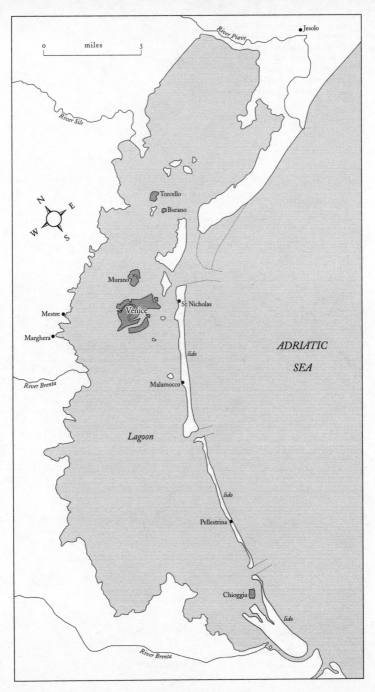

The Venetian Lagoon

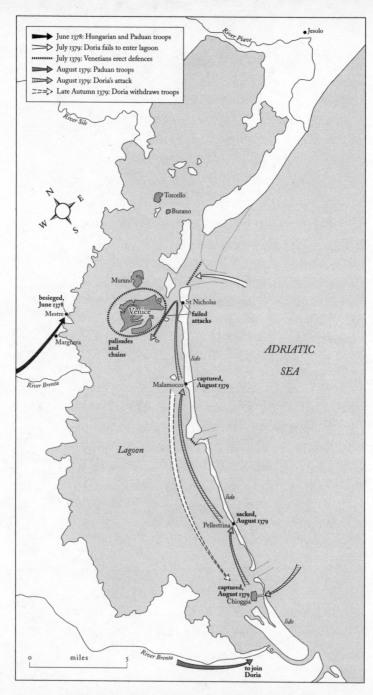

River Piave

Jesolo

River Sile

N
W — E
S

Torcello

Burano

Murano

St Nicholas

**besieged,
June 1378**
Mestre

Venice

**failed
attacks**

Marghera

**palisades
and
chains**

ADRIATIC

SEA

River Brenta

lido

Malamocco

**captured,
August 1379**

Lagoon

lido

**sacked,
August 1379**
Pellestrina

**captured,
August 1379**
Chioggia

lido

0   miles   5

River Brenta

**to join
Doria**

The War of Chioggia June 1378–December 1379

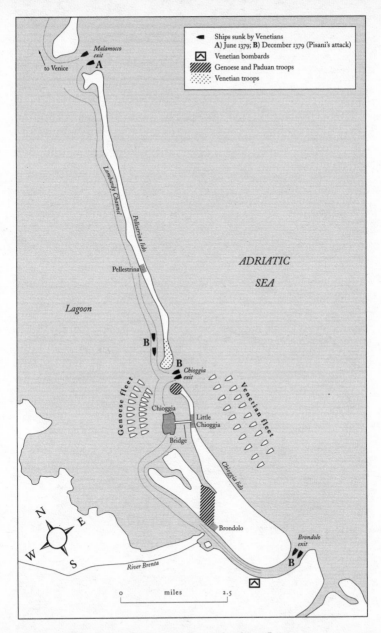

The Siege of Chioggia December 1379–June 1380

Place Names in this Book

I have used a number of place names employed by the Venetians and others during the period covered by this book. This is a list of their modern equivalents:

Acre	Akko (Israel)
Adrianople	Edirne (Turkey)
Brazza	The island of Brač (Croatia)
Butrinto	Butrint (Albania)
Caffa	Feodosiya on the Crimean peninsula (Ukraine)
Candia	Heraklion (Crete). The Venetians also used Candia to refer to the whole island of Crete.
Canea	Chania or Hania (Crete)
Cattaro	Kotor (Montenegro)
Cerigo	The island of Kythira (Greece)
Cerigotto	The island of Antikythira (Greece)
Coron	Koroni (Greece)
Curzola	The island of Korčula (Croatia)
Durazzo	Durrës (Albania)
Jaffa	Now part of Tel Aviv: Tel Aviv-Yafo (Israel)
Lagosta	The island of Lastovo (Croatia)
Lajazzo	Yumurtalık near Adana (Turkey)
Lepanto	Nafpaktos (Greece)
Lesina	The island of Hvar (Croatia)
Modon	Methoni (Greece)
Naplion	Naflio or Navplion (Greece)
Narenta River	Neretva River (Croatia)

Negroponte	The Venetians used this name for both the whole island of Euboea, off the east coast of Greece, and its main town Halkida (or Chalkis)
Nicopolis	Nikopol (Bulgaria)
Ossero	Osor on the island of Cres (Croatia)
Parenzo	Pore (Croatia)
Pola	Pula (Croatia)
Porto Longo	Harbour on the island of Sapienza (Greece)
Ragusa	Dubrovnik (Croatia)
Retimo	Rethimno (Crete)
Rovigno	Rovinj (Croatia)
Salonica	Thessaloniki (Greece)
Santa Maura	The island of Lefkadtha or Lefkas (Greece)
Saray	The now vanished capital of the Golden Horde, on the river Volga, probably at Selitrennoye near Astrakhan (Russia)
Scutari	Shkodër (Albania)
Sebenico	Šibenik (Croatia)
Sidon	Saïda (Lebanon)
Smyrna	Izmir (Turkey)
Soldaia	Sudak on the Crimean Peninsula (Ukraine)
Spalato	Split (Croatia)
Tana	Azov on the sea of Azov (Ukraine)
Tenedos	The island of Bozcaada at the mouth of the Dardanelles (Turkey)
Trau	Trogir (Croatia)
Trebizond	Trabzon (Turkey)
Tripoli	Trablous (Lebanon)
Tyre	Sour (Lebanon)
Zante	The island of Zakynthos (Greece)
Zara	Zadar (Croatia)
Zonchio	Later Navarino, the bay of Pylos (Greece)

Prologue

DEPARTURE

Late in the evening of 9 April 1363, the poet and scholar Francesco Petrarch was writing to a friend. The Venetian Republic had granted the great literary figure of the age an imposing house on the waterfront overlooking the Basin of St Mark, from where he could survey all the rich hubbub of the city's port. Petrarch was drowsing over his letter when he was jolted rudely awake.

It was completely dark. The sky was stormy. I was tired . . . when suddenly the shouting of sailors struck my ears. Remembering the meaning of this from previous occasions, I hurriedly got up and climbed to the top of this house, which surveys the harbour. I looked out. Good God, what a sight! At once touching, marvellous, frightening and exhilarating! Here in the harbour there were some sailing ships which had moored at the marble quayside over the winter, as massive as this great house which the most generous of cities has put at my disposal. Their masts rise as high as its square corner towers. At this very moment, while the stars are muffled by thick cloud, while my walls are shaken by blasts of wind, while the sea roars and bellows horribly, the largest of them casts off on its voyage . . .

If you'd seen this vessel, you would have said it was not a boat but a mountain swimming on the surface of the sea, and so heavily laden with a huge quantity of cargo that the great part of its bulk was hidden beneath the waves. It is setting out for the River Don, for this is as far as our ships can sail on the Black Sea, but many of those on board will disembark and journey on, not stopping until they have crossed the Ganges and the Caucasus to India, then on to farthest China and the eastern Ocean. What is the source of this insatiable thirst for wealth that seizes men's minds? I confess, I was gripped by compassion for these unfortunate men. I understand now why the poets rightly call the sailor's life wretched.

Petrarch the landlubber was awed by the outsized ambition of this enterprise; the humanist poet was disturbed by the fierce materialism that propelled it. For the Venetians themselves such departures were the stuff of daily life. In a city where every man could row, the experience of embarkation – the drift from land to sea – was almost as unconscious as crossing the threshold of your house: a ferry across the Grand Canal, a gondola to Murano or Torcello, a night's crabbing in the eerie reaches of the lagoon, the heady departure of an armed war fleet to the blare of trumpets, the seasonal sailings of the great merchant galleys on the regular run to Alexandria or Beirut – these were deep, cyclical experiences of a whole people. Embarkation was a central metaphor of the city's life, endlessly repeated in art. In St Mark's, a mosaic boat departs with swelling sails to carry the saint's body to Venice; Carpaccio's St Ursula treads a realistic gangplank into a rowing boat while the high-sided merchant ships wait off shore; Canaletto catches Venice setting sail in holiday mood.

Leave-taking was accompanied by elaborate rituals. All seafarers would commit their souls to the Virgin and St Mark. St Nicholas was also a firm favourite and stops would be made at his church on the Lido for a last prayer. Significant enterprises would be prefaced by services, and ships were routinely blessed. Crowds gathered on the waterfront, then the ropes were cast off. For Felix Fabri, a pilgrim on his way to the Holy Land in the fifteenth century, it happened 'just before dinner time; all the pilgrims aboard, and the wind fair, the three sails were spread to the sound of trumpets and horns and we sailed out to the open sea'. Once through the barrier of the sheltering sand bars of the lagoon islands, the *lidi*, ships passed into the open sea and another world.

*

Departure. Risk. Profit. Glory. These were the compass points of Venetian life. Voyaging was a repeated experience. For nearly a thousand years they knew no other. The sea was at once their protection, their opportunity and their fate; secure in their shallow lagoon with its deceptive channels and treacherous mud flats that no invader could penetrate, shielded if not insulated from the surge of the Adriatic, they wrapped the sea around them like a cloak. They changed its gender from the masculine, *mare*, to the feminine *mar* in the Venetian dialect and every year on Ascension Day they married it. This was an act of appropriation – the bride and all her dowry became property of the husband – but it was also one of propitiation. The sea was danger and uncertainty. It could and did smash ships, hasten enemies and periodically threaten to overwhelm the defences of their low-lying city. The voyage could be terminated by an arrow shot or a rising sea or disease; death came in a shroud weighted with stones and dropped into the lower depths. The maritime relationship would be long, intense and ambivalent; not until the fifteenth century did the Venetians seriously question whether the marriage should be with land rather than water and during this time they moved up the gradient from eel trappers, saltpanners and bargemen on the slow inland rivers of north Italy, to merchant princes and coiners of gold. The sea brought the fragile city, existing like a mirage on its tenuous oak pilings, riches beyond measure and a maritime empire as splendid as any. In the process Venice shaped the world.

This book is the story of the rise of that empire, the Stato da Mar they called it in dialect, and the commercial wealth it created. The crusades provided the Republic with its chance to ascend the world stage. The Venetians took the opportunity with both hands and profited hugely. Over five hundred years they became masters of the eastern Mediterranean and nicknamed their city La Dominante; when the sea turned against them, they mounted an exhaustive rearguard action and fought to the last breath. The empire that they constructed was already well advanced by the time Petrarch looked from his window. It was a curious, cobbled-together affair, a collection of islands, ports and strategic bastions, designed solely to harbour its ships and channel goods back to the mother city. Its construction was a story of courage and duplicity, luck, persistence, opportunism and periodic catastrophe.

Above all it is a saga about trade. Alone in all the world, Venice was organised to buy and sell. The Venetians were merchants to their fingertips; they calculated risk, return and profit with scientific precision. The red-and-gold lion banner of St Mark fluttered from mastheads like a corporate logo. Trade was their creation myth and their justification, for which they were frequently reviled by more terrestrial neighbours. There exists no more explicit description of the city's *raison d'être* and its anxieties than the appeal it made to the pope in 1343 for permission to trade with the Muslim world:

Since by the Grace of God our city has grown and increased by the labours of merchants creating traffic and profits for us in diverse parts of the world by land and sea and this is our life and that of our sons, because we cannot live otherwise and know not how except by trade, therefore we must be vigilant in all our thoughts and endeavours, as our predecessors were, to make provision in every way lest so much wealth and treasure should disappear.

Its gloomy conclusion echoes a manic-depressive streak in the Venetian soul. The city's prosperity rested on nothing tangible – no land holdings, no natural resources, no agricultural production or large population. There was literally no solid ground underfoot. Physical survival depended on a fragile ecological balance. Venice was perhaps the first virtual economy, whose vitality baffled outsiders. It harvested nothing but barren gold and lived in perpetual fear that if its trade routes were severed, the whole magnificent edifice might simply collapse.

There is a moment when the departing vessels shrink to vanishing point, and the watchers on the quay turn back to normal life.

Sailors resume their tasks; stevedores heft bales and roll barrels; gondoliers paddle on; priests hurry to the next service; black-robed senators return to the weighty cares of state; the cutpurse makes off with his takings. And the ships surge out into the Adriatic.

Petrarch watched until he could see no more. 'When my eyes could no longer follow the ships through the darkness, I picked up my pen again, shaken and deeply moved.'

It had been arrival however, rather than departure, which launched the Stato da Mar. A hundred and sixty years earlier, in Lent 1201, six French knights were rowed across the lagoon to Venice. They had come about a crusade.

PART I

OPPORTUNITY: MERCHANT CRUSADERS

1000–1204

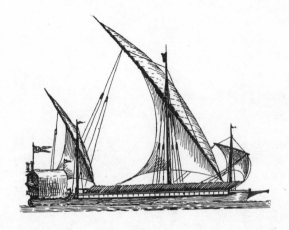

I

Lords of Dalmatia

———— ⌒⌒⌒ ————

1000–1198

The Adriatic Sea is the liquid reflection of Italy, a tapering channel some 480 miles long and a hundred wide, pinched tighter at its southern point where it flows into the Ionian past the island of Corfu. At its most northern point, in the enormous curved bay called the Gulf of Venice, the water is a curious blue-green. Here the River Po churns out tons of alluvial material from the distant Alps, which settle to form haunting stretches of lagoon and marsh. So great is the volume of these glacial deposits that the Po Delta is advancing fifteen feet a year and the ancient port of Adria, after which the sea is named, now lies fourteen miles inland.

Geology has made its two coasts quite distinct. The western, Italian shore is a curved, low-lying beach, which provides poor harbours but ideal landing spots for would-be invaders. Sail due east and your vessel will snub against limestone. The shores of Dalmatia and Albania are a four-hundred-mile stretch as the crow flies, but so deeply crenellated with sheltering coves, indents, off-shore islands, reefs and shoals that they comprise two thousand miles of intricate coast. Here are the sea's natural anchorages, which may shelter a whole fleet or conceal an ambush. Behind, sometimes stepped back by coastal plain, sometimes hard down on the sea, stand the abrupt white limestone mountains that barricade the sea from the upland Balkans. The Adriatic is the frontier between two worlds.

For thousands of years – from the early Bronze Age until well after the Portuguese rounded Africa – this fault line was a marine highway linking central Europe with the eastern Mediterranean, and a portal for world trade. Ships passed up and down the sheltering Dalmatian shore with the goods of Arabia, Germany, Italy, the Black Sea, India and the furthest East. Over the centuries they carried Baltic amber to the burial chamber of Tutankhamun; blue faience beads from Mycenae to Stonehenge; Cornish tin to the smelters of the Levant; the spices of Malacca to the courts of France; Cotswold wool to the merchants of Cairo. Timber, slaves, cotton, copper, weapons, seeds, stories, inventions and ideas sailed up and down these coasts. 'It is astonishing', wrote a thirteenth-century Arab traveller about the cities of the Rhine, 'that although this place is in the far west, there are spices there which are to be found only in the Far East – pepper, ginger, cloves, spikenard, costus and galanga, all in enormous quantities.' They came up the Adriatic. This was the point where hundreds of arterial routes converged. From Britain and the North Sea, down the River Rhine, along beaten tracks through the Teutonic forests, across Alpine passes, mule trains threaded their way to the top of the gulf, where the merchandise of the East also landed. Here goods were transshipped and ports flourished. First Greek Adria, then Roman Aquileia, finally Venice. In the Adriatic site is everything: Adria silted up; Aquileia, on the coastal plain, was flattened by Attila the Hun in 452; Venice prospered in the aftermath because it was unreachable. Its smattering of low-lying muddy islets set in a malarial lagoon was separated from the mainland by a few precious miles of shallow water. This unpromising place would become the entrepôt and interpreter of worlds, the Adriatic its passport.

From the start the Venetians were different. The first, rather idyllic snapshot we have of them, from the Byzantine legate Cassiodorus in 523, suggests a unique way of life, independent and democratic:

You possess many vessels . . . [and] . . . you live like seabirds, with your homes dispersed . . . across the surface of the water. The solidity of the earth on which they rest is secured only by osier and wattle; yet you do not hesitate to oppose so frail a bulwark to the wildness of the sea. Your people have one great wealth – the fish which suffices for them all. Among you there is no difference between rich and poor; your food is the same, your houses are alike. Envy, which rules the rest of the world, is unknown to you. All your energies are spent on your salt-fields; in them indeed lies your prosperity, and your power to purchase those things which you have not. For though there may be men who have little need of gold, yet none live who desire not salt.

The Venetians were already carriers and suppliers of other men's needs. Theirs was a city grown hydroponically, conjured out of marsh, existing perilously on oak palings sunk in mud. It was fragile to the sea's whim, impermanent. Beyond the mullet and eels of the lagoon, and its saltpans, it produced nothing – no wheat, no timber, little meat. It was terribly vulnerable to famine; its sole skills were navigation and the carrying of goods. The quality of its ships was critical.

Before Venice became the wonder of the world, it was a curiosity; its social structure enigmatic and its strategies distrusted. Without land there could be no feudal system, no clear division between knight and serf. Without agriculture, money was its barter. Their nobles would be merchant princes who could command a fleet and calculate profit to the nearest *grosso*. The difficulties of life bound all its people together in an act of patriotic solidarity that required self-discipline and a measure of equality – like the crew of a ship all subject to the perils of the deep.

Geographical position, livelihood, political institutions and religious affiliations marked Venice out. It lived between two worlds: the land and the sea, the east and the west, yet belonging to neither. It grew up a subject of the Greek-speaking emperors in Constantinople and drew its art, its ceremonial and its trade from the Byzantine world. Yet the Venetians were also Latin Catholics, nominal subjects to the pope, Byzantium's anti-Christ. Between such opposing forces they struggled to maintain a particular free-dom. The Venetians repeatedly defied the pope, who responded by excommunicating the whole city. They resisted tyrannous solutions to government and constructed for themselves a republic, led by a doge, whom they shackled with so many restraints that he could receive no gift from foreigners more substantial than a pot of herbs. They were intolerant of over-ambitious nobles and defeated admirals, whom they exiled or executed, and devised a voting system to check corruption as labyrinthine as the shifting channels of their lagoon.

The tenor of their relations with the wider world was set early. The city wished to trade wherever profit was to be made without favour or fear. This was their rationale and their creed and they pleaded it as a special case. It earned them widespread distrust. 'They said many things to excuse themselves . . . which I do not recollect,' spat a fourteenth-century churchman after watching the Republic wriggle free of yet another treaty (though he could undoubtedly remember the details painfully well), 'excepting that they are a quintessence and will belong neither to the Church nor to the emperor, nor to the sea nor to the land.' They were in trouble with both Byzantine emperors and popes as early as the ninth century for selling war materials to Muslim Egypt, and whilst purportedly complying with a trade ban with Islam around 828, they managed to spirit away the body of St Mark from Alex-andria under the noses of Muslim customs officials, hidden in a barrel of pork. Their standard let-out was commercial necessity: 'because we cannot live otherwise and know not how except by trade'. Alone in all the world, Venice was organised for economic ends.

By the tenth century they were selling oriental goods of extraor-dinary rarity at the important fairs at Pavia on the River Po: Rus-sian ermine, purple cloth from Syria, silk from Constantinople. One monkish chronicler had seen the emperor Charlemagne looking drab beside his retinue in oriental cloth bought there from Venetian merchants. (Particularly singled out for clerical tut-tutting was a multicoloured fabric interwoven with the figures of birds – evidently an item of outrageous foreign luxury.) To the Muslims they traded back timber and slaves, literally Slavs until that people became Christians. Venice was by now well placed at the head of the Adriatic to become the pivot of trade, and on the round turning of the millennium, Ascension Day in the year 1000, Doge Pietro Orseolo II, a man who 'excelled almost all the ancient doges in knowledge of mankind', set sail on an expedition that would launch the Republic's ascent to wealth, power and maritime glory.

On the threshold of the new era the city stood finely poised between danger and opportunity. Venice was not yet the compact mirage of dazzling stone that it would later become, though its population was already substantial. No splendid palazzi flanked the great S-bend of the Grand Canal. The city of wonder, flamboyance and sin, of carnival masks and public spectacle lay centuries ahead. Instead low wooden houses, wharves and warehouses fronted the water. Venice comprised less a unity than a succession of separate islets with patches of undrained marsh and open spaces among the parish settlements, where people grew vegetables, kept pigs and cows and tended vines. The Church of St Mark, a plain predecessor of the extraordinary basilica, had recently been badly burned and patched up after political turmoil that left a doge dead in its porch; the square in front of it was beaten earth, divided by a canal and partially given over to orchard. Sea-going vessels that had sailed to Syria and Egypt crowded the commercial heart of the city, the Rivo Alto – the Rialto. Everywhere masts and spars protruded above the buildings.

It was the genius of Orseolo to fully understand that Venice's growth, perhaps its very survival, lay far beyond the waters of the lagoon. He had already obtained favourable trading agreements with Constantinople, and, to the disgust of militant Christendom, he despatched ambassadors to the four corners of the Mediterranean to strike similar agreements with the Islamic world. The future for Venice lay in Alexandria, Syria, Constantinople and the Barbary coast of North Africa, where wealthier, more advanced societies promised spices, silk, cotton and glass – luxurious commodities that the city was ideally placed to sell on into northern Italy and central Europe. The problem for Venetian sailors was that the voyage down the Adriatic was terribly unsafe. The city's home waters, the Gulf of Venice, lay within its power, but the central Adriatic was a risky no-man's-land, patrolled by Croat pirates. Since the eighth century these Slav settlers from the upper Balkans had established themselves on its eastern Dalmatian shores. This was a terrain made for maritime robbery. From island lairs and coastal creeks, the shallow-draughted Croat ships could dart out and snatch merchant traffic passing down the strait.

Venice had been conducting a running fight with these pirates for 150 years. The contest had yielded little but defeat and humiliation. One doge had been killed leading a punitive expedition; thereafter the Venetians had opted to pay craven tribute for free passage to the open seas. The Croats were now seeking to extend their influence to the old Roman towns further up the coast. Orseolo brought to this problem a clear strategic vision that would form the cornerstone of Venetian policy for all the centuries that the Republic lived. The Adriatic must provide free passage for Venetian ships, otherwise they would be forever bottled up. The doge ordered that there would be no more tribute and prepared a substantial fleet to command obedience.

Orseolo's departure was marked by one of those prescient ceremonies that became a defining marker of Venetian history. A large crowd assembled for a ritual mass at the Church of St Peter of Castello, near the site of the present arsenal. The bishop presented the doge with a triumphal banner, which perhaps depicted for the first time St Mark's lion, gold and rampant on a red background, crowned and winged, with the open gospel between his paws declaring peace but ready for war. The doge and his force then stepped aboard, and with the west wind billowing in their sails, surged out of the lagoon into the boisterous Adriatic. Stopping only to receive further blessing from the bishop of Grado they set sail for the peninsula of Istria on the eastern tip of the Adriatic.

Orseolo's campaign could almost serve as the template for subsequent Venetian policy: a mixture of shrewd diplomacy and the precise application of force. As the fleet worked its way down the small coastal cities – from Parenzo to Pola, Ossero to Zara – the citizens and bishops came out to demonstrate their loyalty to the doge and to bless him with their relics. Those who wavered, weighing Venice against the counter threat of the Slavs, were more readily convinced by the visible show of force. The Croats saw what was coming and tried to buy him off. Orseolo was not to be turned, though his task was made harder by the coastal terrain. The pirates' stronghold was well protected, hidden up the marshy delta of the Narenta River and beyond the reach of any strike force. It was shielded by the three barrier islands of Lesina, Curzola and Lagosta, whose rocky fortresses presented a tough obstacle.

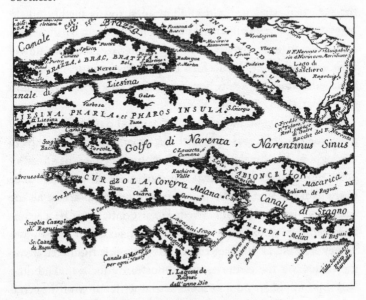

The Narenta River and its barrier islands

Relying on local intelligence, the Venetians ambushed a ship-load of Narentine nobles returning from trade on the Italian shore and used them to force submission from the Croats at the mouth of the delta. They swore to forgo the annual tribute and harassment of the Republic's ships. Only the offshore islands held out. The Venetians isolated them one by one and dropped anchor in their harbours. Curzola was stormed. Lagosta, 'by whose violence the Venetians who sailed through the seas were very often robbed of their goods and sent naked away', offered more stubborn resistance. The inhabitants believed their rocky citadel to be impregnable. The Venetians unleashed a furious assault on it from below; when that failed, a detachment made their way up by a steep path behind the citadel and captured the towers that contained the fort's water supply. The defence collapsed. The people were led away in chains and their pirates' nest demolished.

With this *force de frappe*, Orseolo put down a clear marker of Venetian intentions, and in case any of the subject cities had forgotten their recent vows, he retraced his footsteps, calling at their startled ports in a repeat show of strength, parading hostages and captured banners. 'Thence, passing again by the aforesaid town, making his way back to Venice, he at length returned with great triumph.' Henceforward, the doge and his successors awarded themselves a new honorific title – Dux Dalmatiae – lord of Dalmatia.

If there is a single moment that marked the start of the rise to maritime empire it was now, with the doge's triumphal return to the lagoon. The breaking of the Narentine pirates was an act of great significance. It signalled the start of Venetian dominance of the Adriatic and its maintenance became an axiom for all the centuries that the Republic lived. The Adriatic must be a Venetian sea; *nostra chaxa*, they would say in dialect, 'our house', and its key was the Dalmatian coast. This was never quite straightforward. Over the centuries and almost until its last breath, the Republic would spend enormous resources fending off imperial interlopers, cuffing pirates and quelling troublesome vassals. The

Dalmatian cities – particularly Zara – struggled repeatedly to assert their independence but only Ragusa (Dubrovnik) ever managed it. Henceforward there was no rival naval power to match Venice in the heart of the sea. The Adriatic would fall under the political and economic shadow of an increasingly ravenous city, whose population would reach eighty thousand within a century. In time the limestone coast became the granary and vineyard of Venice; Istrian marble would front the Renaissance palaces on the Grand Canal; Dalmatian pine would plank their galleys and its seamen would sail them out of Venetian naval bases on the eastern shore. The crenellated limestone coast came to be seen almost as an extension of the lagoon.

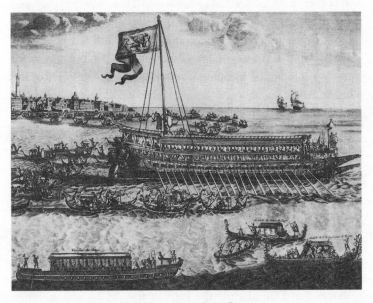

The *Bucintoro* and the Sensa

The Republic, with a Byzantine talent for transforming significant victories into patriotic ceremonies, henceforth performed an annual celebration of Orseolo's triumph. Every Ascension Day, the people of Venice participated in a ritual voyage to the mouth of the lagoon. At the start it was a relatively plain affair. The clergy, dressed in their copes and ceremonial robes, climbed aboard a barge decked with golden cloth and sailed out to the *lidi*, the long line of sand bars that protects Venice from the Adriatic. They took a jar of holy water, salt and olive branches out to where the lagoon opens to the sea at the Lido of St Nicholas, the patron saint of sailors, and waited there, at the meeting of the two waters, for the doge to arrive in the ceremonial galley the Venetians called the *Bucintoro*, the Golden Boat. Rocking on the waves, the priests proclaimed a short and heartfelt prayer: 'Grant, O Lord, that the sea is always calm and quiet for us and all who sail on it.' And then they approached the *Bucintoro* and sprinkled water over the doge and his followers with the olive branches and poured the remainder into the sea.

In time the Ascension Day ceremony, the Sensa, would become greatly elaborated, but in the early years of the millennium it was a simple act of blessing, a propitiation against storms and pirates, based on seasonal sailing rituals as ancient as Neptune and Poseidon. The miniature voyage enacted the whole meaning of Venice. Within the lagoon lay safety, security and peace; in its treacherous labyrinth of shallow channels all would-be attackers floundered and sank. Beyond lay opportunity but also danger. The *lidi* were the frontier between two worlds, the known and the unknown, the world that was safe and the one that was dangerous; in their founding myth St Mark was surprised by a squall and only found peace within the lagoon, but the voyage beyond was not optional. For the Venetians the sea was life and death and the Sensa acknowledged the pact.

Ascension Day marked the start of the sailing season, when sailors could be hopeful of a calm voyage. Yet the waters of the Adriatic were notoriously fickle at any time of year. They could be smooth as silk, or whipped into choppy fury by the *bora*, the north wind. The Romans, no great sailors, were frightened of it; the Adriatic nearly drowned Julius Caesar, and the poet Horace thought there was nothing to equal the terror of the waves dash-

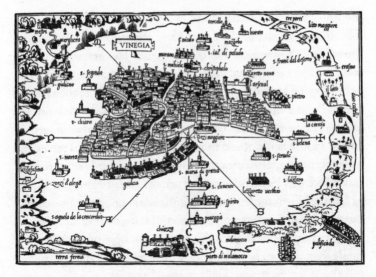

Venice sheltered by its *lidi*

ing the cliffs of southern Albania. Oared galleys could be quickly swamped by a mounting sea; sailing ships running before the wind had little room for manoeuvre in the narrow straits. There is no more vivid historical account of the sea's ferocity than the fate of a Norman fleet crossing to Albania in the early summer of 1081:

There was a heavy fall of snow and winds blowing furiously from the mountains lashed up the sea. There was a howling noise as the waves built up; oars snapped off as the rowers plunged them into the water, the sails were torn to shreds by the blasts, yard-arms were crushed and fell on the decks; and now ships were being swallowed up, crew and all . . . some of the ships sank and their crews drowned with them, others were dashed against the headlands and broke up . . . many corpses were thrown up by the waves.

The sea was tumultuous, dangerous, pirate-infested. The Venetians fought unceasingly to keep their seaway to the world open.

Even the *lidi* were no certain guarantee. Because the Adriatic is a cul-de-sac, it feels the moon's tug with a special force, and when the phases are right and the sirocco, the wind from Africa, pushes the water up the Venetian Gulf and the opposing *bora*, hard off the Hungarian steppes, holds it back, the lagoon itself is under threat. In folk memory, the events of late January 1106 emphasised the force of the sea. People remembered that the sirocco had been blowing up from the south with unusual force; the weather became unnervingly sultry, day after day sucking the energy out of men and beasts. There were unmistakable signs of approaching storm. House walls oozed moisture; the sea started to groan and gave off the strange neutral smell of electricity; birds skittered and squawked; eels leaped clear of the water as if trying to flee. When at last the storm broke, shattering thunder shook the houses and torrential rain hammered the lagoon. The sea rose up from its depths, overwhelmed the *lidi*, poured through the openings of the lagoon and swamped the city. It demolished houses, ruined merchandise, destroyed food stocks, drowned animals, strewed the small fields with sterile salt. An entire island, the ancient town of Malamocco, vanished, leaving ghostly foundations visible through the murky water at low tide. Hard on its heels came devastating fires that ripped through the wooden settlements, leaping the Grand Canal, incinerating twenty-four churches and gutting a major part of the city. 'Venice was rocked to its very core,' wrote the chronicler Andrea Dandolo. Venice's hold on the material world was fragile; it lived with impermanence. It was against such forces that people felt their vulnerability and made sacrificial offerings.

The doges' assumption of their new title, Dux Dalmatiae, marked a moment of unparalleled change in the sea power of the eastern Mediterranean. For four hundred years the Adriatic itself had been ruled from Rome; for another six hundred the sea, and Venice itself, had been subject to its Greek-speaking successor, the Byzantine emperors in Constantinople. By the year 1000, this power was starting to wane and the Venetians were engaged in a stealthy act of substitution. In the small stone cathedrals of Zara, Spalato, Istria and Trau, the Venetian doge was remembered in prayers only after the name of the emperor in Constantinople, but it was purely a ritual formula. The emperor was far away, his power no longer stretched much north of Corfu, at the gates of the Adriatic, and along the Italian shore. The lords of Dalmatia were in all fact the Venetians. The power vacuum created by weakening Byzantine control would allow Venice to move up the scale progressively from subjects, to equal partners and finally, in tragic circumstances, to usurpers of the Byzantine sea. The lords of the Dalmatian coast were embarked on the ascent.

The relationship between Byzantium and Venice was one of intense complexity and longevity, chafed by mutually contradictory views of the world and subject to wild mood swings, yet Venice always looked to Constantinople. This was the great city of the world, the gateway to the east. Through its warehouses on the Golden Horn flowed the wealth of the wider world: Russian furs, wax, slaves and caviar, spices from India and China, ivory, silk, precious stones and gold. Out of these materials, Byzantine craftsmen fashioned extraordinary objects, both sacred and profane – reliquaries, mosaics, chalices chased with emeralds, costumes of shot silk – that formed the taste of Venice. The astonishing basilica of St Mark, reconsecrated in 1094, was designed by Greek architects on the pattern of the mother church of the Holy Apostles in Constantinople; its artisans recounted the story of St Mark, stone by stone, in imitation of the mosaic styles of St Sophia; its goldsmiths and enamellers created the Pala d'Oro, the golden altarpiece, a miraculous expression of Byzantine devotion and art. The whiff of spices on the quays of Venice had been carried a thousand miles from the go-downs of the Golden Horn. Constantinople was Venice's souk, where its merchants gathered to make (and lose) fortunes. As loyal subjects of the emperor, the right to trade in his lands was always their most precious possession. He, in turn, used it as the bargaining chip to rein in his uppity vassals. In 991 Orseolo gained valuable trading rights for Venetian support in the Adriatic; twenty-five years later they were tetchily withdrawn again in a spat.

Differing attitudes to commerce marked a sharp dividing line. From early on the amoral trading mentality of the Venetians – the assumed right to buy and sell anything to anyone – shocked the pious Byzantines. Around 820 the emperor complained bitterly about Venetian cargoes of war materials – timber, metal and slaves – to his enemy, the sultan in Cairo. But in the last quarter of the eleventh century the Byzantine Empire, such a durable presence in the Mediterranean basin, started to decline, and the balance of power began tilting in Venice's favour. In the 1080s the Venetians defended the empire in the Adriatic against powerful Norman war bands, intent on taking Constantinople itself. Their reward was sumptuous. With all the imperial pomp of Byzantine ritual, the emperor affixed his golden seal (the *bulla*) to a document that would change the sea for ever. He granted the city's merchants the rights to trade freely, exempt from tax, throughout his realms. A large number of cities and ports were specified by name: Athens and Salonica, Thebes and Antioch and Ephesus, the islands of Chios and Euboea, key harbours along the coasts of southern Greece such as Modon and Coron – invaluable staging posts for Venetian galleys – but above all Constantinople itself.

Here Venice was given a prize site down by the Golden Horn. It included three quays, a church and bakery, shops and warehouses for storing goods. Though nominal subjects of the emperor, the Venetians had effectively acquired their own colony, with all the necessary infrastructure, in the heart of the richest city on earth under extremely favourable conditions. Only the Black Sea, Constantinople's grain basket, was barred to the avid traders. Quietly echoing among the solemn, convoluted lines of the Byzantine decree was the sweetest Greek word a Venetian might ever want to hear: monopoly. Venice's jostling rivals in maritime trade – Genoa, Pisa and Amalfi – were now put at such disadvantage that their presence in the city was almost futile.

The Golden Bull of 1082 was the golden key that opened up the treasure house of eastern trade for Venice. Its merchants flocked to Constantinople. Others started to permeate the small ports and harbours of the eastern seaboard. By the second half of the twelfth century Venetian merchants were visible everywhere in the eastern Mediterranean. Their colony in Constantinople grew to around twelve thousand and, decade by decade, the trade of Byzantium imperceptibly passed into their hands. They not only funnelled goods back to an avid market in continental Europe, they acted as intermediaries, restlessly shuttling back and forward across the ports of the Levant, buying and selling. Their ships triangulated the eastern seas, shipping olive oil from Greece to Constantinople, buying linen in Alexandria and selling it to the crusader states via Acre; touching Crete and Cyprus, Smyrna and Salonica. At the mouth of the Nile in the ancient city of Alexandria they bought spices in exchange for slaves, endeavouring at the same time to perform a nimble balancing act between the Byzantines and the crusaders on one hand and their enemy, the Fatimid dynasty in Egypt, on the other. With each passing decade Venice was sinking its tentacles deeper into the trading posts of the East; its wealth saw the rise of a new class of rich merchants. Many of the great families of Venetian history began their ascent to prominence during the boom years of the century. It heralded the start of commercial dominance.

With this wealth came arrogance – and resentment. 'They came', said a Byzantine chronicler, 'in swarms and tribes, exchanging their city for Constantinople, whence they spread out across the empire.' The tone of these remarks speaks a familiar language of xenophobia and economic fear of the immigrant. The upstart Italians, with their hats and their beardless faces, stood out sharply, both in manner and appearance, in the city streets. The charges levelled against them were many: they acted like citizens of a foreign power rather than loyal subjects of the empire; they were fanning out from their allotted quarter and were buying properties across the city; they cohabited with or married Greek women and led them away from the Orthodox faith; they stole the relics of saints; they were wealthy, arrogant, unruly, boorish, out of control. 'Morally dissolute, vulgar . . . untrustworthy, with all the gross characteristics of seafaring people', spluttered another Byzantine writer. A bishop of Salonica called them 'marsh frogs'. The Venetians were becoming increasingly unpopular in the Byzantine Empire and they seemed to be everywhere.

In the larger geopolitics of the twelfth century, the relationship between the Byzantines and their errant subjects was marked by ever more violent oscillations between the poles of love and hate: the Venetians were insufferable but indispensable. The Byzantines, who complacently still saw themselves as the centre of the world, and for whom land ownership was more glorious than vulgar commerce, had given away their trade to the lagoon dwellers and allowed their navy to decline; they became increasingly dependent on Venice for maritime defence.

The imperial policy towards the pushy foreigners veered erratically. The emperor's one throttle on them was control of trading rights. Repeated attempts were made over a century to loosen Venice's hold on the Byzantine economy by playing the Republic off against its commercial rivals, Pisa and Genoa. In IIII the Pisans were also granted trading rights in Constantinople; forty-five years later the Genoese were similarly admitted. Each was awarded tax breaks, a commercial quarter and landing stages in Constantinople. The city was a crucible for fierce rivalry between the Italian republics that would, in time, flare into full-scale trade wars. When the Spanish Jew Benjamin Tudela came to the city in 1176 he found 'a tumultuous city; men come to trade there from all countries by land and by sea'. The city became a claustrophobic arena for competition. Ugly brawls broke out between competing nationalities, hemmed into adjacent enclaves along the banks of the Golden Horn. The Venetians were jealous of their monopolies which they felt had been earned in the Norman wars of the last century; they deeply resented the manner in which successive emperors rescinded them or favoured their rivals. The Italians had become, in the eyes of the ruling Greeks, an uncontrollable nuisance: 'a race characterised by a lack of breeding which is totally at variance with our noble sense of order', they pronounced with aristocratic hauteur. In 1171, the emperor Manuel I took the whole Venetian population in his empire hostage and detained it for years. The crisis took two decades to resolve and left a bitter legacy of mutual mistrust. By the time Venetian merchants were readmitted to Constantinople in the 1190s any special relationship was dead.

It was against this background that the pope called for a new crusade in the summer of 1198.

2

The Blind Doge

The Fourth Crusade opened with a furious blast:

After the miserable destruction of the territory of Jerusalem, after the mournful massacre of the Christian people, after the deplorable invasion of the land on which had stood the feet of Christ and where God, our Father, had seen fit before recorded time to work out salvation in the middle of the earth . . . the apostolic seat [papacy], disquieted by the misfortune of such a great calamity, was sorely troubled . . . [it] cries out and raises its voice like a trumpet, desiring to arouse the Christian people to fight Christ's fight and to avenge the outrage against Him who was crucified . . . Therefore, my sons, take up the spirit of fortitude, put on the shield of faith, the helmet of salvation, trusting not in numbers nor in brute force, but rather in the power of God.

The ringing call to militant Christendom, launched by Pope Innocent III in August 1198, came an ominous century after the successful capture of Jerusalem. In the interim the whole crusading project had slid towards collapse. The decisive blow fell in 1187, when Saladin shattered a crusader army at Hattin and retook the Holy City. Neither the Holy Roman Emperor Frederick Barbarossa, who drowned in a Syrian river, nor the English king, Richard the Lionheart, had come close to regaining it. The crusaders were now confined to a few settlements along the coast such as the ports of Tyre and Acre. It fell to the pope to breathe life back into the project.

Innocent was thirty-seven years old – young, brilliant, determined, pragmatic, a master of religious rhetoric and a skilled jurist. His call to arms was both a military venture, a campaign of moral rearmament in a secularising world, and an initiative to reassert papal authority. From the start he made it clear that he intended not only to raise the crusade but to direct it himself, through the offices of his papal legates. While one went to stir up the warrior lords of northern France, the other, Cardinal Soffredo, came to Venice to ask about ships. A century of crusading had taught military planners that the land route to Syria was an arduous trudge and that the Byzantines were hostile to large numbers of armed men tramping across their terrain. With the other maritime republics, Pisa and Genoa, at war, only Venice had the skill, the resources and the technology to transport a whole army to the east.

The immediate Venetian response was startling. They sent their own legates back to Rome to request, as a preliminary, the lifting of the papal ban on trading with the Islamic world, specifically Egypt. The Republic's case framed at the outset the collision of faith and secular necessity that was to haunt the Fourth Crusade. It rested on the prototype definition of Venetian identity. The legates argued the city's unique situation. It had no agriculture; it depended entirely on trade for its survival and was being badly hurt by the embargo, which it faithfully observed. The legates might also have muttered under their breath that Pisa and Genoa had meanwhile continued their trade in defiance of the papacy, but Innocent was not impressed. The city had long existed at an oblique angle to pious Christian projects. Eventually he gave the Venetians a carefully worded permission, framed to exclude transaction in any war materials, which he proceeded to enumerate: '[we] prohibit you, under strict threat of anathema, to supply the Saracens by selling, giving or bartering, iron, hemp, sharp implements, inflammable materials, arms, galleys, sailing ships, or timbers', adding with a lawyer's eye, to snuff out any legal loopholes the devious Venetians might seek to exploit, 'whether finished or unfinished . . .'

. . . hoping that because of this concession you will be strongly moved to provide help to the province of Jerusalem, and making sure that you do not try any fraud against the apostolic decree. Because there can not be the slightest doubt that he who tries fraudulently, against his own conscience, to cheat this order, will be bound tight by divine sentence.

This was not a good start. The threat of excommunication was heavy and Innocent did not trust Venice at all, but practically he had no choice but to bend a little: only the Republic could supply the ships.

So it was that when six French knights arrived at Venice in the first week of Lent 1201, the doge probably had a good idea of their mission. They came as envoys of the great crusading counts of France and the Low Countries – from Champagne and Brie, Flanders, Hainaut and Blois – with sealed charters that gave them full authority to make whatever agreements they saw fit for maritime transport. One of these men was Geoffroi de Villehardouin of Champagne, a veteran of the Third Crusade and a man with experience of assembling crusader armies. It was Villehardouin's account that would form a principal, but highly partial, source for all that followed.

Venice had a long tradition of equating age with experience when it came to appointing doges, but the man the counts had come to see was remarkable by any measure. Enrico Dandolo was the scion of a prominent family of lawyers, merchants and churchmen. They had been intertwined in nearly all the great events of the past century and had built up an impressive record of service to the Republic. They had been involved in reforming the city's church and state institutions in the middle years of the twelfth century and participated in Venice's crusading ventures. By all accounts the male Dandolos were a clan of immense wisdom, energy – and longevity. In 1201 Enrico was over ninety. He was also completely blind.

No one knows what Enrico looked like; his physical image has been shaped by numerous anachronistic portrayals, so it is easy now to imagine a tall, thin, wiry man with a white beard and piercing but sightless eyes, steely in his resolve for the Venetian state, sagacious with experience of many decades at the heart of Venice's life during a century of rising prosperity – an impression for which there is no material substance. Of his personality, contemporary impressions and subsequent judgements have been sharply divided. They would match the divergent views of Venice itself. To his friends Dandolo would become the epitome of the Republic's shrewdness and good government. To the French knight Robert of Clari he was a 'most worthy man and wise'; to Abbot Martin of Pairis, a man who 'compensated for physical blindness with a lively intellect'; the French baron Hugh of Saint-Pol called him 'prudent in character, discreet and wise in making difficult decisions'. Villehardouin, who came to know him well, declared him to be 'very wise, brave and vigorous'. To the Greek chronicler Niketas Choniates, who did not, he was destined to a counter-judgement which has also passed into the bloodstream of history: 'a man most treacherous and hostile to the [Byzantines], both cunning and arrogant; he called himself the wisest of the wise and in his lust for glory surpassed everyone'. Around Dandolo would gather accretions of myth that would define less the man than the way that Venice would be seen both by itself and its enemies.

Dandolo had always been destined for high office, but some time in the mid-1170s he started to lose his sight. Documents that he signed in 1174 show a firm, legible signature well aligned along the page. Another in 1176 bears the tell-tale signs of visual impairment. The words of the Latin formula ('I, Henry Dandolo, judge, have signed underneath in my hand') slope away downhill to the right, as the writer's grasp of spatial relationship falters across the page, each successive letter taking its stumbling position from an increasingly uncertain guess as to the orientation of its predecessor. It appears that Dandolo's eyesight was slowly fading and in time utterly extinguished. Eventually, according to Venetian statute, Dandolo was no longer permitted to sign documents, only to have his mark attested by an approved witness.

The nature, the degree and the cause of Dandolo's loss of sight were destined to become subjects of much speculation and to be held as a key explanation for the events of the Fourth Crusade. It was rumoured that during the Byzantine hostage crisis of 1172, when Dandolo was in Constantinople, the emperor Manuel 'ordered his eyes to be blinded with glass; and his eyes were uninjured, but he saw nothing'. This was held to be the reason why the doge harboured a profound grudge against the Byzantines. In another version he lost his sight in a street brawl in Constantinople. Variants of this tale perplexed the medieval world in all subsequent considerations of Dandolo's career. Some held that his blindness was feigned, or not total, for his eyes were attested to be indeed still bright and clear, and how otherwise was Dandolo able to lead the Venetian people in peace and war? Conversely it was said that he was adept at covering up his blindness, and that this was a proof of the treacherous cunning of the man. It is certain, however, that Dandolo was not blinded in 1172 – his signature was still good two years later – nor did he himself ever apportion blame for it. The only explanation that he subsequently gave was that he had lost his sight through a blow to the head.

However it happened, it did nothing to dim the clarity of his judgement or his energy. In 1192 Dandolo was elected to the position of doge and swore the ducal oath of office to 'work for the honour and profit of the Venetians in good faith and without fraud'. Despite the fact that Venice, always profoundly conservative in its mechanisms, was never given to a heady admiration of youth, the blind man who had to be led to the ducal throne remained an unusual choice; it is possible he was viewed as a stop-gap. Given his advanced years the electors could feel reasonably confident that his term of office would be short. None of them could have guessed that it had thirteen years to run, during which time he would transform the future of Venice – or that the arrival of the crusader knights would be the trigger.

Dandolo welcomed the knights warmly, examined their letters of credence carefully and, being satisfied with their authority, proceeded to the business. The matter was unfolded in a series of meetings. First to the doge and his council, 'inside the doge's palace, which was very fine and beautiful', according to Ville-hardouin. The barons were highly impressed with the splendour of the setting and the dignity of the blind doge, 'a very wise and venerable man'. They had come, they said, because they 'could be confident of finding a greater supply of ships at Venice than at any other port' and they outlined their request for transport – the number of men and horses, the provisions, the length of time for which they requested them. Dandolo was evidently taken aback by the scale of the operation that the envoys outlined, though it is unclear exactly how detailed their projections were. It was a week's work for the Venetians to size up the task. They came back and named their terms. With the thoroughness of experi-enced workmen quoting on a job they stipulated exactly what they would supply for the money:

We will build horse transports to carry 4,500 horses and nine thousand squires; and 4,500 knights and twenty thousand foot soldiers will be embarked on ships; and our terms will include provisions for both men and horses for nine months. This is the minimum we will provide, con-ditional on payment of four marks per horse and two per man. And all the terms we are setting out for you will be valid for a year from the day of departure from the port of Venice to serve God and Christendom, wherever that may take us. The sum of money specified above totals ninety-four thousand marks. And we will additionally supply fifty armed galleys, free of charge, for as long as our alliance lasts, with the condi-tion that we receive half of all the conquests that we make either by way of territory or money, either by land or at sea. Now take counsel among yourselves as to whether you are willing and able to go ahead with this.

The per capita rate was not unreasonable. The Genoese had asked for similar from the French in 1190, but the aggregate sum of ninety-four thousand marks was staggering, equivalent to the annual income of France. From the Venetian point of view it was a huge commercial opportunity, shadowed by considerable risk. It would require the undivided attention of the whole Vene-tian economy for two years: a year of preparation – shipbuilding, logistical arrangements, manpower recruitment, food sourcing –

followed by a second year of active service by a sizeable section of the male population and the use of all its ships. It would commit the Venetians to the largest commercial contract in medieval history; it would mean the cessation of all other trading activity during the span of the contract; failure at any point would mean disaster for the city, because all its resources were involved. It was small wonder that Dandolo had studied the letters of authority so closely, drawn the contract so carefully and asked for half of the proceeds. The two dimensions were time and money; both had been scrupulously weighed. The Venetians were seasoned merchants; contracting was what they did and they believed in the sanctity of the deal. It was the gold standard by which Venetian life operated: its key parameters were quantity, price and delivery date. Such bargains were hammered out on the Rialto every day of the trading year, though never on this scale. The doge might have been surprised that the crusaders agreed so readily after only an overnight consideration. The envoys were particularly impressed by the Venetian offer to contribute fifty galleys at their own expense. It was not without significance. Nor was the seemingly innocuous phrase 'wherever that may take us' inserted in the contract without purpose.

The doge might have been driving the deal, but Venice defined itself as a commune, in which all the people theoretically had a say in the major decisions of the state. In this case their whole future was at stake. It was critical to obtain wide consent for the deal. Villehardouin recorded the process of Venetian democracy at work. The transaction had to be sold to an ever widening audience: first the Great Council of fifty, then to two hundred representatives of the Commune. Finally Dandolo called the general populace to St Mark's. According to Villehardouin, ten thousand people were gathered together in expectation of dramatic news. In the smoky darkness of the great mother church, 'the most beautiful church that might be', wrote Villehardouin, who was evidently as susceptible as anyone to the atmosphere of the place, glimmering like a sea cave shot through with shafts of obscure

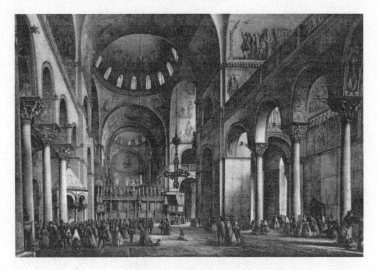

The interior of St Mark's

light and the smouldering gold of its mosaic saints, Dandolo constructed a scene of mounting drama, using 'his intelligence and powers of reason – which were both very sound and sharp'. First he requested 'a mass to the Holy Spirit and to beg God that he might guide them concerning the request the envoys had made to them'. Then the six envoys entered the great doors of the church and walked down the aisle. The Frenchmen, doubtless wearing their surcoats emblazoned with the scarlet cross, were the object of intense interest. People craned and jostled to catch a glimpse of the foreigners. Clearing his throat, Villehardouin made a powerful address to his audience:

My lords, the greatest and most powerful barons of all France have sent us to you. They have begged your mercy to take pity on Jerusalem, which is enslaved by the Turks, so that, for the love of God, you should be willing to help their expedition to avenge Jesus Christ's dishonour. And for this, they have chosen you because there is no nation so powerful at sea as you, and they have ordered us to throw ourselves at your feet and not to get up until you have agreed to take pity on the Holy Land overseas.

The marshal flattered their maritime pride and their religious zeal, as if they had been personally called upon by God to perform this mighty deed. All six envoys fell weeping to the floor. It was an appeal direct to the emotional core of the medieval soul. A thunderous roar swept through the church, along the nave, mounting to the galleries and up into the swirling heights of the dome. People 'called out with one voice and raised their hands up high and cried "We agree! We agree!"' Dandolo was then helped to the pulpit, his sightless eyes sensing the moment, and sealed the pact: 'My lords, behold the honour God has done you, because the finest nation on earth has scorned all others and asked *your* help and co-operation in undertaking a task of such great importance as the deliverance of Our Lord!' It was irresistible.

The Treaty of Venice, as it came to be known, was signed and sealed the following day with all due ceremony. The doge 'gave them his charters . . . weeping copiously, and swore in good faith on the relics of saints to loyally hold to the terms in the charters'. The envoys responded in kind, sent messengers to Pope Innocent and departed to prepare for crusade. Under the terms of the treaty, the crusading army would be gathered on the auspicious St John's Day, 24 June the following year, 1202, and the fleet would be ready to receive them.

Despite the fervent assent of the population, the Venetians were, by nature, a cautious people, in whom the mercantile spirit had bred shrewd judgement, not given to flights of fancy, and Dandolo was a cautious leader. Yet any measured risk analysis of the Treaty of Venice would suggest that it involved hazarding the whole economy of the Commune on one high-stakes project. The number of men and ships required, the sums of money to be laid out – the figures were breathtaking. Dandolo was probably over ninety years old with presumably only a few years to live. He personally was responsible for pushing through this enormous project. On the face of it he had much to lose. Why on earth should he risk his declining years in this gamble?

The answers lay in the Venetian character, its peculiar admixture of the secular and religious, and in the treaty itself. Venice continuously looked back to the precedents of its history for received wisdom to steer the ship of state. Its rise over the previous century had been deeply entwined with the adventure of the crusades. The Venetians had participated in the First Crusade and again in 1123. From both they had profited in material terms; they had acquired a third of the city of Tyre in 1122, ruled directly from the lagoon on terms of tax-free trade, which marked the start of Venice's overseas empire, as well as a foothold in a string of other harbours.

Beneath the pattern of intermittent holy wars, these Palestinian ports provided the Italian republics with new opportunities to acquire goods of the furthest Orient. They found themselves linked to a network of ancient trading routes that stretched all the way to China. Venice was also able to access a world of wealth and luxury within the Levant itself, where sophisticated manufacturing skills and agricultural expertise had been flourishing for hundreds of years. Tripoli was famous for the weaving of silk, Tyre for the vivid transparency of its glass, for its purple and red fabrics dyed in the vats of Jewish artisans, for sugar cane, lemons, oranges, figs, almonds, olives and sesame. Via the port of Acre, one could acquire medicinal rhubarb from the river Volga, Tibetan musk, cinnamon and pepper, nutmeg, cloves, aloe and camphor, ivory from India and Africa, and Arabian dates; in Beirut, indigo, incense, pearls and wood.

The brilliant Levantine light had exposed Europeans to a tumbling world of bright colours and vivid scents. New tastes in goods, clothes, foods and flavours permeated the crusader kingdoms and were carried back in the holds of merchant ships to an increasingly wealthy Europe. In return Venice, and its rivals, also provisioned the crusades; they brought the kingdom of Jerusalem (as well as its enemies in Egypt) the resources of war – arms, metal, wood and horses – and the necessary goods to sustain colonial life on a foreign shore, and ballasted their ships with pilgrims eager to witness the holy places. For Venetian merchants the crusades had proved highly profitable. In the process they deepened their knowledge of how to trade across a cultural divide, which would make them, in time, the interpreters of worlds.

The expeditions to previous crusades had entered the national memory as triumphant episodes in the litany of Venetian glories. They reinforced the city's sense of itself and its expectations. Venice had always looked east into the rising sun: for trade and booty, for material objects with which to embellish the city, for the stolen bones of Christian saints, for the possibility of wealth and military glory – and not least for the remission of sins. Venice's attachment to the East was aesthetic, religious and commercial. The returning argosies set a pattern of expectation: that what would be unloaded at the Basin of St Mark would enrich, ennoble and sanctify the city. A hundred years earlier a doge had raised to the status of patriotic duty the demand that merchant ships returning from the East should bring back antiquities, marbles and carvings for the decoration of the newly rebuilt Church of St Mark. A successful expedition in 1123 had given the Republic lively expectations of the commercial benefits that might be derived from crusade. In the new treaty of Venice, the maritime contract alone would give a good profit, and half of all the spoils might yield unknown wealth.

As a youth, Dandolo had probably personally witnessed the religious fervour and national that had accompanied the departure of crusading fleets and heard the impassioned words of the doge of his childhood, extolling their spiritual and material glory:

Venetians, with what immortal glory and splendour will your name be covered from this expedition? What reward will you gain from God? You will win the admiration of Europe and Asia. The standard of St Mark will fly triumphantly in far-off lands. New profits, new sources of greatness will come to this most noble city . . . Roused by the holy zeal of religion, excited by the example of all Europe, hurry to arms, think of the honour and the prizes, think of your triumph – with the blessings of heaven!

Dandolo had other personal reasons. He came from a family of crusaders; probably a desire to emulate his forefathers struck a deep chord in him. And he was an old man: concern for his soul would also have weighed heavily. The promised absolution of sins was one of the most powerful incentives for crusades. He had impelling national, personal, spiritual and family motives for signing the treaty.

The blind but percipient doge had evidently glimpsed a moment of destiny – as if everything in Venetian history led up to this extraordinary opportunity. But there was something else, buried at the heart of the treaty, which would have lent it considerable appeal. What was kept from all but a handful of signatories and the crusading lords back in France and Lombardy was that the expedition, which had stirred the rank and file vaguely to 'take pity on the Holy Land overseas', had no intention initially of going there. It was bound for Egypt. As Villehardouin confessed in his chronicle, 'It was secretly agreed in closed council that we would go to Egypt, because via Cairo one could more easily destroy the power of the Turks than by anywhere else, but publicly it was just announced that we were going overseas.'

There were sound strategic reasons for this. It had long been recognised by shrewder military tacticians that the wealth of Egypt was a reservoir of resource for the Muslim armies in Palestine and Syria. Saladin's victories had been built on the riches of Cairo and Alexandria. As Richard the Lionheart had realised, 'the keys to Jerusalem are to be found in Cairo'. The problem was that such an oblique approach to recapturing the Holy City was unlikely to stir the popular imagination. The ardently pious sought salvation by fighting for the ground on which Jesus had stood, not strangling Islam's supply lines in the souks of the Nile Delta.

But to the Venetians this offered a further extension of commercial opportunity. Egypt was the wealthiest region in the Levant and another natural access point to the highly lucrative spice routes. It promised richer commercial prizes than the harbours of Tyre and Acre could ever provide. 'Whatever this part of the world lacks in the matter of pearls, spices, oriental treasures, and foreign wares is brought hither from the two Indies: Saba, Arabia, and both the Ethiopias, as well as from Persia and other lands nearby,' wrote William of Tyre twenty years earlier. 'People from East and West flock thither in great numbers, and Alexandria is a public market for both worlds.' In fact Venice had a poor share of this market, despite the recent permission from Pope Innocent. Genoa and Pisa dominated the trade with Egypt. Dandolo had been to Alexandria; he knew at first hand both its wealth and its defensive frailties, and the city held a powerful emotional attraction for the Republic. It was here that St Mark had died and whence Venetian merchants had spirited away his bones. In essence, a victorious campaign in Egypt with half the proceeds as reward gave Venice a glimpse of riches that might far exceed all its previous commercial triumphs. It could, at a stroke, deliver a large part of the commerce of the eastern Mediterranean into its grasp, and permanently discomfit its maritime rivals. Tax-free monopoly trading was an irresistible lure. The potential returns were evidently worth the risk, and this was why the Venetians had thrown in fifty war galleys at their own expense. They were not designed to fight sea battles off the coast of Palestine, but to nose their way up the shallow reedy deltas of the Nile for a strike against Cairo.

This secret agenda was just one worrying co-ordinate of a treaty that was destined to exert a malign influence on the crusade. The others were time – the Venetians had committed themselves finally to a nine months' finite maritime contract, from St John's Day, 24 June 1202 – and crucially, money. It seems likely that the final agreed sum was knocked down to eighty-five thousand marks, still a staggering amount. Even if the per capita rate was reasonable, Villehardouin's estimate of thirty-three thousand crusaders was exceptionally high. Villehardouin had experience of estimating crusader armies but his overnight acceptance of the doge's terms would prove a colossal blunder. He had dramatically miscalculated the number of crusaders who could be assembled; he had also failed to realise that those on whose behalf he had signed the treaty were not themselves bound to it: they were under no obligation to sail from Venice. The crusade was under financial pressure from the start: Innocent had attempted, and failed, to raise funds through taxation. The six delegates had to borrow the first down payment on the deal – two thousand marks – on the Rialto. Though no one knew it at the time, the Treaty of Venice contained the active ingredients for serious trouble, which would render the Fourth Crusade the most controversial event in medieval Christendom.

Villehardouin jingled his way back over the Alpine passes. The crusaders of France, Flanders and northern Italy – the Franks, as the Byzantines referred to them – made their vows and their wills, donned their surcoats and laboriously began the long-winded preparations for departure; in the lagoon, the Venetians set to work preparing the largest fleet in its history.

3

Thirty-four Thousand Marks

The scale of the operation dwarfed any of the city's previous maritime expeditions. It required Dandolo to order the immediate suspension of all other commercial activities and to recall merchant vessels from overseas as the whole population threw itself into the preparations. They had thirteen months to complete the work.

The shipbuilding and refurbishment alone were a huge project, which required immense quantities of wood, pitch, hemp, ropes, sailcloth, and iron for nails, anchors and fixings. The Italian mainland was scoured for resources. Quantities of fir and larch were floated down the rivers that fed into the lagoon; oak and pine came from the Veneto and the Dalmatian coast. The state arsenal, established in 1104, was the industrial hub of the work, but much of it was carried on in private yards scattered across the islands of the lagoon. The air rang with the sound of hammering and sawing, the blows of axes and the rasping of adzes; cauldrons of pitch bubbled and steamed; forges glowed; rope makers paid out hundreds of yards of twisted hemp; oars, pulleys, masts, sails and anchors were shaped, hewed, sewn and forged. Ships started to grow from the keel up; others were refitted or adapted. In the arsenal war machines were under construction – stone-throwing catapults and siege towers in kit form which could be dismantled for the voyage.

The logistical requirements of the crusade demanded vessels of different types. The 4,500 knights and twenty thousand foot soldiers would be carried in round ships – high-sided sailing

Shipbuilding in Venice

vessels with fore and aft castles, of varying sizes from a handful of immense prestige ships, assigned to the nobility, to the standard crusader transports that crammed six hundred men below decks, then down to smaller craft. The 4,500 horses would be carried in 150 specially adapted oared galleys, fitted with hinged landing doors either in the side or the bows, up which the horses could be walked into the belly of the vessels, then secured in slings to counteract the rolling motion of the sea. The doors, which would be below the waterline, had to be caulked shut for the voyage, but could be swung open on a shelving beach to permit a fully armoured knight to ride out, terrifying any unsuspecting foe. In total, the Venetians probably had to provide 450 ships to carry the army and all its impedimenta. Then there were the fifty galleys which the Venetians themselves would provide and the recruitment of sailors and oarsmen to man the fleet. To row and sail thirty-three thousand men across the eastern Mediterranean required another thirty thousand maritime specialists – half the adult population of Venice, or replacements recruited from the sea-going cities of the Dalmatian coast. Many volunteered as crusaders but the numbers still had to be made up. Men from each parish of the city were impressed by a lottery drawn using wax balls – those who drew a ball containing a scrap of paper were ordered to the Republic's service.

A parallel effort of hardly less magnitude was required to provision the armada. The Venetians carefully quantified the provisions for each man for a year: 377 kilos of bread and flour, two thousand kilos of cereals and beans, three hundred litres of wine: the mathematics of provisioning a crusader army stacked up huge numbers. The agricultural hinterland of Venice was scoured for produce; wheat was secured from regional centres – Bologna, Cremona, Imola and Faenza – and double-baked in Venetian ovens to make the durable ship's biscuit which formed the staple of the maritime diet. Not all this food would have been sourced in Venice. Undoubtedly Venetian planners sought to reprovision along the way as they sailed down the coast of Dalmatia, but fulfilling the contract was an enormous challenge.

All this work had to be paid for. The Venetian mint was compelled to produce extra quantities of small silver coins, the *grosso*, to pay the master carpenters, caulkers, rope makers, sail makers, smiths, sailors, cooks and bargees who laboured unceasingly for a year to ready the fleet. In effect, the Republic was living on credit, anxiously awaiting the fulfilment of the contract, and payment.

By early summer 1202, the Venetians had assembled the enormous fleet needed to transport and maintain an army of thirty-three thousand men 1,400 miles across the eastern Mediterranean and maintain it for a year. 'The Venetians had fulfilled their side of the bargain and more so,' acknowledged Villehardouin. 'The fleet which they had prepared was so large and so magnificent that no Christian man had ever seen better.' It was, by any account, an extraordinary feat of collective organisation and a testimony to the effectiveness of the Venetian state, which would in time contribute enormously to the development of the Republic's maritime capabilities.

The fleet was fully prepared for the scheduled departure date, St John's Day, 24 June 1202, but the crusade itself was badly co-ordinated and running late. The word was given for the crusaders to leave their homes at Easter (6 April 1202), but many did not make their final farewells until Pentecost, 2 June. The crusaders arrived in Venice in straggling bands, under their lords and feudal banners. The leader of the whole enterprise, Boniface of Montferrat, did not reach the lagoon until 15 August, but it was already clear by early June that the numbers assembling at Venice fell far short of the contracted thirty-three thousand for whom the Venetians had prepared their magnificent fleet. Some took alternative routes to the Holy Land, shipping from Marseilles or Apulia, for reasons of convenience or lower cost – or perhaps rumour had reached them that the Venetian fleet was intending to strike at Egypt rather than liberate Jerusalem. Villehardouin was quick to heap blame on those who failed to show up because 'these men and many others besides were fearful of the very peril-ous venture on which the army gathered at Venice was engaged'. The truth was otherwise: Villehardouin or the crusading lords to whom he had reported had terribly miscalculated the numbers; nor were those who did muster bound by his agreement to take the longer land route to Venice. 'There was a great shortfall in the number from the army at Venice, which was a grave misfortune – as you will learn later,' he wrote.

There was still not sufficient room to accommodate the cru-sader army within Venice itself and the authorities were wary of armed men in the city's confined spaces. Camps were allotted to them on the desolate sandy island of St Nicholas, the longest of the *lidi*, and which today is known simply as the Lido: 'So the pilgrims went there and set up their tents and quartered them-selves the best they could,' recalled Robert of Clari, a poor French knight who wrote a vivid first-hand account of the crusade, not from the aristocratic viewpoint of Villehardouin but from that of the rank and file, the expedition's foot soldiers.

While a trickle of crusaders continued to arrive, the allotted departure date came and went and the frown on Dandolo's face deepened by the day. The morale of the assembled force was intermittently buoyed up by the arrival of high-profile figures – Baldwin of Flanders arrived in late June, then Count Louis of Blois, each with his own forces; the papal legate, Peter Capuano, reached Venice on 22 July to add spiritual succour to the cause, but the gap between the contract and the force now gathered remained horribly large. By July there were still only twelve thousand men. 'In fact', Villehardouin conceded, 'it was so well provided with ships, galleys and horse transports, that there were enough for three times the assembled army.'

If this was an embarrassment to the crusading lords, it was potentially ruinous for Venice. The Commune had staked its whole economy on the deal, and for Dandolo who had brokered it and advocated and cajoled the population into accepting the treaty it spelled personal catastrophe. Dandolo, like all the merchants of Venice, believed in the sanctity of contracts. This one, above all others, had to be honoured. According to Clari, he turned furiously on the crusader lords:

'Lords, you have treated us badly because as soon as your ambassadors had struck the deal with me and my people, I ordered throughout the land that no merchant should go trading, but all should help to prepare the fleet and they have all applied themselves to this and earned nothing for more than one and a half years. They've lost a great deal, and for this reason my people, and I too, want you to repay the money you owe. And if you don't do so, know that you won't leave this island until the very moment that we've been paid, nor will you find anyone to bring you enough to eat and drink.' When the counts and the crusaders heard what the doge said, they were greatly worried and dismayed.

It is unclear how serious the latter threat was. Clari went on to say that the doge 'was a great and worthy man, and so did not cease from having them brought sufficient to eat and drink', but the lot of the ordinary crusader, marooned on the Lido, was becoming increasingly uncomfortable. They were effectively captives in the hot sun; kicking up the sand on the long sea strand, looking out into the blue-green of the Adriatic on one side, the duller lagoon on the other where Venice shimmered, tantalisingly out of reach, tormenting and exploiting them. 'Here,' wrote one chronicler, evidently no friend of Venice,

after pitching their tents, they awaited passage from the Kalends of June [1 June] to the Kalends of October [1 October]. A *sistarius* of grain sold for fifty *solidi*. As often as it pleased the Venetians, they decreed that no one release any of the pilgrims from the aforementioned island. Consequently the pilgrims, almost like captives, were dominated by them in all respects. Moreover, a great fear developed among the commons.

They had come piously for the salvation of their souls and they found themselves betrayed by their fellow Christians. It was inexplicable. The festering resentment would return later in more tangible forms. Disease broke out; 'the result was that the dead could barely be buried by the living'. And probably not one of them knew that the voyage for which they were so ardently hoping was not destined for the Holy Land anyway. For the poor, the crusade would prove to be a series of broken contracts, made in bad faith by the rich and powerful. Already Venice was being held accountable for the consequences.

When the papal legate, Peter Capuano, reached the city, he released the destitute, the sick and the women from their crusading vows; many others seem to have deserted and gone home of their own accord. Capuano appeared on the scene as the voice and conscience of the pope, rallying the faithful 'in a marvellous manner' with his inspirational preaching, but was quite incapable of solving the fundamental problem. The crusaders could not pay; the Venetians could not release them from their debt. The compression of these two irreconcilable forces would create a climate of continuous crisis management for the crusade and have consequences that no one at the time could foresee.

There was a tense stand-off. The Venetians were furious. The barons leading the crusade, shamefaced by their failure to honour the contract, attempted to get every individual to pay his own passage: four marks for a knight, down to one for a foot soldier. All crusades were bedevilled by the question of ready cash and this was no exception. Many had already paid and refused to contribute more; others could not. The debt remained enormous. In the summer heat of the Lido, fierce disputes broke out amongst the army about how to proceed. Some wanted to leave and seek other routes to the Holy Land. Others were prepared to give all they had for the sake of their souls. The crusade was threatened with shameful disintegration. The aristocratic leaders tried to set an example by handing over their valuables and borrowing more on the Rialto. 'You should have seen the quantity of fine vessels of gold and silver carried to the doge's palace as payment,' recorded Villehardouin self-justifyingly. The gap still remained a staggering thirty-four thousand marks – nine tons of silver. They told the doge they could raise no more.

For Venice and Dandolo the situation was now critical. The doge had personally brokered the deal; he had to manage the crisis. Dandolo was forced to present the situation to the council, and then to the Commune. The mood was ugly; the whole city had bought into this project and everyone had something to lose. Bankruptcy threatened and the people were angry. Time was going by: soon it would be too late in the season to sail anyway and the venture must necessarily collapse; not least of all, Venice was paying host to twelve thousand increasingly restive armed men. Dandolo, with the wisdom of his nine decades and the collective experience of Venetian history behind him, outlined two options; firstly, they could keep the fifty-one thousand marks already collected and abandon the project. This would earn them the opprobrium of all Christendom: 'we shall henceforth always be considered as rogues and cheats'. Alternatively they could temporarily suspend collection of the debt, and this is what he urged: 'rather let us go to them and tell them that if they will repay us the thirty-six thousand [*sic*] marks they owe us from the first conquests that they make for themselves, then we will take them overseas'. Venice concurred, and this was put to the crusaders some time in early September:

. . . they were most happy and fell at his feet for joy and they loyally guaranteed that they would willingly do as the doge suggested. There was such rejoicing that night that there were none so poor that he did not make great illuminations, and they carried flaming torches on the ends of their lances around their tents and lit them within so that it seemed as if the whole camp was ringed with fire.

Seen from Venice, the Lido was a line of lights.

It was probably on the feast of the Virgin – Sunday 8 September – that a large crowd of Venetians, crusaders and pilgrims gathered in the Church of St Mark for mass. Before the service Dandolo climbed up into the pulpit and delivered an emotional address to the people:

Lords, you are allied with the finest nation in the world, on the most noble mission that anyone has ever undertaken. I am just a weak old man, in need of rest and impaired in body, but I see that no one knows how to govern and lead you better than I, your lord. If you will let me take the sign of the cross to protect and lead you, and let my son take my place and guard the city, I will go with you and the pilgrims to live and die.

There was an explosion of assent. Everyone cried out, 'We beg you for God's sake to agree and do so!' The sight of the old doge, blind, ninety years old, undoubtedly close to the end of life, offering to join the crusade, led to mass crying: 'many tears were shed because this noble man, if he had wanted, had plentiful reasons for staying at home. He was an old man, and though he had fine eyes in his head, he could see nothing,' recorded Villehardouin. Descending from the pulpit, Dandolo was led weeping to the high altar, where he knelt and had the cross conspicuously sewn to his doge's *corno* – the large cotton cap that signified his position – 'because he wanted people to be able to see it'. This had a galvanising effect on the Venetian population, who 'began to take the cross in a great throng and large numbers . . . Our pilgrims were filled with joy and great emotion at the doge's cross-taking,' said Villehardouin, 'because of his great wisdom and reputation.' At a stroke the ancient doge had placed himself at the centre of the crusade. Final preparations were hurried on for the departure of the fleet before the end of the sailing season.

The *corno*

Yet again there was more to all this than met the eyes of the pious crusaders. Behind the bland agreement to defer the crusaders' debt 'until God lets us conquer together' lay another layer of secret agreements, under which the crusade would unfold like a series of false drawers. In order to square deferment of the debt with the Venetian guarantee of a concrete benefit, Dandolo had engaged in some lateral thinking and put forward a startling proposal to the crusader high command. It was tied up with Venice's obsession with the geopolitics of the Adriatic, and specifically with the city of Zara on the Dalmatian coast. Venice's domination of the sea, its enforcement of trading restrictions and tax tariffs, continually irked the Dalmatians. Zara, 'an exceedingly rich city . . . situated on the sea', chafed continuously against Venetian control and had made a series of bids for independence since Doge Pietro Orseolo's voyage in the year 1000. In 1181 it yet again threw off the Venetian yoke and signed a protective pact with the Hungarian kings. This was to be a repeated pattern. To the Venetians the Zarans were in breach of their feudal oath; worse still they were also politicking with the Republic's maritime rivals, the Pisans. It is highly likely that Dandolo had no intention of allowing his fleet to sweep down the Adriatic anyway without cuffing the unruly Zarans, but behind closed doors he had put it to the crusader lords that it was too late in the year to sail to the East; if they were to help subdue Zara, the suspension of the debt could be more readily accepted in Venice. Faced with the prospect of the crusade's collapse, they agreed.

This was theologically extremely tricky. The first stop on the crusade was to be the conquest of another Christian – and Catholic – city. Worse still, its new overlord, Emico of Hungary, had himself taken the cross. They would be attacking another crusader. It was true that Emico had shown no sign of actually going on crusade; as far as the Venetians were concerned he had cynically signed up purely for papal protection against such reprisals, but this still smacked of cardinal sin. Furthermore Innocent had been alerted by Emico to such a possibility and had already sent Dandolo an explicit warning 'not to violate the land of this king in any way'. No matter. Dandolo promptly muzzled the papal legate, Peter Capuano, by preventing him from accompanying the fleet as the pope's official spokesman, and continued to ready the ships. The slightly forlorn legate blessed the crusade whilst reserving his position on its objective and hurried back to Rome. Innocent prepared a threatening epistle. His early fears about the treacherous Venetians seemed to be fully confirmed. Within the assembling Christian army word probably leaked out that the first objective was to be a Christian city and Boniface of Montferrat, the titular leader of the crusade, politely excused himself from accompanying the expedition on its initial mission: he evidently wanted no part in Venice's imperial projects, but the whole crusading expedition was caught between a rock and a hard place – it either went to Zara or it disintegrated.

Preparations were now hurried forward. In early October siege machines, weapons, food, barrels of wine and water were laboriously carried, winched or rolled aboard the ships; the knights' chargers were led snorting up the loading ramps of the horse transports and coaxed into the leather slings designed to let them swing with the lurch and roll of the sea; the doors were then caulked shut 'as you would seal a barrel, because when the ship is on the high seas the whole door is underwater'. Thousands of foot soldiers, many of whom had never put to sea before, were crammed into the dark, claustrophobic holds of the troop carriers; the Venetian oarsmen took their places on the rowing benches of the war galleys; the blind Dandolo was led aboard the doge's sumptuous vessel; anchors were raised, sails unfurled, ropes cast off. Venetian history would be strung together on the recital of its great maritime ventures, but few would surpass in splendour the departure of the Fourth Crusade. None would have a deeper effect on the Republic's ascent to empire. It marked Venice out as a power whose maritime capabilities were unmatched in the Mediterranean basin.

For the landlubber knights, it was a spectacle that took the breath away and moved them to hyperbole: 'Never did such a magnificent fleet sail from any port,' was Villehardouin's verdict. 'One might say that the whole sea sparkled on fire with ships.' To Robert of Clari, 'it was the most magnificent spectacle to behold since the world began'. Hundreds of ships spread their sails across the lagoon; their banners and ensigns fluttered in the breeze. Standing out in the massed armada were some enormous castellated sailing vessels, rising like towers over the sea with their high poops and forecastles, each one badged with the glittering shields and streaming pennants of the crusader lords to whom they had been assigned, as symbols of magnificence and feudal power. The names of some of these survive: the *Paradise* and the *Pilgrim*, carrying the bishops of Soissons and Troyes, the *Violet* and the *Eagle*. The sheer height of these vessels was to play a significant part in the events ahead. Crusaders in their surcoats bearing the crosses of their nations – green for Flanders, red for France – crowded the stacked decks. The Venetian galley fleet was led forward by the doge's vessel, painted a significant vermilion, in which Dandolo sat beneath a vermilion canopy, 'and he had four silver trumpets which trumpeted before him and cymbals making a tremendous sound'. Volleys of noise swept across the panoramic sea. 'A hundred pairs of trumpets of both silver and brass which sounded the departure' blared across the water, drums and tabors and other instruments thumped and boomed; the brilliantly coloured pennants streamed in the salt wind; the oars of the galleys dashed the waves; black-robed priests mounted the forecastles and led the whole fleet in the crusader hymn '*Veni Creator Spiritus*'. 'And without exception, everyone, both great and small, wept with emotion and the immense joy that they felt.' With this triumphant din and the pious release of pent-up feelings the crusading fleet swept out of the mouth of the lagoon, past the Church of St Nicholas and the outer spits of the Lido, for so many months a prison, and into the Adriatic.

Yet there were uneasy notes amongst the splendid noise. The *Violet* sank on departure. There were those with profound spiritual doubts about attacking Christian Zara; far away in Rome Pope Innocent was sitting, pen in hand, preparing to excommunicate any crusader who dared to do so. And the missing sum of thirty-four thousand marks would continue to haunt the expedition all the way round the coast of Greece, like an albatross dangling from the tall masts.

4

'A Dog Returning to its Vomit'

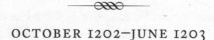

The Venetians had every intention of using this magnificent fleet along the way to reassert their imperial authority in the upper Adriatic, to cuff insubordinate cities, threaten pirates and levy sailors. Where Venice saw this as a legitimate assertion of feudal rights, many of the crusaders, frustrated and impoverished by the long wait on the Lido, already perceived the whole venture as a perversion of crusading vows. 'They forced Trieste and Mugla into submission,' an anonymous chronicler bluntly asserted as the fleet worked its way down the coast, 'they compelled all of Istria, Dalmatia, and Slavonia to pay tribute. They sailed into Zara, where their [crusading] oath came to naught. On the feast of Saint Martin they entered Zara's harbour.' Venetian ruthlessness was not always well received.

The fleet smashed through the harbour chain, forced its way in and proceeded to disembark thousands of men. The doors of the transports were prised open; the groggy, disorientated horses were led blindfolded onto dry land; catapults and siege towers were unloaded and assembled; a host of tents, with banners flying, was pitched outside the city walls. The Zarans surveyed this ominous enterprise from their battlements and decided to surrender. Two days after the fleet's arrival they sent a delegation to the crimson pavilion of the doge to offer terms. The business of Zara was a purely Venetian matter, but Dandolo, either out of scrupulousness or a desire to make the Zarans sweat, declared that he could not possibly accept this until he had conferred with the French barons. He left the delegation kicking its heels.

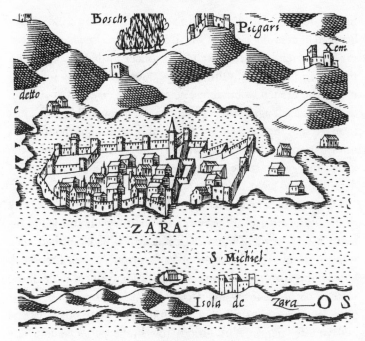

Zara and its harbour

Unfortunately for Dandolo – and as it turned out even more unfortunately for Zara – at almost the same moment a ship arrived from Italy carrying the furious interdict of Pope Innocent. The actual letter is lost but its contents were clearly restated later:

... we took care to strictly enjoin in our letter, which we believe came to your attention and that of the Venetians, that you not be tempted to invade or violate the lands of Christians ...Those, indeed, who might presume to act otherwise should know that they are bound by the fetters of excommunication and denied the indulgence that the [pope] granted the crusaders.

This was extraordinarily serious. Excommunication threatened, at a stroke, to damn the very souls crusading was intended to save. The letter was a grenade thrown into the expedition's uneasy pact and it opened up all the underlying tensions of the enterprise. A dissenting group of French knights, led by the powerful

Simon de Montfort, had always seen the diversion to Zara as a betrayal of crusader vows. While Dandolo was elsewhere discussing the surrender with a body of crusader lords, they called on the Zaran delegation waiting at the doge's tent. They informed it that the French would refuse to attack the city, and 'if you can defend yourself against the Venetians, then you will be safe'. Just to make sure the message got across, another knight shouted this information over the battlements. Armed with this promise the Zaran delegation turned on its heels and went back to the city, determined to resist.

Dandolo, meanwhile, had got the agreement of the majority of the leaders to accept the surrender and they all returned to his tent. Instead of the Zaran delegation, which had vanished, they were confronted by the abbot of Vaux, probably with Innocent's letter in his hand, who stepped dramatically forward with all the force of papal authority and declared: 'Lords, I forbid you, by the pope in Rome, to attack this city; for it is a place of Christians and you are pilgrims.' A furious row broke out. Dandolo was incensed and rounded on the crusader leaders: 'Sirs, by agreement I arranged the surrender of this city, and your men have taken it from me, although you gave me your word that you would help me to conquer it. Now I call on you to do so.' Furthermore, according to Robert of Clari, he was not prepared to back down before the pope: 'Lords, you should be aware that I won't relinquish my vengeance on them at any price, not even for the pope!'

The crusader leaders, more squeamish, found themselves caught between excommunication and the breaking of a secular agreement. Shamefaced and appalled by de Montfort's actions, they decided they had no option but to underwrite their commitment to the Venetian cause – the outstanding debt was tied up in the deal. Otherwise the crusade might just collapse. It was with heavy hearts that they agreed to this unpalatable act: 'Sir, we will help you to take the city despite those who want to prevent it.' The unfortunate Zarans, who had tried to surrender peacefully, now found themselves subjected to overwhelming force. They tried to prick crusader consciences by hanging crosses from the walls. It made no difference. Giant catapults were wheeled up to bombard the walls; miners began to tunnel beneath them. It was all over in five days. The Zarans sued for peace on more humiliating terms. Barring a few strategic executions, the Venetians spared the citizens' lives; the city was evacuated and the victors 'looted the city without mercy'.

It was now mid-November and Dandolo pointed out to the assembled army that it was too late in the year to sail on; the winter could be passed pleasantly enough in the mild climate of the Dalmatian coast. It would be better to wait until spring. It was reasonable enough, unavoidable even, but this suggestion seems to have plunged the crusade into fresh crisis. The rank-and-file crusaders felt they were being yet again shamelessly exploited – and they largely blamed Venice. They had been imprisoned on the Lido, led astray to attack Christian cities, impoverished and deceived. The clock was ticking steadily on the year's contract with Venice and they were no step nearer the Holy Land, let alone Egypt. The spoils of Zara had been largely appropriated by the lords. 'The barons kept the city's goods for themselves, giving nothing to the poor,' wrote an anonymous eyewitness, evidently sympathetic to the plight of the common man. 'The poor laboured mightily in poverty and hunger.' Collectively they still owed thirty-four thousand marks.

Shortly after the sacking of Zara, popular resentment erupted into violence.

Three days later, a terrible catastrophe befell the army near the hour of vespers, because a wide-ranging and very violent fight broke out between the Venetians and the French. People came running to arms from all sides and the violence was so intense that in nearly every street there was fierce fighting with swords, lances, crossbows and spears, and many men were killed or wounded.

It was with considerable difficulty that the commanders regained control of the situation. The crusade was hanging by a thread.

What the ordinary crusaders did not know – and this would have horrified them far more – was that they had now been excommunicated for the attack on the city. In an exercise of creative crisis management, the crusading bishops simply bestowed a general absolution on the army and lifted the ban, which they had no authority to do. Over the winter of 1202–3 the rank and file whiled away the time on the Dalmatian coast in reasonable accord whilst waiting for the new sailing season, blissfully unaware that their immortal souls were still in grave peril. The Frankish barons decided to hurry an abjectly apologetic delegation back to Rome to try to sort the situation out. The Venetians refused point-blank to participate: Zara was their own business; on its capture was built the agreement which would lead to the return of the thirty-four thousand marks and as long as this debt remained outstanding, the whole Republic's position was critical.

Even before this delegation had left for Rome, word of Zara had reached Innocent and he was drafting a furious response. It began tersely enough: 'To the counts, barons and all the crusaders without greeting' and went downhill from there. In a series of battering sentences, like the rhythmic thud of a siege engine, he castigated the crusaders for their 'very wicked plan':

You set up tents for a siege. You entrenched the city on all sides. You undermined its walls, not without spilling much blood. And when the citizens wanted to submit to your rule and that of the Venetians . . . they hung images of the cross from their walls. But you . . . to the not insignificant injury to Him who was crucified, you attacked the city and its people, you compelled them to surrender by violent skill.

He reminded the hangdog delegation when it arrived that the absolution granted by the bishops was absolutely illegal. He demanded repentance and restitution of the spoils. But his ultimate condemnation was reserved for the Venetians who 'knocked down the walls of this same city in your sight, they despoiled churches, they destroyed buildings, and you shared the spoils of Zara with them'. In the biblical analogy of the man who fell among thieves, the Venetians were cast as the plunderers, leading the crusade astray. Innocent also insisted that no more damage be done to Zara – an order the Venetians would roundly ignore – but at the same time, considering the crusaders' plight and his own ardent desire that his crusade should not disintegrate, he established a process by which absolution could be achieved – from which the Venetians were pointedly excluded. Due to the fact that the letter with which the delegation returned plainly stated that the army was, as yet, still under papal ban and that some of its terms, such as the return of the spoils, were simply not going to be met, the contents were again suppressed. It was given out that full absolution had been granted. The pope's ability to manage his crusade was plainly limited.

If Innocent thought that his deepest fears about the snares of a sinful world had been realised, he was wrong. Things were about to get far worse. The propulsive forces that drove the whole enterprise forward – the spiritual thirst, the Venetian debt, the shortage of funds, the secret agreements, the continuous betrayals of the rank and file, the repeated threat of disintegration, the months passing on the maritime contract – these were about to deliver another extraordinary twist to the direction of events. On 1 January 1203, ambassadors came to Zara from Philip of Swabia, king of Germany. They brought with them an enterprising proposal for the crusade to consider. It involved the whole complex back story of Byzantium and its fraught relationship with western Christendom. And like many of the secret deals that ensnared and propelled the crusade, its contents were already known to some of the leading knights.

Put baldly, the ambassadors said this: they had come on behalf of Philip's brother-in-law, a young Byzantine nobleman called Alexius Angelus, to plead for help in regaining his rightful inheritance – the throne of Byzantium – from his uncle. Angelus's father, Isaac, had been deposed and blinded by the present emperor, Alexius III. In fact, by the strict laws of succession, the young man had no rightful claim to the throne, but the niceties of Byzantine imperial protocol were probably lost on the French knights. The ambassadors came with a cunningly framed and carefully timed proposal that suggested an intimate knowledge of the crusaders' plight. It combined a garbled appeal to Christian morality with an offer of hard cash:

Since you campaign for God, right and justice, you must also return the inheritance to those who have been wrongly dispossessed, if you can. And Angelus will give you the best terms that anyone has ever offered to a people and the most valuable help in conquering the land overseas.

Firstly, if God allows you to restore his inheritance to him, he will put the whole of Romania [Byzantium] in obedience to Rome, from which it has been severed. Next, because he understands how you have given everything you have for the crusade so that you are now poor, he will give two hundred thousand silver marks to the nobles and the ordinary people together. And he himself will personally go with you to the land of Egypt with ten thousand men . . . he will perform this service for a year, and for the rest of his life he will maintain five hundred knights in the land overseas at his own expense.

The terms were extraordinarily generous. They seemed to offer everything to everyone. The papacy could achieve one of its most ardent objectives: submission of the Orthodox Church in Constantinople to Rome; the crusaders could not only handsomely repay their debt, they would gain the military resources both to conquer and to retain the Holy Land. The pope, it was suggested, would actually welcome such an action. And it would be easy: Angelus had many supporters in Constantinople; the gates would be flung open to welcome the liberators from his tyrannical uncle, the emperor Alexius III. 'Sirs,' concluded the envoys in the tone of persuasive salesmen offering a once-in-a-lifetime bargain, 'we have full authority to conclude these negotiations should you wish to do so. And you should be aware that such generous terms have never been offered to anyone. He who turns them down obviously has no real appetite for conquest.'

Some of what they said was wish-fulfilment; some was simply

untrue. In fact Angelus had called on Innocent with an outline of this plan the previous autumn and been given a very dusty response. Innocent had already warned the crusaders off supporting such a scheme, which would involve yet another attack on Christian lands, 'lest, by any chance, fouling their hands with the massacre of Christians, they commit a sin against God', and had written to the Byzantine emperor to say that he had done so. Alexius Angelus was young, ambitious and foolish. He was making unwise promises he could not guarantee, telling the crusader lords what they wanted to hear. But an inner circle of Frankish barons was already acquainted with the scheme and they were receptive. Boniface of Montferrat, the leader of the whole venture, had family grievances against the Byzantine emperor. Afterwards Innocent would lay the blame for what ensued squarely on the Venetians, but it was not their idea. It is uncertain if Dandolo knew in advance of the plan to divert the crusade to Constantinople; it is likely that he appraised it with a very cool eye. He certainly knew much more about the inner workings of Constantinople than most of the French barons, and he did not invest much confidence in the young Angelus. As for Angelus, the treaty being put forward in his name would eventually cost him his life.

The decision as to whether to attack a second Christian city on their way to the Holy Land was put to a restricted council of secular and religious leaders at Zara the next day. It immediately reopened furious and schismatic debate, which threatened, yet again, to jeopardise the whole expedition. Opinion was sharply divided. The abbot of Vaux again railed against it 'for they had not agreed to wage war against Christians'; on the other side an iron pragmatism was put forward: the army was short of funds, the debt remained outstanding, this would provide both money and men to retake the Holy Land: 'You should know that the Holy Land overseas will only be recovered via Egypt or Greece [Byzantium], and that if we turn down this offer we will be shamed forever.' Dandolo must have weighed it carefully: the debt would be handsomely repaid and an emperor favourable to their interests would be highly valuable in Constantinople, yet the Venetians also had a lot to lose. The Republic was once more trading profitably there and its resident merchants would again make easy hostages if the bid failed, but poverty was ultimately the driver of events. The crusade could simply fail for lack of money and food; if Angelus could easily be installed, Dandolo reasoned that 'we could have a reasonable excuse for going there and taking the provisions and other things . . . then we should well be able to go overseas [to Jerusalem or Egypt].' After careful consideration he decided to join those in favour, 'partly', declared one anti-Venetian source, 'in the hope of the promised money (for which that race is extremely greedy), and partly because their city, supported by a large navy, was in fact arrogating to itself sovereign mastery over that entire sea'. This was a retrospective judgement of the way things fell out.

Eventually, a powerful caucus of French barons, led by Boniface, overrode all objections and voted to accept the proposal. It was quickly signed and sealed in the doge's residence. Alexius was to arrive two weeks before Easter. It was effectively stitched up – and had possibly been agreed in outline long before the crusade set sail. The common crusaders would be taken wherever their feudal masters wanted and the Venetians sailed. Even Villehardouin had to admit that 'this book can only testify that among the French party only twelve swore oaths, no more could be obtained'. He conceded that it was highly contentious: 'so the army was in discord . . . Know that men's hearts were not at peace, because one of the parties worked to break up the army, the other to hold it together.' There were significant defections. Many of the rank and file 'gathered together and, after having made a compact, swore they would never go there'. A number of high-ranking knights, similarly disgusted, took the same course. Some returned home, disappointed; others sought passage direct to the Holy Land. Five hundred were lost in a shipwreck. Another band was set upon and massacred by Dalmatian peasants. 'So the army continued to dwindle day after day.'

Innocent, meanwhile, as yet unaware of this latest – and more heinous – act of wickedness, followed up his previous threats with an explicit excommunication of the unrepentant Venetians, but his hold over the crusade was weakening by the day. Yet again its leaders simply suppressed the letter. Then, just as the fleet was preparing to sail south, they despatched a half-hearted apology for doing so back to Rome, safe in the knowledge that they would be out of earshot by the time any response could come. It was accompanied by the disingenuous explanation that Innocent would actually have preferred them to suppress his letter than let it lead to the break-up of the expedition! 'We are confident', they wrote, 'that it is more pleasing in your sight, that . . . the fleet remain together than it be lost by a sudden display of your letter.' When Dandolo finally got round to apologising two years later, he would use the same get-out.

On 20 April, with all the equipment, horses and men re-embarked, the bulk of the fleet set sail for Corfu. By this time, the Venetians, far from repentant, had razed Zara to the ground: 'its walls and towers, palaces too, and all its buildings'. Only the churches were left intact. Venice was determined that the rebellious city should be incapable of further defiance. Dandolo and Montferrat remained in Zara; they were waiting for Alexius, the young pretender. He turned up five days later – on St Mark's Day, a carefully timed arrival – 'and was received with a celebration of unmeasurable festivity by the Venetians who were still there'. They then embarked on galleys and followed the army down to Corfu.

The crusade was lurching from crisis to crisis – its need for cash being continuously set against the distasteful means of obtaining it – and the arrival of the young pretender seems to have prompted a further wave of revulsion amongst the faithful. In Corfu Alexius was initially received with all the trappings of imperial majesty by the leading Frankish barons, who 'greeted him and then treated him with great pomp. When the young man saw the high-born men honouring him like this, and the force that was there, he was more joyful than any man had ever been before.

Then the marquis came forward and conducted him to his tent.' And there, according to the count of Saint-Pol, Alexius resorted to his own emotional blackmail: 'on bent knees and drenched in tears, he implored us as a supplicant that we should go with him to Constantinople'. It was a tactic that misfired badly. There was, according to Saint-Pol, 'great uproar and dissent. For everyone was shouting that we should hurry to Acre, and nor were there more than ten who praised the idea of making the journey to Constantinople.' Robert of Clari put the views of the ordinary man more bluntly: 'Bah! What are we doing with Constantinople? We have our pilgrimage to make . . . and our fleet is to follow us for only a year, and half of it has gone by already.'

So furious was the controversy that a large dissenting group of leading Franks left the camp and set themselves up in a valley some distance away. Panic infected the crusader command. According to Villehardouin 'they were mightily distressed and said "Sirs, our situation is dire: if these men leave us . . . our army will be lost."' In a make-or-break attempt to prevent the crusade's total collapse, they set out on horseback to beg the dissidents to reconsider. The atmosphere, when the two parties met, was highly charged. Both groups dismounted and walked cautiously towards each other, uncertain what would happen. Then,

. . . the barons fell at their feet, all weeping, and said that they would not get up until those who were there promised not to leave them. And when the others saw this, they were moved to great compassion and wept bitterly when they saw their lords, their relatives and their friends fall at their feet.

It was an extraordinary piece of manipulation – and it worked. The dissidents were overwhelmed by this raw emotional appeal and agreed to go forward, on strict terms. It was now mid-May and the Venetian ship lease was running out. They would stay at Constantinople only until 29 September. The leaders had to swear that when this time came they would provide ships to the Holy Land at two weeks' notice. They set sail from Corfu on 24

May. According to Villehardouin, always ready to put the most positive spin on events, the day

was fine and clear, the wind soft and gentle and they unfurled their sails to the breeze ... and such a fine sight was never seen. It seemed that this fleet would certainly conquer lands because as far as the eye could see, one could behold nothing but sails, ships and other craft, so that men's hearts rejoiced greatly.

The crusade had survived by the skin of its teeth.

And yet for those who could see, the Corfu stay should have given further pause for thought. Alexius had promised that the Byzantines would recognise the justice of his claim, that the gates of Constantinople would be flung wide to welcome him and then the Orthodox Church would bow to the supremacy of Rome. Nothing at Corfu presaged such an outcome. The citizens remained loyal to the ruling emperor, kept their gates shut and bombarded the Venetian fleet in the harbour, forcing it to withdraw. As for the religious schism, when the Orthodox archbishop of Corfu invited some of his Catholic brethren to lunch, he remarked that he could see no basis for Rome's primacy over his church, other than the fact that it had been Roman soldiers who had crucified Christ.

Back in Rome, Innocent's worst fears had been confirmed. He had now learned that, after sacking Zara, the crusaders were sailing for Constantinople. On 20 June he penned another blast: 'Under threat of excommunication we have forbidden you to attempt to invade or violate the lands of Christians . . . and we warn you not to contravene this prohibition lightly.' Expressing his utter revulsion at the possibility of redoubled sin, he summoned up the most distasteful metaphor at his command: 'A penitent returning to his sin is regarded as a dog returning to its vomit.' The letter makes quite clear whom Innocent held responsible for this state of affairs. Dandolo is likened to Pharaoh in Exodus, who 'under a certain semblance of necessity and the veil of piety' kept the crusaders, as the children of Israel, in bondage. He is 'a person hostile to our harvest', a trifle of leaven 'corrupting the whole mass'. Innocent commanded the crusader leaders to present the letter of excommunication to the Venetians, 'so that they cannot find an excuse for their very sins'. At the same time he was wrestling with the tricky theological problem as to how the crusaders might consort with the excommunicated Venetians on the ships. His elliptically worded solution was startling: they might travel with them to the Holy Land, 'where, seizing the opportunity, you might suppress their malice, insofar as it is expedient'. Decoded, it suggested that the unrepentant Venetians might justifiably be destroyed.

But everyone in the fleet, willingly or otherwise, was in this together, and it was far too late. With a fair wind, the fleet was making steady progress towards the Dardanelles even as Innocent set pen to paper. Four days later, on 24 June 1203, the crusaders were in the Bosphorus, looking up, astonished, at the impregnable walls of Constantinople. Events had drifted well beyond Innocent's control. The following month he sorrowfully acknowledged as much: 'For here the world ebbs and flows like the sea, and it is not easy for someone to avoid being driven hither and thither in the ebb and flow, or for him, who does not stay in the same place, to remain unmoved in it.' The maritime image was telling.

5

At the Walls

Some time on 23 June 1203, the people of Constantinople gazed out from the sea walls to behold an extraordinary sight: an enormous Venetian fleet tacking up the Bosphorus from the west, carrying ten thousand Christian crusaders intent on replacing their emperor. Many were puzzled and stunned; almost all were unprepared. Among the audience of this maritime spectacle was an aristocratic chronicler of the Byzantine court, Niketas Choniates. As he prepared to recall the events about to unfold, Choniates was overcome by emotion. 'Up to now, the course of my history has been smooth and it went along easily,' he wrote of his narrative. 'Now, to tell the truth, I hardly know how to describe what happened next.'

Choniates was scathing about the present emperor, Alexius III, who had deposed and blinded his own brother Isaac, and whose nephew was now coming to demand the throne. 'A man who could not even lead sheep' was perhaps his kindest verdict. The emperor was lazy, pleasure-seeking, complacent and intrinsically unwarlike – though he may also have been lulled by Innocent's letters assuring him that aggressive action from the west was forbidden and would not happen. At any rate, preparations for such an eventuality were minimal. When urged to take precautions against the impending storm, 'it was as though his advisors were talking to a corpse'. The Byzantine navy was almost non-existent – its admiral had sold off the anchors, sails and rigging. Reluctantly the emperor 'began to repair the rotting and worm-eaten small vessels, barely twenty in number'. He preferred to put his faith in the defensive strength of the city's walls and his army. Constantinople occupied the best-fortified position in the medieval world; its thirteen-mile triangular site was guarded by sea on two fronts, the third by a formidable triple wall, which had remained unbreached in eight hundred years. As for forces, he commanded some thirty thousand men – three times the size of the crusader army – backed by the civilian resources of a substantial population.

Many of the Venetians were familiar with the silhouette of Constantinople looming on their port bow; to the landlubber crusaders seeing its walls for the first time, the prospect was extraordinary. It took their breath away. Constantinople was on a scale quite beyond their experience. It was the largest metropolis in the Christian world; the capital of an empire which, although shrunken, controlled most of the eastern Mediterranean, from Corfu to Rhodes, Crete to the shores of the Black Sea, much of Asia Minor and continental Greece. The city's population numbered four or five hundred thousand; Venice's was perhaps sixty thousand, Paris the same. From the water they could see, behind the encircling sea walls, a city dense with impressive buildings, all dominated by the mother church of Hagia Sophia, whose imposing dome looked, as one Greek writer put it, as if it were suspended from heaven.

The European chroniclers struggled to find analogies to convey the scale of the place: 'it has more inhabitants than those who live in the area from the city of York all the way to the River Thames', the parochial English chronicler Ralph of Coggeshall assured his readers. A sense of wonder, awe – and growing trepidation – informs the eyewitness accounts. 'They looked on Constantinople for a long time because they could scarcely believe there could be such an enormous city in all the world,' declared Villehardouin.

They saw its high walls and magnificent towers by which it was enclosed for all its circumference, and the fine palaces and tall churches, of which

Constantinople from the sea

there were so many that none would believe it if he hadn't seen this with his own eyes, as well as the great dimensions of the city, which is the sovereign of all others. Know that there was no one so brave that his flesh did not tremble.

What they could not yet fully grasp was what Constantinople contained: the marble, the broad streets, the mosaics, the icons, the sacred gold, the treasure houses, the ancient statues looted from the classical world, the holy relics and irreplaceable libraries; nor could they fathom the scale of its dark underside: the huddled slum streets of wooden houses on the hills down to the Golden Horn where a downtrodden urban proletariat eked out lives of poverty and riot. Medieval Constantinople was a mirror image of ancient Rome, a place where explosive popular and partisan tensions exposed the melting-pot city to superstition, chronic instability and dynastic upheaval. Above all its people were fiercely loyal to their Orthodox faith and deeply hostile to the rival claims of Rome. A city whose population was given to contemptuously naming their dogs 'Rum Papa' – the Roman pope – was unlikely to respond well to Angelus's confident promise that it would easily submit to its detested rival.

The Venetians had a better understanding of the situation; there were perhaps as many as ten thousand of their compatriots trading within the city, and they did not underestimate the task. Dandolo was a sage adviser and he gave the crusader lords the benefit of his knowledge. 'My lords, I know the situation in this land better than you do, because I have been there before. You have undertaken the most arduous and perilous mission undertaken by any men. For this reason it is critical that you proceed with care.' On 24 June, the day after they first sighted Constantinople, the whole fleet passed close under the city walls. It was John the Baptist's feast day and the fleet made a magnificent array as it sailed by, with banners and pennons streaming in the wind and shields hung from the ships' sides. On the deck the soldiers nervously sharpened their weapons. They passed so close they could see a throng of people watching from the walls, and they loosed arrows at the Greek ships as they went.

As they set up camp on the Asian shore across the water from the city and foraged for food, they waited in confidence for Angelus's supporters to welcome them in as liberators. None came. Instead an ambassador from the emperor arrived to declare he was 'deeply puzzled why and for what purpose you have come to his kingdom ... because he is a Christian and you are also Christians, and he is well aware that you have set out to recover the Holy Land overseas'. The ambassador, an Italian, offered them food and money to speed them on their way, backed by a threat from the emperor: 'If he wanted to do you harm, you would be destroyed.'

A growing uncertainty gripped the crusader command as to

how exactly to proceed. The lack of welcome was unnerving. It was Dandolo again who proposed a way forward; by this time he probably had a good idea of the true state of affairs via Venetian merchants within the city. To break the deadlock he suggested that they should sail up to the city walls, display Angelus to the population and explain that he had come to free them from the tyrant. Ten galleys set out under flag of truce; the young prince was placed in the lead galley with Dandolo and Boniface. As they rowed up and down very close to the walls, the young prince was shown to those watching intently from the battlements above: 'Behold your true lord,' the herald called across the water in Greek. 'Know that we do not come to do you harm, but to protect and defend you.' There was silence; then shouts: 'We do not recognise him as our lord; we do not even know who he is.' On being told that he was the son of Isaac, the former emperor, there was a further riposte: they knew nothing about him. It was probably followed by a sharp volley of arrows for added emphasis. Not a single person had expressed support for the crusaders' champion. 'We were stunned,' recorded Hugh of Saint-Pol. The crusaders had believed utterly in the scenario of instant success that Angelus had painted for them at the outset. They would have been less surprised if they had taken heed of the reaction he had received on Corfu. The Greeks wanted nothing to do with this western puppet who had promised submission to Rome. It did not help that Angelus was visibly under the wing of the unpopular Venetians. 'And so they sailed back to camp and went each to his own quarters.' It was a gloomy moment. The crusaders knew now that they would have to fight their way in if they wanted money and men to win back the Holy Sepulchre. Jerusalem must have suddenly looked a long way off. They prepared for war. And for the first time the crusaders began to look sideways at the young man who had promised them so much – 'a child in mind rather than age', was the disgusted judgement of Choniates.

The day after this failed approach, Sunday 4 July, the crusader barons attended a solemn mass and gathered to formulate their plans. Dandolo, with his detailed knowledge of the city, was probably again instrumental in their choice of tactics. The city's harbour was in the sheltered Golden Horn, a long creek on its eastern flank. It was down by this shoreline that the Venetians had their settlement; the city walls were at their weakest along this stretch. To protect the harbour the Byzantines had a chain of iron links strung across its mouth, from the walls of the city to the tower of Galata, fringed by the settlement of the Jewish community, on the headland opposite. It was decided that the first step must be to land near the suburb of Galata, storm the tower and break the chain, allowing the fleet to sail into the Horn. Time was pressing hard on the crusaders; they were already short of supplies. That evening men confessed their sins and drew up wills, 'since they did not know when God would impose his will on them'. There was much apprehension about undertaking an amphibious landing on a contested shore; 'there was real doubt that they would be able to land at Constantinople', remembered Robert of Clari. They 'were to embark upon their ships and go forward to take the land by force and either live or die'.

Intense preparations were made. The horses were caparisoned and saddled and walked back up the ramps onto the horse transports, accompanied by their knights. Helmets were laced tight, crossbows cranked. It was a fine summer morning just after sunrise. The Venetian galleys rowed out, towing the transports behind them to secure a safe passage across the fast-flowing Bosphorus currents, with Dandolo in charge. Ahead of them went oared barques packed with archers and crossbowmen to clear the shore as they swept in. The attack was accompanied by the tremendous noise of a hundred trumpets, 'of silver and brass', and the heavy thumping of drums. It seemed 'as if all the sea were covered with ships', according to Clari. The emperor had his troops massed on the shoreline ready to push them into the sea. As the armada closed on the beach, a shower of bolts and arrows forced the defenders back; knights with lowered visors splashed heavily through the shallows; archers followed, running and firing; behind them the horse ramps were lowered and the mounted knights came thundering out of the belly of the ships, lances ready, silk banners streaming in the wind. It was probably the psychological impact of this sudden apparition that broke the Greek spirit. The mounted knights lowered their lances for a concerted cavalry charge, with the momentum 'to make a hole in the wall of Babylon', as one Byzantine writer once memorably put it. The emperor's men 'by God's grace withdrew, so that we could hardly reach anyone even by an arrow shot'. For the Greeks, with the advantage of possession, it should have been as fiercely contested as a Normandy beachhead, but they tamely surrendered the position. It was not a good omen for the emperor.

Alexius still held the Galata tower – the key to the sea chain and the Golden Horn – but worse quickly followed. Next morning 'at the hour of terce', the Greeks made a counterattack. Men burst out of the tower and set upon the crusaders on the shore; at the same time a secondary force came across the Horn in boats. Initially the crusaders were caught by surprise but they regrouped and repulsed the Greeks, who attempted to flee back into the tower but failed to close the gate. It was quickly taken. The windlass that controlled the chain was now in the hands of the intruders. Sensing the moment, one of the great Venetian sailing ships, the *Eagle*, on the momentum of the Bosphorus winds, crashed through the chain and surged into the Horn. The puny force of Byzantine vessels gathered at the chain was scattered or sunk by pursuing galleys. The Venetian fleet now sailed into the calm waters of Byzantium's inner harbour, close enough to start making the emperor very uncomfortable indeed. Four days later the crusaders moved closer still. The army marched up the east bank of the Horn and attempted to make a crossing at a small bridge opposite the north-eastern corner of the walls. Here was another opportunity for the Greeks to repel their adversary; they broke the bridge but failed to prevent the crusaders from repairing it and marching across. 'No one came out of the city to oppose them, which was quite extraordinary, because for every man that was in our army, there were two hundred in the city.' The crusader army took up camp on a hill directly opposite the most favoured of the emperor's residences, the Blachernae Palace, set into the massive land walls. The emperor and his enemies could look each other full in the face: 'We were so near', said Hugh of Saint-Pol, 'that our arrows hit the palace roof and went through the windows below, and the arrows of the Greeks hit our tents.'

At last Alexius seemed to have roused himself from his torpor – or complacency – and began to harass the intruders in more determined fashion. Probing sorties were sent out by day and night to test the crusaders' resolve; 'They were never able to relax,' recalled Villehardouin. They were 'kept so hemmed in that six or seven times a day the whole army was called to arms. They could neither sleep, rest nor eat without being armed.' A new sense of desperation infected the crusader camp. The force that had set out so bravely to win back the Holy Land nine months ago now found itself in the inconceivable position of having to do or die outside a Christian city. From their position at the north-eastern corner of Constantinople they could appreciate the size of the task. To the west, the land walls stretched away in an unbroken series of triple defences, cresting the rolling terrain to the horizon. A succession of towers alternated on the inner and outer walls, so close that 'a seven-year-old boy could toss an apple from one turret to the next'. It was 'a terrifying prospect; along the three leagues of Constantinople's land walls, the whole army could only besiege just one gate . . . Never, in any city, had so many people been besieged by so few.'

Hunger was driving the army forward. Alongside the quest for money, the imperative to seek out food was a continual leitmotiv of the crusading venture. They only had three weeks' supplies left, and they were being kept closely confined by the attentions of the Greeks. 'They were unable to search for food more than four crossbow-shots away from the camp, and they had precious little flour and bacon . . . and no fresh meat apart from the horses that they killed.' 'I had become so desperate,' recorded the aristocratic

Hugh of Saint-Pol, 'that I had to exchange my surcoat for bread. However I did manage to hold onto my horses and weapons.' The clock was ticking on their resolve. They needed to bring matters to a head with all possible speed.

Dandolo wanted the whole army to mount a ship-borne attack across the Golden Horn. The walls here were at their lowest – a single defensive line only thirty-five feet high. His plan was to lower 'astonishing and magnificent devices' – improvised flying bridges – from the masts of his tallest ships onto the walls so that men could pour into the city. The Venetians were expert at the practical engineering procedures needed to construct and operate such devices, and comfortable with mounting attacks suspended thirty feet above a pitching deck. These were mariners' skills. The earth-bound knights paled at fighting in mid-air above a rolling sea and made their excuses; they would conduct their own assault on the land wall near the Blachernae Palace using battering rams and scaling ladders. In the end it was agreed to make a simultaneous attack by land and sea on the north-eastern corners.

On 17 July, after days of preparation, the Fourth Crusade readied itself for an all-out assault on a Christian city. The flying bridges had been constructed from the yard-arms of the sailing ships, lashed together and planked to create bridges wide enough for three men to walk abreast. They were covered with hide and canvas to protect the attackers from missiles, and mounted on their largest transports. If Clari is to be believed, these structures were a hundred feet long and were hauled up the masts on a complex system of pulleys. The Venetians also mounted stone-throwing machines on the prows of the transports and winched crossbowmen up to the tops in wicker cages; the decks, packed with archers, were covered with ox hides to protect them against the terrifying effects of 'Greek fire' – jets of burning petroleum projected from flamethrowers. 'They organised their attack very well,' according to Villehardouin. At the land walls, the Franks had mustered scaling ladders, battering rams, mining equipment and their own heavy catapults, ready for a concerted rush.

That morning they moved forward by land and sea. Dandolo had his fleet drawn up in a single line of 'a good three crossbow-shots in length'. It advanced slowly across the placid Horn, protected by a torrent of rocks, crossbow bolts and arrows ripping across the sky at the sea walls. They were met by a similar hail of projectiles back, whipping across the decks, pelting the covered flying bridges. The huge sailing vessels – the *Eagle*, the *Pilgrim*, the *Santa Monica* – surged towards the walls until the flying bridges crashed against the battlements so that 'the men on either side struck at each other with swords and lances'. The noise was extraordinary – the blowing of trumpets, the thudding of drums, the clash of steel, the smashing of rocks hurled by the mangonels, the shouts and screams. 'The roar of the battle was so loud it seemed as if both land and sea shook.'

At the land walls, the crusaders propped up their ladders and attempted to force their way in. 'The attack was forceful, good and strong,' according to Villehardouin, but they were well matched by the emperor's crack troops – the Varangian Guard, long-haired axe-wielding Danes and English – and the resistance was stubborn. Fifteen men made it up onto the walls; there was fierce hand-to-hand fighting but the intruders could make no progress; they were hurled back off the ramparts; two men were taken prisoner and the assault juddered to a halt 'with a lot of men wounded and injured; the barons were extremely disturbed'. Critically, the Venetian attack also started to falter. The fragile low-lying galleys refused to follow the transports in, alarmed by the torrent of missiles being hurled down on them. The whole enterprise hung in the balance.

It was at this moment that the doge made a critical intervention, probably the single most significant action in the whole long maritime history of the Republic. Dandolo, old and blind, was standing 'in the prow of his galley, fully armed and with the banner of St Mark set up in front of him', in the admiring words of Villehardouin. He could evidently hear the sound of battle raging around him – the shouts and cries, the crash and fizz of arrows and missiles; whether he sensed that the Venetians were now hanging back is unclear; more likely he was told. Evidently he realised the seriousness of the situation. The doge peremptorily ordered his galley to row forward and put him ashore, 'or else he would punish them severely'. The vermilion galley rowed hard for the shore, into the barrage of Greek missiles; as it landed, the banner of St Mark was seen being carried onto dry land; the other vessels followed, shamefacedly, in its wake.

After the mosaics that commemorate the body of St Mark sailing to Venice, this is the single most iconic image in Venetian history – the blind doge, standing erect at the prow of his ship with the red-and-gold lion banner of St Mark fluttering in the wind as his ship grounds beneath the menacing city walls; battle rages around him, but the wise old merchant crusader stands unmoved, urging his fleet on. The memory of this moment, endlessly recounted, would send shivers of martial patriotism down the spines of the Venetian people for hundreds of years; it would become the rallying cry in times of intense national danger, cited as the supreme example of the old heroic qualities on which the wealth of the Republic was built. Four hundred years later Tintoretto would be commissioned to recreate the scene in the council chamber of the doge's palace in vivid, if anachronistic, detail. With hindsight the Venetians understood what it meant. Dandolo's initiative made possible, via a train of events that no one could predict at the time, the Republic's ascent to Mediterranean empire. If that day the Venetians had failed by sea, as the French had by land, the whole expedition would probably have collapsed.

But it did not. Shamed by the blind doge, the Venetian galleys surged up onto the beach; the assault was renewed; then the red and gold of St Mark was seen fluttering from one of the towers, probably by the men on the flying bridges. A battering ram was set to the walls. Suddenly overwhelmed, the defenders withdrew, leaving the Venetians to open gates and stream into the city. In a short time they were in control of twenty-five or thirty towers

– a quarter of all the walls along the Golden Horn. They started to push up the hill among the narrow streets of wooden houses, capturing booty, including valuable warhorses.

Now Alexius seems to have stirred himself from a complacent belief in the strength of his defences. For days he had 'sat back as a mere spectator of events', watching passively from the windows of the Blachernae Palace. With the Venetians inside the walls, he now had to act. He sent down detachments of the Varangian Guard to force the intruders out. The Venetians were unable to withstand this counterattack and fell back towards their newly captured towers. Desperate to retain a foothold they began torching the houses as they went, to create a barrier of fire between themselves and the advancing Greeks. In the heat of a July day with a stiff breeze blowing off the Golden Horn, the flames started to eat their way up the lower slopes of the north-eastern sector of the city, ripping through the densely packed streets, 'sending the inhabitants flying in all directions'. The sharp crackle of combusting wood and plumes of ominous smoke filled the air; the wall of fire advanced unpredictably in the erratic breeze; 'everything from the Blachernae hill to the Monastery of Evergetes was consumed by fire', remembered Choniates, and 'rushing flames were carried as far as the district of Deuteron'. By the time the fire was finally halted on the steepening slopes leading to the Blachernae Palace the following day, 125 acres of the city had been reduced to ashes; maybe twenty thousand people had lost their homes. In its place was a great charred open space – an ugly wound within the city's heart. To Choniates, 'That day produced a pitiful spectacle; it demanded rivers of tears to match the terrible fire.' He had as yet seen nothing that fire would inflict on his beloved city in the cause of war.

Meanwhile with the fire raging and the Venetians consolidating their position behind it, the quick-witted Dandolo started to ferry the captured horses up to the French camp. The success at the sea walls put new heart into the despondent crusaders at the land walls. Within the city, the emperor was under pressure.

Constantinople was burning. An ominous murmur reached his ears of the people's discontent: their houses had been destroyed; the Venetians were in control of the walls. 'He saw', observed Choniates, 'the mob stirred up by anger, heaping unrestrained curses and abuse on him.' Given the charged atmosphere, this was a dangerous moment for an emperor. It was time for decisive action.

Alexius drew up his forces and marched them out of the city gates to confront the crusader army on the plain. As the crusaders watched them pour out and form up, the spectacle took their breath away. They were greatly outnumbered: 'So many people marched out', reported Villehardouin, 'that it seemed as if the whole world was moving.' Despite the numerical advantage, Alexius's objective was probably a limited tactical one: to put sufficient pressure on the land army to push the Venetians back from the sea walls they were currently occupying. The Byzantines were wary of heavy western cavalry and had no need to risk battle in open terrain. If they could expel the Venetians, then the walls could still wear down the crusaders' morale.

And the land army was now in a position of supreme peril. Forced back at the walls, short of food, weary from days of feints and alarms around their camp, it seemed that they again had to do or die. Rapidly they lined up their forces in front of the palisaded encampment: lines of archers and crossbowmen, then knights on foot who had lost their horses, then the mounted knights, each of whose horses was magnificently 'adorned over all its other coverings with a coat of arms or a silk cloth'. They were formed up in disciplined order with strict instructions not to break ranks or charge intemperately. Yet the prospect in front of them was daunting. The Byzantine army seemed so huge that 'if they were to go out into the countryside to engage the Greeks, who had such a vast number of men, they would have been swallowed up in their midst'. In desperation, they turned out all their servants, cooks and camp followers, dressed in quilts and saddle cloths for armour, with cooking pots for helmets, brandishing kitchen utensils, maces and pestles in a grotesque parody of a military force

– an ugly Brueghelesque vision of an armed peasantry. These men were tasked with facing the walls.

Tentatively the two armies closed on each other, each side keeping good order. From the walls and the windows of the palace, the ladies of the imperial court looked down on the unfolding spectacle like spectators at the Hippodrome. At the sea walls, Alexius's show of force was having its desired effect. Dandolo 'said that he wanted to live or die with the pilgrims', and ordered the Venetians to withdraw from the sea walls and make their way up to the palisaded camp by boat.

Meanwhile, the crusaders were being drawn forward, away from the detachments guarding the camp. As they did so, it was pointed out to Baldwin, leader of the crusader army, that they would soon be out of reach of help if battle were engaged. He signalled a strategic withdrawal. The command was not well received. Within the chivalric code of knighthood, retreat was a smirch on honour. A group of knights disobeyed and continued the advance. For a short while the crusader ranks were thrown into disarray; a seasoned Byzantine general would have seized the moment to strike hard. The emperor did not; his army watched and waited from beyond a small valley that separated the two sides. Those around Baldwin were shamed by the spectacle of others riding forward in their place. They beseeched him to countermand the order: 'My lord, you are acting with great dishonour by not advancing; you must realise if you do not ride forward, we will not stay at your side.' Baldwin signalled a fresh advance. The two armies were now 'so close together that the emperor's crossbowmen fired directly on our men, at the same time as our archers fired into the emperor's ranks'. There was a tense stand-off.

And then the far larger Byzantine army started to withdraw. Whether it was the resolve of the crusaders that dissuaded the unwarlike emperor, or whether he had achieved his objective of forcing the Venetians out of his city is not clear. In either case it was to prove a public relations disaster with his own people. As his men drew back, they were followed at a wary distance by the enemy, brandishing their spears. It looked, from the lofty walls, like cowardice. 'He returned', wrote Choniates, 'in the most utter and shameful disgrace, having only increased the enemy's pride.'

Yet to the crusaders it seemed more like deliverance than victory. By God's will, they had been mysteriously let off. Their nerves had been strung to breaking point in the presence of the might of the Greek army and they had been lucky to escape from potential disaster. 'There were none so brave that he was not mightily relieved.' They returned to camp 'and took off their armour, because they were exhausted and overcome with fatigue. They ate and drank little because they had few provisions left.' The overall emotion was one of relief rather than elation.

What they did not know was that the city was crumbling from within. The humiliating spectacle of the retreating Byzantine army, played out before a watching audience below the city walls; the burnt houses; the muttering of the people; the slippery allegiances in the whispering galleries of the imperial palace – the emperor returned from the field of battle uneasily aware that his hold on power was precarious. He himself had come to power by blinding his brother Isaac II; Isaac, in his turn, after the mob had strung the emperor Andronicus upside down in the street, in an execution of repulsive fury. Opinion was turning against the emperor; 'It was as if he had actually worked to ruin the city,' was Choniates's scathing judgement. It was time to get out. Overnight, Alexius gathered up a large quantity of gold and precious imperial ornaments and slipped away. The imperial throne was suddenly vacant, the palace factions thrown into confusion. Stunned, they hauled the blinded Isaac back out of his monastery, reinstalled him on the throne and prepared to negotiate with the crusaders. Word was sent to their camp across the Golden Horn that Isaac wanted to make contact with his son, Alexius Angelus.

The crusaders were equally amazed when messengers reached their camp with the news. It seemed to Villehardouin like a vindication from God as to the justness of their cause: 'Now hear how mighty are the miracles of our Lord when it pleases him!' At a stroke it appeared that their troubles were over. The next day, 18 July, they sent four envoys, two Venetians and two Frenchmen, one of whom was Villehardouin, to the imperial palace to discuss terms with the new emperor. Angelus they kept safely back in their own camp, still wary of Byzantine tricks. The envoys made their way up to the Blachernae Palace along a route flanked by the Varangian Guard. Inside they beheld a scene of extraordinary wealth. The blind emperor, richly attired, seated on his throne; around him so many noble lords and ladies, all 'as magnificently dressed as could be'. The envoys, intimidated, or at least wary of this assemblage of people, asked to speak with Isaac in private. Here, before a select few, they outlined the terms that his son had agreed at Zara the previous December. It is clear from Villehardouin's account that the deal the 'foolish youth, ignorant of the affairs of state' had struck with these insistent westerners made Isaac's jaw drop open. The financial promises were outrageous: the two hundred thousand marks of silver, the year's supply of provisions for the Holy Land crusade, a year's campaigning by ten thousand Byzantine troops, a lifetime's maintenance of five hundred knights in the Holy Land. Worst of all was his commitment to place the Orthodox Church under the authority of Rome. The populace would instantly riot at such news. Isaac told them quite bluntly, 'I don't see how it can be honoured.' The envoys were insistent. Caught between a rock and a hard place, Isaac eventually conceded. Oaths were sworn and charters signed. The envoys returned triumphantly to their camp; Alexius Angelus was reunited joyfully with his father; on 1 August in a service of solemn pomp he was crowned co-emperor with his father in Hagia Sophia as Alexius IV.

It seemed as if an end was in sight for all the crusade's problems. The army withdrew, at the emperor's request, back over the Golden Horn, where it was supplied plentifully with food. Its candidate was now astride the Byzantine throne. The crusaders had been promised the resources to complete their pilgrimage to the Holy Land; they could now write confidently back home in the hope that the pope might forgive all their manifold sins. 'We carried out the work of Jesus Christ with his help,' wrote the self-justifying count of Saint-Pol, 'so that the Eastern Church . . . acknowledges herself to be the daughter of the Roman Church.' This was wishful thinking.

Saint-Pol spoke up particularly for the part played by Enrico Dandolo: 'For the Venetian doge, prudent in character and wise in making difficult decisions, we have a great deal of praise.' Without Dandolo, the whole venture might have perished outside the city's massive walls. And the Venetians were now in sight of reimbursement for their maritime efforts. They received eighty-six thousand marks from Alexius, the full amount of their debt; the other crusaders were similarly repaid. It seems that the new co-emperor would fulfil all his obligations to the expedition. The crusaders were free to tour the city which they had attempted to sack. They marvelled at its wealth, its statues, precious ornaments, its holy relics – objects of veneration for the pious pilgrims. Their admiration was both sacred and profane. Here was a city vastly richer than any they had seen in Europe. The westerners were astonished – and covetous.

Yet in this moment of holiday after the fight to survive, there were deep tensions. Constantinople remained taut, unappeased, volatile. Away from the broad thoroughfares and magnificent buildings, the Greek proletariat inhabited pitiful shanty towns; they were unpredictable and fiercely resentful of the imposition of the crusaders. Had they known of their new emperor's promise of submission to the Roman pope they would have exploded. Choniates likened this mood to a kettle coming to the boil. Their animosity was centuries deep, and it was reciprocated by the westerners' view of 'Greek treachery'. 'Their inordinate hatred for us and our excessive disagreement with them allowed for no humane feeling between us,' Choniates later said. The French demanded that a section of wall should be demolished as security for their visitors against hostage-taking. And they were deeply suspicious of the blind Isaac, who had attempted an anti-crusader alliance with Saladin twenty years earlier. From their camp three hundred yards across the Golden Horn, they could even see a mosque, built at that time just outside the sea walls for the use of a small colony of Muslims. It was a provocation.

And time continued to tick away. Despite the upfront payments, Alexius and Isaac were in growing trouble. The contract with Venice was due to expire on 29 September. It was now vital that the crusaders depart imminently. Alexius had no powerbase; he was dependent on the unpopular crusaders for support; he understood enough about the short and violent reigns of emperors to realise what their departure would mean. 'You must know', he frankly told the Venetian and crusader lords, 'that the Greeks hate me because of you, and if you abandon me I will lose this land again and they will kill me.' At the same time he was in financial straits; to keep up the payments he began on a course of action destined to double his unpopularity. 'He profaned sacred things,' howled Choniates, 'he plundered the temples, the hallowed vessels were seized from churches without the slightest qualm, melted down and given to the enemy as common gold and silver.' To the Byzantines, with their long experience of the Italian maritime republics, the westerners' lust for money seemed like a dreadful dipsomania: 'They yearned to drink again and again from a river of gold as if bitten by snakes that make men rabid with a thirst that can never be quenched.'

Confronted with the precariousness of the situation and the shortage of cash, Alexius, like a gambler doubling his stake whilst lengthening the odds, made the crusaders a new offer. If they would stay another six months, until 29 March 1204, this would give him time to establish his authority and meet his financial obligations; it was already late in the season to sail anyway, better to overwinter in Constantinople; he would pay all the provisioning expenses during that time, bear the costs of the Venetian fleet until September 2004 – another whole year – and provide his own fleet and army to accompany the crusade. If it was a desperate gamble by Alexius, it was also a hard proposal for the crusader lords to sell to the put-upon army, which was also still blissfully unaware that it was under excommunication.

Predictably there was uproar. 'Provide us with ships as you swore you would as we want to go to Syria!' they cried. It took considerable cajoling and persuasive argument to talk the bulk of the army round. There would be a further postponement until the spring, and 'the Venetians swore that they would provide the fleet for another year from the feast of St Michael [the end of September]'. Dandolo charged a further hundred thousand marks for the privilege. Alexius continued to melt down church gold 'to appease the ravenous hunger of the Latins'. The doge, meanwhile, wrote a smooth letter to the pope trying to explain the sack of Zara in the hope of getting the excommunication lifted.

The temperature in the kettle was steadily rising. And while Alexius went on a progress of his domains to cement his power-base beyond the city with the protection of a section of the crusader army – who had to be paid handsomely – it boiled over.

6

Four Emperors

Throughout the first assault on Constantinople, a substantial population of Italian merchants had remained within the city. The citizens of Amalfi and Pisa had loyally fought alongside their Greek neighbours when Dandolo attacked the sea walls. The Venetian merchants probably barred their doors and stayed inside. But as the Greek population surveyed the aftermath of this attack – hundreds of homes gutted by fire, an unpopular new emperor installed, a section of their walls demolished to empha- sise the humiliation of their proud city – they erupted in fury. The merchants' quarters were down by the Golden Horn, where they had wharves and warehouses. On 18 August a Greek mob descended on the hated Italians. Their rage centred on Venice but the rampage quickly became indiscriminate. They ransacked all the merchant dwellings, driving out loyal foreigners as well as the treacherous Venetians. 'Not only were the Amalfitans . . . disgusted by this wickedness and recklessness but also the Pisans who had chosen to make Constantinople their home,' reported Choniates in dismay. The Pisans and Venetians disliked each other intensely but mob violence had given them a common cause. Now gath- ered in the crusader camp they had a shared motive for revenge.

The following day a freelance force of Venetian and Pisan merchants and Flemish crusaders commandeered some fishing boats and sailed back across the Horn. The two groups probably had different goals. The crusaders were tempted by the chance to plunder the taunting mosque on the waterfront. The ousted merchants were bent on revenge. When the Muslims called for help, the Greek population ran out to repulse the intruders. Some of the Venetians and Pisans made it through the open gates and set upon the properties of their former Greek neighbours, 'then they fanned out into various places and fired the houses'. It was the height of a long dry summer; an impatient wind was blowing steadily from the north. The close-packed wooden houses on the lower slopes started to crackle and burn. The fire, propelled by the wind, picked up speed and began advancing up the hills into the heart of the city.

Fires were a common hazard in Constantinople, but this, according to Choniates, 'proved all the others to be but sparks'. A wall of flame 'whooshed up unbelievably high'; it leaped gaps across the streets, tacking with the shifting course of the wind, advancing across a front hundreds of yards wide, veering unpredictably to leave areas untouched, then whipping back on itself. As night fell, cyclones of sparks were sucked skywards on the thermal updraft, and 'balls of fire were hurled up from the inferno high into the sky so that remarkably they consumed buildings a good distance away'. The lines of flames divided and came together again 'meandering like a river of fire . . . advancing gradually and leaping over walls to ravage the buildings beyond'.

In the dark, the crusaders looked on in horror from across the water at the long humped silhouette of city hills outlined in fire. Villehardouin watched 'those great churches and rich palaces melt and collapse, and the wide merchant streets consumed by flames'. The noise was deafening. Buildings went up 'like candle wicks' and exploded; marble shattered, iron bubbled and melted like water hissing on fire. Choniates, who himself lost considerable property, witnessed the destruction as the flames tore through some of the ancient and magnificent public spaces of the city.

Porticoes collapsed, the most beautiful buildings in the squares were toppled, the tallest columns consumed like brushwood. There was nothing that could withstand the fury of the fire . . . and the buildings towards the arch of the Milion . . . crashed to the ground . . . the porticoes of Domninos were reduced to ashes . . . and the Forum of

Constantine and everything lying between the northern and southern limits of the city was destroyed.

The fire licked the porch of Hagia Sophia but miraculously turned aside.

The city was divided by 'an enormous abyss, like a river of fire'. Driven by the flames, people struggled to move their valuables to safe ground, only to find that the fire 'taking a winding course and moving in zigzag paths and branching off in many directions and returning to its starting point, destroyed the goods that had been moved . . . The majority of the city's inhabitants were stripped then of their possessions.' Flying embers sucked out over the sea torched a passing ship. In the space of three days the fire cut a dark gash through the heart of urban Constantinople. Sporadic outbursts continued for days, the deep pits of smouldering embers whipped unpredictably back into ignition. From sea to sea, the inhabitants of the city, of whom probably only a small number actually died, found it cut in two by a blackened and smouldering strip of devastation. Choniates summed up the mood of the people with an anguished cry. 'Alas! The most splendid and beautiful palaces filled with beautiful things and the greatest riches, which astonished everyone – all gone.' Four hundred acres of the city had been atomised, and a hundred thousand people lost their homes, including Choniates himself.

Watching from their camp, the crusaders were struck dumb. 'No one knew who started the fire,' Villehardouin disingenuously proclaimed, figuratively staring at his shoes. Others were more honest; Baldwin of Flanders's court poet was later to say quite openly that 'he and we alike bear guilt for the burning of churches and palaces'. And the citizens of Constantinople knew exactly whom to hold responsible. Almost every westerner still residing in the city fled to the crusader camp. More than the treachery, the double-dealing, the mistaken intentions across the cultural divide, the events of 19–21 August marked a firebreak that could henceforth not be crossed. The crusading venture like a zigzag-ging fire was destroying everything in its ambient path. For the Venetians their long maritime adventure seemed to have no end in sight. They prepared to overwinter, drew their ships out of the water onto the banks of the Golden Horn and waited to see what would happen next.

In early November Alexius IV returned from his progress to the lands of Thrace. The expedition had been a relative success. He had subdued some cities previously loyal to his predecessor and mulcted them for cash. On his return he was accorded the welcome befitting a legitimate emperor; the populace and the crusader lords rode out to welcome him as he approached the gates. The Latins noticed a change in his manner; he was more self-confident, or as Villehardouin put it, 'The emperor began to show disdain towards the barons and those who had helped him so much.' The payments to the crusaders slowed down. At the same time his father, Isaac, as co-emperor, was pushed into the background. It was now Alexius's name that was mentioned first in proclamations. Embittered, the older man began to defame his son, claiming, amongst other things, 'that he kept company with depraved men whom he smote on the buttocks and was struck by them in return'. The blind old man fell prey to superstition and the toadying prophecies of monks. He was increasingly fearful of the mob; on the advice of his soothsayers he had one of the great totemic statues of the city – a monumental bronze image of a wild boar with raised bristles – removed from the Hippodrome and set up outside the palace in the belief that 'it could restrain the mad fury of the populace'.

Such presentiments were not misplaced, even if Isaac's mysti-cal defences were unlikely to prove adequate. Constantinople was descending into chaos. 'The wine-bibbing portion of the vulgar masses', as the aristocratic Choniates haughtily dubbed them, marched on the Forum of Constantine in an equally superstitious fury, and smashed to pieces a beautiful bronze statue of Athena, 'because the foolish rabble believed that she was turned towards the western armies'. Alexius meanwhile continued to melt down the valuables of the Church and taxed the nobles increasingly heavily to pay the crusaders. The proceeds were 'simply thrown to the dogs', according to Choniates.

It was not enough. By midwinter, funds were drying up. And in the shadows of the imperial court there waited another player in the game: Alexius Ducas, known colloquially as Murtzuphlus, meaning 'gloomy', because 'his eyebrows were joined together and seemed to hang down over his eyes'. He was a nobleman with a long history of court intrigue. He was ambitious, fearless and totally opposed to pandering to the westerners. Alexius had freed him from prison for plotting against his predecessor; it was to prove a bad mistake. As the winter drew on and the crusaders became more importunate, Murtzuplus emerged as the leader of the increasingly popular anti-western faction. When Boniface of Montferrat made a direct appeal to Alexius to pay what was due, Murtzuphlus's counter-counsel was blunt: 'Ah, sir, you have paid them too much. Don't pay them any more! You have paid so much you have mortgaged everything. Make them go away and then expel them from your land.' Eventually the payments stopped altogether, yet Alexius kept playing for time. He continued to support the crusader camp with food. He was walking a delicate tightrope but events began to spiral beyond his control. On 1 December, there was a further outbreak of mob violence against westerners close to the city walls and an attack on the Venetian ships. To the Greeks it was now clear that the ships were the key to everything; destroy the fleet and the crusaders would be trapped and vulnerable.

Across the Golden Horn the want of money was starting to tell. Dandolo and the crusader lords held a summit; they resolved on an ultimatum. Six leading notables, three crusader lords and three Venetians, were despatched to the palace to deliver a blunt message to the emperor. 'And so the envoys mounted their horses, buckled on their swords and rode together as far as the palace of Blachernae.' This was not a desirable assignment. At the palace gate they dismounted and made their way between the customary lines of Varangian guards into the hall, where they found the twin emperors, father and son, seated on beautiful thrones, surrounded by 'a large number of important lords, and it seemed to be the court of a rich prince'.

Apparently unintimidated, the envoys set out their case. To the feudal crusaders, the failure to pay was a breach of honour; to the bourgeois Venetians it was a broken contract. The words were straightforward. Tellingly they were addressed solely to Alexius: 'You swore to them, both you and your father, to keep the agreement which you had sworn – and [we] have the documents. But you haven't kept the terms as well as you should.' They demanded that the contract be honoured. 'If you do so it will be most agreeable to them. If not, understand that henceforward they will regard you as neither their lord nor their friend . . . Now, you have clearly heard what we have said and you must act as you please.'

To the westerners it was just plain speaking, but the Greeks 'were astonished and outraged at this challenge and said that no one had ever been brazen enough to dare to defy the emperor of Constantinople in his own hall'. There was immediate uproar, expressions of extreme ill-will, hands reaching for sword hilts, shouts and curses. Turning abruptly on their heels the envoys fled to the gate with a rising fury speeding them away. They rode off in palpable relief, lucky to be alive. The breakdown was decisive: if the crusaders wanted the funds to reach the Holy Land, they would have to take them. 'In this way,' Villehardouin recorded, 'the war began.'

But the matter was not quite settled. Dandolo, from the perspective of his ninety years, decided to make one more personal appeal to Alexius's better nature. He sent a messenger to the palace, requesting a meeting at the harbour. Dandolo had himself rowed across in a galley, with three more galleys packed with armed men to guard him. Alexius rode down to the shore. The doge opened abruptly: 'Alexius, what are you thinking of? Remember that it is we who dragged you out of misery and then made you lord and crowned you emperor. Will you not honour your commitments and not do anything more about it?' The emperor's response was firmly negative. Fury overcame the doge. 'No? Contemptible boy,' he spat, 'we hauled you out of the dung heap and we'll drop you back in it. And I defy you. Be fully aware that from now on I will pursue you to your utter destruction, with all the power at my disposal.' With these words the doge left and returned to camp.

Initially, there was skirmishing along the shores of the Golden Horn, without particular advantage to either side, but the Greeks knew where the weakness of the crusaders lay. They continuously eyed the ships. Some time probably in mid-December, they launched a night attack on the Venetian fleet. A number of fireships were prepared, laden with dry timber and oil, and with a stiff breeze blowing across the Horn, they were ignited and cut loose 'and the wind drove them at great speed towards the fleet'. It was only quick thinking by the Venetians which prevented disaster; rapidly boarding their own vessels they manoeuvred them out of the way of the guttering fireships. On the night of 1 January 1204, with conditions again favourable, the Greeks made a second attempt. The wind was again blowing hard towards the Venetian fleet; seventeen large ships were filled with timber, hemp, barrels and pitch. At the depths of midnight they set fire to the vessels and watched the fiery squadron surge across the harbour in a chained line. At the first call of the trumpets, the Venetians scrambled to their stations, cast off and tackled the approaching vessels. 'And the flames burned so high', recorded Villehardouin, 'that it seemed that the whole world was burning.' It was now that Venetian seafaring skill was put to the test.

A huge mass of Greeks came down onto the shoreline and hurled abuse at the detested Italians, 'and their shouts were so loud that it seemed that the earth and sea shook'. Some climbed into rowing boats and shot at the Venetian vessels as they put out from the shore. Undaunted, the Venetians gingerly approached the fiery armada and managed to attach grappling hooks to the line, and 'by brute force towed them out of the harbour in the face of their enemies', where they released the fireships and the strong Bosphorus current swept them away flaming into the night. Without Venetian skill, Villehardouin acknowledged that 'if the fleet had been burned they would have lost everything, because they would have been unable to depart by land or sea'.

Despite these determined assaults Alexius himself was conspicuous by his absence in the front line. The emperor was still trying to manage two counter-pressures, fearful that if the mood inside the city turned ugly, he might need to make yet another appeal to the crusaders. And they needed him alive too: it was Alexius with whom the deals had been struck all the way back in Corfu the previous spring. But Alexius's equivocation was keenly felt by his own subjects.

The people of the city, who were at least brave, demanded of their emperor that he should be as loyal as they were and use his strength to resist the enemy alongside the army – unless, of course, he was only paying lip service to the Byzantine cause and deep-down favoured the Latins. But his posturings were meaningless, for Alexius shrank from taking up arms against the Latins.

Furthermore, according to Choniates, who watched all this unfold with aristocratic alarm, 'The disgruntled populace, like a vast sea whipped up by the wind, contemplated revolt.'

Into this power vacuum, the shaggy-browed Murtzuphlus started to insert himself, energetically pressing forward with patriotic fervour in defence of the city, 'burning with desire to rule and to gain the citizens' favour'. On 7 January, 'displaying proof of outstanding courage', he led an attack on the hated intruders outside the walls. The Greeks were forced back and Murtzuphlus's horse stumbled and fell; he was only rescued by a company of archers, but this attempt demonstrated his willingness to defend the mother city. Alexius meanwhile seemed happy to sit behind the walls and watch, while the Venetians used their galleys to plunder the shores of the Golden Horn and employed fire, now the most hated form of war, to inflict further damage on the city. When the crusaders embarked on a two-day punitive raid across the surrounding countryside, plundering and despoiling, the exasperation of the mob finally exploded: the boiling kettle began 'to blow off steam of abuse against the emperors'.

On 25 January a rowdy crowd descended on the mother church of Hagia Sophia; under its domed and mosaicked canopy, they forced the senate and clergy to convene and demanded the appointment of a new emperor. Choniates was one of the city dignitaries present. The nobility were frozen with fear and indecision by this eruption of violent democracy. They refused to appoint any of their number; none wanted to be nominated, 'for we realised full well that whoever was proposed for the election would be led out the very next day like a sheep to slaughter'. Recent history had thrown up such ephemeral emperors whose reigns, like the gaudy life of dragonflies, had passed before sunset. The mob refused to budge from the church without a candidate. Eventually they seized a hapless young aristocrat, Nicholas Kannavos, led him to the church, placed a crown on his head, proclaimed him emperor and retained him there. It was now 27 January. The city descended into factional chaos. With Kannavos in the church, blind Isaac now dying and Murtzuphlus waiting in the wings, Alexius did what Choniates predicted he would. He played his last card. He called on the crusaders to enter the palace and secure his position. That day Baldwin of Flanders came to discuss this plan.

Murtzuphlus was party to these deeply unpatriotic deliberations. He knew that a moment had come. He secretly called on the palace power brokers, one by one. He won over the chief eunuch with the promise of new positions; he then gathered the Varangian Guard 'and told them about the emperor's intention and convinced them to consider taking as the right action that which was desirable and pleasing to the [Byzantines]'. Finally he went to deal with Alexius.

According to Choniates, at the dead of night on 27 January he burst into the emperor's chamber informing him that the Varangian Guard was massing at the door, 'ready to tear him apart' because of his friendship with the hated Latins. Terrified, confused and barely awake, Alexius begged for help. Murtzuphlus threw a robe over the emperor by way of disguise, led him out through a little-used door to 'safety' with the emperor gabbling pathetic thanks, and threw him, chained by the legs, into 'the most awful of prisons'. Murtzuphlus donned the imperial regalia and was proclaimed emperor. In the swirling confusion there were now four emperors in the city: the blind Isaac, Alexius IV Angelus in prison, Alexius V Murtzuphlus in the palace, Kannavos as the plaything of the mob in Hagia Sophia. The elaborate dignity of the great empire had completely collapsed. Murtzuphlus moved fast to clear up the mess. When the Varangian Guard burst into Hagia Sophia, Kannavos's protectors simply melted away. On 2 February, the innocent young noble, apparently a man of integrity and talent, was taken off and decapitated; on the fifth, Alexius V Murtzuphlus was crowned in Hagia Sophia with the customary splendour. The blind Isaac, when he was told of the palace coup, was seized by terror and conveniently died. Or he may have been strangled.

Outside the walls, the news of the coup was greeted as final proof of Byzantine duplicity: Murtzuphlus was not a legitimate emperor, he was a usurper – and a bloodthirsty one at that. According to the more lurid accounts, when he captured three Venetians he had them hung up by iron hooks and roasted alive, 'with our men looking on, and they could not be spared from such a horrible death by any prayer or payment'. More prosaically, he cut off the crusaders' food supply. The change of regime returned the crusaders to a state of chronic need. 'Once again,' one of the sources records, 'there was a time of much scarcity within our ranks and they ate many horses.' 'The prices in the camp were so high', reported Clari, 'that a *sestier* of wine was sold there for twelve sous, fourteen sous, even at times fifteen sous, a hen for twenty sous and an egg for two cents.' The crusaders embarked on another extensive raid to provision the army. They attacked the town of Philia on the Black Sea and were returning on 5 February with booty and cattle when Murtzuphlus, whose support now rested on the pledge rapidly to drive the Latins into the sea, rode out to intercept them. He took with him the imperial banner and a precious miracle-working icon of the Virgin, one of the most revered relics of the city, whose presence ensured victory in battle. In a fierce clash, the Greeks were rebuffed and the icon captured. Murtzuphlus rode back with a report that the battle had been won. Questioned as to the whereabouts of the icon and banner, he became evasive, declaring that they had been put away for safe-keeping. The following day, in an attempt to humiliate the upstart emperor, the Venetians put the imperial and sacred items on a galley and sailed up and down the city walls, taunting him with their trophies. When the Greeks saw this they turned on the new man; Murtzuphlus remained resolute. 'Don't be dismayed, for I will make them pay heavily and will fully avenge myself on them.' He was already being backed into a corner.

A day later, 7 February, Murtzuphlus tried a different tack. He sent messengers to the crusader camp to ask for a parley at a site up the Golden Horn. Dandolo again had himself rowed across in a galley, while a party of horsemen came round the top of the Horn for extra security. Murtzuphlus rode up to meet the doge. The crusaders now felt no hesitation in speaking plainly to one who had, according to Baldwin of Flanders, 'shut up his lord in prison and had snatched away his throne, after having disregarded the sanctity of an oath, fealty and a covenant – matters that are firmly binding even among infidels'. Dandolo's requests were blunt: release Alexius from prison, pay five thousand pounds of gold, swear obedience to the pope in Rome. To the new anti-western emperor these conditions were of course 'punitive and completely unacceptable'. While they were engrossed in these negotiations, 'putting aside all other thoughts', the crusader cavalry suddenly bore down on the emperor from the higher ground.

Giving free rein to their horses, they closed on the emperor, who wheeled his horse and scarcely managed to escape the danger, while some of his companions were captured.' This treacherous ruse confirmed what Choniates and the Greeks already felt, that 'their immense hatred for us and our great quarrel with them prevented there being any reasonable relations between us'.

And it was reciprocated the following day. Murtzuphlus had drawn one conclusion from the meeting with Dandolo: that as long as Alexius was still alive, he provided a cause for the troublesome intruders and a threat to himself. On 8 February, according to Choniates, he went twice to offer Alexius, chained in his dungeon, a cup of poison. It was refused. He then, according to the unreliable Baldwin, strangled him with his own hands, 'and with unheard-of cruelty, he tore apart the sides and ribs of the dying man with an iron hook that he held in his hand'. The Latins were ever ready to add extra gore to the blood-spattered chronicles of Constantinople. Choniates delivered a measured, if theologically more hair-raising account. Murtzuphlus 'cut the thread of his life by having him strangled, squeezing out his soul, so to speak, through the strait and narrow way, and sprang the trap leading to hell. He had reigned six months and eight days.' Within the context of the times, it was to prove quite a long reign.

Murtzuphlus gave out that Alexius had died, and buried him with honour. The crusaders were not deceived. Messages attached to arrows were shot over the walls to their camp proclaiming Murtzuphlus a murderer. To some, his death evoked no more than a shrug of the shoulders: 'A curse on anyone who regrets that Alexius is dead.' They merely wanted the resources to go on their crusade. But Alexius's death provoked a new crisis. Murtzuphlus ordered them to depart and vacate his land, or 'he would kill them all'. Now the Venetians had no hope of recouping their maritime costs and the Holy Land was receding by the day. The whole venture had been beset by continuous crisis management; the spring of 1204 was just a further astonishing twist. Time was now pressing hard on their heels: in March, the patience of the rank and file would finally expire; they would insist on being taken to Syria. They could not go back to Italy without acquiring undying shame; they did not have resources to attack the Holy Land; food was running out; the only course was to press forward: 'Perceiving that they were neither able to enter the sea without danger of immediate death nor delay longer on land because of their impending exhaustion of food and supplies, our men reached a decision.' Constantinople must be stormed.

This required yet another theological U-turn: if the taking of Zara had been a sin, Constantinople was a magnification of it. None of the leaders of the venture were unaware of the pope's final prohibition: even if the Greeks did not bow to the Catholic Church in Rome, he had placed an absolute ban on using this as justification for attacks on their fellow Christians: 'Let no one among you rashly convince himself that he may seize or plunder the Greeks' lands on the pretext that they show little obedience to the Apostolic See.' They were now going to do just that.

Dandolo, the crusader barons and the bishops met in yet one more crisis session. Moral justification was required for this further perversion of the crusaders' pledge. Murtzuphlus had given them one and the clergy dutifully endorsed it: such a murderer had no right to possess lands, and all those who had consented to the crime were complicit in it. And, above and beyond all this, the Greeks had withdrawn from obedience to Rome. 'So this is why we tell you', said the clergy, 'that the war is right and just and if you have a strong determination to conquer this land and bring it into obedience to Rome, those of you who die confessed will receive the same indulgence as has been granted by the pope.' In plain words, taking the city could be counted as fulfilling the crusaders' vows. Constantinople, by sleight of hand, had become Jerusalem. This was, of course, a lie – but it was swallowed, because it had to be. 'You should know', said Villehardouin, ever keen to airbrush the facts, 'that this was a considerable comfort both to the barons and the pilgrims.' The crusaders once more prepared to attack the city.

7

'The Works of Hell'

Both sides had learned from the attack on Constantinople ten months earlier that while the land walls were invulnerable, the sea wall along the Golden Horn was low and fragile, given the Venetians' naval skill. The hostilities were to be a complete rerun – for the Venetians it must have seemed like running in a dream.

The two opposing armies prepared accordingly. The Venetians readied their ships, reconstructed their flying bridges and shipboard catapults. The Franks rolled out their own siege engines and wheeled shelters that would allow their troops to work away at the base of the wall, protected from bombardment from above. This time there were refinements. The Venetians prepared wooden frames over their ships and covered them with nets made from vines 'so that the stone-throwing catapults could not shatter the ships into pieces or sink them'. They had hides soaked in vinegar draped over the hulls to lessen the risk from flaming arrows and firebombs, and they loaded siphons of Greek fire onto their ships.

Murtzuphlus however had also analysed the problem of the low sea wall and devised an ingenious defence. On top of the regular line of battlements and turrets the Greeks now built grotesque wooden structures of immense height – sometimes seven storeys high, with each storey hanging pendulously further out, like fantastical medieval houses crowding over a street. The overhang was critical. It meant that anyone propping a ladder against the wall from below would be confronted with an insuperable obstacle, and the task was made more daunting by trapdoors in the floors of the towers from which rocks, boiling oil and missiles could be rained down on the enemy. 'There was never any city so well fortified,' declared Villehardouin. The new emperor overlooked nothing. The turrets were protected with soaked hides; all the gateways were bricked up and Murtzuphlus erected his command headquarters, a vermilion tent, on a prominent hill in front of the monastery of Christ Pantepoptos – the All-seeing – which afforded him a panoramic strategic overview of the battlefield below.

These feverish preparations lasted most of Lent; the banks of the Golden Horn on both sides were abuzz with the sound of hammering and banging, the sharpening of swords on the blacksmiths' anvils, the caulking of hulls, the fitting of the complex superstructures to the Venetian ships. In March the crusader leaders convened to work out a set of ground rules for a positive outcome: what would happen if they won? It was crucial to predetermine a division of spoils and the future of the city; experienced commanders knew well that medieval sieges could descend into fractious chaos at the moment of apparent victory. The March Pact set down rules for the division of booty: the Venetians to get three quarters of the proceeds until their debt of 150,000 marks was paid off; thereafter the spoils to be divided equally; an emperor to be chosen by a committee of six Venetians and six Franks; the crusaders to remain in Constantinople for another year. There was a further clause that was of little regard to the feudal knights of Europe but critical to the merchants from the lagoon: the chosen emperor would permit no trade with anyone at war with Venice. This provided the Venetians with a lockout of their maritime competitors – the Pisans and the Genoese. It was a potential goldmine.

In an attempt to impose discipline, the army was made to swear on sacred relics that they would hand in all booty worth five sous or more, 'that they would use no violence against women or tear off their clothes, for whoever did so would be put to death ... nor lay hands on any monks, cleric or priest, except in self-defence, and that they would not sack church or convent'. Pious words. The army had been outside the walls for eleven months. They were hungry and angry; they had been detained here against their will; they had seen the immense wealth of the city for themselves; they knew the customary rewards for taking a city by storm.

By early April everything was ready. On the evening of Thursday the 8th, ten days before Easter, the men were confessed, and boarded their ships; the horses were loaded onto the horse transports; the fleet lined up. The galleys were interspersed among the transports. The great ships with their high poops and forecastles towered over them all. As dawn approached they cast off to make the short crossing of the Horn, a distance of a few hundred yards. It was an extraordinary sight – the fleet strung out along a mile front with the outlandish flying bridges protruding from their masts, 'like the tilting beam of a scale's balance', the great ships each with the flags of its lord fluttering in the wind as proudly as when they left the lagoon nine months earlier. Handsome rewards were offered for scaling the walls. From the decks the men could look up at the overhanging wooden superstructures,

each containing a multitude of men . . . [and] either a petrary [a stone-throwing siege engine] or a mangonel was set up between each pair of towers . . . and atop the highest storey platforms were extended against us, containing on each side ramparts and bulwarks, with the tops of the platforms at a height slightly less than a bow could shoot an arrow from the ground.

On the rising ground behind they could see Murtzuphlus directing operations from in front of his tent, 'and he had his silver trumpets sounded and his snare drums beaten and they made a mighty racket'. As they neared the shore, the ships slowed and winched themselves in; men started to disembark, splashing through the shallows and trying to advance ladders and battering rams under their sheltering roofs soaked in vinegar.

They were met by volleys of arrows and 'enormous stone blocks ... dropped on the siege engines of the French ... and they began to crush them, shattering them to pieces and destroying all their devices so effectively that no one dared stay in or under the siege equipment'. The Venetians swung their flying bridges up towards the castellated battlements but were finding it difficult to reach the tall superstructures – or to steady their ships in a stiff contrary wind that forced the ships back from the shore – and the defence had been carefully organised and well stocked with weapons. The attack started to falter; the men ashore could not be supported by the buffeted ships pushed back by the wind; eventually the signal was given to withdraw. From the ramparts there were loud hootings and jeerings; trumpets and drums thundered; in a final gesture of triumphal mockery some of the defenders climbed up onto the highest platforms 'and dropped their breeches and showed their backsides'. The army retired in despair, convinced that God did not want the city to fall.

That evening there took place in a church an agonised confer-ence between the crusader lords and the Venetians about how to proceed. The problem was the opposing wind, but it was also morale. A proposal to attack the sea walls outside the Horn was opposed by Dandolo, who was well aware of the strong current along that shore. 'And know', declared Villehardouin, 'that there were those who wanted the current or the wind to take the ships down the straits – they did not care where so long as they left the land and went on their way – and this was no wonder for they were in grave peril.' The chronicler continuously brought a charge of cowardice against those with a distaste for the manner in which the crusade had been hijacked.

To raise morale, the ever obliging clergy resolved on a cam-paign of theological vilification of their fellow Christians within the city. On Palm Sunday, 11 April, all the men were called to service, where they heard the leading preachers in the camp deliver a unified message to each national group, 'and they told them that because [the Greeks] had killed their rightful lord, they

were worse than the Jews . . . and that they should not be afraid
of attacking them for they were the enemies of the Lord God'.
It was a message that drew on all the prejudicial motifs of the
age. The men were bidden to confess their sins. In a short-term
gesture of virtuous piety all the prostitutes were expelled from the
camp. The crusaders repaired and re-armed the ships and prepared to launch a new assault the following day: Monday 12 April.

They adjusted their equipment for this second attempt. It was
clear that a single ship throwing its flying bridge forward to attack
a tower had not worked: the defenders could bring all the weight
of numbers to bear on the one spot. It was now decided to link the
high-sided sailing ships, the only vessels with the height to reach
the towers, in pairs, so that the flying bridges could grapple with
a tower from both sides like twin claws. Accordingly they were
chained together. Again, the armada sailed out across the Horn
to the din of battle. Murtzuphlus was plainly visible in front of
his tent directing operations. Trumpets and drums sounded; men
shouted; catapults were cranked up – the waterfront was quickly
engulfed in a storm of noise, 'so loud', according to Villehardouin,
'that the earth seemed to shake'. Arrows thocked across the water;
gouts of Greek fire spurted up from the siphons on the Venetian
ships; enormous boulders, 'so enormous that one man couldn't lift
them', were hurled through the air from the sixty catapults ranged
on the walls; from the hill above, Murtzuphlus shouted directions
to the men, 'Go here! Go there!' as the angle of attack altered. The
defensive arrangements of both sides worked well. The Greek fire
fizzled out against the timber superstructures on the ramparts,
which were protected by leather casings soaked in vinegar; the
vine nets absorbed the force of the boulders which struck the
ships. The contest was as inconclusive as the day before. And
then, at some point, the wind shifted to the north, propelling the
giant sailing ships closer to the shore. Two of these vessels which
had been chained together, the *Paradise* and the *Pilgrim*, surged
forward, their flying bridges converging on a tower from both
sides. The *Pilgrim* struck first. A Venetian soldier clattered up the

walkway, sixty feet above the ground, and leapt onto the tower. It was a gesture of doomed bravery; the Varangian Guard advanced and cut him to pieces.

The flying bridge, responding to the surge of the sea, disengaged and closed on the tower for a second time. This time a French soldier, Andrew of Durboise, took his life in his hands and leapt the gap; scarcely grabbing the battlements, he managed to haul himself inside on his knees. While he was still on all fours, a group of men rushed forward with swords and axes and struck him. They thought that they had dealt him a death blow. Durboise, however, had better armour than the Venetian. Somehow he survived. To the astonishment of his assailants, he climbed to his feet and drew his sword. Appalled and terrified by this supernatural resurrection, they turned and fled to the storey below. When those on that level saw the flight, they in turn became infected with panic. The tower was evacuated. Durboise was followed onto the ramparts by others. They now had secure control of a tower and tied the flying bridge to it. The bridge however continued to dip and rear with the movement of the ship against the sea. It threatened to pull down the whole wooden superstructure. The bridge was untied, cutting off the small band of soldiers on their hard-won foothold. Further down the line, another ship struck a tower and managed to take it, but the crusaders on the two towers were effectively isolated, surrounded by a swarm of men on the towers either side. The contest had reached a critical point.

However, the sight of flags flying from these towers put new courage into the attackers now landing on the fore shore. Another French knight, Peter of Amiens, decided to tackle the wall itself. Spotting a small bricked-up doorway, he led a charge of men to try to batter it open. The posse included Robert of Clari and his brother, Aleaumes, a warrior monk. They crouched at the foot of the wall with their shields over their heads. A storm of missiles pelted down on them from above; crossbow bolts, pots of pitch, stones and Greek fire battered on the upturned shields whilst the men beneath desperately hacked away at the gate 'with axes and good swords, pieces of wood, iron bars and pickaxes, until they made a sizeable hole'. Through the aperture they could glimpse a swarm of people waiting on the other side. There was a moment of pause. To crawl through the gap was to risk certain death. None of the crusaders dared advance.

Seeing this hesitation, Aleaumes the monk thrust his way forward and volunteered himself. Robert barred the way, certain his brother was offering to die. Aleaumes struggled past him, got down on his hands and knees and started to crawl through with Robert trying to grab his foot and haul him back. Somehow Aleaumes wriggled and kicked his way free to emerge on the far side – to a barrage of stones. He staggered to his feet, drew his sword – and advanced. And for a second time the sheer bravery of a single man, fuelled by religious zeal, turned the tide. The defenders turned and ran. Aleaumes called back to those outside, 'My lords, enter boldly! I can see them withdrawing in dismay. They're starting to run away!' Seventy men scrambled inside. Panic rippled through the defence. The defenders started to retreat, vacating a large part of the wall and the ground behind. From above, Murtzuphlus saw this collapse with growing concern and tried to muster his troops with trumpets and drums.

Whatever the new emperor may have been he was no coward. He spurred his horse and started down the slope, probably virtually unaccompanied. Peter of Amiens ordered his men to stand their ground: 'Now, lords, here is the moment to prove yourselves. Here comes the emperor. See to it that no one dare to give way.' Murtzuphlus's advance slowed to a halt. Unsupported, he drew back and returned to the tent to rally his forces further back. The intruders demolished the next gate; men started to flood inside; horses were unloaded; mounted knights galloped through the open gates. The sea wall was lost.

Meanwhile Peter of Amiens advanced up the hill. Murtzuphlus abandoned his command post and rode off through the city streets to the Bucoleon Palace, two miles away. Choniates bewailed the behaviour of his fellow countrymen: 'The cowardly thousands, who had the advantage of a high hill, were chased by one man from the fortifications they were meant to defend.' 'And so it was', wrote Robert of Clari from the other side, 'that my lord Peter had Murtzuphlus's tents, chests and the treasures which he left there.' And the slaughter began: 'There were so many wounded and dead that there seemed no end to them – the number was beyond computation.' All afternoon the crusaders plundered the surrounding area; further north refugees started to stream out of the land gates.

At the day's end the crusaders drew to a halt 'exhausted by fighting and killing'. They were wary of what lay ahead: in the dense tangle of city streets, the soldiers and citizens could put up a spirited defence, street by street, house by house, raining missiles and firepots down on them from the rooftops, ensnaring them in guerrilla warfare which might last a month. The crusaders ferried all their men across and camped outside the walls, with detachments controlling the red tent and surrounding the well-fortified imperial palace of Blachernae. No one knew what was happening in the city's labyrinth or how the four hundred thousand population would react, but if they would neither surrender nor fight, it was decided to wait until the wind was right and burn them out. They now knew how vulnerable the city was to fire. That night a fire was started pre-emptively by twitchy soldiers near the Horn, tearing out another twenty-five acres of housing.

In the heart of Constantinople, there was chaos. People wandered aimlessly about in despair or took to removing or burying their possessions, or left the city, heading north across the wide plain. Murtzuphlus rode here and there, trying to persuade them to stand their ground, but it was hopeless. Shaken by the rippling succession of disasters – the repeated attacks, the devastating fires, the short-lived and violent ends of successive emperors – they could summon no loyalty to the present incumbent. Fearing that he would, as Choniates put it, be 'fed into the jaws of the Latins as a banquet if he were captured', he abandoned the palace and boarded a fishing boat and sailed away from the city – yet another emperor at loose in the Greek back country, having reigned for two months and sixteen days. Choniates was a stickler for the dates. Once more 'the ship tossed by storms' lacked a captain.

What was left of the ruling clique struggled to absorb each fresh blow. There was a scrabbled attempt to find yet another emperor; early on 13 April, the tattered remnant of the imperial administration and the clergy convened at Hagia Sophia to elect the successor. There were two candidates, evenly matched young men, 'both modest and skilled in war'. The choice was made by drawing lots, but the winner, Constantine Lascaris, refused to put on the imperial insignia – he was not prepared to be identified as emperor if resistance proved futile. Outside the church, the Varangian Guard drew up in formation nearby at the Milion, the golden milestone, a ceremonial arch surmounted with the figure of Constantine the Great. This was the epicentre of Byzantium, the point from which all distances in the empire were measured. They stood there, axes in hand, awaiting orders from the new emperor, according to tradition.

It did not start well for Lascaris. He harangued the large number of people gathered at the ancient heart of the city, 'cajoling them to resist . . . but none of the crowd were swayed by his words'. The Varangians asked for a pay rise to fight. This was granted. They marched off, but never fulfilled their orders, quickly realising the odds were against them, so that 'when the heavily armed Latin troops appeared, they promptly scattered and sought safety in flight'. Lascaris had already realised all was hopeless. The briefest of all the brief reigns in Constantinople was over within hours. The 'emperor' entered the palace, just a few hours after Murtz-uphlus had vacated it, and followed suit: he took a boat across the Bosphorus to Asia Minor, where Byzantium would live to fight again.

Down by the Horn, the crusaders started a perplexing day. They nervously prepared for the hard street fighting ahead. Instead they encountered a religious procession coming down the hill from

Hagia Sophia to their camp. The clergy advanced with their icons and sacred relics, accompanied by some of the Varangian Guard, 'as was the custom in rituals and religious processions', and a host of people. In a city undergoing a period of repeated civil wars this was practised procedure: to welcome in a new emperor deposing the old. They explained that Murtzuphlus had fled. They had come to acclaim Boniface as the new emperor – to honour him and lead him to Hagia Sophia for his coronation.

It was a moment of tragic misunderstanding. To the Byzantines this was customary regime change. To the Franks it was abject surrender. And there was no emperor – according to the March Pact that had still to be decided – only an ugly, angry, desperate army to whom the idea had been preached, not two days before, that the Greeks were treacherous people, worse than the Jews who had killed Christ, worse than dogs.

They started to advance into the heart of the city. It was true: there was no opposition; no trumpets or defiant martial clamour. They quickly found that 'the way was open before them and everything there for the taking. The narrow streets were clear and the crossroads unobstructed, safe from attack.' Stupefied, 'they found no one to resist them'. The streets were apparently lined with people who had turned out 'to meet them with crosses and holy icons of Christ'. This pacific, abject, trusting, desperate ritual was horribly misjudged. The crusaders were utterly unmoved: 'At this sight their demeanour remained unchanged, nor did the slightest smile cross their faces, nor were their grim and furious expressions softened by this unexpected spectacle.' They just robbed the bystanders, beginning with their carts. Then they started a wholesale sack.

At this point the chronicle of Niketas Choniates breaks out into an anguished cry of pain: 'O City, City, eye of all cities . . . have you drunk at the hand of the Lord the cup of his fury?' Over the space of three days Choniates watched the devastation of the most beautiful city of the world, the destruction of a thousand years of Christian history, the plunder, rape and murder of its citizens. His account, frequently descending into a threnody of semi-articulate pain, unfolds in a series of vivid snapshots as an eyewitness to profound tragedy. He barely knew where to start: 'Which actions of these murderous men should I relate first, and which should I end with?'

To the Byzantines, Constantinople was the sacred image of heaven on earth, a vision of the divine made manifest to man, a vast sacramental icon. To the crusaders it was a treasure house waiting to be stripped. The previous autumn they had visited Constantinople as tourists and seen the extraordinary wealth of the place. Robert of Clari was one of many open-mouthed at the glimpse of riches afforded to the warrior class of underdeveloped western Europe: 'For if anyone should relate to you even a hundredth of the richness, beauty and magnificence that was there in the convents, monasteries, abbeys and palaces of the city, he would be taken for a liar and you would not believe him.' Now it all lay at their mercy.

The two crusader leaders, Boniface and Baldwin, hurried to secure the richest prizes – the sumptuous imperial palaces, the Bucoleon and the Blachernae, 'so rich and so magnificent that no one could describe it to you', where the crusader deputations had been repeatedly overawed by the wealth of the Byzantine court. Elsewhere there was indiscriminate plunder. All the vows made before the attack were forgotten. The crusaders targeted both churches and the mansions of the rich. The Greek accounts are vivid with rhetorical anguish:

Then the streets, squares, two-storeyed and three-storeyed houses, holy places, convents, houses of monks, and nuns, holy churches (even God's Great Church), the imperial palace, were filled with the enemy, all war-maddened swordsmen, breathing murder, iron-clad and spear-bearing, sword-bearers and lance-bearers, bowmen [and] horsemen.

They battered their way into Hagia Sophia and started to strip the place. The high altar, fourteen foot long, 'so rich that no one could estimate its value', whose surface was 'made of gold and precious stones broken and ground up all together', 'blazing with every sort of precious material and wrought into an object of extraordinary beauty, astonishing to everyone' – this was hacked to pieces. The overarching canopy, supported on slim columns, all of solid silver, was dragged down and broken up; the hundred silver chandeliers suspended each by a great chain 'as thick as a man's arm', the columns studded with 'jasper or porphyry or some other precious stone', the silver altar rails, the golden censers and sacrificial vessels – 'and the pulpit, a wonderful work of art, and the gates . . . completely faced with gold', all were chopped into transportable lots. Axes, crowbars and swords hacked, wrenched and prised out. Every corner of the church was probed for the valuables it might contain, the monks tortured for hidden treasures, casually despatched for trying to protect a venerated icon or particular relic; women were raped there, men were killed.

To the Greeks it was if these crusaders who had come in the name of God were filled with a kind of terrible madness,

baying like Cerberus and breathing like Charon, pillaging the holy places, trampling on divine things, running riot over holy things, casting down to the floor the holy images of Christ and His holy Mother and of the holy men who from eternity have been pleasing to the Lord God, uttering calumnies and profanities, and in addition tearing children from mothers and mothers from children, treating the virgin with wanton shame in holy chapels, viewing with fear neither the wrath of God nor the vengeance of men.

Mules and asses were led into Hagia Sophia to carry away the loot but were unable to keep their footing on the polished floors of ancient polychromatic marble and slipped and fell; somehow maddened by this difficulty, the looters slashed the terrified animals open with their knives. The floor became slippery with blood and the muck of excrement from their punctured bowels. A prostitute, evidently not expelled from the camp, was set on the patriarch's throne 'and started to sing a wretched song and danced about, spinning and turning'.

Some of this ecclesiastical looting was nominally in a religious cause. Abbot Martin of Pairis learned that the Church of the Pantocrator Monastery housed an extraordinary collection of relics. Hurrying there with his chaplain, he entered the sacristy – the depository of the most sacred objects – where he encountered a man with a long white beard. 'Come faithless old man,' bawled the prelate, 'show me the more powerful of the relics you guard. Otherwise understand that you will be punished immediately with death.' The trembling monk showed him an iron chest, containing a trove of treasures, 'more pleasing and more desirable to him than all the riches of Greece'. 'The abbot greedily and hurriedly thrust in both hands, and as he was girded for action, both he and the chaplain filled the folds of their habits with sacred sacrilege.' With their robes stuffed with religious treasure, the two men waddled back to their ship, with the old monk in tow. 'We have done well . . . thanks be to God,' was the abbot's laconic reply to passers-by.

An extraordinary list of the religious treasures of the Orthodox world made it back to the monasteries of Italy and France: the Holy Shroud, hair of the Virgin Mary, the shinbone of St Paul, fragments of the crown of thorns, the head of St James – the venerated objects were carefully itemised in the chroniclers' accounts. Dandolo obtained for Venice a piece of the True Cross, some of Christ's blood, the arm of St George and part of St John's head. Many of the great icons and valued religious talismans of the Byzantine Church were just lost in the rampage – probably smashed to pieces by men intent only on precious metal. By the Church of the Holy Apostles, where Constantine himself and all the emperors were buried, they plundered all night, 'taking whatever gold ornaments, or round pearls, or radiant, precious and incorruptible gems were still preserved within'; crowbarring open the tombs, they gazed on the face of the great Justinian, builder of Hagia Sophia, dead for seven hundred years. His corpse was not decomposed in the airtight tomb. They looked upon this sight as if it were a miracle – then looted the body for its valuables. And everywhere there were acts of terrible molestation:

They slaughtered the new-born, killed prudent matrons, stripped elder women, and outraged old ladies; they tortured the monks, they hit them with their fists and kicked their bellies, thrashing and rending their reverend bodies with whips. Mortal blood was spilled on holy altars, and in place of the Lamb of God sacrificed for the salvation of the universe, many were dragged like sheep and beheaded, and on the holy tombs the wretches slew the innocent. Such was the reverence for holy things of those who bore the Lord's Cross on their shoulders.

The murders and rapes appalled:

There was no one spared grief – in the wide streets and the narrow lanes; there was wailing in the temples, tears, lamentations, pleas for mercy, the terrible groaning of men, the screams of women, the tearing to pieces, the obscene acts, enslaving, families torn apart, nobles treated shamefully and venerable old men, people weeping, the rich stripped of their goods.

'Thus it went on,' continued Choniates, thunderous with rage, 'in the squares, in corners, in temples, in cellars – everywhere terrible deeds.' 'The whole head', he said, 'was in pain.' In a final taunting gibe, he contrasted the generous treatment by Saladin at the recapture of Jerusalem seventeen years earlier. 'They allowed everyone to go free and left them everything they possessed, content with just a few gold coins' ransom on each head ... thus the enemies of Christ dealt magnanimously with the Latin infidels.'

There were just a few brief moments of human sympathy. The crusaders looting the Church of St George of Mangana were stopped dead in their tracks by the spiritual presence of the saintly figure of John Mesarites, a bearded ascetic, who told the intruders that his purse was so empty that he feared no thieves. They stood before him in silence. Led to the baron in charge, he sat on the floor. The baron placed him in the seat of honour and knelt at his feet. His unearthly sanctity impressed the Norman warriors. He was fed, according to his brother's sardonic account, 'like some ancient saint by thievish, man-eating magpies'.

Choniates, who himself showed considerable personal courage, was also the recipient of acts of extraordinary humanity. His palace had been destroyed in the devastating fire of the previous year. At the moment of the sack he was living quite humbly. 'My house, with its low portico, was difficult to approach because of its cramped location', hidden away near Hagia Sophia. Despite his detestation of the Venetian invaders, this polished aristocrat obviously had sympathetic personal relations with some resident foreigners. Most had fled before the final attack, but he had taken into his household a Venetian merchant and his wife and protected them. When the looters finally reached the house, Domenico the merchant acted with considerable presence of mind. Donning armour so that he looked like one of the invading Italians, he resisted all attempts to sack the house, claiming that he had already gained possession of it for himself. The intruders gradually became more insistent, particularly the French, 'who were not like the others in either character or physique'. Realising that he could not hold out indefinitely, and fearing the rape of the women, Domenico moved them all to the house of another Venetian. The net closed on this house too. Domenico moved them again. The servants fled.

The proud Byzantine nobles found themselves reduced to the status of common refugees. Abandoned by their servants, 'We had to carry the children who could not walk on our shoulders and a baby boy, still a suckling, in our arms; thus we were compelled to make our way through the streets.' Domenico ingeniously dragged them along as if they were his captives. Choniates realised that it was essential to leave. On 17 April, five days after the siege, a small group of nobles started the dangerous walk up the main thoroughfare towards the Golden Gate – a distance of three miles. They wore ragged clothes to conceal their origins; the patriarch, with no sign of his rank as archbishop, took the lead. It was a wet and windy day. Choniates's wife was heavily pregnant and some of the young women in the group were temptingly beautiful to the French soldiers lounging about; the men cordoned the girls in the middle of the party, 'as if in a sheep pen', and instructed them to rub mud into their faces to disguise their looks. 'We passed through the streets like a line of ants,' said Choniates. All went well until they passed a church. Suddenly 'a lecherous and wicked barbarian' thrust himself into the band of refugees and snatched a girl, the young daughter of a judge, and dragged her away. The judge, who was ageing and ill, tried to run after him but stumbled and fell in the mud. Lying there he called on Choniates to free the girl.

Choniates took his life in his hands. 'Immediately I turned on my heels in pursuit of the abductor.' In tears, he called out to passing soldiers to take pity and help, and even grabbed some by the hand and persuaded them to follow. The whole party and a group of soldiers followed the abductor back to his lodging where he had secured the girl and barred the door. He now defied the crowd to do their worst. And there Choniates made an impassioned speech, wagging his finger at the potential rapist, shaming the crusaders he had gathered with a ringing address, reminding them of their vows before God, appealing to them to remember their families and the precepts of Christ. Somehow it worked. Enough was transmitted across the barrier of language. He incited their anger and won them round. The crowd threatened to hang the villain on the spot. Sulkily he surrendered the girl to her father, who was weeping with joy.

And so they made it out of the Golden Gate. From there they could look back along the rippling line of defensive land walls, intact for eight hundred years, now powerless to prevent this disaster. For Choniates the moment was too much. 'I threw myself headlong on the ground face down and cursed the walls, because they were completely untouched by the disaster, neither did they weep, nor had they collapsed in a heap, but were still standing, insensible.'

In the immediate aftermath, Constantinople witnessed a lewd and grotesque carnival. 'The beef-eating Latins', as Choniates dubbed them, roamed through the streets, 'riotous and indecent', mimicking the dress and customs of the Byzantines. They dressed themselves in Greek robes, 'to mock us and placed women's headdresses on their horses' heads, and tied the white bands which hang down their backs round their beasts' muzzles', and planted the distinctive Greek hats on their horses' heads and rode through the streets with abducted women on their saddles. Others, 'holding scribes' reed pens and inkwells, mimicked writing in books, mocking us as secretaries'. To Choniates's refined palate, these men were barbarians, guzzling and carousing all day long, gorging themselves on delicacies and their own disgusting, crude, pungent food – 'the chines of oxen boiled in cauldrons, chunks of pig mixed with bean paste and cooked up with a marinade of garlic paste and foul-smelling garlic'.

To this debauchery would be added the wholesale destruction of a thousand years of imperial and religious art. In the aftermath, the conquerors, with their hunger for precious metals and the copper and bronze from which to mint coins, cast into the furnace an extraordinary catalogue of statuary, much of which was ancient even at the city's founding in the fourth century, collected from across the Roman and Greek world by Constantine the Great. To Choniates the destruction was endless, 'like a line stretching out to infinity'. Under the blows of hammers and axes they felled the giant bronze figure of Hera, so immense that it took four oxen to cart the head away, and an enormous equestrian statue from its plinth in the Forum of the Bull, carrying a rider who 'extended his right hand in the direction of the chariot-driving sun . . . and held a bronze globe in the palm of his hand'. All these were melted down for coins.

The Venetian role in this rape and pillage goes largely unrecorded, though one German chronicler, keen perhaps to point a finger elsewhere, declared that the Italian merchants expelled from the city, particularly the Venetians, were responsible for the slaughter in a spirit of revenge. Choniates, who loathed Dandolo as a sly cheat largely responsible for the catastrophe, picked out the French crusaders as the most muscular pillagers of his beloved city – and owed the safety of himself and his family to the courage of a Venetian merchant. The Venetians at least had perhaps a more discerning attitude to the works of art that they plundered.

All the parties had solemnly sworn that the booty would be centrally collected and equitably divided according to clearly agreed rules. Baldwin of Flanders wrote that 'an innumerable amount of horses, gold, silver, costly tapestries, gems and all those things that people judge to be rich is plundered'. Much was never handed in; the poor, according to Robert of Clari, were again cheated. But the Venetians received the 150,000 marks owed to them under the terms of the agreements, and another hundred thousand to share amongst themselves. In material terms Dandolo's gamble seems to have paid off.

When it came to appointing a new emperor, Dandolo, in his nineties, excused himself from consideration, judging that, apart from his age, the election of a Venetian would be enormously contentious. There were two rival candidates, the counts Baldwin and Boniface. The Venetians probably threw their weight behind Baldwin, judging his rival too closely tied to Genoa. Venice's prime concern was above all to secure stability for its trading interests in the eastern Mediterranean, but the Latin Empire of Constantinople, as it came to be known, was shaky from the first; it was beset by internal squabbles between the feudal lords and outside pressure from the Byzantines and the neighbouring Bulgarians. For most of the surviving protagonists it would end badly. Murtzuphlus, who had escaped from the city, was treacherously blinded in exile by the other exiled rival, Alexius III; recaptured by the crusaders, he was prepared for a special end, reputedly devised by Dandolo. 'For a high man, I will detail the high justice one should give him!' He was taken to the base of the tall column of Theodosius, prodded up the internal steps to the platform at the top; sightless, but grasping his imminent fate, and watched by an expectant crowd, he was pushed off. Baldwin, the first emperor of the Latin Kingdom of Constantinople, died slowly in a Bulgarian ravine, his arms and legs chopped off at the joints; his rival, Boniface, also killed in a Bulgarian ambush, had his skull despatched to the Bulgarian tsar as a gift.

The blind doge survived, shrewd to the last. With a cool head, he masterminded a successful withdrawal of a crusader army almost encircled by the Bulgarians in the spring of 1205. Everyone who came in contact with the old man recognised his unique powers of discrimination and prudence. His superior judgement had saved the crusade from repeated disaster. He was, according to Villehardouin, 'very wise and worthy and full of vigour' to the end. Even Pope Innocent paid a kind of backhanded tribute to a man whom he heartily loathed. The Venetians had committed to stay at Constantinople until March 1205. A resident population remained to occupy their share of the city, but with the year up many more prepared to sail home. Dandolo, knowing that the end of his life was near, applied to the pope for release from his crusader vows and to be allowed to return too. Innocent had the last laugh – insisting that the aged old doge should proceed with the army to the Holy Land, to which it would never now go. 'We are mindful', he began smoothly,

that your honest circumspection, the acuteness of your lively innate character, and the maturity of your quite sound advice would be beneficial to the Christian army far into the future. Inasmuch as the aforesaid emperor and the crusaders ardently praise your zeal and solicitude and among [all] people, they trust particularly in your discretion, we have not considered approving this petition for the present time, lest we be blamed . . . if, having now avenged the injury done to you, you do not avenge the dishonour done Jesus Christ.

It must have afforded Innocent some impious satisfaction to gain the advantage, though he finally lifted the sentence of excommunication on the old man in January 1205. Dandolo spent his last days a long way from the lagoon. Like his father before him, he died in Constantinople. In May 1205 he breathed his last and was buried in Hagia Sophia, where his bones would remain for 250 years, until another convulsion racked the imperial city.

Innocent had initially applauded the deeds of the crusaders in bringing the Byzantines under the Catholic Church. Dandolo had been dead for two months before the truth about the city's fall finally reached him. His verdict fell on the crusaders like a scourge. Their enterprise had been 'nothing but an example of affliction and the works of hell'. The sack of Constantinople burned a hole in Christian history; it was the scandal of the age and Venice was held to be deeply complicit in the act. It would reinforce papal views of the merchant crusaders, who traded unapologetically with Islam, as enemies of Christ. The label would be regularly reapplied down the centuries. But for Venice it was an extraordinary and unlooked-for opportunity. They had set out in the autumn of 1203, banners flying, to conquer Egypt. The fortunes of the sea had carried them away to unforeseen destinations. As for their actual part in the proceedings they kept silent. There are no contemporary Venetian accounts of the crusade that was intended to take Jerusalem via Cairo but ended up in Christian Constantinople.

On 1 October 1204, the Byzantine Empire was formally divided among the victorious parties. The merchant crusaders returned from Constantinople with a rich array of trophies, marbles and holy relics. Where the Frankish crusaders hacked up and melted down, the Venetians picked their plunder like connoisseurs, carrying back to the lagoon intact works of art to beautify and ennoble the city. Along with the bodies of saints – Lucia, Agatha, Simeon, Anastasius, Paul the Martyr – they acquired caskets, icons and jewelled treasures, statues, marble columns and sculptured reliefs. Much of this went to adorn St Mark's; a pair of ancient bronze doors was installed at its entrance; a Roman statue was used to form the body of St Theodore with his crocodile atop one of the twin columns nearby; Dandolo himself was said to have selected from the Hippodrome the four bronze-gilt horses caught in dramatic and frozen motion with nostrils flaring and hooves raised, which came, along with the lion of Venice, to define the

The spoils of war

Republic's sense of itself: proud, imperial – and free. Dandolo had ensured that the Venetians, alone of all the participants in the Fourth Crusade, did not pay homage to its new emperor; they kept themselves clear of the whole edifice of feudal obligation.

Along with their exquisite spoils of war, winched ashore on the quays of Venice after the sack of 1204, the city acquired something else. Overnight it had gained an empire. Of all the parties that had set out in the autumn of 1202, it was the Republic that had profited most handsomely. Dandolo had taken the opportunity and shaped, for the lagoon dwellers, an extraordinary advantage.

PART II

ASCENT: PRINCES OF THE SEA

1204–1500

8

A Quarter and Half a Quarter

1204–1250

By the partition of Byzantium in October 1204, Venice became overnight the inheritor of a maritime empire. At a stroke, the city was changed from a merchant state into a colonial power, whose writ would run from the top of the Adriatic to the Black Sea, across the Aegean and the seas of Crete. In the process its self-descriptions would ascend from the Commune, the shared creation of its domestic lagoon, to the Signoria, the Serenissima, the Dominante – the dominant one – a sovereign state whose power would be felt, in its own proud formulation, 'wherever water runs'.

On paper the Venetians were granted all of western Greece, Corfu and the Ionian islands, a scattering of bases and islands in the Aegean Sea, critical control of Gallipoli and the Dardanelles, and most precious of all, three eighths of Constantinople, including its docks and arsenal, the cornerstone of their mercantile wealth. The Venetians had come to the negotiating table with an unrivalled knowledge of the eastern Mediterranean. They had been trading in the Byzantine Empire for hundreds of years and they knew exactly what they wanted. While the feudal lords of France and Italy went to construct petty fiefdoms on the poor soil of continental Greece, the Venetians demanded ports, trading stations and naval bases with strategic control of seaways. None of these were more than a few miles from the sea. Wealth lay not in exploiting an impoverished Greek peasantry, but in the control of sea lanes along which the merchandise of the east could be channelled into the warehouses of the Grand Canal. Venice came in time to call its overseas empire the Stato da Mar, the territory of the sea. With two exceptions it never comprised the occupation of substantial blocks of land – the population of Venice was far too small for that – rather it was a loose network of ports and bases, similar in structure to the way stations of the British Empire. Venice created its own Gibraltars, Maltas and Adens, and like the British Empire it depended on sea power to hold these possessions together.

This empire was almost an accidental construct. It contained no programme for exporting the values of the Republic to benighted peoples; it had little interest in the lives of these unwilling subjects; it certainly did not want them to have the rights of citizens. It was the creation of a city of merchants and its rationale was exclusively commercial. The other beneficiaries of the partition of 1204 concocted scattered kingdoms with outlandish feudal titles – the Latin Empire of Constantinople, the kingdom of Salonica, the despotate of Epirus, the megaskyrate of Athens and Thebes, the triarchy of Euboea, the principality of Achaea, the marquisates of Boudonitza and Salona – the list was endless. The Venetians styled themselves quite differently. They were proud lords of a Quarter and Half a Quarter of the Empire of Romania. It was a merchant's precise formulation, coming in total to three eighths, like a quantity of merchandise weighed in a balance. The Venetians, shrewdly practical and unromantic, thought in fractions: they divided their city into sixths, the capital costs of their ships into twenty-fourths and their trading ventures into thirds. The places where the flag of St Mark was raised and his lion carved on harbour walls and castle gates existed, in the repeated phrase, 'for the honour and profit of Venice'. The emphasis was always on the profit.

The Stato da Mar allowed the Venetians to ensure the security of their merchant convoys and it protected them from the whims of foreign potentates and the jealousy of maritime rivals. Crucially, the treaty afforded unequalled control of trade within the centre of the eastern Mediterranean. At a stroke it locked their competitors, the Genoese and the Pisans, out of a whole commercial zone.

Theoretically Byzantium had now been neatly divided into discrete blocks of ownership, but much of this existed only on paper, like the crude maps of Africa carved up by medieval popes. In practice it was far messier. The implosion of the Greek empire shattered the world of the eastern Mediterranean into glittering fragments. It left a power vacuum, the consequences of which no one could foresee –the irony of the Fourth Crusade was that it would advance the spread of Islam, which it had set out to repel. The immediate aftermath was less an orderly distribution than a land grab. The sea became a Wild East for adventurers and mercenaries, pirates and soldiers of fortune from Burgundy, Lombardy and the Catalan ports. It was a last Christian frontier for the young and the bold. Tiny principalities sprang up on the islands and plains of Greece, each one guarded by its desolate castle, engaging in miniature wars with its neighbours, feuding and killing. The history of the Latin kingdoms of Greece is a tale of confused bloodshed and medieval war. Few of them lasted long. Dynasties conquered, ruled and vanished again within a couple of generations, like light rain into the dry Greek earth. They were dogged by continuous, if uncoordinated, Byzantine resistance.

Venice knew better than most that Greece was no El Dorado. True gold was coined in the spice markets of Alexandria, Beirut, Acre and Constantinople. They impassively watched the feudal knights and mercenary bands hack and hatchet each other and pursued a careful policy of consolidation. They hardly bothered with many of their terrestrial acquisitions. They never claimed western Greece, with the exception of its ports, and unaccountably failed to garrison Gallipoli, the key to the Dardanelles, at all. Adrianople was assigned elsewhere for lack of Venetian interest.

The Venetians' eyes remained fixed on the sea but they had to fight for their inheritance, continuously dogged by Genoese adventurers and feudal lordlings. This would involve them in half a century of colonial war. Venice was granted the strategic island of Corfu, a crucial link in the chain of islands at the mouth of the Adriatic, but they had to oust a Genoese pirate to secure it and then lost it again five years later. In 1205, they bought Crete from the crusader lord Boniface of Montferrat for five thousand gold ducats, then spent four years expelling another Genoese privateer, Henry the Fisherman, from the island. They took two strategic ports on the south-west tip of the Peloponnese, Modon and Coron, from pirates, and established a foothold on the long barrier island of Euboea, which the Venetians called Negroponte (the Black Bridge), on the east coast of Greece. And in between they occupied or sublet a string of islands round the south coast of the Peloponnese and across the wide Aegean. It was out of this scattering of ports, forts and islands that they created their colonial system. Venice, following the Byzantines, referred to this whole geographic area as Romania – the kingdom of the Romans, the word the Byzantines used for it – and divided it up into zones: Lower Romania, which constituted the Peloponnese, Crete, the Aegean islands and Negroponte, and Upper Romania, the lands and seas beyond, up the Dardanelles to Constantinople itself. Further still lay the Black Sea, a new zone of potential exploitation.

The cardinal points of the system were the twin ports of Modon and Coron (so frequently linked in Venetian documents as almost to constitute a single idea), Crete and Negroponte. This triangle of bases became the strategic axis of the Stato da Mar, and over the centuries Venice would fight to the death for their retention. Modon and Coron, twenty miles apart, were Venice's first true colonies, so critical to the Republic's maritime infrastructure that they were called 'the Eyes of the Republic' and declared to be 'so truly precious that it is essential that we provide whatever is required for their maintenance'. They were vital stepping stones on the great maritime highway and Venice's radar stations. Information was as invaluable for the merchants on the Rialto as ready coin; it was compulsory for all ships returning from the Levant to stop there and pass news of pirates, warfare and the price of spices.

Modon, with its encircling harbour 'capable of receiving the largest ships' capped by a fort fluttering the flag of St Mark,

Modon

animated by turning windmills, bastioned by towers and thick walls to shield it from a hostile hinterland, provided arsenals, ship repair facilities and warehouses. 'The receptacle and special nest of all our galleys, ships and vessels on their way to the Levant', it was labelled in official documents. Here ships could mend a mast, replace an anchor, hire a pilot; obtain fresh water and trans-ship goods; buy meat and bread and watermelons; venerate the head of St Athanasius or try the heavily resinated local wines, which 'are so strong and fiery and smell of pitch so that they can't be drunk', one passing pilgrim complained. When the merchant fleets pulled in on their way east, the ports were transformed into vivid fairs where every oarsman with a little merchandise under his rowing bench would set up his wares and try his luck. Modon and Coron were the turntables of the Venetian sea. From here one route headed east. Galleys could tip the spiked fingers of the Peloponnese, drifting past the ominous headland of Cape Matapan, once the entrance to the underworld, and head for Negroponte, on the way to Constantinople. The other, more essential trunk route led south via the barren stepping-stone islands of Cerigo and Cerigotto to Crete – hub of the Venetian system.

The bases, harbours, trading posts and islands that Venice inhabited after 1204 were part of the commercial and maritime network that sustained its trading activities. If taxed heavily, they were generally ruled lightly. Crete however was different. The Great Island, ninety miles long, lying across the base of the Aegean like a limestone barrier buffering Europe from the African shore, resembled less an island than a complete world; a harsh intractable series of separate zones, spined by three great mountain ranges, intercut with deep ravines, high plateaus, fertile plains and thousands of mountain caves. Crete spawned Zeus and Kronos, the primitive gods of the Hellenic world; it was a landscape of wildness, banditry and ambush. For Venice, its occupation was like a snake attempting to swallow a goat. Crete's population was five times that of Venice and its people fiercely independent, utterly loyal to the Orthodox faith and the Byzantine Empire, in whose destruction the Venetians were deeply complicit. Crete had been cheap to buy. Owning it would cost a fortune in money and blood.

From the start, there was spirited resistance. It took a dozen years to oust the Genoese in military ventures that cost Dandolo's son, Ranieri, his life. Venice then embarked on a process of military colonisation. It tried to remake the island as an enlarged model of itself, breaking it into six regions, the *sestieri*, as in Venice, and inviting settlers from each Venetian *sestiere* to settle in the area that was given the same name. Waves of colonists left their home city to try their luck in this new world with promises of land holdings in return for military service. The outflow of population was considerable. In the thirteenth century, ten thousand Venetians settled on Crete, out of a population that never numbered more than a hundred thousand, and many of the aristocratic names of the Republic, such as Dandolo, Querini, Barbarigo and Corner, were represented. Still, the Venetian presence on the island was always small.

Crete was Venice's full-blown colonial adventure, which would involve the Republic in twenty-seven uprisings and two centuries of armed struggle. Each new wave of settlers sparked a fresh revolt, led by the great Cretan landowning families, deprived of their estates. The Venetians, essentially urban people, consolidated their hold on the three principal cities on the northern coast: Candia (the modern Heraklion), the hub of Venetian Crete, and further west the cities of Retimo and Canea. The countryside nominally pinned down by a series of military forts was more tenuously held, and among the limestone fastnesses of Sphakia and the White Mountains, where warrior clans lived by banditry and heroic song, no Venetian writ ran at all. Venetian rule was harsh and indifferent; the island was managed directly from the mother city by a duke, answerable to the Republic's senate, a thousand miles away. Venice mulcted Crete with particular ferocity, worked its peasantry hard to extract grain and wine for the mother city, and repressed the Orthodox Church. Fearful of Byzantine national sentiment, which burned most brightly among the Orthodox clergy, spreading across the Aegean, they banned all priests from outside the island. The Republic practised an uncompromising policy of racial separation. No man could hold a post in the island's administration unless he was 'flesh of our flesh, bone of our bone' as the formula ran; the fear of going native echoes through the Venetian records. Conversion to Orthodoxy meant immediate loss of a Venetian's land holdings. The colonists were fond of quoting St Paul's unflattering words on the Cretans: 'always liars, evil beasts, slow bellies'. The Cretan peasantry were downtrodden and poor – and continued so for all the 450 years of Venetian rule.

The Cretans, arbitrarily taxed, exploited and stripped of their privileges, rose again and again: the revolts of 1211, 1222, 1228 and 1262 were just a prelude; the period 1272–1333 saw a wave of major national uprisings under the feudal Cretan lords – the Chortatzises and the Callergises – rendering Crete at times almost ungovernable. The duke of Crete was killed in an ambush in 1275; Candia was under siege in 1276; the following year pitched and bloody battles were fought on the Mesara plain, Crete's great fertile crescent; the mountaineers of Sphakia massacred their garrison in 1319; in 1333 the Callergises rose over taxes for a galley fleet.

The Venetians poured money and men into military response, interspersed with unfulfilled promises. Their reprisals were harsh and swift; they burned villages and sacked monasteries; beheaded rebels, put suspects to the torture, exiled women and children to Venice, tore families apart. When they finally captured Leo Callergis in the 1340s, they dropped him in the sea, tied in a sack, following the sombre formula applied in Venice. ('This night, let the condemned be conducted to the Orfano canal, where his hands bound and his body loaded with a weight, he shall be thrown in by an officer of justice. And let him die there.') The Republic's colonial policy remained unbending.

Despite this, Cretan resistance seemed ineradicable. Time and again only clan feuding saved the Venetian project. The areas that rose up and were sacked followed a timeless pattern of resistance. The warrior culture ran uninterrupted down the centuries. The same villages would be burned again by the Turks and yet again in the Second World War. By 1348 Venice had endured 140 years of Cretan defiance. It still had the most shocking revolt to come.

The cost was high. 'The perfidious revolt of the Cretans monopolises the assets and resources of Venice,' the senate complained, but whenever it stopped spluttering about the price and contemplated the alternatives it could never bring itself to sail away. Crete was an axiom. If Modon and Coron were the eyes of the Republic, Crete was its hub, 'the strength and courage of the empire', the nerve centre of its maritime kingdom, 'one of the best possessions of the Commune'. The ponderous superlatives ring through the official registers. Nowhere else was the Venetian lion carved more proudly on gateways and harbour walls. Crete was twenty-five sailing days away from the doge's palace – as far off as Bombay from London to the British Empire of 1900 – but in the imagination of the lagoon, distance was telescoped. Crete loomed large. Misshapen maps of its long low profile, hooked upward

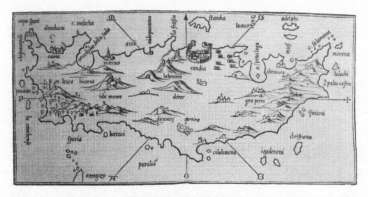

Venetian map of Crete

slightly at the eastern end, would be endlessly repeated down the long centuries of its occupation; news about Crete on the Rialto was a critical indicator of mercantile fortunes.

The island was at the crossroads of the Republic's two great trading routes – those that led to Constantinople and the Black Sea, and those that went on to the spice markets of Syria and Egypt. It was the back station for supplying the crusader ports of the Holy Land; the place for warehousing and trans-shipping goods; for repairing and reprovisioning the merchant galleys; for naval operations throughout the Aegean in times of war. Groggy pilgrims bound for the Holy Land stepped ashore here for a brief respite from the sea. Merchants resold silk and pepper, dodging the intermittent papal bans imposed on trading with the infidel; news was exchanged and bargains struck. After 1381, when the practice was banned in Venice, Crete became the illicit hub of the Republic's slave trade. In the great barrel-vaulted galley sheds of Candia and Canea, the duchy of Crete kept its own fleet to patrol the coast against pirates, crewed by press-ganged Cretan peasants. Candia itself was a faithful replica of the Venetian world, with its Church of St Mark fronting the ducal palace across a main square, its Franciscan friary, its loggia and its Jewish quarter pressed up against the city walls. From the main thoroughfare, the *ruga maestra*, running gently downhill to the harbour, the sea was an abiding presence, sometimes whipped into grey fury by the north wind pummelling the breakwater, sometimes calm. From here homesick townsfolk and anxious merchants could watch the ships making the awkward turn into the narrow entrance of Candia's harbour, and could see them depart again down the sea roads to Cyprus, Alexandria and Beirut; above all to Constantinople.

The maritime trunk route to Constantinople was critical in the map of Venetian trade. It passed via Crete through the scattered islands of the central Aegean – the Archipelago – fragments of rock speckling the surface of the sea. At the centre of these lay the Cyclades, the Circle the Greeks called them, grouped around Delos, once the religious centre of the ancient Hellenic world, now a haven for pirates drawing water from its sacred lake. The islands, separated by a few miles of flat sea, comprised a set of individual kingdoms. Naxos, large and well-watered, famous for its fertile valleys, was the most promising of the group; then volcanic Santorini; Milos famous for obsidian; Seriphos, the best harbour in the Aegean, so rich in iron ore that it confused the compasses of passing ships; pirate-haunted Andros.

Venice had been gifted all these islands by the treaty of 1204, yet it had neither the resources nor the keen economic interest to occupy them as a state enterprise. They were too small and too many to be garrisoned by Venetian forces, yet neither could they be ignored. Their harbours provided shelter in a storm, places to take on fresh water and heave to; unoccupied they represented danger from pirates, threatening the seaways north. With a keen eye to cost–benefit analysis, the Republic threw them open to private venture. Some time around 1205, Marco Sanudo, nephew of Enrico Dandolo, resigned his position as a judge in Constantinople, equipped eight galleys with the support of other enterprising nobles, and sailed forth to carve out his own private kingdom in the Cyclades. He was determined to do or die, not for the glory of the Republic, but for his own cause. Finding the castle at Naxos – the jewel of the central Aegean – occupied by Genoese pirates, he resolved that there would be no retreat. He burned his boats, besieged the pirates for five weeks, ousted them, and declared himself the Duke of Naxos. Within a decade the Cyclades had morphed into separate micro-kingdoms, property of a swarm of aristocratic adventurers, keen for the individual glory on which Venice tended to frown. Marino Dandolo, another nephew of the old doge, held Andros, the Ghisi brothers Tinos and Mykonos, the Barozzi occupied Santorini. Some possessions were doled out whimsically; Marco Venier was granted Kythera, which the Italians called Cerigo, the reputed birthplace of Venus, on the basis of the similarity of names. In each place, the owners constructed castles out of ransacked Greek temples and carved their coats of arms above the door, maintained miniature navies with which they fought each other, built Catholic churches and imported Venetian priests to chant the Latin rite.

An exotic hybrid world grew up in the central Aegean. The majority of the Greeks remained loyal to their Orthodox faith but generally tolerated their new overlords; the Venetian adventurers at least provided some measure of protection against the scourge of piracy, which ravaged the islands of the sea. Despite the prospect of a gold rush which the opening up of the Archipelago seemed to create, the islands contained precious little gold.

The saga of the Venetian Aegean was colourful, violent and, in places, surprisingly long-lasting. The duchy of Naxos did not expire until 1566; the most northern island of the group, Tinos, remained faithful to Venice until 1715. The Republic, however, was to find these freebooting duchies not always to its liking. Marco Sanudo, conqueror of Naxos, lived the life of a charmed adventurer, seeking advantage where he could. He helped suppress a rebellion on Crete, but finding the rewards not forthcoming, changed sides and made cause with the Cretan rebels until he was chased back to Naxos. Undeterred, he ill-advisedly attacked Smyrna, where he was captured by the emperor of Nice; his charm was such that he managed to exchange a dungeon for the hand of the emperor's sister. The Ghisi, at least, were loyal to the Republic in the nearby fortress of Mykonos. They burned a large candle in their island church on St Mark's day and sang the saint's praise. More often, the dukes of the Archipelago launched their tiny fleets across the summer seas and fought petty wars. The Cyclades became a zone of intermittent privatised battle, and its lords were by turns quarrelsome, treacherous and mad. Some were ruled by absentee landlords on Crete; Andros from a Venetian palazzo; Seriphos by the unspeakable Nicolo Adoldo, given to inviting prominent citizens of the island to dinner, then hurling them from the castle windows when they refused his demands for cash. When the crescendo of complaints grew too loud Venice was forced to intervene. Adoldo was banished from Seriphos for ever and languished for a while in a Venetian gaol. But Venice tended to be pragmatic in these matters – Adoldo was piously buried in the church he endowed in the city; it winked at the murder of the last Sanudo to rule Naxos by a usurper more favourable to itself. Nor was it averse to direct intervention. When an heiress to the duchy of Naxos took a fancy to a Genoese nobleman, she was abducted to Crete and 'persuaded' to marry a more suitable Venetian lord. This strategy of occupation by proxy had its drawbacks – and in time Venice would be forced to accept direct ownership of many of these places – but at least the petty lordlings of the Aegean damped down the level of piracy and ensured the merchant fleets a more steady passage through the ambush zones of the Archipelago.

Beyond it all lay Constantinople. When the Venetian fleet made its way up the Dardanelles in the summer of 1203 and gazed up at the sea walls of the city, they were confronted with a daunting and hostile bastion. After 1204, the city was Venice's second home. Venetian priests sang the Latin rites in the great mosaic church of Hagia Sophia; Venetian ships tied up securely at their own wharfs in the Golden Horn, unloading goods into tax-free warehouses. The Republic's erstwhile competitors, the Genoese and the Pisans, with whom it had brawled repeatedly under the wary gaze of the Byzantine emperors, were barred from the city's trade. And, for the first time, Venetian ships also had the freedom to pass up the straits of the Bosphorus into the Black Sea and seek new points of contact with the furthest Orient. Thousands of Venetians flooded back into the city to trade and live. So powerful was the attraction of Constantinople, that one doge, Jacopo Tiepolo, for a time *podesta* (mayor) there, was said to have proposed moving the centre of Venetian government to the city. Venice, once the puny satellite of the Byzantine Empire, idly contemplated replacing it. And the steady, if hard-fought, consolidation of its colonies and bases across the eastern Mediterranean promised to turn the sea into a Venetian lake. Its merchants were everywhere. Tiepolo established trading agreements with Alexandria, Beirut, Aleppo and Rhodes. He articulated a consistent policy and a continuity of effort that would last for hundreds of years. Venetian objectives remained frighteningly consistent – to secure trading opportunities on the most advantageous terms. The means, however, were endlessly flexible. The Venetians were opportunists born for the bargain, ready to sail wherever the current would run.

Destiny lay in the East, in its spices, its silks, its marble pillars and its jewelled icons, and the riches of the Orient flowed back, not only into the coffers of Venetian merchants, stored in the barred ground-floor warehouses of their great palazzos fronting the Grand Canal, but also into the visual imagery of the city. The mosaicists who decorated the Church of St Mark in the thirteenth century imaged the biblical world of the Levant. They reproduced the lighthouse from Alexandria; camels with tasselled reins; merchants leading Joseph into Egypt. An oriental note also starts to pervade the grand architecture of the city.

By the time that Renier Zeno became doge in 1253, Easter was celebrated with the splendour of Byzantine ritual. The doge walked in solemn procession the short distance from the ducal palace to the Church of St Mark. He was preceded by eight men holding banners of silk and gold bearing the saint's image; then two maidens, one carrying the doge's chair, the other its golden cushions, six musicians with silver trumpets, two with cymbals of pure silver, then a priest carrying a huge cross of gold and silver, embedded with precious stones, another an ornate gospel; twenty-two chaplains of St Mark's in golden copes followed, singing psalms, and then the doge himself walking beneath the ritual umbrella of gold cloth, accompanied by the city's primate and the priest who would sing the mass. The doge, looking for all the world like a Byzantine emperor, wore cloth of gold and a crown of jewelled gold and carried a large candle, and behind came a noble carrying the ducal sword, then all the other nobles and men of distinction.

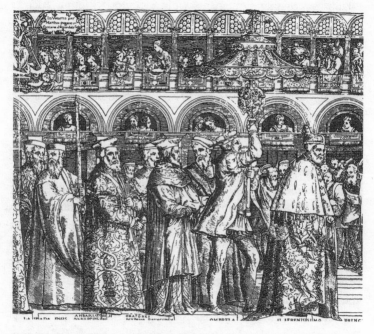

The procession of a doge

As they processed along the facade of the church, past the porphyry columns taken from crusader Acre and those plundered from Constantinople, it was as if Venice had stolen not only the marble, icons and pillars of Constantinople, but its imperial imagery, its love of ceremonial, its soul. In the submarine gloom of the mother church, Easter was celebrated with words that linked sacred and profane, the risen Christ and the Venetian Stato da Mar: 'Christ conquers!' went up the cry. 'Christ reigns! Christ rules! To our lord Renier Zeno, illustrious doge of Venice, Dalmatia and Croatia, and lord of a quarter and half a quarter of the empire of Romania, salvation, honour, life and victory! O, St Mark, lend him aid!'

The events of 1204 amplified Venice's sense of itself. A growing assumption of imperial grandeur began to possess the little Republic, as if in the shimmering reflection of the spring canals, Venice was morphing into Constantinople.

The acclamation of the Stato da Mar would be followed a few weeks later each year by a claim to ownership of the sea itself at another great ceremony: the Sensa, on Ascension Day. When Doge Orseolo had departed from the lagoon in the year 1000, this had been a simple blessing. After 1204, it became an increasingly elaborate expression of the city's sense of mystical union with the sea. The doge, ermine-robed and wearing the *corno*, the pointed hat that symbolised the majesty of the Republic, was piped aboard his ceremonial barge at the quay in front of his palace. Nothing expressed the city's maritime pride so richly as the *Bucintoro*, the Golden Boat. This majestic double-decker vessel, ornately gilded and painted with heraldic lions and sea creatures, covered by a crimson canopy and rowed by 168 men, pulled away from the quay. Golden oars dashed the waters of the lagoon. In the prow a figurehead representing justice held aloft a set of scales and a raised sword. The swallow-tailed banner of St Mark billowed from the masthead. Cannon fire crashed; pipes shrilled; drums beat a rapt tattoo. Accompanied by an armada of gondolas and sailing boats, the *Bucintoro* rowed out into the mouth of the Adriatic. Here the bishop uttered the ritual supplication: 'Grant, O Lord, that for us and all who sail thereon, the sea may be calm and quiet,' and the doge took a golden wedding ring from his finger and tossed it into the depths with the time-honoured words: 'We wed thee, O Sea, in token of our true and perpetual dominion over thee.'

Despite the rhetoric, the sea which Venice mythologised, and the wealth that it carried, would prove harder won. The Genoese, excluded from easy access to rich trading zones, were snapping continuously at Venice's heels. They waged an unofficial war of piracy against their maritime rivals. Three years before Doge Renier Zeno walked in the solemn Easter procession, an incident occurred in the crusader port of Acre on the shores of Syria: a Genoese citizen was killed by a Venetian. Three years later, the Mongols sacked Baghdad. In the aftermath of these disconnected events the two maritime republics would be drawn into a long-running contest for Mediterranean trade, which would lead them both to immense wealth and the edge of ruin. The arena would stretch from the steppes of Asia to the harbours of the Levant. It would encompass the Black Sea, the Nile Delta, the Adriatic, the Balearic Islands and the shores of Greece. Brawls would take place as far away as London and the streets of Bruges. Along the way all the peoples of the eastern Mediterranean would be caught up in its slipstream: the Byzantines, the Hungarians, rival Italian city states and the towns of the Dalmatian coast, the Mamluks of Egypt and the Ottoman Turks – all became entwined in the contest for their own advantage or defence. It would last 150 years.

9

Demand and Supply

—— ∞∞ ——

1250–1291

Venezia e Genova: Venice the Most Serene, Genoa the Proud. The two maritime republics were mirror images; even their names were echoes. Like Venice, Genoa, symmetrically positioned on the western flank of Italy at the top of its own gulf, was a natural point of trans-shipment from sea to land. It had easy access to the upper reaches of the Po valley and the wealthy markets of Milan and Turin, as well as routes through the Alpine passes into France. It too depended on the sea. Huddled about by mountains which offered plentiful wood for shipbuilding but no rich agricultural hinterland, Genoa looked to the Mediterranean as its escape from poverty and imprisonment. It had a good sheltered port and a climate more equitable than the malarial lagoon. Genoese sailors were as hardy as the Venetians, their merchants as avid for profit. Like their Adriatic rivals, the Genoese were pushy, pragmatic and ruthless.

In political temperament however they were quite different. Where Venetians submitted themselves to government control and worked by communal enterprise, born out of the city's precarious physical position, the need for co-operation to prevent its islands from being flooded and its lagoon silting up, the Genoese were marked by a strong streak of individualism and a preference for private enterprise. It was a distinction not lost on unsympathetic outside observers. In an analogy unflattering to both peoples, the Florentine Franco Sacchetti likened the Genoese to donkeys:

Genoa

The nature of the donkey is this: when many are together, and one of them is thrashed with a stick, all scatter, fleeing hither and thither, so great is their vileness ... The Venetians are similar to pigs and are called 'Venetian pigs', and truly they have a pig's nature, for when a multitude of pigs is confined together and one of them is hit or beaten with a stick, all draw close and run unto him who hits it; and this is truly their nature.

It was out of these contrasts in character that a fierce commercial rivalry would develop.

Genoa shared the same goals as Venice: to grab share and monopolise markets, but its means were different. From the start the Genoese maritime empire was largely privatised – the fleet that beat the more cautious Venetians to the First Crusade and gained preferential trading rights in the new crusader kingdom was got up by individual initiative. Intrepid Genoese risk-takers staked claims earlier and adopted technologies faster. Genoa was the first to many of the commercial and practical innovations that revolutionised international trade. Gold currency, marine charts, insurance contracts, the use of the stern rudder, the introduction of public mechanical clocks – the Genoese were using these decades earlier than the Venetians. Having gained a head start in the Levant trade during the First Crusade, Genoa initiated a lucrative galley route to Flanders fifty years before Venice and notwithstanding the singular fame of Marco Polo pushed faster and further into the Orient than their Adriatic rivals. Facing west towards the Atlantic gave the Genoese an amplified sense of the possibilities beyond the Mediterranean basin and better access to ocean-going ship technologies. As early as 1291 two Genoese brothers sailed out of the Gates of Gibraltar to seek a route to India. It was no accident that it should be the Genoese sailor Christopher Columbus (Cristóbal Colón) who touched the New World in 1492. Intrepid, creative, risk-taking, innovative – these were hallmarks of the individualistic genius of Genoa.

It was also characteristic that one of Columbus's prime objectives in crossing the Atlantic was to find a fresh stock of human beings to enslave. Linked to this energetic individualism was a dark side to the Genoese temperament. The ruthless materialism of the Italian maritime republics, their 'insatiable thirst for wealth' commented on by Petrarch, startled and repulsed the pious medieval world. Both were frequently castigated by the papacy for trading with Islam; the Byzantines found them odious and the Muslims despised them. But if Pope Pius II thought the Venetians were hardly further up the scale of nature than fish, and the words 'Venetians' and 'bastards' sounded identical to Syrian Arabs, Genoa generally enjoyed a slightly worse reputation: 'cruel men, who love nothing but money' was the curt judgement of one Byzantine chronicler. They were enthusiastic slavers – there were more slaves in Genoa than any other city in medieval Europe. The Genoese also had a fatal weakness for chaotic violence; the internal politics of the city were riven by repeated bouts of factional infighting so exhausting that the people periodically begged outsiders to govern the city; it was an object lesson in political instability that made the prudent Venetians shudder. On the high seas they acquired a similar notoriety for piracy and privatised plunder. For Genoa there was a particularly thin line between warfare and buccaneering.

Like the Venetians they were everywhere; by the start of the fourteenth century Genoese traders could be found from Britain to Bombay, establishing trading posts, shifting cargoes by camel or mule train, packing spices into ships, buying and selling wheat and silk and grain. 'So many are the Genoese,' wrote a patriotic city poet, 'and so spread out throughout the world, that wherever one goes and stays, he makes another Genoa there.' By 1250, Genoa was booming; its population, about fifty thousand, was one of the largest in Europe, though always smaller than that of Venice – and furiously competing for the goods of the world.

The contest with Venice – and its other close rival Pisa – had started with the opportunities of the early crusades. All the Italian maritime republics aspired to be monopoly traders, keen to lock out competitors and to strike exclusive deals with the host lords of the Levant. The quarrelsome merchant settlements, frequently barricaded in adjacent quarters like miniature forts, made tiresome guests. Nowhere was this more marked than in Constantinople where the bickering between rival colonies drove the Byzantine emperors to call a plague on all their houses and periodically to expel the lot.

Everything changed after 1204. The fall of Constantinople gifted the Venetians a dominant position. At a stroke the Genoese were excluded from some of the richest markets of the east. Venice controlled the Aegean, gained a first foothold in the Black Sea, won Crete – and above all was co-owner of Constantinople. For Genoa it represented a huge setback. Its privateers harried the triumphant Venetians wherever they could; Henry the Fisherman made a bold grab for Crete; Genoese pirates methodically began to plunder Venetian merchant fleets as an alternative form of war. The great wave of prosperity that Venice experienced in the half-century after 1204 intensified profound jealousy elsewhere in the Mediterranean. It exploded into open warfare in the crusader port of Acre on the shores of Syria.

Here, in a dense walled town with its encircling harbour, the two republics occupied adjoining colonies and competed fiercely for lucrative trade with the Islamic world. For Genoa, Acre and its adjoining port of Tyre, represented a heartland: they had established a presence here earlier than Venice and they looked to establish a compensating monopoly for Venetian control of Constantinople. The atmosphere was heavy with commercial rivalry. In 1250 an incident took place in Acre that led to a riot; the riot became a battle, and the battle provoked a war that would spread across the whole of the eastern Mediterranean.

The causes were small but multiple. There was a dispute over a shared church that lay between the two mercantile quarters; a Genoese seaman turned up in the harbour with a ship which the Venetians, with their suspicious eye for piracy, thought was one of theirs taken by theft; a private quarrel between two citizens turned into a fight that left the Genoese dead. At a certain temperature the powder keg exploded. A Genoese mob descended on the harbour and sacked Venetian ships, then pillaged their quarter and slaughtered its inhabitants.

When word got back to Venice, the doge demanded satisfaction. Not getting it, the Venetians armed thirty-two galleys under Lorenzo Tiepolo, the son of a former doge, and sailed off to the Levant. In 1255, Tiepolo's fleet hove into view off Acre, crashed through the chain which the Genoese had strung across its mouth and burned their galleys. Descending on the nearby stronghold at Tyre, the Venetians redoubled the humiliation, capturing the Genoese admiral and three hundred citizens who were transported back to Acre in chains. The town became a cauldron of street violence, split down the middle and sucking all the other resident nationalities into the contest. Both sides used heavy siege equipment to bombard rival fortifications. The Venetians sent for more ships from Crete; 'every day the contest was fierce and bitter', according to the Venetian chronicler Martino da Canal. When news reached Genoa of their citizens being led through Acre in chains, there was an outpouring of patriotic fury: 'there were calls for vengeance such as have never been forgotten. Women said to their husbands: "Spend our dowries on revenge."' Both sides fed in more ships and men, but the Venetians managed to press forward street by street, taking the contested church and a key hill within the town. The Genoese were forced back to their bazaar area. It was a bitter, slow-motion contest – the foretaste of things to come.

Back in Genoa and Venice new forces were enrolled. In 1257 the Genoese despatched a larger fleet of forty galleys and four round ships under a new admiral, Rosso della Turca. Getting wind of this, the Venetians hurried out matching ships of their own under Paolo Faliero. In June, della Turca's fleet showed up off the Syrian coast to the immense joy of the beleaguered Genoese. From a tall tower in their quarter they hung the banners of all their allies in the fight and made a triumphant din, raining down insults on the Venetians below; in the colourful (and prejudicial) words of the Venetian chronicler: 'Slaves, you're all going to die! . . . flee the city that will be your death. Here comes the flower of Christianity! Tomorrow you will all be killed, either on sea or land!'

Della Turca's fleet bore down on Acre for a definitive collision. As they approached, the ships lowered their sails and dropped anchor to threaten the harbour. The wind was too strong for the Venetian ships to sally forth. Night fell and the Genoese in the town 'made great illuminations with candles and torches . . . They were so emboldened and made such great boasting and such a din that the most mild-mannered seemed like a lion, and they continually threatened the Venetians.'

Next morning at dawn, both sides prepared themselves for the inevitable sea battle. The Venetian commanders attempted to put spirit into their men with a singing of the Evangelists' psalm. 'And when they had sung, they ate a little and then they weighed anchor and roared, "Pray for us with the help of our Lord Jesus

Christ and St Mark of Venice!" And they began to row forward.'
Back in the town the Genoese garrison sallied out to confront
the Venetian *bailo* [governor] and his men. Cries of 'St Mark!'
and 'St George!' rang across the sea as the two fleets closed, with
the gold lion of Venice and the flag of Genoa – a red cross on a
white background – fluttering in the wind, 'and the battle on the
high sea was huge and extraordinary, hard fought and bitter'. The
Genoese had slightly the larger fleet but the Venetians had hired
extra men from the mixed populations of Acre. It was to be the
first of many maritime encounters and it ended with a ringing
Venetian victory. The Genoese hurled themselves into the sea or
turned their ships in flight; the Venetians took twenty-five galleys,
1,700 men drowned in the sea or were taken. Seeing the annihila-
tion of their fleet, the Genoese garrison laid down its arms and
surrendered, and the crusader knight Philip de Montfort, coming
up the coast from Tyre to help the Genoese, turned back in disgust at the spectacle with the remark that 'the Genoese are empty
boasters who more resemble seagulls, diving into the sea and
drowning. Their pride has been laid low.' The Genoese lowered
the flags on their tower and surrendered. They were expelled from
Acre; their tower was razed to the ground; chained prisoners were
paraded in St Mark's Square and confined to the dungeons of
the doge's palace. It took the pleading of the pope to secure their
release. As a souvenir, the Venetians also carried home from their
enemy's quarter the squat stump of a porphyry column which
was set up in St Mark's Square at the corner of the church. It
became known as the Pietra del Bando, the proclamation stone,
from which the laws of the Republic were read out, and on which
the freshly severed heads of traitors who broke them were put on
display. ('The smell of them', one later visitor complained, 'doth
breed a very offensive and contagious annoyance.')

The contest at Acre set the tone for a long series of Venetian–
Genoese wars – driven by profit but sustained by patriotic fervour
and visceral hate. Genoa was bitterly discomfited by the defeat
but did not submit. It simply altered its angle of attack; it decided

to use diplomatic methods to strike at the eastern hub of Venetian sea power – Constantinople itself.

From the start the Latin Empire of Constantinople had been a sickly creature: starved of long-term supplies of manpower, short of funds, hemmed in by resentful and unassimilated Greeks. By the middle of the century its position was critical. The Latin emperor, Baldwin II, controlled little more than the footprint of the city itself. He was so short of cash that he sold off the copper from the palace roofs and pawned the city's most precious relic, the crown of thorns, to Venetian merchants – who sold it on to the king of France. Only the Venetians, for whom the city was both a second home and a trading base of enormous value, worked wholeheartedly to sustain Baldwin's position; the permanent presence of a Venetian fleet in the Golden Horn was the best guarantor of the Latin emperor's survival. Sixty miles over the water in Asia, the Byzantine emperor in exile, Michael VIII, was biding his time in the lakeside town of Nicaea, when an unexpected Genoese deputation called on him in the autumn of 1260.

The Genoese arrived with a proposition. They offered the emperor the services of their fleets for the reconquest of the city. To Michael this was providential. He knew how weak Baldwin's position was; he also knew how hard the Latins would be to displace with the Venetian navy unchecked. A deal was hammered out. The Genoese would supply fifty ships, the running costs (for which they set a high price) to be paid by Michael, to win back Constantinople. In return they were to supplant the Venetians in the city with all the tax-free trading rights, land and commercial infrastructure – the quays and warehouses – which their rivals presently enjoyed. Free trade and self-governing colonies were to be granted in a scattering of key trading locations across the Aegean, such as Salonica and Smyrna; they would also become the rightful owners of Venice's most precious colonies – Crete and Negroponte. So keen was Michael for the deal he also granted an unprecedented additional favour: access to the trade of the Black Sea, from which the Byzantines had always been careful to exclude Italian merchants. In effect Genoa would supplant Venice in the eastern Mediterranean. The Treaty of Nymphaion, signed on the coast of Asia Minor on 10 July 1261, opened up new imperial prospects for Genoa and a second front in the maritime war.

In the event, the end came fifteen days later without the Genoese firing a shot. On 25 July 1261, the Venetian fleet made a sally up the Bosphorus to attack a Byzantine position; Michael meanwhile despatched a small contingent to study Constantinople's defences. Inside knowledge informed the raiders of an underground passage and a scalable wall. While Baldwin was asleep in his palace on the other side of the city, a band of men slipped into the city, hurled a few surprised guards off the ramparts and opened the gates. It was so abrupt, so opportunist that Baldwin had to flee to a Venetian merchant ship without his crown and sceptre. By the time the Venetian fleet hurried back to the Golden Horn, they found their whole quarter on fire, their families and their compatriots crowding the waterfront like bees smoked out of their hives, arms outstretched, begging for rescue. Perhaps three thousand were taken off. The refugees, who had lived in the city for generations, watched their lives and their fortunes guttering down to the water's edge and called out farewells to the city they considered home. Many died of thirst or starvation before the dangerously overcrowded ships reached Negroponte. Back in Venice the news was received with astonishment and dismay. Venice had propped up the Latin Empire for fifty years; its commercial loss was a catastrophe, doubled by the sudden preferment of the hated rival. The Genoese methodically destroyed the Venetian headquarters in Constantinople and shipped its stones home as a trophy to construct a new church to St George. Such national taunts mattered.

The sea war ground on for nine more attritional years. The Venetians won the pitched battles, but found themselves unable to counter Genoese privateers harrying their merchant convoys.

Such hit-and-run tactics were discomfiting and potentially inexhaustible. Venice preferred defined, short sharp wars and a return to peaceful business; for a city dependent on the sea endemic piracy had the potential to inflict grave damage. Underlying this first Genoese war was a profound truth: neither side had the resources to win the sea by conventional means – they could only exhaust themselves in the endeavour. Peace, when it came in 1270, was little more than a truce imposed on embittered foes. The resumption of war was merely a matter of time, but the idea of inflicting a maritime knockout blow was potent: Genoa did just that to Pisa in 1284. It remained the elusive goal of both Genoa and Venice for another century.

When the Venetian refugees gazed back at their burning quarter from the choppy waters of the Bosphorus in the summer of 1261 they might have thought that they had seen Constantinople for the last time. It looked too as though the Republic's imperial and commercial expansion had come juddering to a halt as it braced itself for the Byzantine and Genoese backlash. Genoese merchants hurried back to the city, took over their rivals' locations and began to exploit the new commercial concessions in the Black Sea.

Yet none of Venice's worst fears ever quite came to pass. Though Michael unleashed a swarm of privateers across the Aegean, Venice was too deeply entrenched to be dislodged. A few small islands were lost. Crete, Modon–Coron and Negroponte held firm. And the Genoese quickly became as unpopular as ever the Venetians had been; all the Byzantine hauteur about the arrogance and greed of the Italian traders resurfaced: 'a foreign land peopled by barbarians of the utmost insolence and stupidity' remained the considered view. Worse still the Genoese were caught plotting for a different reinstatement of a Latin empire within the city. The Genoese, in their turn, were temporarily banished, then reinstated – but this time outside the city walls. They were granted a separate settlement across the Golden Horn in the suburb of Galata –

and the Venetians were allowed back into Constantinople in 1268 with a resumption of permitted trading rights and equal access to the Black Sea. The two troublesome republics were to be kept physically apart and played off against each other.

It was a typical piece of Byzantine diplomacy but it concealed an uncomfortable fact. The Treaty of Nymphaion, signed with the Genoese in 1261, would prove to be a stepping stone to disaster. By overtly recognising the need for Italian naval support, allowing the Genoese an autonomous, fortified settlement at Galata and throwing open the Black Sea to foreign trade, Byzantium's key prerogatives were given away and its naval power progressively undermined. Twenty years later, the emperor Andronicos disbanded the Byzantine fleet altogether as a cost-cutting measure. Henceforward Venice and Genoa would usurp naval control over her seas, ports, straits, grain supplies and strategic alliances. The war between the two republics would be fought in the Bosphorus, beneath the walls of Galata, in the Black Sea and the shores of the Golden Horn, while the Byzantine emperors watched helplessly from behind their walls or were dragged in as hapless pawns. The enmity between the maritime republics would remain a malign force within Constantinople to the very last day of its Christian life, and it muffled the stealthy advance of another emergent power in the region – the Turkic tribes now moving west across the land mass of Asia Minor.

In the city's hippodrome there was a remarkable column, erected by Constantine the Great at the city's founding eleven hundred years earlier. Even then it was ancient. It had once stood in the temple of Apollo at Delphi as a monument to Greek freedom, commemorating the defeat of the Persians at the battle of Plataea in 479 BC; it was said to have been cast from the shields of the Persian dead. The bodies of three intertwined serpents formed a tightly coiled column cresting into flaring heads, finely worked in polished bronze. After 1261, the intertwined creatures might as well have represented, not freedom, but entanglement, the serpent head of the Byzantine Empire hopelessly intertwined with those of Genoa and Venice in an embrace from which henceforth it could never extricate itself.

The game that was now being set out across the waters and shores of the Byzantine Empire was being played for high stakes. Venice and Genoa were involved in a contest for both survival and wealth. By the thirteenth century Europe was in the middle of a long boom from which the Italian maritime republics were uniquely placed to profit. Between classical times and 1200 no western city had a population that surpassed twenty thousand. By 1300 there were nine cities in Italy alone of more than fifty thousand. Paris swelled from twenty thousand to two hundred thousand in a century; Florence had 120,000 by 1320, Venice a hundred thousand, fed by immigration from the Dalmatian coast. The population of northern Italy was immense. It would continue to climb until an ominous day some time in early 1348 when an unknown ship from the Black Sea tied up near Petrarch's house in the Basin of St Mark. It would not be surpassed again until the eighteenth century.

Italian urban centres such as Milan, Florence and Bologna were unable to feed themselves, no matter how closely they dredged the agricultural resources of the Po valley. Like ancient Rome, the growing metropolises depended on the import of food by sea. Genoa and Venice were now poised to dominate its provision. Venice, the landless city which had always lived solely on import, had an unsurpassed understanding of food supply. It was as dense as any city on earth; by 1300 almost all available land had been built on; the islands had been linked by bridges. Hunger like the threat of the sea was a constant. The records of the various Venetian governing bodies reveal a near obsession with grain. The orders, the prices, the quantities, the damping down or increase of supply are monotonous but crucial entries in the state registers. Grain not only preserved the serenity of the city, but the *biscotto* – literally the 'double-cooked' long-lasting dry ship's biscuit – was the carbohydrate that powered the merchant galleys and war fleets without which it could not be secured. Venice had an office for grain, as it did for other staples, whose activities were scrupulously regulated as a matter of national security. Grain officials had to report every month to the doge on the city's stocks, which were subject to delicate controls. (It was a fine balance – if levels were too low, the want would be felt; too high, grain prices would fall, inflicting losses on the Commune.) After 1260 with the inexorable rise in the populations of both Genoa and Venice, the competition for grain would spill over into the contested waters of the Byzantine world. In other commodity foodstuffs – oil, wine, salt, fish – Venice and Genoa had the opportunity to profit as critical middlemen to the clamouring markets on their doorsteps.

Symbols used by individual Venetian merchants
to mark their goods

If there was one trade in hunger, there was another in luxury. The thirteenth century also witnessed a commercial revolution that promised the restless merchant cities of Italy a steadily rising tide of wealth. More coin was in circulation than ever before; people were moving from payments in kind to payments in cash; to investing rather than hoarding; to the legitimate loan of money; to international banking; to credit and bills of exchange; double-entry bookkeeping and new forms of entrepreneurial organisation. The invention of novel instruments of transaction facilitated the development of trade on an unprecedented scale. While twenty-five per cent of the urban population might be destitute, there arose a desire to consume among the courts, churchmen and the rising middle class of urbanising Europe that found its expression in a demand for distant luxuries – and the means to pay for them. Venice traded not just in staples, but in conspicuous consumption. And this trade was largely orientated towards the incomparably richer, better provided East.

Pepper

Nothing encapsulated the development of consumerism more acutely than the appetite for spices. They performed no necessary function in food preservation, only salt did, but the galaxy of comestibles that medieval people classed as spices – pepper, ginger, cardamoms, cloves, cinnamon, sugar and dozens more – made food more appealing and expressed a certain desire for culinary interest and displays of wealth. Across the barriers of holy war, the crusades had given Europeans a taste for oriental refinement. Spices were the first manifestation of a world trade and its ideal commodity. They were lightweight, high in value, low in bulk, and almost imperishable; they could be readily transported over long distances by boat or camel, rebagged into smaller lots, stored almost indefinitely. At the far western end of a long supply chain the peoples of the Mediterranean were largely ignorant of how and where they grew – Marco Polo was the first European to leave an eyewitness account of the cultivation of pepper in India – but they were fully aware that the spices were landed in Egypt and the Arabian peninsula and that the total trade passed through the hands of Muslim middlemen. The spice routes would alter their course according to the rise and fall of kingdoms further east, but during the thirteenth century, the ports of the shrinking crusader kingdom in Palestine were a crucial outlet to the Mediterranean. It was this that made the competition at Acre so fierce. After Genoa was ousted, its merchants concentrated their trading colony forty miles up the coast at Tyre. And while the Mamluk dynasty in Egypt was slowly reducing the crusader castles of Palestine one after another, both the Genoese and the Venetians were also simultaneously trading with it within the Nile Delta. When it came, the Mamluk counterstrike against the crusades seriously altered the fortunes of both republics and turned their contest in a new direction.

In April 1291, the Mamluk sultan al-Ashraf Khalil drew up a huge army outside the walls of Acre, determined finally to snuff out the infidel presence within the lands of Islam. The Muslims, embittered by the long centuries of holy war, had come with a grim determination to leave not a Christian alive. Al-Ashraf had prepared his campaign carefully, dragging with him from Cairo an array of giant catapults and other war machines, among them two huge specimens, ominously named the Victorious and the Furious, and a posse of efficient smaller engines called the Black Oxen. Acre was a substantial city of some forty thousand people drawn from all the crusading states in Europe: French and English, Germans, Italians, the crusading orders (the Templars, Hospitallers and Teutonic knights) and the commercially minded Venetians and Pisans. Many had been residents for a long time. On 6 April the catapults began to hurl giant rocks against the tall medieval walls and the sultan's engineers started methodically mining beneath them with horrible efficiency. After centuries of squabbling between the various Christian factions, the final defence was conducted with a bravery and sense of unity born of desperation.

Both the Venetians and Pisans fought valiantly; their skills in constructing and operating their own catapults were employed to great effect, but day after day the continuous bombardment relentlessly degraded the defensive ring. Attempts at a negotiated truce were rebuffed. The sultan was implacable. He remembered a massacre of Muslim merchants in the city the previous year and pressed on. On Friday 18 May, he ordered a final assault on the stricken town. To the sound of arrows whipping through the air, the crash of rocks, the beating of drums and the blaring of trumpets, the Mamluk army forced its way into the city and put it to the sword. The final hours of Acre were pitiful and squalid. The Templars and Hospitallers went down almost to the last man. Women and children, young and old, rich and poor crowded the quays as the Muslims advanced over the bodies of the indiscriminately slain. At the waterfront civilisation collapsed. Venetian merchants clutching their gold begged for passage but there were not enough vessels to take them off. Overcrowded rowing boats capsized and sank, drowning their occupants; the strong seized control of ships and held the imploring citizens to ransom. The ruthless Catalan adventurer Roger de Flor, commandeering a Templar galley, became fabulously rich on the proceeds of one day's work, extorting jewels, pearls and sacks of gold from the noblewomen of the city. Those unable to pay were left pitifully at the water's edge, waiting to be killed or enslaved. When Acre fell, the sultan systematically reduced it to ruins. The remaining Christian strongholds, Tyre, Sidon, Beirut and Haifa, were all stormed or surrendered in quick succession. The Muslims scorched the whole coast against the possibility of a Christian return. They razed the cities to the ground. After two centuries, the crusading footholds in the Holy Land had been swept away.

To Christian Europe this was a profound shock; there were immediate plans for fresh crusades – and recrimination. The papacy was well aware who had been providing the Mamluks with military supplies. Venice and Genoa had always maintained a complex position on Islamic trade. As the Victorious and the Furious hurled giant rocks at the walls of Acre, Italian merchants were buying silk and spices, flax and cotton in Alexandria, selling back worked woollen goods from the new looms of Italy, furs from the Russian steppes – and other more contentious materials which had directly affected the course of the wars. Iron and timber – al-Ashraf's giant catapults may well have been constructed from wood carried on Christian ships – were war materials; even more serious to the papacy, many of the troops who burst through the gates of Acre were military slaves shipped from the Black Sea in Christian vessels. In 1302 Pope Boniface VIII demanded a trading ban with the Mamluks in Egypt and Palestine which gradually squeezed the maritime republics. Specific commodities were expressly forbidden under pain of excommunication. Some of the military trade continued illicitly; the purely mercantile exchange in spices and cloth certainly did, but the papal stance hardened progressively. It became increasingly desirable to bypass the Islamic world in securing the luxury products – the spices, pearls and worked silk – that originated from beyond Christendom. In a daring response to circumstance, some enterprising Genoese armed two galleys and sailed out into the Atlantic just as Acre fell. Their objective was to discover a direct route to outflank Arab middlemen (and the Venetians) and source spices direct from India. The enterprise was two hundred years premature; they were never seen again. But within the Mediterranean basin the fall of Acre realigned the competitive pressure between Genoa and Venice. It pitched them into new theatres of war. Henceforward the battleground would swing north again into a contest for the Bosphorus and the Black Sea.

10

'In the Jaws of our Enemies'

1291–1348

The Bosphorus, the seventeen-mile strait which links the Mediterranean to the Black Sea, is one of the strategic waterways of the world. A narrow maritime corridor twisting through high hills, it was formed in the last ice age, when the landlocked Black Sea burst out of its confines. The straits are governed by unique hydraulic forces. The powerful current pushing the fresher water of the Black Sea down towards the Mediterranean at a speed of five knots is reversed forty metres down by a submarine countersurge forcing heavier salty water up the Bosphorus, so that a ship lowering a fishing net may be dragged back northwards against the apparent run of the sea. In the late summer, during the breeding season, millions of fish used to migrate up the straits, so many that you could catch the bonito, the greater mackerel, in the Golden Horn with your bare hands, according to the Greek geographer Strabo, or idly scoop them in nets from the windows of waterside houses. In winter the Bosphorus was a zone of fog and snow; icy winds funnelled off the Russian steppes; the occasional iceberg bumped against the walls of Constantinople. The Bosphorus, as the later French traveller Pierre Gilles pointed out, was the reason for the city's existence – 'with one key [it] opens and closes two worlds, two seas'. And at the end of the thirteenth century, with the loss of Acre and the shutting down of the souks of the Nile Delta, the Bosphorus became the centre of the great competitive game between Genoa and Venice. The lock which it now opened was access to the second world, that of the Black Sea.

The ancient Greeks described it as pleasant, in the hope of

appeasing its fierce squalls and ominous depths, but the Black Sea has a dark heart. Below two hundred metres, the sea drops away into silence. These lower reaches lock up the world's largest reservoir of toxic hydrogen sulphide. There is no oxygen. The water is dead; wood remains perfectly preserved. The ghostly hulls of thousands of years of maritime disasters lie undecayed on the sea bed; only their iron fittings – anchors, nails, weapons and chains – have been eaten away by the poisonous depths. The Venetians called it the Greater Sea and it frightened them. Its centre is a blank; there are no island stepping stones, as in the Aegean, to provide anchorage in a storm; most shipping preferred to creep round its edge or darted across at its narrowest point.

Yet along its northern shore the sterility of the open water is offset by an astonishing coastal shelf, where four great river deltas debouch millions of tons of nutrient-rich sediment into the sea. The level bird-haunted swamps of reed and mud at the mouth of the Danube sustained, until modern times, a wealth of marine life. Salmon came to spawn here in vast numbers and sturgeon the size of small whales. The offshore shallows seethed with fish – anchovy, mullet, whiting and turbot. The fish stocks of the Danube, the Dnieper, the Dniester, and the Don – tucked into the tributary Sea of Azov in its north-east corner – fed Constantinople for a thousand years; caviar was a food of its poor, and the migratory bonito so crucial that it featured on Byzantine coins. Along the estuarine gulfs fish were salted, smoked, barrelled up and shipped west to supply the largest population in the late medieval and early modern world. When the Spanish traveller Pero Tafur arrived in the Black Sea in the fifteenth century he watched the packing of caviar: 'they put the eggs into casks and carry them all over the world'. Beyond, the black earth of the level Ukrainian steppes provided Constantinople's grain basket – and the gateway to yet another world.

To the Europeans the shores of the Black Sea were the frontiers of civilisation; the steppes beyond were the province of barbarian nomads, where distance was only marked by the tumuli of the ancient Scythians, long buried with their slaves, their women, horses and gold. Early travellers felt not only the blast of the restless steppe wind and the physical cold but a deeper discomfort of the soul. 'I was now come into a new world,' wrote the early steppe traveller William of Roubruck. Two centuries later Pero Tafur was more easily dismayed. He found it 'so cold that ships freeze in the harbour. Such is the bestiality and deformity of the people that I was glad to give up the desire to see more, and return to Greece.'

But it was here, in coastal settlements fringing the ominous sea and backed by the steppe wilderness, that the Greeks had settled since Mycenaean times and traded with the nomads. Until the fall of Constantinople in 1204 the Byzantines kept the Bosphorus straits firmly closed. The Black Sea provided the grain without which the city could not survive; the Italians were barred. It was the sacking of the city in 1204 which sprung the lock. Unhindered, the Venetians began to make forays into the Greater Sea. In 1206, they established a modest trading post at Soldaia on the Crimean peninsula and started trading with the local chiefs. They were at first discouraged by the violence and instability of the steppe dwellers beyond their walls, but the same year, two thousand miles to the east, an event was taking place that would reshape the trade routes of the world. The war lord Temuchin, Genghis Khan, managed to unite 'the people with felt tents' – the warring tribal peoples of the Mongolian steppe – into a coherent force to thunder west across the great Eurasian grasslands. Within thirty years the Mongols had blitzed their way from China to the plains of Hungary and the frontiers of Palestine. After the devastation – the deaths of millions of Persian peasants, the sacking of Baghdad and the great Muslim cities of the Euphrates, the burning of Herat, Moscow, Cracow – an extraordinary peace settled on the Eurasian world. The Mongols created a unified kingdom that stretched five thousand miles west from China; the old silk routes reopened; trading posts sprang up. Under the Pax Mongolica travellers could traverse the blue horizons without fear of banditry or arbitrary taxation. And the Mongol khans were keen to make contact with the West. From about 1260 a highway opened into the heart of Asia that created new opportunities for trans-continental trade. For the merchants of Europe it dangled the tantalising possibility of cutting out Arab middlemen and sourcing the luxury goods of the furthest Orient direct.

The western terminus of these routes was the Black Sea. By land, camel trains jogged from caravanserai to caravanserai out of central Asia; by sea the spices of Java and the Moluccas were routed round India to the Persian Gulf, trans-shipped across land to the roadheads at Trebizond on the southern shore of the Sea – or further west to Lajazzo on the Mediterranean. From Saray on the Volga, in the western kingdom of the Mongols, the Golden Horde exerted a peaceful pressure on the petty princelings of the Black Sea. Suddenly a doorway opened that would last a century. Through it slipped adventurous European merchants. The elder Polos, Matteo and Nicolo, set out from Soldaia in 1260 with jewels for the khan of the Golden Horde at Saray; twenty years later Marco would follow in their footsteps. With the fall of Acre and the papal ban on Islamic trade, the Black Sea became the displaced centre of world trade – the axis of a series of long-range routes for exchange from the Baltic to China – and the epicentre of the commercial rivalry between Venice and Genoa. It was an opportunity that would enrich and wreck medieval Europe.

Genoa quickly established a winning lead. After the fall of the Latin kingdom in 1261 they were granted free access to the sea. Venice was barred. The Genoese pushed energetically into the new zone and began to ring the coasts with settlements. They established trading posts on the north shore with a headquarters at Caffa on the Crimean peninsula, which brought them into close contact with the khans of the Golden Horde. They were soon able to control the grain trade at the mouth of the Danube; they struck deals with the small Greek kingdom of Trebizond and from there travelled overland to the important Mongol market at Tabriz. Genoa was ideally placed: backed by its secure base at

Galata across the Golden Horn from Constantinople, it strived for commercial monopoly. Suddenly Venice was playing catch-up. The Venetians were hungry for Black Sea grain and struggled to develop their own footholds. When Acre fell in 1291 and the pope banned trade with the Muslim lands, the stakes in the game increased; they would double again in 1324 when the papal ban became absolute. For fifty years – from the 1290s until 1345 – the emporia of the Black Sea became the warehouse of the world. Both republics realised instantly what was stake. Genoa was intent on maintaining a monopoly; Venice on finding a way in.

With the squeezing of opportunities elsewhere, the commercial competition in the Black Sea intensified. It only took an inopportune meeting of two armed and competitive merchant convoys, a flung insult, a sea brawl, an exchange of derogatory diplomatic notes with financial demands to lead to hostilities. A second Genoese war broke out in 1294 and lasted five years. It was the mirror image of the first; this time Genoa won the set-piece sea battles but suffered huge commercial damage. The engagements involved random, chaotic and opportunistic acts of piracy across all the zones of commercial competition from North Africa to the Black Sea. Each went for its rival's mercantile assets. Genoa sacked Canea on Crete; Venice burned ships at Famagusta and Tunis. The Genoese in Constantinople hurled the Venetian *bailo* out of a window and massacred so many merchants 'that it has become necessary', reported back a contemporary, 'to dig huge deep trenches everywhere to bury the dead'. When this news reached the lagoon, the cry went up: 'War to the knife!' Ruggiero Morosini, ominously nicknamed Malabranca (the Cruel Claw), was despatched with a fleet to gut the Genoese colony of Galata while its inhabitants cowered behind the walls of Constantinople and dragged the Byzantines into the fight. A Venetian fleet advanced into the Black Sea and ransacked Caffa, but stayed too long and got iced in. A Genoese squadron got as far as the Venetian lagoon and attacked the town of Malamocco; the Venetian privateer Domenico Schiavo forced his way into Genoa's harbour, where he was said to have coined gold ducats on the city's break-water as a calculated insult. The war was conducted beyond the point of tactical reason and was immensely damaging to both parties. When the pope attempted to arbitrate and even offered to meet half the costs of the Venetian claims personally, the Republic was seized by irrational emotions and refused.

Both sides were able to put out substantial fleets at great cost. None equalled the ostentatious but futile Genoese display of 1295, when they despatched 165 galleys and thirty-five thousand men. It would be three hundred years before the Mediterranean would see such a show of maritime force again, but the Venetians evaded it and the armada was forced to slink home. In 1298, when the two finally met off the island of Curzola in the Adriatic, 170 galleys were involved. It was the largest maritime battle the republics ever fought. This time the Genoese won a startling victory: only twelve of Venice's ninety-five galleys survived; five thousand prisoners were captured. Andrea Dandolo, the Venetian admiral, shamed beyond indignity at the prospect of being led through Genoa in fetters, beat his brains out against the gunwales of a Genoese ship. Yet it was a hollow victory too. So many Genoese died at Curzola that when the victorious admiral, Lamba Doria, stepped ashore at Genoa, he was met by silence – no rejoicing crowds, no church bells. The people just mourned their dead. And it would be Venice that gained the posthumous glory. Among those Venetian prisoners unloaded at Genoa was a wealthy merchant who had got up a galley at his own expense. The Venetians mockingly called him Il Milione – the teller of a million tales. Ensconced in some comfort as a rich man, he struck up friendship with another prisoner, Rustichello da Pisa, a writer of romances. As Il Milione started to talk, Rustichello spotted a business opportunity. He took up his pen and began writing. Marco Polo had time to talk himself back down the Mongol highway all the way to China. The gold, the spices, the silk and the customs of the furthest Orient, as well as the tall stories, were transmitted to a fascinated European audience.

One year after Curzola both sides were led sullenly back to the negotiating table. The Peace of Milan in 1299 solved nothing. Its terms left the matter of the Black Sea unresolved. The search for food and raw materials from its shores, the access to the trade routes of central Asia, intensified the unofficial war. The Venetians worked hard to build their position; the Genoese to shoulder them out. Through diplomacy and patience, Venice slowly gained footholds. On the Crimean peninsula the two republics confronted each other across a distance of forty miles; the Venetians at Soldaia, the Genoese at the much more powerful commercial hub at Caffa. It was an unequal contest. The Genoese had absolute control of Caffa; it was a well-fortified city whose magnificent harbour, according to the Arab traveller Ibn Battuta, contained 'about two hundred vessels in it, both ships of war and trading vessels, small and large, for it is one of the world's most celebrated ports'. The Genoese worked to smother the Venetian upstart at Soldaia. In 1326 Soldaia was sacked by local Tatar lords beyond Mongol control and abandoned. On the southern shores, the republics competed more directly at Trebizond – the roadhead of the second path to the Orient, via the land route to Tabriz and the Persian Gulf. Here, as at Acre, they occupied adjacent barricaded colonies by permission of the Greek emperor of the tiny kingdom and could stoke up a healthy hatred.

Venice worked to ratchet up the pressure on the northern shore. In 1332 its ambassador, Nicolo Giustinian, journeyed across the winter steppes to the Mongol court at Saray to request an audience with the khan of the Golden Horde. Approaches to the Mongol overlords were occasions of trepidation: Venetian state registers reported ruefully on the lack of volunteers. The khan was a Muslim – 'the exalted Sultan Muhammad Uzbeg Khan', Ibn Battuta titled him,

exceedingly powerful, great in dignity, lofty in station, victor over the enemies of God . . . his territories are vast and his cities great . . . [he holds audience] in a pavilion, magnificently decorated, called the Golden Pavilion . . . constructed of wooden rods covered with plaques of gold, and in the centre of it is a wooden couch covered with plaques of silver gilt, its legs being pure silver and their bases encrusted with precious stones. The sultan sits on this throne.

Bowing low before the khan, Giustinian presented his suit. He had come to beg the khan to allow the establishment of a trading colony and to grant commercial privileges at the settlement of Tana on the Sea of Azov – the small, shallow offshoot in the north-west corner of the Black Sea, shaped like its miniature replica.

Tana and the Sea of Azov – a later print

Here, where the River Don reaches the sea through a wide marshy delta, the Venetians hoped to regain an effective presence in the Russian and oriental trade. Tana was well situated at the heart of the western Mongol kingdom, ideally placed for journeys north to Moscow and Nizhni Novgorod, the river routes of the Don and the Volga, and at the very head of the great trans-Asian silk route: 'The road you travel from Tana to Cathay is perfectly safe, whether by day or by night,' the Florentine merchant Francesco Pegolotti assured the readers of his merchant's handbook a few years later. The Mongols were not uninterested in trade with the west and the great khan granted the request. In 1333, the year of the monkey, he gave the Venetians a site on marshy ground beside the river with permission to build stone houses, a church, warehouses and a palisade.

In many respects Tana was better placed than the powerful Genoese centre at Caffa, 250 miles to the west and located on the spur of the Crimean peninsula. Genoa maintained a colony at Tana too but it was subsidiary to its powerful hub, and it certainly had no wish to see Venice develop a foothold. The Venetians also had particular advantages in exploiting this new opportunity. The Sea of Azov was familiar terrain – an estuarine lake with a mean depth of eight metres, whose channels and hidden shoals made navigation difficult; the lagoon-dwelling Venetians with their shallow-draughted galleys managed to nose their way up to Tana with greater ease than the Genoese in their heavier ones. According to the Florentine chronicler Matteo Villani, 'the Genoese could not go to the trading post at Tana in their galleys as they did at Caffa, to where it was more expensive and difficult to get spices and other merchandise overland than to Tana'. From the start, Tana was a thorn in Genoese flesh – an intrusion into their zone of private monopoly. It became a cornerstone of Genoa's policy to dislodge Venice from the northern shores of the Greater Sea: 'there shall be no voyages to Tana' was the mantra of their diplomacy. The Venetian response was equally robust. According to treaty, the Black Sea was common to all and they intended, as the doge roundly declared in 1350, 'to maintain free access to the sea with utmost zeal and the employment of all their powers'. Out of this collision of interests would come two more bloody wars.

At Tana a small core of resident Venetian merchants established themselves to manage the hinterland trade across the Russian steppe and the luxury exchanges with the distant East. Marco Polo, from the perspective of his vast, fifteen-year journey to the

Pacific, could afford to treat the Black Sea with disdain as being almost on the doorstep of Venice. 'We have not spoken to you of the Black Sea or the provinces that lie around it, although we ourselves have explored it thoroughly,' he wrote. 'It would be tedious to recount what is daily recounted by others. For there are so many others who explore these waters and sail upon them every day – Venetians, Genoese, Pisans – that everybody knows what is to be found there.' Yet to the resident consul and his merchants it was the outermost rim of the Venetian world. It felt like an exile. Educated Venetians, watching ice freeze up the shallow alluvial sea for another winter, hunkering down in their ermine furs and squinting into the blizzards being swept on the thousand-mile winds, might have longed for the lights of Venice reflected in their domestic canals.

A note of homesickness, frequent in merchant reports from beyond the Stato da Mar, haunts their letters. It was a three-month round trip for the great merchant fleets from the mother city that set out in spring, touched Tana for a mere few days and vanished again. They left the residents to the vastness of the steppes, watching the nomads moving from horizon to horizon in long processions beyond their settlement, as the merchant Giosafat Barbaro did:

First, herds of horses by the [hundreds]. After them followed herds of camels and oxen, and after them herds of small beasts, which endured for the space of six days, that as far as we might see with our eyes, the plain every way was full of people and beasts following on their way . . . and in the evening we were weary of looking.

Chronic insecurity was the lot of all Venetian trading posts perched on foreign soil. The whims of the local potentates had to be continuously appeased by watchful diplomacy, lavish presents – and whatever physical barricades they were permitted to erect. None was more dependent on goodwill than Tana. Unlike the Genoese settlement at Caffa, which was a fortress ringed by double walls, Venetian Tana had no meaningful defence in the early years beyond a flimsy wooden stockade. It was dependent on the stability of the Golden Horde. The senate viewed Tana as being precariously positioned 'at the limits of the world and in the jaws of our enemies'. The Venetians walked on eggshells. Cooped up for months close to the detested Genoese, their community was so small that Venice gave unusual permission to grant citizenship to other European merchants. Yet back in Venice, Tana was vividly imagined. It gave its name to the Tana, the rope factory in the state arsenal which used Black Sea hemp in its manufacture. It was Tana too that Petrarch was thinking about as he vicariously shivered from the safety of his writing desk, watching the ships depart for the mouth of the Don and speculating on the fierce commercial energy that impelled the Venetians to such outlandish parts.

What drove them on were the possible returns, the 'insatiable thirst for wealth' that baffled the scholarly Petrarch so much. At Tana they acquired both the portable, lightweight, high-value luxury items of the furthest Orient and the bulk commodities and foodstuffs of the steppe hinterland: precious stones and silk from China and the Caspian Sea; furs and skins, sweet-smelling beeswax and honey from the glades of Russian forests; wood, salt and grain and dried or salted fish in infinite varieties from the Sea of Azov. In return they shipped back the manufactured goods of a developing industrial Europe: worked woollen cloth from Italy, France and Bruges; German weapons and iron utensils; Baltic amber and wine. On the opposite shore at Trebizond they accessed raw materials – copper and alum, as well as pearls from the Red Sea, ginger, pepper and cinnamon from the Indies. In all these transactions the trade imbalance was huge – Asia had more to sell than the infant industrial base of medieval Europe could offer in return. It had to be paid for with bars of ninety-eight per cent pure silver; large reserves of European bullion drained away into the heartlands of Asia.

There was one other highly profitable item in which the Venetian merchants came to deal, although its business was always outstripped by the Genoese. Both Caffa and Tana were active centres of slave trading. The Mongols raided the interior for 'Russians, Mingrelians, Caucasians, Circassians, Bulgarians, Armenians and divers other people of the Christian world'. The qualities of the ethnic groups were carefully distinguished – different peoples had different merits. If a Tatar was sold (expressly forbidden by the Mongols and the source of repeated trouble) 'the price is a third more, since it may be taken as certain that no Tatar ever betrayed a master'; Marco Polo brought back a Tatar slave from his travels. Generally slaves were sold young – boys in their teens (to get the most work out of them), the girls a little older. Some were shipped to Venice as domestic and sexual servants, others to Crete in conditions of plantation slavery, where village names such as Sklaverohori and Roussohoria still record the legacy and origin of this commerce. Or they were sold on in an illicit trade, expressly forbidden by the pope, as military slaves to the Mamluk Islamic armies of Egypt. Candia, on Crete, formed one hub of this secret business, where the final destinations of the 'merchandise' were usually suppressed. Most of these Black Sea slaves were nominally Christian.

Pero Tafur recorded the practice at the slave markets in the fifteenth century:

The selling takes place as follows. The seller makes the slaves strip to the skin, males as well as females, and they put on them a cloak of felt, and the price is named. Afterwards they throw off their coverings, and make them walk up and down to show whether they have any bodily defect. The seller has to oblige himself, that if a slave dies of the pestilence within sixty days, he will return the price paid.

Sometimes parents came selling their own children, a practice which affronted Tafur, though it did not prevent him acquiring 'two female slaves and a male, whom I still have in Cordoba with their children'. Though slaves usually only made up a small portion of a Black Sea cargo, there were cases when whole shipments of human merchandise would be entrusted to the holds in a manner similar to that of the later Atlantic slave trade.

To the Republic, Tana mattered hugely. 'From Tana and the Greater Sea,' a Venetian source wrote, 'our merchants have gained the greatest value and profit because they were the source of all kinds of goods.' For a time merchants there could monopolise almost the entire China trade. The Tana convoys were intricately interlocked with the rhythm of the returning galleys from London and Flanders four thousand miles away, so that they could carry Baltic amber and Flemish cloth to the Black Sea and return with rare oriental goods for Venice's winter fairs. Exotic produce from the Orient added weight to Venice's reputation as the market of the world, the one place where you might find anything. For at least a hundred years foreign merchants – particularly Germans – had been coming to Venice in large numbers, bringing metals – silver, copper – and worked cloth to buy these oriental goods.

From the fruits of the long boom of the thirteenth and fourteenth centuries, Venice was transforming itself. By 1300 all the separate islets had been joined by bridges to form a recognisable city, which was densely inhabited. The streets and squares of beaten earth were progressively paved over; stone was replacing wood for building houses. A cobbled way linked the centres of Venetian power – the Rialto and St Mark's Square. An increasingly wealthy noble class constructed for themselves astonishing palazzos along the Grand Canal in the Gothic style, tempered with elements of Islamic decoration to which the travelling merchants had been exposed in Alexandria and Beirut. New churches were built and the skyline punctuated with their brick campaniles. In 1325 the state arsenal was enlarged to meet the increased requirements for maritime trade and defence. Fifteen years later work was begun redeveloping the doge's palace into the masterpiece of Venetian Gothic, a delicate traceried structure of astonishing lightness and beauty that seemed to express the effortless serenity, grace, good judgement and stability of the Venetian state. The facade of the basilica of St Mark was gradually transformed from plain Byzantine brick into a rich fantasy of

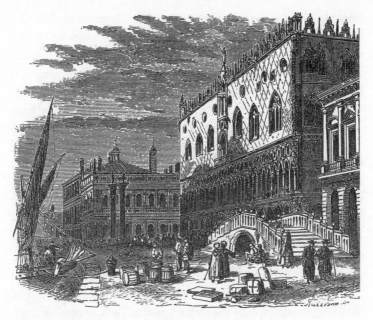

Venetian gothic: the doge's palace and the waterfront

marble and mosaic, incorporating the plunder of Constantinople and the East, and topped with domes and oriental embellishment that took the viewer halfway to Cairo and Baghdad. Some time around 1260 the horses of the Constantinople hippodrome were winched into place on its loggia as a statement of the city's new-found self-confidence. Out of maritime trade, Venice was starting to dazzle and bewitch.

Meanwhile in the Black Sea the Venetians at Tana began to steal a march on Genoese Caffa. The state registers bear running testament to the close attention paid to their trading post. After permission for a settlement was granted in 1333, a consul was immediately despatched who 'is allowed to trade' – an unusual concession – 'and must keep in his service a lawyer, four servants and four horses'. In 1340 he was instructed to seek another abode because of the closeness to the Genoese and the frequent fights; ambassadors were sent back to Uzbeg Khan for the purpose. The

consul was later barred from trading but his salary rose in rec-
ompense. The behaviour of the Venetian merchants was often
a cause for concern. In the summer of 1343 it was noted that 'a
lot of merchants are fraudulently avoiding the [tax] imposed
by the khan. This is not without risk to the colony. The consul will henceforth insist that all merchants swear that they have
actually paid.' Gifts of carefully stipulated amounts were to be
presented to the khan. A later curt directive to the consul states
that 'the Venetians must stop taxing the merchandise of foreign
merchants: this could displease the Tatar government and end up
damaging Venetian interests'. The thin margin between tolerance
and xenophobia worried the authorities back in the lagoon.

Despite the careful prescriptions of the Venetian senate the
fragile balancing act at Tana collapsed. In 1341 Uzbeg died. His
thirty-year reign had been the longest and most stable Mongol
administration. Venice was quick to analyse the dangers: 'The
death of Uzbeg exposes the trading post at Tana to difficult days;
the consul will choose twelve Venetian merchants to consider the
new circumstances and make obeisance to the new [khan].' This
model diplomacy was almost immediately undone – as so often
in Venetian trading posts – by the ill-discipline of an individual
merchant. It came against the usual brawling rivalry between
Venetian and Genoese residents in confined places – men were
killed in these contests – which irked the local Tatar governor,
unable to tell the two groups of citizens apart. There were other
matters too: the tax evasion, the failure to give adequate presents,
the accustomed arrogance of the unruly foreigners. Venetian self-
confidence was particularly high in September 1343 when armed
galleys put in at the mouth of the Don. A personal altercation
led to an eruption of violence. An important local Tatar, Haji
Omar, apparently struck a Venetian, Andriolo Civrano, in a dispute. Civrano's response was premeditated: he ambushed Haji
Omar at night and killed him along with several members of his
family. Aghast, the Venetian community braced itself and tried
to return the body and pay blood money. First they called on the

Genoese to take a united stance in confronting the crisis. The Genoese did no such thing. They attacked and plundered Tatar property themselves and sailed away, leaving the Venetians to face the consequences. In the ensuing violence, sixty Venetians were killed. The new khan, Zanibeck, descended on Tana and sacked it, destroyed all their goods and took some of the merchants hostage. The survivors fled to Genoese Caffa in their ships where they begged for safe haven. All contact with the Asiatic world was now concentrated on this Genoese fort.

The crisis at Tana spread. If Zanibeck was irked by the Venetians, he was more deeply so by the Genoese at Caffa, which had become a direct colony outside the khan's control, taxing other foreign merchants as it pleased. Zanibeck decided to wipe the troublesome Italians from his domain. He descended on Caffa with a large army. It led to a rare moment of Genoese and Venetian co-operation. The Venetians were granted tax-free concessions and they stood shoulder to shoulder behind the city's impressive defences. Over the icy winter of 1343, the Mongol army bombarded the city's walls, but the advantage of the sea was with the Genoese. In February 1344 a fleet raised the siege; the Mongols retreated, leaving fifteen thousand dead. The following year Zanibeck was back, more determined than ever to expel the Genoese.

The two rival republics agreed on a joint trade embargo in all the realms of the Mongols. In 1344, the Venetian senate forbade 'all commerce with the regions ruled by Zanibeck, including Caffa'. The decree was read out on the steps of the Rialto to ensure that the message was clearly understood, with the threat of heavy fines and the forfeit of half the cargo. At the same time, with the agreement of the Genoese, they sent conciliatory ambassadors back to Saray to attempt to resolve the crisis. It was in vain. The only response was the whipping flight of Tatar arrows over the city walls, the tensioning creak and thunder of catapults. The siege of Caffa went on into 1346.

By the 1340s the Black Sea had become the warehouse of the world. The rolling siege of Caffa and the destruction of Tana brought trade to a standstill, like ice freezing the winter sea. The effects were felt throughout the hungry cities of the Mediterranean basin. There was famine in the eastern Mediterranean – lack of wheat, salt, fish in Byzantium; shortage of wheat in Venice and a rocketing of prices in luxury goods: silk and spices doubled throughout Europe. It was these effects that made the Black Sea so crucial and the competition between the maritime republics so fierce. The returns encouraged the merchants to endure all the difficulties of trade on the edge of the steppe. Coupled with the ongoing papal embargo on the Mamluks, world trade was grinding to a halt. There was now no outlet in the East for the manufactured goods of Italy and the Low Countries. In 1344 the Venetians made an anguished appeal to the pope:

... at this time ... the trade with Tana and the Black Sea can be seen to be lost or obstructed. From these regions our merchants have been accustomed to derive the greatest gain and profit, since it was the source of all trade both in exporting our [wares] and importing them. And now our merchants know not where to go and cannot keep employed.

The pope began to permit a gentle relaxation of trade with Egypt and Syria; it was start of a process that would gradually switch the spice trade back to the Mediterranean basin.

But in Caffa the siege took an unexpected turn. The Tatars outside the wall started to die. According to the only contemporary account:

Disease seized and struck down the whole Tatar army. Every day unknown thousands perished ... they died as soon as the symptoms appeared on their bodies, the result of coagulating humours in their groins and armpits followed by putrid fever. All medical advice and help was useless. The Tatars, exhausted, astonished and completely demoralised by the appalling catastrophe and virulent disease, realised that there was no hope of avoiding death ... and ordered the corpses to be loaded into their catapults and flung into Caffa, so that the enemy might be wiped out by the terrible stench. It appears that huge piles of dead were hurled inside, and the Christians could neither hide, flee nor escape from these corpses, which they tried to dump in the sea, as many as they

could. The air soon became completely infected and the water supply was poisoned by rotting corpses.

It is unlikely that the Black Death was transmitted from just this single event, but it was soon carried west on merchant ships. Only four out of eight Genoese galleys sailing the Black Sea in 1347 made it back to the city; on the others all the crew died and the ships vanished. The plague was in Constantinople in December; it reached Venice some time around January 1348, almost simultaneously with a series of portentous earthquakes which set all the church bells ringing and sucked the water out of the Grand Canal. By March plague had Venice in its grip; by May, as the weather warmed up, it was out of control. No city on earth was more densely populated. It now faced catastrophe. According to the Venetian chronicler Lorenzo de Monacis, the plague exceeded all proportions:

[It] raged so fiercely that squares, porticoes, tombs, and all the holy places were crammed with corpses. At night many were buried in the public streets, some under the floors of their own homes; many died unconfessed; corpses rotted in abandoned houses . . . fathers, sons, brothers, neighbours and friends abandoned each other . . . not only would doctors not visit anyone, they fled from the sick . . . the same terror seized the priests and clerics . . . there was no rational thought about the crisis . . . the whole city was a tomb.

It became necessary to take the bodies away at public expense on special ships, called pontoons, which rowed through the city, dragging the corpses from the abandoned houses, taking them . . . to islands outside the city and dumping them in heaps in long, wide pits, dug for the purpose with huge effort. Many of those on the pontoons and in the pits were still breathing and died [of suffocation]; meanwhile most of the oarsmen caught the plague. Precious furniture, money, gold and silver left lying about in the abandoned houses were not stolen by thieves – extraordinary lethargy or terror infected everyone; none seized by the plague survived seven hours; pregnant women did not escape it: for many, the foetus was expelled with their innards. The plague cut down women and men, old and young in equal measure. Once it struck a house, none left alive.

During the summer of 1348 the black-draped pontoons punted slowly through the foetid canals. The terrible cry rose up: 'Dead bodies! Dead bodies!' Every house was compelled by punitive edicts to bring out its corpses. Extraordinary measures were put in place to try to stem the death rate. A special health committee was convened; ships suspected of being infected were burned; all trade ground to a halt; the sale of wine was prohibited, taverns closed; criminals were let out of prison for lack of warders. The Rialto, the docks, the busy canals fell silent. Venice was gripped in gloom. Out on the distant islands of the lagoon the dead went on being tipped into pits – a layer of earth, then a layer of bodies, then another layer of earth – 'just like lasagne' as one Florentine writer unnervingly put it.

By the time the plague had burned itself out, possibly two thirds of the Venetian population had perished; fifty noble families ceased to exist. The survivors were literally treading on the dead. For centuries, unwary fishermen stepping ashore on certain deserted islands deep in the lagoon scrunched on the whitening bones of the hastily buried victims. The Black Death radically altered the outlook of Venetian merchants. For 150 years, Venice had advanced on a rising tide of European prosperity, growing wealth and booming populations. Maritime ventures, characterised by an optimistic culture of risk-taking, had brought rich returns. But it was the rampant materialism, the expansion of trade routes, the commercial connections across vast distances that had brought not only silk, spices, ivory and pearls, grain and fish, but also the plague bacillus from inner Asia. It was the Italian maritime republics who were charged with carrying death to Europe; the consequences were taken to be divine judgement for cupidity and sin. The contemporary chronicler Gabriele de Mussis set out the charge in an imaginary dialogue between God and the merchants:

'Genoa, confess what you have done ... Venice, Tuscany and the whole of Italy, say what you did.'

'We Genoese and Venetians are responsible for revealing God's judgement. Painfully, we set sail to our cities and entered our homes ...

and alas, we carried with us the darts of death, and at the very moment that our families hugged and kissed us, even as we were speaking we were compelled to spread poison from our mouths.'

By the end of 1350, as a by-product of the Black Sea trade, probably half of Europe's population had died. The figure in the Mediterranean basin was perhaps as high as seventy-five per cent in places. The Black Death jolted a whole continent into new ways of thinking and acting, wrenching it away from a communal medieval past. Venice, whose materialistic drive had affronted Petrarch, was the harbinger of multiple new worlds, identities and mindsets. Afterwards the mercantile mood of Italy would itself darken. Melancholy tinged the bright prospects for wealth and trade: 'Nothing is more certain than death,' became the popular sentiment, 'nor is anything more uncertain than the hour of it.' Merchants became more risk-averse, more conservative, more aware of sudden reversals of fortune; in the stock phrase of maritime enterprise, *fortuna maris*, the fortune of the sea, made men increasingly cautious. Henceforth Venice was patrolling the plague frontiers of Europe.

But the competition in the Black Sea went on regardless. The trade boycott was breached by both parties. In 1347, the Venetians overtly broke ranks and acquired new concessions from Zanibeck to trade at Tana. Genoa, determined that 'there shall be no sailing to Tana', prepared to retaliate. Its proud declaration that Venetian voyaging in the Black Sea was ever only with the express permission of Genoa made new wars inevitable. They would take both players to the brink of ruin.

II

The Flag of St Titus

The Black Sea remained an unresolved problem, which plague had done nothing to ease. It merely reduced the available manpower and the protagonists' naval capabilities. Within a year of losing two thirds of their populations, Genoa and Venice were at war again. In the aftermath, the contest moved back to the Bosphorus, the choke point that controlled access to the markets of central Asia. War returned again to the sea walls of Constantinople, a repeated point of destiny in Venice's maritime adventure.

By the late 1340s it was clear that the reconstituted Byzantine Empire had never recovered from the trauma of the Fourth Crusade. Racked by civil war, harassed by the inexorable advance of the Turks across the Anatolian land mass, totally incapable of managing its maritime frontiers, the city had no means of controlling the predatory instincts of Venice and Genoa. The two republics became kingmakers, backing differing factions in the city's internal power struggles. In this respect, the Genoese were far better placed. From their strongly fortified trading town at Galata with its sheltered harbour, just across the water from the city, they were uniquely positioned to squeeze the Greek emperor. Constantinople was entirely dependent on Genoese ships for access to the wheat of the Black Sea, and Galata had stolen much of the city's trade. By 1350 its customs revenues were seven times those of Constantinople. The entwined snakes of Constantine's column had become parasites threatening to overwhelm the host body. Constantinople found itself helplessly entangled in the running fight between the two cities for commercial dominance. War advanced remorselessly to its doorstep;

The Genoese acted with impunity. In 1348 they mounted an attack on the city; the following year, when the Byzantines attempted to construct a new fleet they destroyed it in the Golden Horn; they helped themselves to strategic Byzantine bases along the coast of Asia Minor; in 1350, they occupied a castle on the Bosphorus which gave them absolute control over the entrance to the Black Sea. When they seized Venetian ships at Caffa, war with Venice became inevitable.

The third Genoese war, which started in 1350, was in most respects scarcely distinct from its predecessors; a chaotic, wide-ranging and visceral maritime brawl, involving hit-and-run tactics, piracy, raids on bases and islands and pitched sea battles. The difference lay in the size of the fleets. The Black Death had devastated the manpower resources of both cities; seafarers had been particularly badly affected. In 1294, Venice had manned some seventy galleys in a matter of months; in 1350 it was hard pushed to fill the rowing benches of thirty-five. Already a small step-change was starting to take place in attitudes among the ordinary citizens towards the sea-going life. The plague had left its survivors better off. They had inherited considerable wealth and the scarcity of labour forced up the asking price. A rift was also opening up between the classes which would become dramatic in fleet matters a generation later. The ordinary seamen began to feel they were not sharing the same risks and conditions as their aristocratic commanders. When it came to conscription, there were complaints that whereas the captains fed on good bread, the oarsmen subsisted on indigestible millet. As a result many of the conscripted men preferred to hire substitutes from among the colonial subjects of Greece and the Dalmatian coast. The solidarity, the discipline, the sense of shared life among the citizens was starting to fray, with long-term consequences for Venetian sea power.

However, if the fleets were now smaller, the contests grew in bitterness. With each returning cycle of war, Venetian–Genoese hatred increased; and in 1352 the two maritime powers were to fight a battle off the walls of Constantinople which would pass down in Venetian memory as one of the nastiest they ever experienced.

In 1351 Venice signed a pact with the Byzantine emperor, John V, for the express purpose of expelling Genoa from the Bosphorus and releasing its throttling grip on the Black Sea. To compensate for its shrunken fleet, the Venetians also enrolled the support of the king of Aragon, in faraway Spain, who had his own reasons for discomfiting the Genoese. He contributed a Catalan force of thirty galleys, twelve of which Venice paid for out of its own pocket. The Venetian command passed to its most experienced admiral, Nicolo Pisani. He was well matched by the Genoese commander, Paganino Doria, scion of a noble maritime family, in a rivalry which would be handed down through the generations. There were initially months of skirmishing in which the protagonists kept missing each other; at one point Pisani, chased back to Negroponte with an inferior force, scuttled his galleys in the harbour rather than risk a fight. Doria was forced to withdraw. Pisani refloated his ships and sailed on.

Early in 1352, a joint Venetian, Byzantine and Catalan fleet finally hunted down their rivals in the mouth of the Bosphorus. On Monday 13 February the two fleets prepared for battle off the city walls of Constantinople. Here the Fourth Crusade had launched its first assault on the city 150 years earlier under very different conditions. It was afternoon when the two fleets finally closed, the depth of winter, bitterly cold, the weather blustery, the sea chopped into fury by a strong wind blowing up from the south and the Bosphorus current running against it with a powerful surge.

Ship-handling was extremely difficult. There were only a few hours of daylight left. In these conditions Pisani considered it wise to hold off for a fresh day, but the Catalan admiral was convinced of easy victory. Sword in hand, he declared he would fight and gave the trumpet call for the attack. Pisani had little option but to follow him in. As they raised anchor, the wind increased its velocity; the sea began to mount into castling peaks and vertiginous troughs. It became impossible to bear down on the Genoese fleet in any kind of order. Doria drew his ships back into the mouth of a sheltered creek, and the allied vessels, propelled by the force of the gale, shot past unable to engage; with huge difficulty they turned about, the rowers straining at the oars, to make a second attempt.

Galley wars

A hundred ships were now wedged into the neck of the Bosphorus at a point only a mile wide. Bucking and rearing, with neither side able to organise its lines, they attempted to engage. The strait was jammed with ships, colliding, crashing into each other, driven ashore by the force of the wind. Rather than a sea battle, it was a series of incoherent micro-fights, small groups of five, six, seven ships tearing at each other blindly in the wind. Night fell abruptly over the violent sea. Confusion increased. It became impossible to tell friend from foe. Venetian ships tried to board each other; Genoese rained arrows down on their own vessels; men fell overboard; galleys lost their steering systems; their oars were shattered in the impact of the battle; vessels floated away rudderless on the current. Once fire caught a ship it blazed like tinder in the fierce gale and was swept away flaring and guttering into the dark. The wind, the biting cold, the splintering of wood, the confused cries, the men staggering along their decks, trying to fight, driven forward by an appalling madness: it looked like a version of hell. There was no strategy or control. Outcomes were decided by luck. Locked together, ships crashed onto the coast; their crews leaped ashore and continued to batter and stab at each other so that in places the sea battle became a land battle. The men from seven Catalan galleys just ran away; the Greeks, perhaps more wisely, hardly engaged at all and retreated into the Golden Horn. Men fought to the death with demented fury. They killed their own side as often as the other.

Dawn broke on a scene of devastation. Empty hulls floated on the water or lay wrecked on the shore; the sea was littered with corpses, spars, the detritus of battle. No one could tell who had won. Both sides claimed the victory. The casualties were huge. Franciscan friars from Galata tried to arrange a prisoner exchange. When they visited the Venetian fleet, they found so few captives that they decided not to return, fearing that when the Genoese learned of their losses they would slaughter their own prisoners out of hand.

Yet in the aftermath advantage remained with Genoa. The Venetian and Catalan fleet withdrew, unable to sustain the assault on Galata. And the Genoese now had military aid from the Ottoman sultan, Orhan. The Byzantines had no choice but to sign a peace treaty with Genoa, under the terms of which Greek ships should have no entry to the Black Sea without Genoese permission. In addition, the Genoese were confirmed in their possession of Galata, which they now fortified more strongly as a sovereign colony. Byzantium was being slowly strangled, not only by the

avid maritime republics, but also by the advancing Ottoman Turks. For Venice, the strategic consequences were severe. What they learned from the Battle of the Bosphorus was that without a strategic fall-back point at the approaches to the Black Sea they would never be able to exercise any concerted pressure on the trade to the furthest East. They cast an acquisitive eye over the small island of Tenedos, strategically positioned at the mouth of the Dardanelles.

There was little rejoicing in Genoa either. 'I saw no annual commemoration of this triumph,' wrote the Genoese chronicler, 'nor did the doge visit any churches to give thanks, as is the normal custom; perhaps, because so many brave Genoese fell in the fight, the victory of that day is best forgotten.'

The war went on. It moved west and continued, through a series of oscillating mood swings that drove each republic in turn from manic joy to the brink of despair, like the dip and lurch of a huge sea. With smaller fleets and diminished resources of manpower, the effects of naval defeat were more keenly felt. When Pisani and the Aragonese wiped out a Genoese fleet off Sardinia the effects inside the city were dramatic. People wept in the streets; with Genoa cut off from its sources of wealth and grain, humiliation, starvation, and abject surrender seemed at hand. The citizens resorted to desperate measures. They made voluntary submission to Venice's terrestrial rival, Giovanni Visconti, the powerful lord of Milan, as a protective shield. Victory was snatched from Venice's hands. Visconti despatched Petrarch, at this time a diplomat in his court, to attempt to woo the Venetians. Using all his literary skill, he called flatteringly upon 'the two most powerful peoples, the most flourishing cities, the two Eyes of Italy' to make peace. And he pointed out that Venetian over-confidence might yet be punished: 'the dice of fortune are ambiguous. It cannot but be that if one of the Eyes is put out, the other will be darkened. For to hope for a bloodless victory over such an enemy, beware less it betoken a fatuous and fallacious confidence!'

The warning went unheeded. The doge, Andrea Dandolo, sent a blunt reply:

... the aim of the Genoese is to snatch from us the most precious of all possessions – our liberty; and in meddling with our rights they drive us to arms ... the quarrel is an old one ... Thus we have undertaken war, merely that we may secure our country, which we hold dearer than life. Farewell.

Petrarch was left to mutter at the mercantile republic's uncouth response: 'No words of mine, not even of Cicero himself, could have reached ears that were stubbornly stopped, or opened obstinate hearts.' And he repeated his warning about the dangers of internecine war: 'Do not fool yourself that if Italy disintegrates Venice will not also fall: for Venice is part of Italy.' Venice would beg to differ – it held itself distinct from the mainland, though by now more deeply involved than it liked to admit.

But as the contest went on the dice did indeed start to roll the other way. It was now Venice's turn to be infected with fear. The Genoese constructed a new fleet and Doria returned to inflict a shattering defeat on Pisani at Porto Longo on the island of Sapienza, near Modon in the southern Peloponnese. It was a catastrophe as total as the Republic had ever experienced. All its galleys were lost. Six thousand men, the flower of Venice's seafaring people, were taken prisoner and a huge amount of booty lost. Nicolo Pisani, his son Vettor and a detachment of sailors made it to Modon. Pisani was deprived of all further public office and lived the remainder of his days a broken man. Vettor was acquitted, but memory of the defeat at Porto Longo would cling to the family like a dark stain and return to haunt the Venetian lagoon twenty-five years later. The doge died two months before this disaster, 'sparing him', Petrarch wrote, with the smug satisfaction of a man who had been proved right, 'the sight of his country's bitter anguish and the still more biting letters that I should have written him'.

Unlike in Genoa however, defeat did not create civil unrest or constitutional collapse in Venice, though within a few months

Doge Dandolo's successor, Marino Faliero, had been executed for an attempted coup. In June 1355, the duke of Milan imposed a new peace on the warring republics, to the relief of Venice and the fury of Genoa. It amounted, in effect, to little more than a ceasefire. Both parties agreed to keep out of the Sea of Azov for three years – a short-term setback to Venice, unable now to use Tana, but welcome to Genoa, whose primacy at Caffa was restored. Venice counted down the months to June 1358 with intense interest; meanwhile it embarked on a new round of diplomatic initiatives with all the trading nations of the hemisphere – the great khan of the Golden Horde, Flanders, Egypt and Tunis.

The war had proved indecisive but both sides had in turn glimpsed the possibility of an elusive final victory, only to have the ultimate prize snatched away by the meddling duke of Milan; each had penetrated deep into the other's waters and taken its opponent to the brink. Twenty-five years later the same war would be refought with the same tactics, reversals, hopes and fears, in the same waters but with magnified consequences. Next time it would be fought to a finish.

In the Vatican they wrung their hands in exasperation at the running hostility of the maritime republics. Successive papal attempts at crusading ventures were repeatedly stymied by their rivalry, as only the protagonists possessed the resources to transport troops. What outsiders realised, and Venice herself was keenly aware of, was that in the interstices of these exhausting wars and the Byzantine collapse, the Ottoman Turks were inexorably advancing. The worst day's work the Genoese ever did themselves, or the rest of Christendom, came in November 1354 when they ferried an Ottoman army across the Dardanelles into Europe. They charged a ducat a head. It was a handsome rate but a terrible bargain. Once established in Gallipoli, the Turks became impossible to dislodge. They were in Europe for good – a fourth snake entwined in the politics of Constantinople and its hinterland.

*

These wars also had deepening repercussions in the Stato da Mar. The Republic's maintenance of its seaways and maritime defences, under the pressure of competitors, drew increasingly heavily on the resources of its colonies. All its outposts, ruled directly from the centre, felt the weighty presence of the Dominante – especially in fiscal matters. The Venetians were masters of a complete vocabulary of taxation, refining and implementing with obsessive scrutiny models derived from their Byzantine predecessors. They levied the *capinicho*, the *acrosticho* and the *zovatico* – direct taxes – on households, land holdings and animals; indirect taxes, the *arico*, the *commerclum* and the *tansa*, fell on the sale of oil and wine, on exports of cheese and iron, on skins and salted fish and the mooring of ships (according to function and tonnage), on the transport of wine even within Crete, and countless other commodities and economic functions. The *angariae* – taxes in kind levied for the construction of fortifications, guard duty, the supply of fodder and firewood – were particularly irksome to the townspeople of Crete; monopoly purchase by the state of core commodities, especially wheat below the market rate, aggravated landowners. There were also special levies to cope with military emergencies and pirate attacks. Wherever the banner of St Mark flew, the Republic's economic demands were felt. Taxes were levied impersonally on all its colonial subjects. They fell on Venetians and indigenous people alike, on foreigners, on clergy and laity, on peasants and townspeople – though Jews were taxed with singular zeal.

Nowhere felt these fiscal burdens more keenly than Crete. The island was the nerve centre of empire. Every commercial and maritime enterprise to the east passed through its harbours. It lay in the front line of crusade and maritime war. Its wheat was vital to the lagoon. It was responsible for arming galleys and levying their manpower, for supplying double-baked biscuits for the Republic's war fleets, for soldiers and oarsmen. When Venice participated in a crusade to Smyrna in 1344 to discomfit the Turks, it was Crete that paid for it. It was Cretan wheat that was

Images of empire: the Venetian domination of Crete

monopolised by the Republic at discount prices. Furthermore the island was expensive to run. The increasing predations of Turkish pirates from the coast of Asia Minor called for military defence, fortifications and galley patrols. The walls of Candia were repeatedly damaged by earthquakes, and its vital man-made harbour and long protecting mole were subject to furious battering from the sea. All this required money and Crete had to pay. Decade after decade a slowly accumulating grudge against the tax demands of the distant mother city grew in strength – not just amongst the Greek population, who had rebelled frequently, but also amongst their landed Venetian overlords, the feudatories, now settled in the island for generations. In the summer of 1363 this dissatisfaction plunged the Venetian imperial project into turmoil.

On 21 July 1363, the Venetian records noted a judgement by the Council of Ten, one of the state's powerful governing bodies. It was against one Marco Turlanio, who had 'permitted an armourer, not named, to go to Padua to practise his craft, notably the making of crossbows. This action is extremely damaging to Venetian interests. The Ten therefore condemn Turlanio to permanent exile and banishment to the island of Crete.' Padua was a hostile city and the defection of craftsmen with specialised military or industrial skills was taken extremely seriously in Venice – salt- or glass-workers risked having their right hands cut off or their lips and noses (in the case of women), or being hunted down and assassinated. Three months later, the registers record that Turlanio was still in Venice: the punishment had been suspended. What happened in between was a convulsion that shook Venice's empire to the core.

On 8 August, the Venetian feudatories learned that the senate was intending to introduce a new tax for the maintenance and cleaning of the harbour at Candia. It was the straw that broke the camel's back. The feudatories objected strongly; it was felt that the work was being undertaken solely for the benefit of the merchant fleets passing through Crete to the shores of Egypt and Syria. They assembled at Candia and demanded the right of appeal to the doge in Venice. The duke of Crete, Leonardo Dandolo, refused to budge; the tax must be paid. He despatched heralds across the city to proclaim this – pointedly to the Church of St Titus, Crete's patron saint, where the chief objectors were gathered. The duke's message was blunt: pay the tax or face confiscation of property and death. There were nineteen Venetian ships in the harbour and around five hundred sailors; Dandolo was advised to call on these men to seize control of the main square and disperse the demonstration. He refused, fearing that this might add fuel to the fire. The sailors stayed in the port.

But Dandolo's edict failed to cower the landlords. The following day they gathered in the central square, backed by an aggrieved mob of townspeople, servants and soldiers, and attempted to storm the ducal palace. The doors held firm. The duke inside was obdurate but personally brave and ordered the gates to be opened. He commanded the feudatories to disperse or face death. Enraged, one of the ringleaders, Tito Venier, cried out, 'It is you who will die, traitor!' Dandolo was saved by his courage. Several other protesters stepped forward and shielded him, but by the end of the day he was under arrest, along with other leading dignitaries of the administration loyal to Venice.

Within a week, the rebels had created a mirror government for an independent Crete, with the Venetian landowner Marco Gradenigo appointed governor and rector, supported by four advisers and a council of twenty. Crete had risen repeatedly in revolt against its Venetian masters for 150 years, but the rebellion of 1363 exposed a far deeper fault line in the Republic's maritime empire. Previously all uprisings had been the work of dispossessed Greek landlords. This was different. For the first time, the Venetian colonists rebelled. They included some of the great names of the Republic's history, noble families such as Gradenigo, Venier, Grimaldi, Querini and Dandolo, which had provided doges, administrators, admirals and merchant princes during the upward curve of expansion. The Republic had always pursued a strict policy of segregation between subject peoples and Venetian colonists and administrators, whom it hedged about with restrictive clauses and prohibitions. Its watchword was ethnic purity; its deepest fear assimilation. In the time-honoured phrase, however far-flung Venetian citizens might be – in Tana, London, Alexandria, Constantinople, Bruges, Lisbon or Candia – they were 'flesh of our flesh, bones of our bones' – loyal and patriotic participants in the communal venture that comprised the Most Serene Republic of St Mark, and whose magnetic north was the lagoon.

Yet on Crete, after 150 years of occupation, in which generations had lived on the island, this aloofness had softened. They spoke Greek as well as their own Venetian dialect, some had intermarried into the leading Greek clans, a few had leant towards the mystical beauty of the Orthodox rite: Crete was starting to conquer the conquerors. The tenor of this revolt was set by the debate over the standard that should now fly over the newly independent island, in an episode related by the heavily anti-Cretan Venetian chronicler de Monacis:

On 13 August the rebels in the palace discussed whether to raise the customary flag of St Mark, or that of St Titus. The crowds ran into the square shouting 'Long live St Titus!' So it was decreed that the figure of St Titus should be raised on flags on land and sea, and be publicly flown everywhere.

The events became known as the Revolt of St Titus. It marked the emergence of a new yearning for independence. But its inception was also marked by ill-omen. 'That same day, the flag of St Titus was raised up high at the top of the campanile to the shouts of the crowd, but upside down with the feet of the saint's image higher than his head. This portent frightened many of the faithful.'

Despite this portent, the 'administration of the magnificent Marco Gradenigo, governor and rector, and his council' proceeded with a surge of optimism. The Venetian feudatories reached out to the Greek population. Greeks were admitted to the ruling council and restrictions on the ordination of Greek Orthodox clergy, who had been tightly controlled by Venice, were lifted.

Sixty miles west, in the small Venetian harbour town of Canea, there was no immediate overthrow of the Republic's administration. The rector (governor) there was Vettor Pisani. The noble Pisani family were no strangers to both glory and disgrace in Venice's service; Vettor's father, Nicolo, had won and lost battles in the previous war with Genoa and been permanently excluded from public office after the disaster at Porto Longo. Vettor himself, an experienced sea captain and naval commander, was also under a cloud. The previous year he had been arrested in the streets of Venice, sword in hand, trying to murder a magistrate. He was fined two hundred gold ducats and stripped of the plum post of *provveditore* of Candia. As rector of Canea, Vettor began to rehabilitate himself; his management of the local Venetian population seems to have been astute. They refused to rise against St Mark; he wrote back to Venice accordingly that 'the landlords of this district have remained faithful to the motherland, resisting all appeals put to them by the rebels of Candia'. It was only when the rebels descended on the town that opposition crumbled and Pisani found himself imprisoned, along with all the other figures of the Venetian administration. Yet the episode revealed him to be a man who could command loyalty. Eighteen years later the proud and temperamental sea captain would emerge as one of the great heroes of Venetian history.

Within a short time the whole of Crete was in the rebels' hands. The banner of St Titus flew from turrets and the masts of ships; in an attempt to shore up its military defences against a Venetian backlash the council took the fateful decision to release from prison men described unflatteringly by de Monacis as 'murderers, thieves, brigands, plunderers and others who had carried out terrible deeds', in return for six months' unpaid military service. It introduced a further unstable element into the revolutionary mix. There were feudatories who began to wonder at the wisdom of the revolt; one Jacobo Mudazzo dared to voice opposition. His house was fired. A few days later his only son was set upon in the street and killed. The Venetian sailors who had been persuaded to lay down their arms under truce were robbed and imprisoned; three galleys of the Venetian fleet were detained along with their crews and oarsmen. Giovanni of Zara, proprietor of a merchant galley, abandoned his vessel and slipped away to Modon in a light cutter. From there the news was sped up the Adriatic. On 11 September the Venetian senate realised that their principal colony, 'the pivot of empire', was in full revolt.

Venice was incredulous. That day the doge outlined an appeal to be made to the feudatories:

. . . it is with sadness and astonishment that we have learned of the uprising in Candia; it seemed unbelievable; the feudatories belong to the same community and come from the same stock; everything possible will be done to bring them back into agreement; an ambassador will be sent to learn the causes of their discontent and take adequate measures; the doge begs his dear sons to listen and return to obedience.

The next day a delegation was appointed with a precise twelve-point remit and a further layer of secret instructions: not to let slip any information on the senate's intentions. Simultaneously Venice was preparing for the eventuality of war. It should have become apparent to this mission as soon as it stepped ashore at Candia that a patronising tone would not go down well. The ambassadors walked the three hundred yards up the long sloping thoroughfare from the harbour to the ducal palace under armed guard. As they passed, the populace leaned out from the flat roofs of their houses and rained curses down on their heads, 'which struck the ambassadors with terror'. Pulling themselves together they delivered an oily oration to the rebel council, trotting out the stock phrases: they understood that children might chafe against their parents . . . but as flesh of their flesh they could return to their former obedience . . . the prodigal son could be forgiven . . . the kindness of the doge, etc., etc. They were met with intransigence. Surrounded by armed men and with the cries of the mob still ringing in their ears, they beat a hasty retreat to their ships and the long sea miles home.

Venice was rocked by the true state of affairs on Crete. The crisis was as serious to its colonial interests as the contest with Genoa. The loss of Crete spelled potential catastrophe for the Stato da Mar. Without its hub, the whole imperial venture might disintegrate. Two particular possibilities haunted them: firstly that the Genoese might find Crete advantageous to their interests – and the rebels were already exploring this avenue; the second was that the revolt might spread across the Aegean and trigger uprisings across all Venice's Greek-speaking possessions. This was also soon confirmed. On 20 October the senate learned that 'the rebels have sent representatives to Coron and Modon, also to Negroponte, to encourage the inhabitants of these territories to join them'. What had seemed at first like a small local difficulty was developing into a major crisis.

The executive apparatus of the Venetian Republic swung into a state of emergency. Increasingly, Venice was replacing the description of its government as a commune with the grander notion of a *signoria*, implying lordship over wide realms. Its response was determined and unequivocal: 'The Signoria cannot give up the great island, pivot of its overseas empire: an expedition will be organised to reconquer it.' A flurry of terse orders was despatched from the doge's palace. The first was to seal Crete off from the world. A series of clipped memoranda to the Collegio (the Venetian council concerned with the day-to-day dissemination of information) set down the plan. On 8 October:

The Collegio will communicate to foreign powers the intention of the Signoria with regard to the Cretan rebels: 1 Venice has decided to use all the means in its power to take back Crete; 2 an expedition is being prepared; 3 Foreign powers are requested to order their subjects to cut off all relations with the rebels, especially commercial ones.

The state registers bristle with urgency and tension. Ambassadors' and messengers' boats were sent to Rhodes, Cyprus, Constantinople, the *baili* of Coron, Modon and Negroponte – and above all to the pope, who was hoping that the Venetians would support a crusading project. And they sent envoys to the Genoese, in the belief that the pope would also pressurise their rival into staying its hand in the name of Catholic unity. Additionally ten galleys were ordered to blockade Crete from the outside world. In Coron and Modon, people were expressly forbidden to buy Cretan goods already available there. The island was to be strangled.

With brisk efficiency the Republic set about preparing an armed response. It publicly declared that 'Crete will be besieged and conquered as quickly as possible'. It cast about for a suitable *condottiere* to lead an army. While Venice only ever managed naval expeditions itself, land wars were sub-contracted by law. One candidate, Galeotto Malatesta, was rejected on cost grounds – 'his pretentious demands are exorbitant', the senate complained. They finally secured the services of a skilled Veronese soldier, Luchino dal Verme, and raised a professional army: two thousand foot soldiers, mining engineers from Bohemia, Turkish cavalry, five hundred English mercenaries, siege engines, thirty-three galleys including horse transports, twelve round ships laden with supplies and siege engines. Venice was accustomed to being paid to carry other people's armies across the eastern seas. Raising and transporting its own was highly costly – 'the perfidious revolt of the Cretans is highly damaging to the goods and resources of Venice' was the complaint – but the Republic was determined to strike fast and with an iron fist. It still took eight months to ready the fleet. On 28 March 1364 dal Verme swore his oath of office and received his war banner from the doge in an elaborate ceremony. On 10 April, after a grand review of troops on the Lido, the fleet set sail. By 6 May it was rocking at anchor in a small bay six miles west of Candia.

Long before dal Verme stepped ashore, news of Venice's armada had begun to throw the rebellion into disarray. Some of the dissident Venetians started to think again. Murderous rifts appeared between factions: town against country, Venetian against Greek, Catholic against Orthodox. One of the Gradenigo clan, Leonardo, who had embraced Orthodoxy with the zeal of the convert, hatched a plan, in conjunction with a Greek monk called Milletus, to kill the waverers. Its remit widened to the murder of all Venetian landlords living outside the safety of the city walls. Milletus prepared a night of the long knives, targeting the isolated farms and country houses of the Italians. De Monacis gave a vivid description of this new wave of terror:

... in order to avoid suspicion of this plot, Milletus stayed with Andreas Corner ... formerly his closest friend, in the house at Psonopila. When night fell, Milletus with his partners in crime burst their way into the house. Terrified, Andreas Corner said to him: 'My friend, why have you come like this?' Milletus replied, 'To kill you.' .... Andreas said: 'Have you stooped to such a great crime that you would kill your family friend and benefactor?' He replied, 'It must be so; friendship gives way to religion, liberty and the eradication of you schismatics from this island, which is our birthright.' .... Having said this, they killed him.

The scene was repeated across the Cretan countryside: the knock on the door, the gasp of surprise, the sudden blow. 'That night right through until morning they killed Gabriele Venerio in his house at Ini, Marino Pasqualigo, Laurentio Pasqualigo, Laurentio Quirino, Marco and Nicolo Mudazzo, Jacobo and Petro Mudazzo ...' The list was long. A shiver ran through Venetian Crete. It was no longer safe to live outside the walls of Candia, Retimo or Canea. The rebellion threatened to spiral out of control. Candia itself lapsed into confusion, stirred by the combustible mixture of Greek patriotism and the newly formed rabble army. A mob attempted to storm the prison and kill the duke of Crete and the Venetian sailors. It was restrained by the city's administration. Even Leonardo Gradenigo was alarmed by the turn of events. It was decided that the monk Milletus was too dangerous an ally for the Venetian rebels. He was lured to a monastery near Candia, captured and hurled off the roof of the duke's palace, where the fickle mob finished him off with swords.

With the gathering news of a Venetian fleet and a growing fear of the Greeks, the debates inside the palace became more intense. What the Venetians and the urban Greeks of Candia feared alike was the stirring of a peasants' revolt – the flaring of centuries of oppression by a downtrodden people. To manage an uprising they could no longer control, an extreme solution was put forward: 'in order to rein in the Greek rebellion, to subject Crete to an external lord, namely the Genoese'. To many of the Venetian lords this was a betrayal too far; tugged by conflicting loyalties, some proposed that it was time to beg for Venice's mercy. One of the proposers, Marco Gradenigo, was summoned back to the duke's palace to discuss the matter – in fact to an ambush. Twenty-five young men had been hidden in the palace chapel. Gradenigo was killed. All the others who opposed the Genoese initiative were rounded up and imprisoned. The council was packed with additional Greek members and the vote carried. A galley flying the flag of St Titus set sail for Genoa, but eight dissenters managed to smuggle a message back to Venice, warning that their rivals were now being invited to enter the fray.

All this was in train when dal Verme anchored his fleet on 6 or 7 May 1364 and disembarked a few miles west of Candia. The terrain ahead was broken and rocky, cut by rivers and gorges, through which only narrow paths led to the city. In this landscape the rebel army lay in wait. Dal Verme despatched an advanced guard of a hundred to scout the terrain. Picking their way through the rocky passes, they were quickly ambushed and massacred. When the main force followed up behind, they stumbled upon a ghastly scene. The bodies had been horribly mutilated. According to de Monacis, keen to colour up Greek atrocities, the rebels had left the bodies with 'their genitals in their mouths and had cut off their tongues and pushed them up their backsides. This atrocity greatly enraged the Italians.' Both sides drew up their forces to gain control of the pass, but it soon became clear that the rabble army was no match for professional soldiers who had fought their way through the city wars of northern Italy – and who were now bent on avenging their fallen comrades. The rebels quickly broke and ran. Many were killed and captured; others took to the mountains. Within a few hours the army was plundering the suburbs of Candia; shortly after, the city surrendered. The keys were carried out by penitent officials to dal Verme. The towns of Retimo and Canea rapidly followed suit. Tito Venier, one of the original instigators of revolt, joined the Greek Callergis clan in the mountains. The revolt of St Titus had collapsed almost as abruptly as it arose. Its flag was torn down; once again the lion of St Mark fluttered gruffly from the ducal palace. In the main square of Candia, the executions began.

The news reached Venice on 4 June. Its arrival was recorded in a memorable letter written by Petrarch.

It was about midday . . . I was standing by chance at a window looking at the wide expanse of sea . . . suddenly we were interrupted by the unexpected sight of one of those long ships they call galleys, all decorated with green foliage, which was coming into port under oars . . . the sailors and some young men crowned with leaves and with joyful faces were waving banners from the bow . . . the lookout in the highest tower signalled the arrival and the whole city came running spontaneously, eager to know what had happened. When the ship was near enough to make out the details, we could see the enemy flags hanging from the stern. There was no doubt that the ship was announcing a victory . . . When he heard this Doge Lorenzo . . . together with all the people wanted to give heartfelt thanks to God throughout the whole city but especially in the basilica of St Mark, which I believe is the most beautiful church there is.

There was an explosion of festive joy within the city. Everyone understood how much Crete mattered. It was the hub of the whole colonial and commercial system, on which Venice depended for trade and wealth. There were church services and processions to give thanks for the victory, and expressions of civic generosity. Convicts were released from prison; dowries allotted to poor servant girls; the whole city, according to de Monacis, was given over to days of ceremonial and spectacle. Petrarch watched tournaments and jousting in St Mark's Square, sitting beside the doge on the church loggia under an awning with the four horses breathing down his neck:

... they seemed to be neighing and pawing the ground as if alive ... below me there wasn't an empty spot ... the huge square, the church itself, the towers, roofs, porticoes and windows overflowed with spectators jammed together, as if packed one on another ... On our right ... was a wooden stage where four hundred of the most eligible noble women, the flower of beauty and gentility, were seated.

Celebrations after the recapture of Crete

There was even a visiting party of English noblemen present to enjoy the proceedings.

With victory came retribution. The senate was determined to eradicate the guilty parties from its domain. Punishment came with many refinements: death by torture or decapitation; the tearing apart of families; the exile not just from the island of Crete but from 'the lands of the emperor of Constantinople, the duchy of the Aegean, the Knights of St John on Rhodes, the lands of the Turks'. Venice sought to expunge Cretan branches of families such as Gradenigo and Venier from its records. For home consumption, some were brought back to Venice in chains. Paladino Permarino had his hands chopped off and was hanged between the twin columns as an inspiration and a warning.

Both celebration and exemplary punishment proved to be premature. The towns of Crete had been restored to fealty; in the countryside the embers of revolt kept bursting into flames that proved hard to stamp out. In the mountains of western Crete a small rump of dissident Venetian rebels, including Tito Venier, one of the original ringleaders, joined forces with the Greek clan of Callergis, backed by a truculent peasantry, to continue guerrilla warfare against the Venetian state. They targeted isolated farms, killing their occupants, burning their vineyards, destroying fortified positions so that Venetian landlords were forced back into the towns and the countryside became a zone of insurrection and danger; small military detachments were ambushed and wiped out. Venice had to devote increasing numbers of men and rotate their military commanders in a search for closure. It was a dirty, protracted war eventually won by cruelty and perseverance. It took four years. The Venetians employed a scorched-earth policy, backed by rewards for turning in rebels. As the Greek peasants starved, they began to co-operate, handing over captured rebels, their wives and children – and sacks of bloody heads. With their support base shrinking, the rebels were forced further and further back into the inaccessible recesses of mountain Crete. In the spring of 1368, Tito Venier and the Callergis brothers made a last stand at Anopoli, the most remote fastness in the south-west. Patiently they were tracked down by the Venetian commander and betrayed by the local populace. In a cave on a rocky hillside, Cretan resistance lived its final moments. Holed up and surrounded, Giorgio Callergis continued to fire defiant arrows at the Venetian soldiers, but his brother realised that further resistance was pointless. In a symbolic act of defeat, he broke his bow, saying that it was no longer needed. Venier, wounded in the ear, stumbled out to surrender. When he asked for a bandage, someone replied: 'Your wound doesn't need treatment; it's utterly incurable.' Venier realised what was being said and just nodded. Shortly afterwards he was beheaded in the public square in Candia.

Crete, exhausted and ruined, sank back into peace. There would be no further major rebellions. The Venetian lion would fly from the duke's palace in Candia for another three hundred years; the Republic ruled it with an iron hand. Those areas that had provided centres of rebellion, the high, fertile upland plateau of Lasithi in the east, Anopoli in the Sphakian mountains, were desertified. Cultivation was forbidden on pain of death. They remained in this state for a century.

In all this turmoil, Genoa stayed its hand. When the rebel galley reached the city in 1364 and begged for aid, it was refused. Venice had sent ambassadors to request a united front against rebellion; Genoa probably resisted the temptation more because the pope had demanded Catholic unity than because of any active spirit of co-operation between the two rivals. It was only a temporary ceasefire. Five years after the final surrender war broke out yet again.

12

Bridling St Mark

1372–1379

The trigger was ominously familiar: the presence of rival merchants in a foreign port, then an exchange of words, a scuffle, a brawl, finally a massacre. The difference lay in the outcome – where previous wars had ended in uneasy truce, the resulting contest was fought to the finish. In the last quarter of the fourteenth century both sides went for the jugular. The War of Chioggia, as it is known to history, brought together all the choke points of commercial rivalry – the shores of the Levant, the Black Sea, the coasts of Greece, the troubled waterways of the Bosphorus – but it was decided within the Venetian lagoon.

The flashpoint was the port of Famagusta. Cyprus, ruled by a fading dynasty of French crusaders, the Lusignans, was a crucial trading hub for both republics. Venice had strong commercial interests there in cotton and sugar growing, and the island was a market for the exchange of goods and a way station on the route to the Levant. Famagusta, lying among palm trees beside a glittering sea, was only sixty miles from Beirut. Here, at the coronation of a new Lusignan king, Peter II, the jostling rivalries of Venice and Genoa suddenly exploded. The issue was petty precedence. The Venetians seized the reins of the king's horse as he was led to the cathedral; at the subsequent banquet a dispute broke out as to which consul should have the honoured place at the king's right hand. The Genoese started throwing bread and meat at their hated rivals, but they had also come with concealed swords. The Cypriots turned on them and hurled their consul out of a window, then descended on the Genoese quarter and ran-

1 The doge's palace, the Molo and the Basin of St Mark, with the line of sheltering *lidi* on the horizon
2 The capture of Constantinople in 1204, an iconic moment in Venetian history, as depicted by Tintoretto nearly 400 years later.

3 Departure: passengers prepare to board high-sided cogs, the bulk carriers of Venetian trade.

4 Return: fast, sleek and very low, a Venetian war galley pulls into port. The *galeotti* furl its sails.

5 The Senza. The doge boards the *Bucintoro*. The Basin of St Mark is a
hubbub of ships and festive trade.

6 Venice, the golden city. The horses of Constantinople are on proud display. Merchants land produce, buy and sell. Marco Polo departs by ship for distant lands, portrayed at the bottom of the picture.

7 The gateway of the arsenal, the 'Forge of War'

8 Arsenal carpenters fashion keels and masts, and plank out ships. Finished hulls are dry stored in sheds behind.

9 & 10 Possessions of the Stato da Mar. TOP: Rovigno (Rovinj, Croatia), a miniature replica of the mother city, held for 500 years. BOTTOM: the fortress of Modon (Methoni, southern Greece), the priceless 'Eye' of the Republic.

11 The sea fortress at Candia (Heraklion) on Crete, guarding its harbour
12 The lion of St Mark, the badge of empire, on the sea walls of Famagusta, Cyprus

13 The exotic orient: the reception of the Venetian ambassador by the
Mamluk governor at Damascus

14 The battle of Zonchio: the ships of Loredan and d'Armer grapple with
the huge Ottoman vessel (centre), just as flames start to engulf them all.

sacked it. For Genoa this was an insufferable insult. The following year a substantial fleet descended on the island and seized it.

The Venetians were not expelled from Cyprus but this turn of events ratcheted up the tension. It made them strategically anxious. They were in danger of being squeezed out of crucial trading zones. This feeling was soon compounded by affairs back in Constantinople, where the Italian republics were meddling furiously in the interminable dynastic struggles for the Byzantine throne. They had become rival kingmakers in the city. Venice supported the emperor, John V Palaeologus; the Genoese backed his son Andronicus.

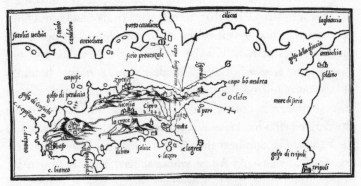

Cyprus

Both acted with ruthless self-interest. Venice was particularly keen to maintain its access to the Black Sea, which Genoa continued to dominate. When John visited the city in 1370, they held him prisoner for a year over an unpaid debt. Six years later they demanded the island of Tenedos with menaces – a war fleet in the Bosphorus – in return for his crown jewels, which they held in hock. Tenedos, a small rocky island off the coast of Asia Minor, was strategically critical; twelve miles from the mouth of the Dardanelles, it surveyed the straits to Constantinople and beyond. As such it was 'the key to the entrance for all those who wanted to sail to the Black Sea, that is Tana and Trebizond'. The Republic wanted it as a throttle on Genoese sea traffic.

The emperor surrendered the island. Genoa's reply was equally prompt. They simply deposed him, replaced him with his son and demanded the island back. However, when they despatched their own fleet to claim their prize, they were met with a forth-right response. The Greek population sided with the Venetians and refused; the intruders were repelled. Andronicus arrested the Venetian *bailo* in Constantinople. Venice demanded the release of their officials and restitution of John V, now lingering in a gloomy dungeon on the city walls. On 24 April 1378 the Republic declared war.

The fleets that both sides could put out were still small in the long shadow of the Black Death. What amplified the contest were the terrestrial allies that the maritime rivals could now enlist. Venice was increasingly involved in the complex power politics of the city states of Italy. For the first time, the Republic had not only a *stato da mar* but also a modest *stato da terra* – holdings of land on mainland Italy, centred on the city of Treviso sixteen miles to the north. From the surrounding area, the Trevigiano, the city derived vital food supplies, floated down the River Brenta to the Venetian lagoon near the town of Chioggia. Three great riv-ers, the Po, Brenta and Adige, whose alluvial deposits, drawn out of the distant Alps, had formed the Venetian lagoon, debouched into the sea near this strategic point. These waterways, along with an interconnecting web of cross-canals, were the arterial trade routes into the heart of Italy, and Venice guarded them all at their point of exit. The Republic was able to apply vice-like economic pressure on northern Italy, controlling salt supplies, taxing river traffic, pushing its own goods upstream on the slow waters in flat-bottomed boats under monopoly conditions. To its immedi-ate neighbours – Padua to the west, the king of Hungary to the east, nervous for his control of the Dalmatian coast – Venice was too powerful, too rich, too proud. If the Republic was a source of admiration, it also evoked envy and fear. The letters that passed between Genoa, Padua and Hungary voiced the profound dis-quiet 'that if [the Venetians] were allowed to establish a firm foothold on the Italian mainland, as they had on the sea, they would in a short time make themselves lords of all Lombardy, and finally of Italy'. Genoa, Francesco Carrara, lord of Padua, and Louis, king of Hungary, signed a pact to encircle Venice by land and sea 'for the humiliation of Venice and all her allies'.

For Genoa this alliance promised new strategic options. Not only could a land war snuff out vital river traffic to Venice, but access to Louis's ports on the Dalmatian coasts, particularly Zara, offered Genoese fleets a base from which to strike Venice at close range. The threat was considerable. Venice lined up her own allies; the king of Cyprus constituted no more than moral support. More significant was his prospective father-in-law, the duke of Milan.

To the expense of a new sea war, the Republic now had to add the cost of defending its land territories. For this, as was traditional, it scoured Italy for a competent *condottiere*. This was always a tricky matter. As Machiavelli would point out, satisfaction from mercenaries was variable. They were both expensive and unreliable: 'disunited, ambitious and without discipline, unfaithful, raliant before friends, cowardly before enemies; they have neither the fear of God nor fidelity to men . . . for in peace one is robbed by them, and in war by the enemy'. Venice would certainly have trouble enough with its hired hands in the months ahead. The city tried to buy the best, the Englishman Sir John Hawkwood – Giovanni Acuto (the Sharp) the Italians called him – a man with a bloody reputation for over-fulfilling his contracts. At Cesena the previous year he had ordered the massacre of five thousand people. Hawkwood however was too expensive for the now cash-strapped Venetians and too closely tied to the lord of Padua; instead they opted for Giacomo de Cavalli of Verona, at seven hundred ducats a month.

The prospect of a land war also introduced the use of new technologies. Two years earlier the Venetians had used gunpowder weapons at a siege for the first time. The cannon was new fangled in Italy: 'a great instrument of iron,' one contemporary writer described it, 'with a hollow bore in its whole length, in which a black powder, made of sulphur, saltpetre, and charcoal, is placed, and above that powder, being ignited through a touchhole, the stone is discharged with enormous force'. Giant bombards, enormous hooped tubes of cast iron, highly unreliable, firing no more than one shot a day, would have their part to play in the contest to come.

In the days before the declaration of war, the city chose as its naval commanders two of the most colourful adventurers to cross the stage of Venetian history. On 22 April 1378 the seventy-two-year-old doge, Andrea Contarini, conferred the office of captain-general of the sea (the overall naval commander in time of war) on Vettor Pisani in an elaborate ceremony in St Mark's. Handing Pisani the Venetian banner of war, the doge declaimed,

You are destined by God to defend with your valour this republic, and to retaliate upon those who have dared to insult her, and to rob her of that security which she owes to the virtue of our progenitors. Wherefore we confide to you this victorious and dread standard, which it will be your duty to restore to us unsullied and triumphant.

The Pisani family knew well the vicissitudes of fortune in the Republic's service. Vettor had been at his father's side during the disastrous defeat at Porto Longo twenty years earlier. Vettor himself divided opinion: outspoken, fearless, patriotic, touchy and short-tempered, he was a naval commander who led from the front. He was an immensely effective leader of men, loved by his crews, disliked by some of his fellow nobles in equal measure. Apart from a charge of attempted murder, he had physically attacked one of his fellow officials whilst he was governor of Crete in 1364, yet his experience at sea was incomparable. He would prove to be a controversial but inspired choice.

At the same time, the Republic gave command to another noble adventurer, Carlo Zeno – Zen in the Venetian dialect. By the age of forty-five Zeno had lived a life of extraordinary risk and adventure across the Stato da Mar. Orphaned as a child after his father was killed in battle, befriended by a pope, Zeno had been by turns a scholar, a musician, a priest, a gambler, a soldier of fortune, a married man. He had been left for dead by robbers when a student at Padua. A few years later he was nearly buried alive in Patras: grievously wounded during a Turkish siege, he was considered a corpse, wrapped in a shroud and placed in a coffin. The lid was about to be nailed shut when signs of life were detected. He was reputed, by unreliable family memoir, to have attempted the release of the Byzantine emperor John V by climbing up into the prison in Constantinople on a rope, only to find the emperor unwilling to abandon his sons, who could not be freed. He had been instrumental in the defence of Tenedos. In the popular imagination he was indestructible. If the ordinary people of Venice referred to Pisani as Father, Zeno was the Unconquered. He was despatched to the eastern Mediterranean as governor of Negroponte with eighteen galleys and orders to inflict maximum damage on Genoese shipping. The maritime safety of Venice was to be entrusted to these semi-legendary noble adventurers.

Venice proceeded without hesitation. While vassals of the duke of Milan were closing in on Genoa by land, Pisani worked his way up the west coast of Italy, sacking ports and spreading terror. In late May he met a Genoese fleet off Anzio and routed it. When the news reached Genoa there was panic: any day now Pisani might be at the unguarded harbour walls; Milanese soldiers were ravaging the back country. The doge was deposed and replaced in one of the periodic upheavals that bedevilled the Genoese state. However Pisani judged his fleet too small to follow up this early success and turned east again to attend to the Adriatic. Over the summer he ranged widely over the seas, blindly hunting small squadrons of Genoese privateers, bombarding Famagusta, escorting grain convoys from Puglia, responding to jumpy and contradictory orders from the war committee in Venice.

And that war was moving closer. By June, five thousand Hungarian troops had marched round the Gulf of Venice and joined up with Francesco, lord of Padua; by early July they were besieging Mestre on the shores of the lagoon just ten miles from Venice. They failed to take it; the Venetian defence held firm against overwhelming odds. According to the chroniclers, the Venetians positioned beehives on their ramparts, which discouraged the invaders from the final assault. It was a heartening victory against large odds and the people of the city knew that as long as their enemy was confined to land the lagoon would protect them. When news reached the city that Genoa had launched a new fleet under Luciano Doria, they thought again.

Pisani meanwhile had been tracking restlessly up and down the Dalmatian coast. He bombarded Zara but the city was too well defended to attack; he moved south to reduce other Hungarian bases. The port of Cattaro was stormed and put to the sword with Pisani fighting in the front line 'like a simple captain'. The booty was shared amongst the whole crew – it was gestures such as this that won the utter loyalty of his men. At this point the orders to Pisani became increasingly insistent: stop Doria entering the Adriatic and above all prevent him from reaching Zara, which would give him both direct contact with the Hungarians and a base just 150 miles from the lagoon. The apparently inexhaustible Pisani positioned his ships in the Sicilian channel to catch Doria's fleet off the toe of Italy. He was outwitted; the Genoese slipped round the south of the island. Pisani doubled back, trying to second-guess what Doria would do next, trawling for news across the mouth of the Adriatic. Doria was glimpsed repeatedly but could not be caught. The autumn was employed in a game of cat and mouse, Pisani keeping his fleet between the Genoese and Zara, returning to bombard the city again, sacking the port of Sebenico and finally running Doria to ground in the heavily fortified harbour at Trau, from which he could not be winkled out. An attack there was beaten back with great loss of life. Doria was determined to bide his time. Pisani turned north to bombard Zara once more.

It was now the end of a punishing year of naval manoeuvres. The ships had been at sea for nine months. Despite his inspirational leadership, the fleet was frustrated at being unable to get to grips with their elusive foe and exhausted by the attempt;

Trau   Sebenico

morale was at a low ebb. Pisani requested permission to return to the lagoon. It was refused. The war committee was desperate for Doria to be dislodged, fearful that he might still slip past towards the lagoon and enclose the city in a pincer movement, menaced by land and sea. Pisani was ordered to overwinter at Pola to protect the inner Gulf of Venice.

It was a disastrous decision. The winter of 1378–9 was exceptionally cold. Snow fell heavily; frosts were sharp and the incessant winter wind off the Hungarian steppes made conditions wretched. Hunger, disease, cold and fatigue thinned the crews; men lost hands and feet to frostbite; soldiers and crossbowmen deserted; oarsmen languished in the cold. The men begged to be allowed to raise anchor rather than idle and die. Only loyalty to Pisani kept the fleet reasonably intact. The admiral returned the sick to Venice with yet another request for release. It was again refused; well-founded fear of the enemy fleet was compounded by the spite of Pisani's noble rivals, keen to inflict continuous hardship on the long-suffering commander. The supply of grain to the city was becoming critical; in the dead days of January Pisani was ordered across the Adriatic to Puglia to escort food supplies to Venice. All the weight of expectation lay with him now. The doge wrote personally to beg him to endure. Step by step Genoa's land allies were snuffing out the arterial supply routes into the city. Treviso itself lay under siege. Pisani careened his galleys and set out from Pola again. Disease, death and desertion continued apace. By the start of February his serviceable galleys had been whittled down from thirty-six to twelve.

That month, despite energetic opposition, Pisani was re-elected captain-general of the sea; two new commissioners, Carlo Zeno and Michele Steno, were appointed to assist him. With them came much-needed food supplies and twelve more galleys, some of them built and paid for privately by personal support-ers. Throughout the spring the reinvigorated fleet responded to a flurry of conflicting orders: to attack Doria in Trau again, to convoy grain, to damage the Dalmatian coast. The game of hide and seek went on; the Genoese only engaged in skirmishes. Their aim was to throttle Venice's food supplies. In one incident Pisani took an arrow in the stomach but Doria slipped away. The news from the terra firma worsened. Treviso was hardly holding out; the forces of Padua tightened their grip on the river traffic. In an attempt to loosen the enemy's hold, Zeno was detached with a squadron of galleys to ravage the coast around Genoa itself. The hope was that a threat close to home would shift the theatre of war and force Doria to withdraw his fleet.

In the short run it made no difference. Doria refused to fight until the moment of his choosing; Pisani, hamstrung by the ongoing deficiencies in his fleet and the plethora of commands, was powerless to act. And then, on 7 May 1379, Doria's fleet sud-denly showed up in the sea road off Pola, where the Venetian fleet was enduring yet another outbreak of disease. The Venetians were completely unprepared. Doria's fleet advanced in line of bat-tle, taunting the enemy to come out and fight. After months of fruitless search in which the fleet had wasted its strength it was an irresistible provocation; 'The soldiers and sailors, like chained mastiffs panting to bite the passers by, began to clamour to be led out to fight, and the captains and commissioners added their vote of confidence.'

Moral pressure was applied to the captain-general: not to fight would be a contempt of the Venetian flag. Pisani was cautious –

and suspicious. He almost certainly had fewer ships; they were in bad shape; they were tucked into a safe haven and Zeno was away. He soberly remembered the defeat at Porto Longo – the result of taking ill-considered advice – and argued that they bide their time until Zeno's return. Preservation of the fleet was tantamount. There was a furious debate. Raised voices. Insults. Shouts. Finally Michele Steno taunted Pisani beyond the point of forbearance, 'that it was not mere opinion, but cowardice and terror that he wanted to avoid battle'. Pisani's hand flew to his sword hilt. Riled over personal honour, he gave way: they would sail out. Commands were given; ships set in order; hawsers released. With the ringing Venetian battle cry, 'He who loves Saint Mark, follow me!' he ordered the attack.

Luciano Doria had prepared his ambush well. He had ten more galleys concealed behind an outer point. His visible fleet fell back little by little before the spirited Venetian advance, drawing his opponent out to sea, then spinning smartly about as the hidden ships caught the Venetians on the flank and from behind – 'and our men, surprised and terrified, went in a flash from bravery to abject terror', ran the sober Venetian report. Panic led to a rout. One of the commissioners, Bragadino, formerly eager for battle, now terrified and trying to shelter from bombardment by the entrapping ships, fell overboard. Twelve experienced sea captains were killed or drowned; five were taken prisoner. With the tattered remnants of the Venetian fleet still engaged but close to flight, Luciano Doria over-confidently flipped up his visor and shouted, 'The enemy are already beaten; we're only a step away from complete victory!' A Venetian captain hurtled forward in the blur of battle and pinioned him through the throat. Doria dropped dead on the spot. It was small consolation. Pisani tried to rally the remaining galleys but it was far too late. Seeing them slip away, including Steno, he gave up the unequal struggle and followed. Five ships made it to Parenzo thirty miles up the coast.

On 9 May, the new Genoese commander wrote to Padua totalling the extent of the victory:

... we won [it] in a very short space of time – just an hour and a half
... of their twenty-one galleys we took fifteen with noble captains on
board, three transport ships laden with grain and salted meat; we have
2,400 prisoners . . . over and beyond these prisoners we believe that
seven to eight hundred died, either in battle or drowned in the sea.

On the 11th Francesco, lord of Padua, and all the people made a
procession to the mother church 'singing and thanking God for
the victory over the Venetians . . . and there was great joy and
revelry, many great feasts in the city, the ringing of church bells,
and in the evening fires and illuminations in the open spaces and
throughout the whole district'.

To Pisani fell the heavy obligation to report the defeat. There was
no time to waste. A ship was despatched to Venice, another to the
colonies in the Levant. The news struck the city dumb. There was
amazement, consternation, fear. People wept for the loss of their
relatives – and for the imminent danger to the city itself. There
was now no fleet to protect it. Many of its most highly skilled
captains and trained crews were either captives of Genoa or dead;
Pisani's fleet had been all but annihilated; Zeno's was far out of
reach somewhere on the high seas. There was sharp awareness of
public calamity, linked to deep-held aristocratic grudges against
the Pisani family. A universal chill descended on the lagoon. The
order was sent out to Parenzo to arrest him 'for having lost the
Republic not only the backbone of its navy, the freedom of the
sea, navigation, commerce, public taxes and the confidence of its
citizens . . . in a single day, even in a single hour'.

On 7 July Pisani clanked down the gangplank on the quay by St
Mark's Square, bound in chains hand and foot. The reception was
mixed – from the common people consolation, from the nobility
nothing but malevolence. Still chained, he laboriously climbed
the steps of the palace, to give his explanation before the doge
and senate. There was no opportunity. He was hustled away into
the darkness of the state prison. The prosecutors began the case
against him. They demanded death – the mandatory sentence for

a commander fleeing in battle: he should be led between the two columns and decapitated 'as an object lesson for the citizens'. The senate rejected the sentence – Pisani had lacked firmness, not courage: it was Steno who had originally incited the attack and then cut and run. The sentence was commuted to six months in prison and five years' exclusion from public office. If this pleased the wounded nobility, it stirred a sullen discontent within the sailors and ordinary people of the city which would soon burst into open defiance.

While Pisani languished in the dungeons, the Genoese were moving closer. Another Doria, Pietro, succeeded the dead Luciano. With forty-eight galleys, he retook all the Dalmatian cities taken by Pisani; moving north into the Gulf of Venice, he recaptured Rovigno, Grado and Caorle, within seventy-five miles of the city. At the start of August Doria appeared off the Lido of St Nicholas and snatched a merchant ship with a cargo of Egyptian cotton, watched impotently by the population. Working his way down the *lidi* he attacked other settlements along the sandbanks that protected the lagoon, then departed trailing the banners of St Mark behind him in the water. It was a very potent demonstration of public humiliation; not only had Doria shown that Venice was unable to protect even its home waters, it underlined the certainty that as long as Genoa controlled the sea, Venice might be starved into defeat. On 25 June, Doria captured two grain ships from Puglia, while the Hungarians and Paduans were throttling the river traffic to Venice. Even the lagoon no longer seemed a secure refuge. The Genoese had also taken their time to reconnoitre the channels and take soundings.

The city was gripped by a sense of national emergency. Pisani's rival, Taddeo Giustinian, was made captain-general of the sea; troops and commanders were apportioned to sectors of the defence. Two of the entrances to the lagoon were blocked with chains. Stout sailing ships were anchored as floating forts. Fortifications, wooden towers, palisades and earthworks were thrown up along the shores of the *lidi*. Giacomo de Cavalli's expensively bought mercenaries, who included a quarrelsome troop of Englishmen, were stationed there to man the defences. A war committee was on twenty-four-hour call in the doge's palace and a system of alarm calls, radiating out from the bells of St Nicholas on the Lido, was put in place, so that at the first sight of a Genoese fleet, peals of church bells rippling across all the parishes of the city would summon the armed militia to St Mark's Square, the nerve centre of whatever last stand the patriotic citizens of the Republic might be compelled to make. For good measure, the Venetians did what they had done in a similar emergency six hundred years earlier. They removed all the *briccole* – the stakes which marked the navigable channels of the lagoon – wiping its surface back to a primeval labyrinth in which nothing snagged the eye.

At the same time as military defence, the Republic had already resorted to diplomacy. Was it possible to split the triple alliance of Padua, Genoa and Hungary? Padua was too bitter a recent foe but Hungary, with troubles of its own elsewhere, might be detached. Ambassadors were hurried to Buda. The response was demoralising: the Hungarians had sensed a unique moment to strike down the Republic. They demanded a huge indemnity – half a million ducats – on top of an annual tribute of a cool hundred thousand and the surrender of Trieste, plus the acceptance of the doge and all his successors as vassals of the Hungarian crown. To add insult to injury, they helpfully suggested that if ready cash were in short supply they would accept the keys of half a dozen towns as a down payment, including Treviso and Mestre on the shores of the lagoon, plus the doge's jewelled cap – the ultimate symbol of a free republic. 'These demands are completely unworthy,' reported back the ambassadors, 'impossible to accept.' If it were to be a choice between humiliation and death, the Republic would go down fighting. A ship had already been despatched with orders to find Zeno's fleet and bring it back. The problem was that no one had any idea where he was.

On 6 August, the bells of St Nicholas started to clang ominously. A small fleet of six ships flying the red and white of Genoa had been sighted on the horizon. Taddeo Giustinian decided to sally forth with an equal number to confront the intruders. As the ships closed, the Venetians spotted a man swimming towards them. He was Hieronimo Sabadia, a Venetian sailor captured at Pola, who had jumped overboard from one of the approaching ships to warn his compatriots not to advance; the six Genoese galleys were a decoy for the main fleet of forty-seven vessels lying over the horizon. It was on such patriotic actions that Venice's hopes now rested. Giustinian turned smartly about; the chain was raised; he sailed back into the lagoon.

There were three principal entrances through the *lidi* into the lagoon; two had been blocked with chains and anchored hulks; the third, at the southern end of the lagoon, the entrance and exit to Chioggia, had been left open. It was here that Pietro Doria proposed to make his strike. The island of Chioggia was a miniature replica of Venice, protected from the open sea by its own *lido*, to which it was connected by a wooden bridge. There was another settlement on this *lido*, known as Little Chioggia, and further south the more substantial village of Brondolo. Chioggia's strategic importance to Venice was immense; it commanded the mouths of the Brenta and the Adige, which linked Venice by water with central Italy, but which, with every passing day, were passing more firmly into the hands of the advancing Hungarian and Paduan troops. The Paduans had prepared a hundred well-armed barges to float supplies downstream to their naval allies.

By taking Chioggia, Doria hoped both to link up with the advancing land forces and to establish a base from which finally to destroy the rival republic. Set in the fringes of the lagoon, within marshes, saltpans, reed beds, sandbanks, narrow excavated channels, secret waterways, Chioggia was the place where a century of maritime warfare was destined to reach its resolution. Venice's imaginative world, habitually vast, had now shrunk to the defence of a few square miles of floundering marsh.

At Chioggia, the Venetians determined to make a resolute stand. They armed a series of isolated outlying forts, water mills and towers along the Brenta and on the shores of the lagoon. The *podesta* (mayor) of Chioggia, Pietro Emo, blocked the river approaches with rocks. Implacably the Paduans overcame all obstacles. With large resources of manpower, they hauled their barges overland, cutting diversionary channels round the obstructions, snuffing out isolated forts. By early August they had secured the strategic Bebbe tower at the mouth of the Brenta, just four miles from Chioggia itself. They established bastions controlling the approach canals and waterways and fought off counterattacks by convoys of small armed boats. Only one fortress held out, that of the Salt Beds, standing on the very edge of the lagoon. Chioggia was effectively cut off, though the Venetian knowledge of the shallow backwaters stood it in good stead: 'Secretly by night many small boats came and went between Venice and Chioggia by tiny channels towards the castle of the Salt Beds, carrying letters and advice.'

On 8 August, the Paduan soldiers and their armed supply boats joined up with Doria's fleet standing in the roadstead of Brondolo, bringing thousands of men, large supplies of food, and the promise of much more downstream from Padua. The allies now had twenty-four thousand men. Within Chioggia there were perhaps 3,500 in total, out of a population of twelve thousand, many of whom guarded the bridgehead which linked the island to its *lido* at Little Chioggia. The Genoese landed on the *lido* and unloaded their siege equipment – mangonels and bombards. In a short time Little Chioggia was taken; the armed hulk guarding the Chioggia channel was fired and destroyed. On 12 August they started to attack the bridgehead, which was defended by a stout bastion. For four days the fighting continued with the Genoese suffering great losses. On the 16th, desperate for a breakthrough, a reward of 150 ducats was offered to any man who could fire the bridge. According to the Genoese chroniclers, there was one enthusiastic volunteer:

. . . a Genoese soldier at once stripped off his armour, got into a small boat with straw and gunpowder and started rowing towards the bridge.

When he was close to it, he set fire to the straw, jumped into the water and started pushing the boat towards the bridge . . . so that it was enveloped in flames. The Venetians were unable to defend the bridge any longer and so abandoned it.

In their haste they failed to raise the drawbridge behind them. 'We pursued [the Venetians] with fire and with great losses on their side as far as the piazza of Chioggia. There was great destruction . . . the piazza was stained red with Christian blood and the grievous and cruel massacre of the Venetians.'

Eight hundred and sixty Venetians were killed; four thousand were taken prisoner; the women and children cowered in the churches. Doria brought his galleys into safe anchorage inside the lagoon. The Genoese now had a secure foothold within reach of Venice, to which it was directly connected by the Lombardy Channel, a deep-water arterial route through the lagoon down which even the deeper-draughted Genoese galleys could access the city. Doria was just twelve miles from St Mark's Square. The flag of St George fluttered in the piazza of Chioggia; the lord of Padua's from its ducal palace; Hungary's from an adjacent tower. Francesco Carrara of Padua entered the city and was carried shoulder-high into the main square by Genoese soldiers, shouting, 'Carro! Carro!' They eyed the larger prize with the anticipation of a sack to equal that of Constantinople.

The news reached Venice at midnight. The bells of the campanile started to clang loudly; soon all the parishes were repeating the alarm. People came armed, running to St Mark's Square to learn of the collapse at Chioggia. There was terror and panic, weeping and chaotic shouting, expectations that a Genoese war fleet would come nosing up the Lombardy Channel at any minute. The citizens began to bury their goods in anticipation of inevitable sack. Others were more resolute, declaring that 'the state would never be lost so long as those who remain can man a galley or handle a weapon'. Gradually the old doge quietened the crowd with calm words and a steadfast face. The following day he sent three ambassadors to Chioggia under safe conduct to sue for peace. After a lengthy oration they handed Doria a piece of paper setting out their conditions for peace. It was blank. The Genoese could write their own terms so long as Venice remained free. But Doria had come to destroy the hated rival. His reply was haughty: 'There will be no peace until first we have put a bridle on those horses of yours on the portico of St Mark's . . . then we shall be at peace. This is our intention and that of our Commune.' Then, referring to the Genoese prisoners, he casually went on, 'I don't want them. Keep them locked up, because I intend to come and rescue all your prisoners in a few days.' Venice would have to fight to the last gasp.

Within the city the bell was rung to call the popular assembly to hear the response. The gathered crowd was now given an unvarnished account of their plight. A year earlier, Genoa's defeat at the sea battle of Anzio had nearly torn that city apart. This was to be a similar test of Venice's character, its patriotism and class coherence. The mood was initially resolute. They would go down fighting rather than die of starvation: 'Let us arm ourselves; let us equip and mount what galleys are in the arsenal; let us go forth; it is better to perish in the defence of our country than to perish here through want.' Everyone prepared for sacrifices. There was to be universal conscription. Salaries of magistrates and state officials were suspended; new patriotic state loans were demanded; business and commerce were abandoned; property prices fell to a quarter of their previous value. The whole city was mobilised in a desperate bid for survival, so that its bronze horses, looted in their turn from Constantinople, could continue to paw the humid Venetian air unfettered. Emergency earthworks were hastily thrown up on the Lido of St Nicholas; a ring of palisades erected in the shallow water around the city; armed boats ordered to patrol the canals night and day; signal arrangements redefined. The arsenal set to unceasing work, refitting mothballed galleys.

Yet this show of patriotic unity under the banner of St Mark concealed dangerous fault lines. At the point of sacrifice the unbearable haughtiness of the noble class stuck in the popular gullet. The people wanted to be led by commanders who shared the same conditions and dangers. The crews declared they would not now man the new trenches on the Lido of St Nicholas unless the nobles went too, and the appointment of Taddeo Giustinian as commander of the city's defences brought the city to the edge of revolt. He was evidently detested; there was only one man they would accept. 'You want us to go in the galleys,' went up the cry in St Mark's Square, 'give us our Captain Pisani! We want Pisani out of prison!' The crowd grew in strength and became increasingly vocal in their disapproval. According to popular hagiography, Pisani could hear the cries from the ducal prison. Putting his head to the bars, he called out 'Long live St Mark!' The crowd responded with a throaty roar. Upstairs in the senatorial chamber a panicky debate was underway. The crowd put ladders to the windows. They hammered the chamber door with a rhythmic refrain: 'Vettor Pisani! Vettor Pisani!' Thoroughly alarmed, the senate caved in: the people would be given Pisani. It was now the end of a nerve-racking day, but when Pisani was told of his release he placidly replied that he would prefer to pass the night where he was, in prayer and contemplation. Release could wait for the morrow.

At dawn on 19 August, in one of the great popular scenes from Venetian history, the unshackled Pisani stepped free from prison to the roar of the crowd. Hoisted onto the shoulders of the galley crews with people climbing up onto ledges and parapets to get a glimpse of the hero, raising their hands to the sky, shouting and cheering, he was carried up the steps of the palace and delivered to the doge. There was an immediate reconciliation; a solemn mass. Pisani played his part carefully, pledging himself humbly to the Republic. Then he was again raised aloft on the shoulders of the crowd and carried away to his house.

It was an exhilarating moment, but also a dangerous one. It was only twenty-four years since a doge had been beheaded for an attempted coup and Pisani was wary of personal adulation. On his way home, he was stopped by an old sailor who stepped forward and called out in a loud voice, 'Now is the time to avenge yourself by seizing the dictatorship of the city. Behold, all are at your service; all are willing at this very moment to proclaim you prince, if you choose!' Pisani turned and dealt the man a stinging blow. Raising his voice, he called, 'Let none who wish me well say "Long live Pisani!" – rather, "Long live St Mark!"'

In fact, the senate, piqued by this popular revolt, had been more grudging with their favours than the crowd at first understood. Pisani was not appointed captain-general, only commander of the *lido* defences. The crews were still ordered to report to the detested Taddeo Giustinian. When this fact sank in there was a further wave of popular dissent. They threw down their banners and declared they would rather be cut to pieces than serve under Taddeo. On the 20th the senate caved in again. Pisani was declared overall commander of the city's defence. At an emotional service in St Mark's he vowed to die for the Republic.

The confirmed appointment had a galvanic effect on morale. The following day the customary recruiting benches were set up near the two columns; the scribes could not enter the names of volunteers fast enough. Everyone enrolled: artists and cutlers, tailors and apothecaries. The unskilled were given rowing lessons in

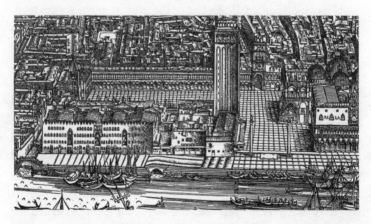

The waterfront at St Mark's. Recruiting benches were set up on the Molo – the quayside in front of the two columns

the Giudecca Canal; stone fortifications were erected by masons on the Lido of St Nicholas at lightning speed; thirty mothballed galleys were re-equipped; palisades and chains encircled the city and closed the canals; every sector of the city's defences was detailed to particular officers. They were to be manned night and day. Many gave their savings to the cause; women plucked the jewellery from their dresses to pay for food and soldiers.

None of this was a moment too soon. In darkness on 24 August Doria mounted a two-pronged attack. One force attempted a galley landing on the Lido of St Nicholas. A second pushed in a swarm of light boats to attack the palisades that protected the city's southern shore. Both were beaten back, but the defenders were compelled to abandon other towns along the *lidi*. Doria established himself at Malamocco, from where he could bombard the islands of the southern lagoon. The red-and-white flag could be seen from the campanile of St Mark's.

Venice was almost completely cut off; there was now just one land route by which it could receive supplies. The sea was sealed. Yet the balance had shifted slightly. Doria had missed a moment. If he had struck out for Venice as soon as Chioggia fell, the city must have capitulated. The brief hesitation had allowed Pisani to regroup and the failure on the 24th gave Venice brief hope. The lord of Padua, disgusted by the failure to force home the advantage, politely took his troops off to the siege of Treviso. Doria decided on attrition. He would starve Venice to death. With winter coming on he withdrew his men from the *lidi* back to Chioggia. Within Venice, supplies started to run low; desperate schemes were proposed to abandon the city and emigrate to Crete or Negroponte. They were instantly rejected. Patriotic Venetians declared that 'sooner than abandon their city, they would bury themselves under her ruins'.

13

Fight to the Finish

Slowly, relentlessly, Venice was being squeezed dry because 'the Genoese held [the city] locked tight, both by sea, and by land from Lombardy'. As autumn wore on the price of wheat, wine, meat and cheese rose to unprecedented levels. Attempts at replenishment proved disastrous; eleven light galleys loading grain further down the coast were caught and destroyed. The strain of guarding the palisades by night and day, waiting for the ringing of church bells, serving in the trenches on the Lido as the weather worsened, all started to take their toll. The Genoese meanwhile continued to receive plentiful provisions down the river routes from Padua. But after the eruption of popular anger at the fall of Chioggia, the patricians realised that it was in their better interest to take regard for the suffering of the poor. 'Go,' the people were told, 'all who are pressed by hunger, to the dwellings of the patricians; there you will find friends and brethren, who will divide with you their last crust!' A fragile solidarity persisted.

The only hope of relief was the return of Zeno, still far over the horizon. In November it was learned he was off Crete, after months of plundering Genoese shipping on a wide track between the coast of Italy and the Golden Horn. Yet another ship was despatched with all haste to call him back. Knowledge of his whereabouts raised a small hope.

Pisani's seamen attempted to damage Doria's supply chain. They used their knowledge of the inner lagoon, its creeks and secret channels, sandbanks and reed beds, to intercept the supply boats coming down the Brenta. With information passed by spies within Chioggia, teams of small boats probed the shallows, lying low at twilight to catch unwary merchants delivering grain or wine. Near the Castle of the Salt Beds, the beleaguered Venetian outpost close to Chioggia, they ambushed sufficient boats to force the Paduans to supply armed escorts, and to discourage merchants from making the voyage. They also had the advantage over the deep-draughted Genoese galleys, uncertain of the channels and liable to grounding if the water was low or they missed their way. Watching the movement of these ships closely, ambitious plans were made to trap isolated vessels, like hunters trying to down an elephant. Lying up at evening in the reed beds, using the cover of the fog and closing night to surprise a foe unable to manoeuvre, landing detachments of archers to shoot from the shelter of the clustering trees, setting fire to the reeds to confuse and obscure, taking short cuts to head off their prey, darting out from nowhere in rowing boats to the sudden blaring of trumpets and drums, they began to play on their enemy's nerves. They had an emboldening success when they cornered and destroyed an enemy galley, the *Savonese*, and captured its noble commander.

It was a small triumph which had disproportionate effects on morale. Upping the stakes, Pisani attempted to snare three galleys on their way to bombard the Castle of the Salt Beds, but the plan was spoiled when the ships spotted the soldiers' banners behind the reeds. Back-paddling furiously and under a bombardment of missiles from the banks, they slipped away. And Pisani had his outright failures; trying to reconnoitre Chioggia's defences with increasing curiosity, he lost ten small boats and thirty men, including the doge's nephew killed in the skirmish. But his close observation of the position of the enemy and the entrances and exits of the lagoon convinced him of the possibility of a daring strike. The disparity between the two forces was huge. The enemy had thirty thousand men, fifty galleys, between seven and eight hundred light boats, ample food supplies, access to timber, gunpowder, arrows, crossbow bolts. But they also had one hidden weakness, which he was certain they had not foreseen.

Some time in late autumn he put forward a proposal to the doge and the war committee for positive action. The city had its back to the wall. Zeno's whereabouts were unknown; the people were wilting both from a lack of hope and a shortage of food; rather than let their morale dwindle to nothing, it was better to die on their feet. The plan was supported by Venice's hired general, Giacomo de Cavalli. The senate accepted it and, perhaps still mindful of the sailors hammering on the chamber door, published a remarkable decree to harness all the resources of patriotic goodwill of a languishing people. For a hundred years, entry to the Venetian nobility had been closed to newcomers. Now the senate published a proclamation offering to ennoble fifty citizens who provided the most outstanding service to the Republic in its hour of need.

The resulting influx of money, resources and goodwill had a short-term galvanising effect on the mood of the people. The work fitting out the galleys was pushed forward in the arsenal; there was rowing practice in the Grand Canal for the inexpert oarsmen who volunteered for the operation, but it was touch and go. The sharpness of deprivation drove people wailing into the piazza. When would Zeno come? There was fear that any delay could prove fatal to the willpower of the city. It was impossible to wait for the missing fleet, and news from Chioggia that the Genoese and Paduans had fallen out over the distribution of booty suggested that the time was ripe. The old doge declared that he would lead the expedition as captain-general with Pisani as vice-captain.

Compulsion was also required: it was announced that all the oarsmen and soldiers should be boarded by noon on 21 December, under pain of death. The doge, Andrea Contarini, gathered the people beneath the banner of St Mark in the piazza; there was vespers in the church, then with great pomp the expedition prepared to sail. There were thirty-four galleys under their noble captains, sixty barks, four hundred small boats – and two large cogs, hulking merchantmen, whose role in the operation was crucial to its success. It was eight o'clock on the evening of the shortest day, the depth of midwinter, but the night was clear and mild, the sea calm, just a light breeze blowing. Contarini ordered the great Venetian banner of war to be unfurled. In silence, hawsers were untied and the expedition set out. The ships were divided into three parts. In the vanguard, Pisani with fourteen galleys and the two cogs; in the rearguard, ten more galleys; the doge took up the centre with essential equipment and the more experienced soldiers.

Pisani's plan was simple but highly risky. He had closely observed the comings and goings of the Genoese; they had become complacent. Doria believed he held Venice in an iron grip, and that little more was required now to squeeze the remaining life out of a starving enemy. There were three maritime exits from Chioggia. Two, at either end of its *lido*, led directly out to sea; the third, the Lombardy Channel, ran behind the island and through the lagoon. Pisani's idea was to block these exits, hemming the enemy in. The besiegers would become, in their turn, besieged.

Under the long hours of darkness the fleet moved forward unseen. For a short while a thick fog obscured everything, causing temporary dismay, then cleared as suddenly as it came. By ten o'clock they were off the Chioggia opening – the first objective. There were no ships; no disturbance; no guard. At dawn on 22 December, the galleys began to ferry men ashore on the Chioggia *lido*. Four thousand eight hundred troops were landed, along with carpenters and trenchers. Pisani meanwhile manoeuvred the cogs towards the mouth of the channel.

On the *lido*, the men started to erect a defensive bastion. The noise of the carpenters attracted the attention of a small detachment of Paduan soldiers lying low in the sand dunes, and battle was joined. Hungarian and Paduan troops advanced from Brondolo. Others poured across the bridge from Chioggia, and the Genoese fleet began a bombardment. The Venetians were pushed back and massacred as they tried to retreat to the ships. As they fled, six hundred were killed, drowned or taken captive. The bastion was quickly demolished, but in the meantime, under this distraction the cogs were being hauled into position – one near the shore, the second blocking the main channel. The first was bombarded and sunk; some Genoese swam out to the second and set it on fire. It burned down to the waterline and also sank. 'And transported with pleasure at this deceptive victory, which prevented them from perceiving the difficulty, full of joy, they returned to Chioggia.' Doria was complacent with success: 'What the Venetians do in a day, I can undo in an hour,' was his smug comment. But he had understood neither the enemy's tactics nor the unintended effect of his own soldiers' actions. The sunken cogs had effectively blocked the channel anyway. The doge proceeded to return with two more cogs laden with rocks, marble and large millstones, which were tipped into the submerged hulks, then wrapped with chains. They were now immovable barriers.

On the 24th the fleet moved down to block the southern exit to the sea – that of Brondolo. Two more cogs were towed into place. Too late Doria woke up to the gradual encirclement. He sent out galleys to destroy the Venetian task force, bombarding it with gunfire from his land batteries at Brondolo, but the Venetians again managed to sink the boats, and reinforced the barrier with tree trunks, ships' masts and chains. Under heavy fire, engineers began the construction of a fort, the Lova, on the shore of Fossone opposite Brondolo. By 29th December it was well on the way to completion. On Christmas Day, or the day after, sailing round the *lidi*, Pisani completed his work by blocking the Lombardy Channel. Chioggia was now hemmed in; its only access was inland, via the rivers of central Italy.

As the channels were closed one after another, anxiety and desperation started to grip the Genoese. It was essential that they break the barricades. For the blockaders, despite their success, morale remained parlous. The galleys had to maintain an alert presence, day and night, on the lee shore. In the trenches at Fossone and on the tip of the *lido* of Pellestrina, adjacent to Chioggia, the Venetians were subjected to continuous bombardment. Food was in short supply; the winter cold was taking its toll on morale. Many of the men were civilian volunteers, artisans, merchants and craftsmen, rather than soldiers used to the vicissitudes of war. The English mercenaries, under their captain William Cook – Il Coqquo – were particularly vociferous. The doge tried to lead by personal example, swearing on his sword that he would never return to Venice unless Chioggia was taken. Despite this, the Venetians began to crack. There was no sign of Zeno. The men wanted to return to the city. On 29 December their misery reached its nadir: short of food, cold, under fire, forced to wade through the winter canals, they were at breaking point. Danger; tiredness; sleep deprivation; death; the now hateful lagoon – the murmuring became ominous. Many wanted to forsake Venice altogether for the Stato da Mar and sail away to Negroponte or Crete. Pisani attempted to rally the troops: if they disengaged, the chance of victory would be gone for ever. He argued that help was near; Zeno was on his way. Eventually the doge and his vice-general struck a bargain with the dissenters. If Zeno had not returned by 1 January they would lift the siege and return to Venice. There were forty-eight hours to save the city. It was known too that Doria was expecting further naval reinforcements.

The 30th and 31st passed in the cold and an agony of expectation. The dawn came up on 1 January. For the Venetians it was not the significant start of a new year – in their calendar this was celebrated on 1 March – but the breaking day was greeted with rapt anxiety. As the feeble winter light grew, fifteen sails could be seen on the southern horizon. They were too far out to determine the flags – the lion of St Mark or the cross of St George. The Genoese watched from the towers of Chioggia, the Venetians from their ships and trenches. Impatient, and deeply worried, Pisani sent out light boats to reconnoitre. As they drew within line of sight, they could see the flag of St Mark run up a masthead. It was Zeno, back from a damaging run across the eastern seas, inflicting huge losses on Genoese commerce. He had blocked the flow of reinforcements and supplies to Doria by sea and taken seventy ships including an immensely rich merchantman, which he towed behind his galleys. It was a decisive turn of events and it signalled a profound psychological shift in the fortunes of war.

Faced by these naval reinforcements the Genoese now struggled with increasing desperation to find a way out. The two seaward exits from the town, at Brondolo and the Chioggia channel, were guarded by Zeno and Pisani respectively. They needed to keep a force of galleys on station, day and night, against the threat of a breakout. The winter weather was ferocious; the onshore winds and strong currents threatened continuously to sweep the vessels onto the enemy coast. One evening, towards dusk, with the sirocco blowing hard up from the south and a boisterous current, Zeno's ship was torn from its moorings and pushed towards the Genoese forts. Instantly it was met with a hail of missiles; Zeno was hit by an arrow in the throat. The ship was wallowing in the swell, drifting slowly into the jaws of death. The crew, cowering under the bombardment, begged their stricken commander to strike the flag and surrender. The indestructible Zeno would have none of it. He plucked the arrow from his throat and barked out an order to a sailor to dive overboard with a tow rope and swim back to the mooring. Cuffing his crew into silence, he ran across the deck, fell down an open hatch, landed on his back and knocked himself out. Bleeding from a head wound, he started to choke on the blood; close to death from suffocation, he came dimly to and turned himself over. He lived to fight on.

Given the appalling conditions, and the narrowness of the Brondolo channel, it was decided to keep just two galleys on station; the remainder were harboured a mile down the coast, within trumpet call, if the need arose. Seeing this, on the night of 5 January Doria made a determined attempt to remove the obstructions. Three Genoese galleys armed with large grappling hooks and stout cables advanced in line up to the entrance on the channel. Their aim was to drag the sunken ships, spars and tree trunks out of the mouth. As the first one reached the entrance, the leading Venetian galley sounded its trumpet and advanced to attack. The Venetians managed to board the first vessel, but the other two, coming up behind, attached hooks to their Venetian opponent and passed the cables to the banks of the canal, where a large body of men hauled the helpless ship back towards the port of Brondolo before aid could arrive. The second Venetian galley, forced back by a volley of arrows, could do nothing. Many of the Venetians threw themselves overboard and drowned as the triumphant Genoese reeled in their prize. Zeno arrived too late.

So began a pattern of moves and countermoves in the narrow waterways and marshlands at the edge of the lagoon. The Genoese tried continuously to find a way out of the steel net; the Venetians to keep it drawn tight. The following day the Hungarian troops made a determined assault on the Chioggia channel. They were driven back. In Genoa, news of the sudden reversal of fortune caused alarm. On 20 January they despatched a new fleet of twenty galleys under Matteo Maruffo; like Zeno however, the Genoese admiral took a wide view of his brief, roving across the sea, capturing Venetian grain ships, sacking ports. He would not reach Chioggia for another four months.

Venice held the exits closed but had failed to prevent river traffic resupplying the stricken town. It was also desperately in need of supplies itself. Three galleys were sent up the Po with a detachment of soldiers to retake the strategic castle of Loredo, which controlled river access to the city of Ferrara. Its capture allowed men and supplies to be floated down to Venice. As news spread that the Republic now encircled Chioggia, merchants began to risk sending wine, cheese and grain back to the city again. Prices were still high but hope rose.

The fortress at Loredo had been reduced with the help of two massive bombards, individually named the Trevisana, which fired a stone ball of 195 pounds, and the slightly smaller Victoria, with a shot of 120 pounds. These two primitive cast-iron tubes, banded with iron hoops to reinforce them against the threat of explosion, were unloaded at the fort opposite Brondolo. The practice was to load the cannon in the evening – a lengthy process of lugging an enormous stone ball into its chamber – and fire them as dawn broke, when the Genoese would still be concentrated in Brondolo. This wake-up call was accompanied by a heavy bombardment of rocks from catapults. The bombards were notoriously inaccurate, but against large static objects at reasonable range the chances of a hit were good. On the morning of 22 January the Trevisana scored a major success. Its mighty stone bullet struck the campanile of Brondolo. A large chunk of masonry collapsed in the square, killing Pietro Doria and his nephew. 'With great laments and grief the bodies were taken to Chioggia and salted so that they could be returned to Genoa.' The following day falling masonry killed another twenty men. Many more died when the bombards hit a monastery taken over by the troops. Doria was replaced by Gaspare Spinola, but day by day the grip was tightening: 'Neither their galleys nor their supply ships could leave harbour, with the bombards and catapults always firing and damaging them.' And Venice knew the tide was turning. Pushing their resources to the limit, they hired five thousand Milanese and English mercenaries at the start of February to drive home the advantage before help could arrive. It was now the Genoese who stared anxiously out to sea for sight of a relieving fleet; they were still able to get supplies downriver from Padua but they could not escape. Unable to force the maritime blockade, they began cutting a new channel across the Brondolo *lido* to the sea. As soon as it was finished, they aimed to slip galleys out at night to Zara for supplies.

Across Italy the war between the maritime republics was yet again causing disquiet and the papacy started on one of its periodic attempts to separate the warring parties. Venice showed interest – the outcome of the fight was still far from clear – but negotiations with the allies involved a slow-motion round of Hungary, Padua and Genoa.

The escape channel being dug across the *lido* worried Venice. A decision was taken to snuff out the menace with an attack on Brondolo. On 18 February Zeno was appointed general-in-chief of the land forces of the Republic with orders to take the village and its command post in the monastery. He had fifteen thousand men at his disposal. As the galleys and the troops massed before dawn the following day there was a change of plan. It was decided instead to tackle the tower and bastion at Little Chioggia which controlled the bridgehead to Chioggia itself, to prevent reinforcements coming across. Fighting at the bridgehead quickly grew fierce. A large Genoese detachment advanced from Brondolo; more were rushed across from Chioggia; both were repulsed by the Venetian troops. The Genoese scattered. Some fled through the reed beds, waded the canals or drowned; more turned and fled back across the bridge in blind panic. So many crowded onto the wooden structure that it cracked and collapsed

. . . at the deep point of the canal, and there remained a thousand on the bridge who were killed with a bombardment of stones or captured; and many threw themselves into the water to get away. Some drowned, others were wounded or killed with the bombardment of rocks. Those who were on the bridge when it collapsed, sank to the bottom from the weight of their armour on their backs; if any crawled out of the canal, as soon as they got out of the water, they were killed with missiles . . . and if the bridge had not given way, the Venetians could have entered Chioggia after the fleeing men and retaken it in the same way that they lost it.

It was a sudden and catastrophic collapse of Genoese morale. It was said afterwards that 'anyone who wished for a suit of armour for a few shillings might have bought as many as he liked from those who stripped the dead'. After this disaster Brondolo was untenable. The Genoese sent their bombards by galley to Chioggia. Two hours before dawn the next day they fired the monastery, burned their siege engines and departed in galleys – some to Chioggia, but many of the Paduans abandoned the siege altogether. Brondolo was taken without a shot fired. Pisani managed to save two galleys that the Genoese had tried to fire 'and many barks and small boats and other things abandoned in the rush'. Zeno now set up camp hard across the canal from Chioggia itself and drew up bombards and catapults, 'which hurled huge rocks day and night into the town, shattering housing and killing people'. 'I remember', wrote one eyewitness, 'that our galleys were sometimes so close to Chioggia that stones were thrown into it without number.'

At this critical moment the Venetians were affected by the same indecision as had overtaken Doria early in the siege. 'The common opinion was that the Venetians could then have taken Chioggia, if they had attacked it at once; but they did not risk it.' In a neat symmetry, they preferred to starve it into submission, squeezing the passes and waterways towards Padua 'so that not a letter or a single thing might go from Chioggia to Padua, and that the Genoese, being unable to escape, would use up all their supplies'. The failure to capitalise on the rout at the bridge had an unexpected effect within the town. It actually improved Genoese morale. They expelled the Venetian women and children to eke out supplies and sat down to wait. The contest dragged on through the spring. The lord of Padua continued to besiege the key Venetian city of Treviso; down the coast at Manfredonia the slowly approaching Genoese relief fleet captured an entire Venetian grain convoy; a Venetian spy, dressed as a German, was discovered and tortured to reveal the Republic's war plans. The pope went on pressing for peace.

The hope in Chioggia now rested on a Genoese naval rescue and the lord of Padua. Despite Venetian efforts, supplies still managed to make their way downriver. In a daring pass, when the river was full, forty barges were floated downstream loaded with food, weapons and gunpowder. They forced their way past a feeble river guard and made it into the town. The Venetians responded by blocking all the approaching waterways with palisades and doubling their armed boats. When the supply boats tried to return they were met with fierce resistance and had to turn back. The marshland and waterways behind Chioggia became the terrain for amphibious warfare: boatloads of men fighting in the rivers; infantry floundering through canals; ambushes among the sedge. The Genoese held a string of fortified water mills, which the Venetians assaulted. On 22 April they launched a major attack on a mill but were pushed back, 'and because of this victory those in the mill greatly rejoiced and lit fires, by which those in Chioggia learned what had happened'. The following day battle was rejoined. The Venetians again attacked the mill, while the Genoese despatched eighty boats from the town to destroy the palisades and reopen the waterway to Padua. Warned of the approach, the Venetians suspended the attack on the mill; going stealthily through the cover of the reeds they ambushed the Genoese breakout, 'and with wild shouts and the firing of many bombards and arrows they began a fierce battle'. The boat crews abandoned their vessels and fled through the reed beds and dry channels. Only six boats got away. It was an ill-omened day for Genoa: 23 April was the feast day of St George. Henceforward no further supplies could reach the beleaguered town.

Despite continued minor successful counterattacks, the pressure on Chioggia was now unrelenting. The Venetians could sense that the end was near. The old doge, who had been in temporary camp on the Pellestrina *lido* for four winter months, had written to the standing war committee on 22 April, pleading age and infirmity and requesting to be allowed to return. The Venetians, as unbending to state servants as to enemies, politely refused. Contarini was the 'life blood, the security, the morale' of the whole enterprise. He remained at the siege. And no concessions were given to the hated enemy. Supplies inside Chioggia were running low. There was discord between the Genoese and their allies, many of whom wanted to lay down their weapons and depart. The Venetians roundly declared they would hang anyone whom they caught leaving the town. They wanted to starve Chioggia as fast as possible, before a Genoese relief fleet could appear. Inside, ammunition was giving out. The defenders were reduced to eating rats, cats, crabs, mice, seaweed. The water, lifted from badly made cisterns, was foul. They stared anxiously out to sea. It remained a blank.

Desperate negotiations ensued. The defenders agreed to surrender so long as they were allowed to go free. Venice refused: surrender would be unconditional and a deadline fixed – after that date, everyone captured would be hanged. The deadline passed. The Genoese kept watching the sea. On 6 June, 'at the hour of terce', Maruffo's fleet was sighted. People climbed on the house roofs, crying, shouting, waving flags. The Genoese admiral fired a shot challenging Pisani to battle; the invitation was refused. Every day Maruffo reappeared with the same challenge. Eventually Pisani sailed out and chased the Genoese several miles down the coast. From the rooftops, the defenders watched with unspeakable pain the flag of St George recede.

The guns had fallen silent in Chioggia. The powder was used up. The defence was at its last gasp. Venetian and Genoese officers began parleying over the walls. The pope's legates again tried to arrange a truce, but the Venetians folded their arms. Maruffo returned from Zara on 15 June with an augmented fleet, yet again dangling his galleys off Chioggia. A last effort was made to break out. Makeshift boats were constructed from any available wood – crates, beds, house timbers. A message was sent to Maruffo to send his ships off the *lido* for a rescue attempt. It failed hopelessly; the ramshackle craft were impeded by the ring of palisades in the canals. They were intercepted, captured and sunk. Maruffo withdrew. On 17 June, the Genoese released their prisoners and sent three ambassadors to Zeno's camp. They made one final attempt to wriggle free, trying to cut a side deal with the mercenary troops: Chioggia could be sacked in return for a safe conduct. The mercenaries had to be appeased with the right to sack the town anyway as long as all the prisoners were given up. One dissenting *condottiere* was hanged between the two columns to keep the hired men in line.

On 21 June, a deputation to the doge's camp was forced to accept unconditional surrender. The following day the commander, Spinola, hoisted the flag of St George for the last time; the impotent Genoese fleet sailed up yet again. Spinola ordered the flag to be struck as a signal of surrender. Maruffo replied with a smoke signal, begging the defenders to hold out just a little longer. There was no reply. 'They understood that it was all over at Chioggia. They returned [to harbour] completely downhearted.'

On 24 June, the doge entered the shattered town; after ten months the banner of St Mark was raised over Chioggia once more, and the defenders, haggard, hollow-eyed, cadaverous, more dead than alive, staggered out to surrender. The victors carefully sorted their prisoners; they used a shibboleth to separate the Paduans, Hungarians and mercenaries from the Genoese. Asked to pronounce the word *capra* (goat), the Genoese could only accurately reproduce their dialect version, *crapa*. Four thousand Genoese were marched off to makeshift prison camps where many died; those who could say *capra* were freed.

On 30 June 1380 the doge was finally allowed to return to Venice. He made his entry in the *Bucintoro*, ornately dressed and decorated for the occasion. It was rowed by a hundred captured oarsmen and followed by seventeen dejected Genoese galleys, their flags trailing in humiliating defeat. They were the sole remnant of the fleet that had set out to bridle the horses of St Mark. Accompanied by Pisani, the Golden Boat returned in triumph to the city among a swarm of small craft, the clanging of bells, the firing of guns, the boom and thunder of victorious noise. So thick was the throng of jubilant people that it was almost impossible to force a way through the crowd for the ducal procession to St Mark's, where the thanksgiving for the deliverance of Venice was celebrated with a solemn mass.

*

For the Venetians there was a saddening afternote. Pisani died six weeks later, chasing the remnant of Maruffo's fleet across the Adriatic. After being at sea almost continuously for over two years, he succumbed to wounds and fever on 15 August at Manfredonia. The people of the city were grief-stricken. No Venetian admiral was ever loved so much or mourned so deeply. He was the subject of popular clamour to the last; his funeral procession to the Church of St Anthony inspired an explosion of popular emotions. A band of sailors shouldered their way through the crowd and hijacked the bier, shouting, 'We his children are carrying our brave captain to our father St Anthony!'

But when peace came at the Treaty of Turin the following year, it was less a victory than the avoidance of defeat. Venice regained her land territory in the Trevigiano, but the Dalmatian coast remained in Hungarian hands. Restored at Constantinople, Venice was again excluded from the Sea of Azov. Competition between the two republics would continue as before. And the almost forgotten island of Tenedos, which had sparked the whole conflict, was demilitarised. Its fortress was demolished, the Greek population forcibly resettled on Crete. It was a solution that would please no one but the Turks, who now used the abandoned harbour as a base for piracy.

Venice had outlasted Genoa less through military supremacy than through the durability of her institutions, the social cohesion of her people and their patriotic adherence to the flag of St Mark. After the humiliation of Chioggia, Genoa imploded. Ten successive doges were deposed in five years; in 1394 the city handed itself to the French kings. For Venice such surrender was unthinkable. It would prefer to drown in its own lagoon. By the sixteenth century, when Veronese added a painting to the ducal palace of the doge's triumphant return, the meaning of Chioggia was clearer. On the rebound of almost catastrophic defeat, Venice would eventually win the contest for Mediterranean trade. The enmity would remain but the Genoese contention was progressively enfeebled.

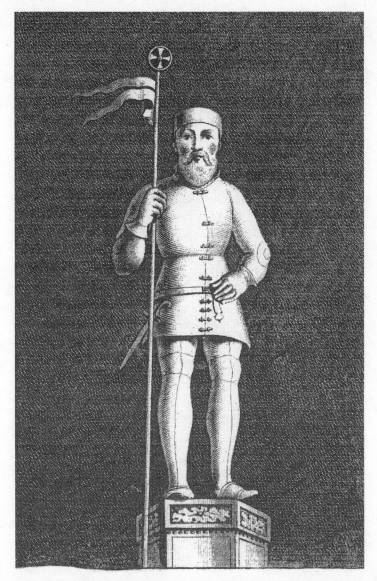

Effigy of Pisani from his tomb

There were other consequences for both republics still over the horizon, like a storm brewing far out to sea. The Genoese–Venetian wars repeatedly stalled papal plans to scotch the growing Ottoman threat. By 1362 the Ottomans had virtually encircled Constantinople; in 1371 they shattered the Serbs; by the end of the fourteenth century their territories stretched from the Danube to the Euphrates.

14

Stato da Mar

1381–1425

Venice had been taken to the limit by the slogging contest in its own lagoon. For two years all trade ceased. The fleet was ruined, the treasury emptied; naval supremacy of the Adriatic was formally gifted away to Hungary in the treaty of 1381. The Genoese wars, plague, Cretan rebellion and papal trade bans had made the fourteenth century a testing time. Yet the Republic had survived. And in the wake of Chioggia the city was able to stage an extraordinary recovery. In the half-century after 1381, the Stato da Mar underwent a burst of colonial expansion that would carry the Republic to the height of maritime prosperity and imperial power. Venice returned to astonish the world.

On the turn of the fifteenth century the eastern Mediterranean was a mosaic of small states and competing interests. The Byzantine Empire continued to decline; the kings of Hungary were losing their grip on the Balkans; the Ottomans were pushing west in their place; the opportunist Catalans, who had been a scourge of the eastern sea, were starting to withdraw. Elsewhere Genoa, Pisa, Florence and Naples, along with an assortment of adventurers and freebooters, held a string of islands, ports and forts. As Hungary's hold on the Adriatic weakened and the Ottomans drew ever nearer, many of the small cities on the Dalmatian coast that had once struggled so hard against Venice came to seek its protection. When the Ottomans in their turn were thrown into turmoil by civil war, the Republic prospered. Between 1380 and 1420 Venice doubled its land holdings – and almost as importantly its population. Many of these acquisitions were in mainland Italy, but it was the strengthening of its maritime empire that enabled Venice to cement its position as the dominant power in the sea and the axis of world trade.

The methods it used to annex new possessions were highly flexible: a mixture of patient diplomacy and short sharp applications of military force. Where the city had obtained an empire by job lot after 1204, these new acquisitions were piecemeal. Ambassadors were despatched to guarantee the safety of a Greek port or a Dalmatian island; an absentee landlord could be tempted to sell up for ready cash; a couple of armed galleys might persuade an embattled Catalan adventurer it was time to go home or swing a factional dispute in a Croatian port; a wavering Venetian heiress might be 'encouraged' to marry a suitable Venetian lord or to bestow her inheritance directly on the Republic. If its techniques were patient and variable, the Republic's underlying policy was frighteningly consistent: to obtain, at the lowest cost, desirable forts, ports and defensive zones for the honour and profit of the city. 'Our agenda in the maritime parts', the senate declared in 1441 like a corporation setting out its strategic plan, 'considers our state and the conservation of our city and commerce.'

Sometimes cities submitted to Venice voluntarily to avoid unwelcome pressures from the Ottomans or Genoese. In each case Venice ran the slide rule of cost–benefit analysis over the application, like merchants eyeing the goods. Did the city have a secure harbour? Good water sources for provisioning ships? An agricultural hinterland? A compliant population? What were its defences like? Did it control a strategic strait? And negatively, what would be the loss if it fell to a hostile power? Cattaro, on the Dalmatian coast, made six requests to submit before the Republic agreed. Patras applied seven times. On each occasion the senators listened gravely and shook their heads. When it came to outright purchase they waited for the stock to fall. Ladislas of Hungary offered his claim to Dalmatia in 1408 for three hundred thousand florins. The following year, with his cities in revolt, Venice sealed it for one hundred thousand. And sometimes the choice was money or compulsion; the carrot and the stick were applied in equal measure. By patience, bargaining, intimidation and outright force, Venice extended the Stato da Mar.

One by one the red-roofed ports, green islands and miniature cities of Dalmatia and the Albanian coast dropped, almost effortlessly, into its hands: Sebenico and Brazza, Trau and Spalato, the islands of Lesina and Curzola, famous for shipbuilding and sailors, 'as bright and clean as a beautiful jewel'. The key to the whole system was Zara, over which Venice had struggled to maintain its dominance for four hundred years. Now it submitted to Venice by free will, with cries of 'Long live St Mark!' To be quite certain, its troublesome noble families were moved to Venice, then offered positions in other cities along the coast. Once again the doge could style himself lord of Dalmatia. Only Ragusa, proudly independent, escaped permanently the embrace of St Mark.

The value of this coast was inestimable. Venetian galley fleets could thread their way up the sheltered channels of its coast; protected by its chain of islands from the Adriatic's unpredictable winds – the sirocco, the *bora* and the *maestrale* – they could put in at its secure harbours. The Republic's ships would be built from Dalmatian pine and rowed or sailed by Dalmatian crews. Manpower was as important as wood, and the maritime skills of the eastern shore of the Adriatic would be at the disposal of Venice for as long as the Republic lasted.

If Zara was important, the acquisition of Corfu was more so. They bought the island from the king of Naples in 1386 for thirty thousand ducats and with the ready acceptance of its populace, 'considering the tempest of the times and the instability of human affairs'. Corfu was the missing link in a chain of bases. The island – which Villehardouin had found 'very rich and plenteous' when the crusaders stopped there in 1203 – occupied an emotional place in the city's history. Here the Venetians had lost thousands of men in sea battles against the Normans in the eleventh century; they were gifted it in 1204, held it briefly, then lost it again. Its position, guarding the mouth of the Adriatic, also

The fortress of Corfu

provided critical oversight of the east–west traffic between Italy and Greece. Across the straits, Venice acquired the Albanian port of Durazzo, rich in running water and green forests, and Butrinto just ten miles away. This triangle of bases controlled the Albanian coast and the seaway to Venice.

Corfu itself, verdant, mountainous, watered by the winter rains, became the command centre of Venice's naval system and its choice posting. They called it 'Our Door' and stationed a permanent galley fleet in its secure port under the captain of the Gulf; in times of danger his authority would be trumped by the all-powerful captain of the sea, whose arrival was announced with belligerent banners and the blare of trumpets. All passing Venetian ships were mandated to make a four-hour stopover at Corfu to exchange news. They came gladly, seeing the outline of the great island floating up out of the calm sea, like a first apprehension of Venice itself. Corfu provided fresh water and the delights of port. The prostitutes of the town were renowned, both for their favours and the 'French disease'; and sailors on the homeward run, being pious as well as frail, also stopped further up the coast at the shrine of Our Lady of Kassiopi to give thanks for the voyage.

The Ionian islands south from Corfu were added in this new wave of empire: verdant Santa Maura, craggy Kefallonia, and 'Zante, *fior di Levante*' (Flower of the Levant) in the Italian rhyme. Lepanto, a strategic port tucked into the Gulf of Corinth and potentially attractive to the Ottomans, was taken by despatching the captain of the Gulf with five galleys and emphatic orders to storm or buy the place. Faced with the choice of decapitation or a safe conduct and 1,500 ducats a year, its Albanian lord went quietly.

The gold rush of new acquisitions stretched round the entire coast of Greece. Zonchio, a well-protected harbour close to Modon, was bought in 1414; Naplion and Argos in the Gulf of Argos came by bribery; Salonica begged for protection from the Turks in 1423. Shrewd in their moves and cognisant of their manpower shortages, untempted by feudal ambition and landed titles in a landscape that yielded so little, the senate refused the submission of inland Attica. What mattered and only mattered was the sea.

Further south, the barren islands of the Cyclades, offered to Venetian privateers after 1204, had become an increasing problem. The Republic had repeated difficulties with their overlords, by turns treacherous, tyrannical, even mad. Turkish, Genoese and Catalan pirates also plundered the islands, abducted their populations and rendered the sea lanes unsafe. As early as 1326, a chronicler wrote that 'the Turks specially infest these islands . . . and if help is not forthcoming they will be lost'. The Florentine priest Buondelmonti spent four years in the Aegean in the early 1400s and travelled 'in fear and great anxiety'. He found the islands wretched beyond belief. Naxos and Siphnos lacked any sizeable male population; Seriphos, he declared, offered 'nothing but calamity', where the people 'lived like brutes'. On Ios the whole population retreated into the castle each night for fear of raiders. The people of Tinos tried to abandon their island altogether. The Aegean looked to the Republic for protection, 'seeing that no lordship under heaven is so just and good as that of Venice'. The Republic started to reabsorb these islands, but as ever its approach was fiercely pragmatic.

The empire that Venice acquired in this second wave of colonial expansion was held together by muscular sea power. To its triangle of priceless keystones – Modon–Coron, Crete and Negroponte – was now added Corfu. But beyond, the Stato da Mar was a shifting, supple matrix of interchanging locations, flexible as a steel net. The Venetians lived permanently with impermanence and many of their possessions came and went, like the moods of the sea. At one time or another they occupied a hundred sites in continental Greece; most of the Aegean islands passed through their hands. Some slipped from their grasp only to be regathered. Others were quite ephemeral. They held the rock of Monemvasia, shaped like a miniature Gibraltar, on and off for over a century and they were in and out of Athens. They had a foothold there in the 1390s, when they watched Spanish adventurers stripping the silver plates from the Parthenon doors, then ruled it themselves for six years. Fifty years later they were offered it again, but by then it was too late.

Nowhere exemplified reversals of colonial fortune as sharply as Tana, on the northern shores of the Black Sea. After Venice was ousted by the Mongols in 1348, a merchant settlement was restored in 1350 and maintained for half a century. But Tana was so far away that news was slow to reach the centre. The galley fleets made their annual visit then vanished again over the sea's rim. Silence gripped the outpost for long months. When Andrea Giustinian was sent to Tana in 1396, he was staggered to discover nothing there – no people, no standing buildings – just the charred remains of habitations and the eerie crying of birds over the River Don. The whole settlement had gone down in fire and blood before an assault by Tamburlaine, the Mongol warlord, the previous year. In 1397 Giustinian appealed to the local Tatar lords for permission to build a new, fortified settlement. Venice simply started again. Tana was that important.

But in the centre of the eastern Mediterranean, Venice ran an imperial system of incomparable efficiency. Throughout the region, wherever the flag of St Mark was flown, the propaganda symbols of Venetian power – economic, military and cultural – were visible: in the image of the lion, carved into harbour walls and above the dark gateways of forts and blockhouses, growling at would-be enemies, offering peace to friends; in the bright roundels of its gold ducats, on which the doge kneels before the saint himself, whose purity and credibility undermined all its rivals; in the regular sweep of its war fleets and the spectacle of its merchant convoys; in the sight of its black-clad merchants pricing commodities in the Venetian dialect; in its ceremonies and the celebration of feast days; in its imperial architecture. The Venetians were omnipresent.

The city exported itself across the sea. Candia was styled *alias civitas Venetiarum apud Levantem*, 'another city of the Venetians in the Levant' – a second Venice – and it replicated its buildings and its emblems of power. There was the Piazza San Marco, faced by the Church of St Mark, a clock tower flying the saint's flag, which like the bells of the campanile in Venice signalled the start and end of the working day, and the ducal palace and the loggia for conducting business and the buying and selling of goods. Two columns stood beside the palace for the execution of criminals, echoing those on the Venetian waterfront, reminding citizens and subjects alike that the writ of exemplary Venetian justice ran in the world. Here the Venetian state was reproduced in miniature: the chamber for weighing wholesale commodities using Venetian weights and measures, the offices dealing with criminal and commercial law, the antechambers and sub-departments of the Cretan administration, similar to those of the doge's palace. Through half-closed eyes a travelling merchant could believe himself transported to some reflection of Venice, remade in the brilliant air of the Levant, like an image by Carpaccio repainting Venice on the shores of Egypt, or an English church in the Raj. Outsiders remarked on this trick of the light. 'If a man be in any territory of theirs,' wrote the Spanish traveller Tafur, 'although at the ends of the earth, it seems as if he were in Venice itself.' When he stopped at Curzola, on the Dalmatian coast, he found that even the local inhabitants had fallen under the Venetian sway: 'The men dress in public like the Venetians and almost all of them know the Italian language.' Constantinople, Beirut, Acre, Tyre and Negroponte all had a church of St Mark at one time or another.

Such features made the travelling merchant or the colonial administrator feel that he occupied his own world; they fended

Imperial monuments: the clock tower at Retimo

off homesickness and projected Venetian power to their subjects, be they speakers of Greek, Albanian or Serbo-Croat. This
was reinforced by the ritual elements of Venetian ceremonial.
The formally orchestrated ceremonies so carefully detailed in
fifteenth-century paintings were exported to the colonies. The
arrival of a new duke of Crete, stepping from his galley to an
announcement of trumpets under a red silk umbrella, met at the
sea gate by his predecessor and walked in solemn procession up

the main street to the cathedral and the anointment with holy water and incense – these were highly scripted demonstrations of Venetian glory. The stately processions, the banners of St Mark and the patron saints, the oaths of loyalty, submission and service to the Republic by subject peoples, the singing of the Lauds service in praise of the duke on the great feast days of the Christian year – these rituals fused secular and religious power in displays of splendour and awe. The pilgrim Canon Pietro Casola witnessed such ceremonial at a handover of the Cretan administration in 1494, which was 'so magnificent that I seemed to be in Venice on a great festival'.

Colonial administration was organised in hierarchical tiers with regulated salary structures, privileges, obligations – and a litany of carefully differentiated titles. At its crest – the most powerful post in the system – was the duke of Crete; matching him for salary (a thousand ducats a year), to reflect the strategic importance of the place, was the *bailo* of Constantinople. Corfu and Negroponte were also governed by a *bailo*, Modon and Coron by two *castellani*, Argos and Naplion by a *podesta*. The islands of Tinos and Mykonos and the other towns of Crete were overseen by rectors; settlements on foreign soil – Tana or Salonica – were the province of consuls. These nabobs of the imperial system were elected, involuntarily, from the nobility of Venice, mandated to their posts and punished for refusal to serve. Beneath these titled people there fell away descending ranks of state servants: counsellors and treasurers, admirals of the colonial arsenals, notaries, scribes and judges, all of them sworn to act for the honour and profit of Venice, each of them apportioned certain rights, responsibilities and restrictions.

For all the pomp and gravitas invested in these state officers their freedom of manoeuvre was carefully circumscribed. Everyone felt the gravitational pull of Venice; even a consul in Tana three months' sailing time away was subject to weighty regulation. The Republic was a centrist empire; everything was ruled, dictated, regulated from the lagoon and precisioned in an endless stream of edicts. An expectation of patriotism was hard-wired into the Venetian psyche; all its colonists came from the same few square miles of the lagoon; all were expected to act with unflinching patriotism for the Signoria. The Republic was obsessed with the racial purity of its citizens. Fear of going native, particularly after the Cretan revolt of 1363, haunted their edicts. Citizenship was rarely granted to foreigners and the frontiers of race were strictly patrolled. Intermarriage and defection to the Greek Orthodox Church were heavily frowned upon, and in the case of Crete actively penalised. High-ranking colonial officials were rotated on a two-year cycle to limit their potential for local contamination, and the centre worked hard to maintain cultural distinctions. At Modon, the Venetians were forbidden to grow beards; their citizens were to remain clean-shaven, distinguishable from the hirsute Greeks.

The conditions under which they served were closely defined. Governors were strictly instructed, under the terms of their commission, on the number of administrators in their retinue, the number of servants and horses that they must maintain for their prestige and use (the state was particular about the horses, neither fewer nor more), their pecuniary allowances and the limitations of their power. They were forbidden to engage in any commercial activity, or to take with them any relatives, and were bound by stern oaths. The Republic was wary of individual aggrandisement – an aversion to personal ambition was deeply ingrained in this most impersonal of states – and intolerant of corruption. Giovanni Bon, sent to Candia to manage its finances in 1396, not only swore the usual oath to act for the honour of Venice, he was bound to rent out the goods of the state at the highest price, to account in minute detail to the duke and his counsellors on an annual basis on everything that he dealt with and noticed during the previous year, to accept no services or gifts; both he and his employees were forbidden all commercial transactions or to offer any banquets to anyone, be they Greek or Latin, either in Candia or within a radius of three Venetian miles.

In a system where the doge himself was expressly barred from accepting gifts of any value from a foreign agency, such injunctions were standard. Its principles were continuous oversight and collective responsibility. No officer was to act alone. It required three keys, each held by a different treasurer, to open the Candia counting house. The duke of Crete required the written agreement of three counsellors to ratify a decision. Everything was built on documentary evidence. The secretarial corps toiling in the bowels of the doge's palace, recording and despatching senatorial decrees to the Stato da Mar, was replicated at the local level. Every Venetian colony had its own notaries, scribes and document store. All decisions, transactions, commercial agreements, wills, decrees and judgements were set down in literally millions of entries, like an infinite merchant's ledger, which formed the historic memory of the state. Everyone was accountable. Everything was written down. By the time of the death of the Venetian state, its archives ran to forty-five miles of shelving.

The records bear witness to the exhaustive central management of the imperial system – an endless struggle against corruption, nepotism, bribery and occasional acts of state treason. 'The honour of the Commune demands that all its rectors be excellent' was its mantra. The frequency with which commissions were accompanied by the injunction not to engage in trade suggests that breaches were many and various – and pursued with dogged persistence. Colonial officials at all levels had plentiful opportunity to feel the severe, impartial scrutiny of Venetian audit. Justice was patient, implacable and inexorable. No one was free from investigation. It fell on a duke with the same impersonal force as on a blacksmith. Its methods were exhaustive. At regular intervals, the syndics or *provveditori* – state inquisitors – made inspections. The sight of these black-robed functionaries stepping down the gangplank at Negroponte or Candia to ask questions and run the rule over the ledgers might strike anxiety in the most puffed-up colonial dignitary. Their powers were almost limitless. In the remit of May 1369 the *provveditori* are reminded that as well as auditing lower-level officials

A *provveditore*: auditor of the Stato da Mar

... their mission in the Levant has an equal bearing on the misdeeds of the governors themselves which might damage the state's interests; the governors cannot refuse to respond about misdeeds with which they are charged, under any pretext, even if invoking the terms of their commissions. The *provveditori* are authorised to turn up wherever they think useful; their freedom of movement is limitless. Nevertheless [a typical Venetian caveat] they must endeavour to limit their travel costs. If an official happens to have committed an act of such seriousness that the *provveditori* suspect that he will not agree to go willingly to Venice to meet the charge, it will be necessary, after discussions with the local governor, to seize the guilty official and forcibly send him.

Accounts would be scrutinised, complaints heard, correspondence confiscated and dissected. The *provveditori* had a year on return to present their findings, to call further witnesses and impeach the guilty. And in a further dizzying level of audit, the inquisitors themselves, despatched usually in groups of three, were forbidden to trade, receive presents, even to lodge separately. The Stato da Mar ran on suspicion.

It was a month to Crete, six weeks to Negroponte, three months to Tana, but anyone could feel the long arm of the Venetian state. At times its reach could be very long indeed. In the spring of 1447, the senate received clandestine word that the duke of Crete himself, Andrea Donato, was consorting treacherously with the Milanese *condottiere*, Francesco Sforza, and taking bribes. The orders to detain him were brief and ruthless:

To Benedetto da Legge, galley captain, charged with arresting the duke: 1. He will go with all possible speed to Candia – all stops are forbidden. 2. At Candia he will anchor in the bay without landing. He will not allow anyone to disembark or come aboard. 3. He will send a trusted person to Andrea Donato, requesting him to come aboard to confer. 4. The pretext for the conversation will be to get information on the Levant situation, because the captain will pretend that he is going to Turkey to the sultan. 5. When Donato is on board, Benedetto will retain him, affirming that it is essential for him to come to Venice, without giving his reasons. 6. Before leaving Candia he will send the letter with which he is entrusted to the captain and counsellors of Crete. 7. In case Donato refuses to come aboard, or can't, Captain Legge will send another letter, with which he is furnished, to the captain and counsellors, so that the duke will certainly come. 8. Once Donato is on board, the galley will depart for Venice at once, where . . . [the captain] will conduct him to the torture chamber. 9. During the whole voyage it is forbidden to speak to the prisoner; in the case that it is essential to put ashore, Donato must not land under any pretext whatsoever.

The accompanying sealed orders to the counsellors read: 'In the case that Andrea Donato refuses to go on board the galley, the captain and counsellors must use physical force; they will put the duke under arrest and conduct him aboard so that he can be taken to Venice without delay.' Da Legge made the journey in record time, plucked the duke off the island and hurried him back to Venice for torture. The round trip took a record forty-five days. The message was clear.

The Venetian state waged continuous war against the malfeasance of its officials; the registers ring with thunderous rebukes, inquiries, fines, impeachments and requests to torture. 'It is forbidden . . .' begin numerous entries, and the lists that follow are long and repetitive – to employ family members, sell public property, trade, and so forth. 'Too many *baili*, governors and consuls obtain favours, allowances and various exemptions. This is intolerable and these practices are formally forbidden.' A duke of Crete is arraigned for a grain scam; a chancellor of Modon–Coron is guilty of extortion; an official is fined for failing to take up a post; another is ordered back to account for a missing sum; the castellan of Modon, Francesco da Priuli, is arrested and snatched from his post – the vote to torture him is carried by thirteen to five, with five abstentions. Conversely, loyalty to the Republic was recognised and rewarded.

Venice applied its adamantine system to all the other subjects of the Stato da Mar. The governors were enjoined to deliver justice to all – to its Venetian colonists and subjects alike. The local populace, the Jews and other resident foreigners were subject to the same governance. By the standards of the times, the Republic possessed a strong sense of fairness which it wielded with considerable objectivity.

The Venetians were lawyers to their fingertips who operated the system with a fierce logic. In cases of murder there were fine gradations. Homicide was distinguished between simple (manslaughter) and deliberate, and divided into eight sub-categories, from self-defence and accidental, through deliberate, ambush, betrayal and assassination; judges were required to establish the motives as scrupulously as possible. (Actions of the secret state were of course exempt from such strictures: the registers for July 1415 record an offer to assassinate the king of Hungary. The assassin, 'who wishes to remain anonymous, will also kill Brunezzo della Scala if he is found in the king's company. The offer is accepted'.) The Republic could and did resort to hideous punishments; they used torture readily to procure the truth – or at least a confession – and they measured their judgements relative to state interests. In January 1368, one Gestus de Boemia was brought before the ducal court at Candia for theft of treasury money. His punishment was intended to be exemplary: amputation of his right hand, public confession of his crime, then hanging outside the treasury which he had raided. The following year, the Cretan Emanuel Theologite also lost a hand and both his eyes for letting a rebel prisoner escape. Toma Bianco had his tongue cut out for uttering insulting remarks against the honour of Venice, followed by imprisonment and perpetual banishment.

Venetian justice was also marked by moral repulsion: a butcher, Stamati of Negroponte, and his accomplice, Antonio of Candia, were condemned to death for male rape of a minor in January 1419; four months later Nicolo Zorzi was burned alive for the same offence. Capital sentences were carried out in the name of the doge for the edification of the populace – in Candia, between two columns in imitation of those in the Piazzetta of St Mark in Venice – yet within this harsh retributive framework decisions could be finely nuanced. Minors below the age of fourteen and the mentally handicapped were exempt from capital punishment, even in cases of assassination. The mentally ill were confined, and branded to advertise their condition. Everyone had right of appeal to Venice; witnesses could be called back to the mother city; cases could be reopened years later; even the Jews, marginalised subjects of the Venetian state, could expect a reasonable respect before the law. Justice ground slowly but with implacable respect for due process. In 1380, when the Venetian fleet was stationed at Modon one Giovannino Salimbene was found guilty of murdering Moreto Rosso. The judgement against Salimbene was deemed to have been 'very badly handled, because of the circumstances, and above all the lack of witnesses'. Four years later the case was reopened with the order for 'a new examination of the officers of the city's night police'.

In this system, cases could be dismissed, mitigating circumstances allowed or judgements overturned on the vote of the relevant appeal body. In March 1415 a fine imposed on Mordechai Delemedego, 'Jew of Negroponte', is reversed – 'the syndics do not have the right to act against the Jews'. The same year a similar fine imposed by the syndics on Matteo of Naplion, at Negroponte, for renting the Republic's property whilst an officer of the state is annulled; 'It has been proved that Matteo had resigned his post when he undertook these transactions' 'A judgement against Pantaleone Barbo – banned from public life for ten years – is reconsidered as 'too severe for a man who has committed his life to the service of the Signoria, with exemplary loyalty'; Giacomo Apanomeriti, a Cretan, fined or alternatively sentenced to two years for raping a woman and refusing to marry her, is given a chance of reprieve. 'The judges of appeal had examined this case: given the youth and poverty of the boy, he is released from all penalties if he marries the girl straight away.'

With its mixed populations of Catholics, Jews and Orthodox Christians, the Republic was concerned above all to keep a social balance. The Stato da Mar was essentially a secular state. It had no programme for the conversion of peoples, no remit to spread the Catholic faith – beyond the occasional leverage of papal support for particular advantage. Its opposition to the Orthodox

Church on Crete was a fear of pan-Greek, nationalist opposition, rather than religious zealotry; elsewhere it could afford to be lenient. On docile Corfu, Venice decreed that the Greeks should have 'liberty to preach and teach the holy word, provided only that they say nothing about the Republic or against the Latin religion'. It was equally alarmed by outbursts of undue fervour from the Catholic monastic orders who trailed in the wake of its conquests, and sometimes appalled. 'The night watch have had to arrest four [Franciscans],' it was reported from Candia in August 1420. 'These men, holding a cross, processed completely naked, followed by a great crowd of people. Such acts are disagreeable.' The Franciscans threatened a delicate cultural and religious balance. Any kind of civil unrest was to be feared. Two years later the doge wrote directly to the administration of Crete about

the sometimes scandalous reports on the behaviour of certain clerics of the Latin Church; this behaviour is all the more dangerous on Crete; one has just learned, in particular, that certain priests preach . . . to the detriment of the Signoria; the scandal has rebounded on the Venetians of the isle; the authorities will take immediate and rigorous measures against these priests, so that peace and tranquillity are restored on Crete.

Deep down Venice wished to keep the balance between its subjects: peace and tranquillity, honour and profit – the ideals went hand in hand.

But if the Republic could afford to be lenient in social matters, as far as security and civil peace allowed, economic pressure was felt everywhere. The colonies were zones of fiscal exploitation, taxed thoroughly and continuously, with the heaviest weight falling on the Jewish population. In matters of money the oppressive presence of the Dominante was inescapable. The central administration was endlessly concerned with collecting taxes. It had little concern as to how they were raised at the local level and there was almost no local say in how the proceeds were spent. The state managed its money like good merchants, accruing as much as possible, spending as little as necessary. Resource extraction was a central preoccupation.

From the Stato da Mar, Venice sought food, manpower and raw materials – sailors from the Dalmatian coast, Cretan wheat and hard cheese (a staple of the sailor's diet), wine, wax, wood and honey. For the hungry urban population of the lagoon, these resources were vital. Crete was a critical support during the Chioggia war. Everything was funnelled directly back to the lagoon under strict conditions – even inter-colonial trade came via the mother city – and goods could only be transported in Venetian ships. Cargoes were scrupulously examined and heavy fines apportioned; each landfall at the customs house earned a small ingredient of state tax. The key products – salt and wheat – were commodity-traded at fixed prices, whose tariffs formed a subsidiary grievance of Cretan landowners, aware of greater gains to be made on an open market. The state registers minuted the operation of this oppressive system. The Dominante stipulated where, when, what and at what price goods could be transported across the Aegean and the Adriatic. It insisted on the use of its weights and measures and forced its currency on subject peoples. The ducat became as potent a symbol of Venetian power as the armed galley.

The effects of these central controls were keenly felt. The economic development of the shores of Greece was stifled, industry stunted (with the exception of Cretan shipbuilding), the opportunity for the growth of a local entrepreneurial class severely curtailed. Instead, Venice concentrated on the agricultural exploitation of its key domains. The terrain was unpromising: large areas of the Stato da Mar were mountainous, barren, short of water and hit by desiccating winds, but in the fertile valleys of Crete, Corfu and Negroponte, the Venetian administrations worked assiduously on irrigation and conservation of fertility. The Lasithi plateau, abandoned by edict under the revolts of the previous century, was brought back into cultivation. When Francesco Basilicata visited in 1630 it was described as 'a very beautiful, flat area and an almost miraculous work of nature'.

The agricultural development of the Stato da Mar was always hampered by a shortage of manpower. People vanished from the fields. Plague and famine and the generally high mortality in the harsh landscapes took a heavy toll; the downtrodden peasantry sought continuously to evade oppressive Venetian control; slaves escaped; pirates snatched whole populations – the continuous draining away of human resources was a running complaint. In 1348, the Signoria could lament that 'the pitiful epidemic which has just ravaged Crete and the resulting high number of deaths require steps taken to repopulate. In particular it is necessary to give confidence to fleeing debtors so that they return to work their land. The landlords lack men.' By the late fourteenth century slaves from the Black Sea were being imported to work the land in a plantation-style system. For the indigenous Greek peasantry life had always been hard; under its colonial overseers it became no easier. Venetian rule paid scant attention to its rural workforce; they were a resource, like wood or iron, used without curiosity. When later, more compassionate observers visited Crete they were startled by what they saw. Four hundred years of Venetian rule produced few gains for its subjects: 'the deprivation of the Cretan people defies credibility,' wrote a seventeenth-century observer. 'There must be few in the world who live in such miserable conditions.' What Venice offered back was just some measure of security against pirate raids.

Colonial administration was a work of continuous oversight, microcosmically managed from the distant lagoon. The exhaustive detail of the state registers bears witness to the attention that Venice paid to the Stato da Mar. The millions of entries set out its preoccupations and obsessions. Here are precise instructions for galley fleets – when they can sail, how long they can land for, what they can sell – price incentives for shipping Cretan wheat, permits to trade, taxes for repairing city walls, accounts of corruption and street brawls, Turkish pirates and shipwrecks. Losses are lamented and blame apportioned. There are the persistent and endless demands for restitution. No detail seems too small for the telescopic vision of the state, recorded by inky clerks toiling in the windowless bowels of the doge's palace: a murder is documented in Constantinople; a Genoese privateer noted in the Cyclades; a hundred crossbowmen are ordered to Crete; 4,700 sacks of ship's biscuit must be prepared for the galleys; the chancellor of Negroponte has too much work; a courageous galley commander loses an arm in battle; the widow of the duke of Crete has purloined two gold cups and a carpet belonging to the state.

Proficium et honorem – profit and honour – are the two persistent accusatives that echo through the record of this colossal and exhaustive enterprise. If profit was the ultimate driver, the Republic gloried in the naming of its colonies and counted them proudly like gold ducats in a merchant's chest. It bestowed on them swelling titles that emphasised their structural importance – 'the Right Hand of our city', 'the Eyes of the Republic' – as if they were organic parts of the Venetian body. To its inhabitants Venice was less a few finite miles of cramped lagoon than a vast space, vividly imagined, extending 'wherever water runs', as if from the campanile of St Mark, distance were foreshortened and Corfu, Coron, Crete, Negroponte, the Ionian Isles and the Cyclades were plainly visible, like diamonds on a silk sea. Damage to the Stato da Mar was felt like a wound; losses like an amputation.

The Stato da Mar was the city's unique creation. If it drew on Byzantine tax structures, in all other respects its management was the reflection of Venice itself. The empire represented Europe's first full-blown colonial experiment. Held together by sea power, largely uninterested in the well-being of its subjects, centrifugal in nature and economically exploitative, it foreshadowed what was to come. It probably cost Venice more than was ever directly extracted in taxes, food and wine, but ultimately it was worth it. Beyond the produce and revenue, it provided the stepping stones across the eastern sea, the naval bases to protect its fleets, the stopping places for its galleys, the entrepôts and marts for storing goods, the back stations to retreat to in hard times. And this second wave of imperial expansion allowed Venice to do something else: to dominate, for a time, the trade of the world.

15

'Like Water in a Fountain'

1425–1500

A merchant galley bound for Alexandria in the fifteenth century sensed the coast long before it came into view. From far out, the sea was muddied by the outflow of Nile silt; at twenty-five or thirty miles a lookout could sight the crumbling lighthouse – the Pharos – the last surviving wonder of the ancient world, then the granite finger of Pompey's Pillar spiking the sea's rim; finally the city itself rose trembling out of the morning haze, glittering with marble, fringed with palm trees, like a vision of the East. Close to the shore, depending on the direction of approach, the vessel might pass a swimming hippopotamus washed out to sea and catch the hot blast of desert wind.

The ship would be quickly spotted. A signal flag on the harbour tower alerted port officials to row out and interrogate the approaching vessel as to its origin, cargo, passengers and crew. On deck they carried a bird cage. Having gathered the necessary information, they would release two carrier pigeons – one to the emir of Alexandria, a second marked with the special insignia of the Mamluk sultan himself, for his personal attention in Cairo 110 miles south. The vessel would then be allowed to proceed into harbour, where its rudder and sails were handed over, its passengers searched 'to our very shirts' by probing customs officers hunting for hidden ducats or gems, its merchandise unloaded, rummaged through and stored in bonded warehouses, landing fees and duty paid, and the new arrivals led wandering through the crowded streets to one of the *fondaci* – the secure lodging houses reserved for Christian visitors. Alexandria was the portal to another world.

The Venetians came to this landfall with centuries of experience. They were here, purportedly, in 828 when two enterprising merchants stole the body of St Mark; pilgrims to the city in the Middle Ages were shown the broad street where the saint was stoned and the church on whose site he was martyred and buried. The city and Egypt had an intense hold on the imagination of Venice; their motifs were brilliantly reproduced in the mosaics of St Mark's – palm trees and camels, deserts and Bedouin tents, Joseph sold into Egypt and the Pharos, reproduced in green and gold, ruby and blue. The city was both spiritually significant – it was here that the Bible was translated into Greek – and, like Constantinople, one of the great hubs of trade. Again and again over the centuries Venetian merchants had steered their ships east from Candia in search of risk and return. The traffic had been subject to frequent interruptions from crusades, papal bans and the shifting of trade routes further east. The relationship with the Fatimid and Mamluk dynasties of Egypt was always fraught, but the potential gains were huge.

By the time Andrea Giustinian stared at the melancholy ruins of Tana on the northern shores of the Black Sea in 1396, that great stream of trade from the furthest Orient was in the process of changing its course. For a hundred years, the Mongol trans-Asian highway and the markets of Persia had diverted the flow of goods north. By the end of the fourteenth century, the Mongol Empire had fragmented; in China it had been replaced by the Ming dynasty which turned its back on the outside world. The spice route reverted to its traditional southern path. Indian dhows trans-shipped their goods at Jeddah on the Arabian shore, from where they were ferried across the Red Sea in small coastal craft, landed on the Sinai peninsula and packed onto camel trains – 'so many I cannot give an account of them, laden' according to the Spaniard Pero Tafur, who claimed to have travelled this route, 'with spices, pearls, precious stones and gold, perfumes and linen and parrots and cats from India'.

Some of this wealth flowed north into the Syrian cities of

Damascus and Beirut. For most of it the destination was Cairo, from where goods were reloaded into flat-bottomed boats and floated down the Nile to Alexandria, the bridgehead with the infidel world. It was here, after the war of Chioggia, that Venice particularly concentrated its commercial efforts and proceeded to crush its rivals, not by warfare, but by patience, commercial acumen and superior organisation. In the century after the peace with Genoa in 1381, the Republic fine-tuned all the unique mechanisms of its mercantile system to dominate oriental trade. What came together was the potent combination of Venice's unique collective endeavour, maritime evolution and the flowering of commercial and financial techniques.

Trading was hard-wired into the Venetian psyche; its heroes were merchants, the myths that it constructed for itself accentuated these values. Its historians conjured a past trading golden age, when 'every man in Venice, both rich and poor, bettered his property . . . The sea was empty of robbers, and the Venetians brought goods to Venice, and merchants of all countries came to Venice and brought there merchandise of all kinds and took it back to their countries.' Its iconic moments were framed in commercial terms – the same chronicler, Martino da Canal, cast Dandolo's final rallying speech before the walls of Constantinople in 1204 in words that entwine religion and profits as conjoined values: 'Be valiant, and with the help of Jesus Christ, my lord St Mark and the prowess of your bodies, you shall tomorrow be in possession of the city, and you shall be rich.' The natural right to gain was the Venetian foundation myth.

By the Middle Ages, the mercantile republics of Italy had unshackled themselves from any lingering theological stigma attached to trade. Christ, rather than turning the money-changers out of the temple, could now be seen as a trader; piracy not usury was the Venetian idea of commercial sin. Profit was a virtue. 'The entire people are merchants,' observed a surprised visitor from feudal, land-holding Florence in 1346. Doges traded, so did artisans, women, servants, priests – anyone with a little cash in hand could loan it on a merchant venture; the oarsmen and sailors who worked the ships carried small quantities of merchandise stashed beneath their benches to hawk in foreign ports. Only colonial officials during their periods of office were excluded. There was no merchant guild in the city – the city was a merchant guild, in which political and economic forces were seamlessly merged. The two thousand Venetian nobles whose senatorial decrees managed the state were its merchant princes. The city expressed a development in human behaviour that struck outsiders forcefully with the shock of modernity and not without alarm. The purity of the place was unmissable, as if it expressed an entirely new phenomenon; 'It seems as if . . . human beings have concentrated there all the force of their trading,' reported Pietro Casola. As the diarist Girolamo Priuli bluntly put it, 'Money . . . is the chief component of The Republic.'

Venice was a joint-stock company in which everything was organised for fiscal ends. It legislated unwaveringly for the economic good of its populace, in a system that was continuously adjusted and tweaked. From the start of the fourteenth century it evolved a pattern of overseas trade, communally organised and strictly controlled by the state with the consistent aim of winning economic wars: 'Nothing is better to increase and enrich the condition of our city than to give all liberty and occasion that commodities of our city be brought here and procured here rather than elsewhere, because this results in advantage both to the state and to private persons.' It was through the application of sea power that it sought monopoly. A century of nautical revolution – the development of charts and compasses, novel steering systems and ship designs – had opened up new possibilities. From the 1300s ships were able to sail the short choppy seas of the Mediterranean in both summer and winter. A larger merchant galley was evolved, principally a sailing vessel with oars to manoeuvre in and out of ports and in adverse seas, which increased cargo sizes and cut journey times. A galley that could carry 150 tons below deck in the 1290s had enlarged to a carrier of 250 tons by the 1450s. This

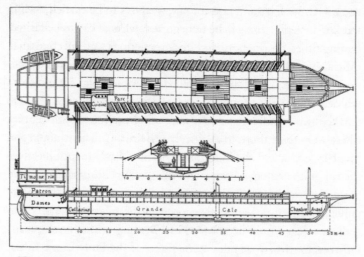

The merchant galley. Its central hold was adapted to form a dormitory
on pilgrim voyages to the Holy Land

galea grossa was heavy on manpower. It required a crew typically
of over two hundred, including 180 oarsmen who could also fight
and twenty specialist crossbowmen as a defence against pirates,
but it was comparatively fast, manoeuvrable and ideal for the safe
transport of valuable cargoes. Alongside these were the cogs and
carracks, high-sided sailing vessels manned by small crews, used
mainly for transporting bulk supplies, such as wheat, timber, cotton and salt. It was the sailing ships that provided the staples to
keep Venice alive; galleys coined the gold.

The merchant galleys, built in the arsenal, were property of the
state, chartered out by auction each year to bidders. The aim was
to manage entrepreneurial activity for the good of both people and
state and prevent internecine competition of the sort that wrecked
Genoa. Every detail of this system was strictly controlled. The
patrono (organiser) of the winning syndicate had to be one of the
two thousand nobles whose families were enrolled in the Golden
Book, the register of the Venetian aristocracy, but the sailing captain was a paid employee of the state, responsible for the ship's safe

return. Crew sizes and rates of pay, weapons to be carried, freight rates to be paid, goods to be transported, ports of call to be visited, sailing times, destinations and stopover periods were all stipulated. Maritime legislation was heavy and precise, as were the penalties for abuse. The galleys travelled set routes, like a timetabled service, the details of which, set down in the early 1300s, were to last for two hundred years. At the end of the fourteenth century there were four: those to Alexandria, Beirut, Constantinople and the Black Sea, and the long-range Atlantic haul, an arduous five-month round trip to London and Bruges. A century later this had expanded to seven, visiting all the major ports of the Mediterranean. After 1418 Venice also cornered the pilgrim market. Two galleys a year would depart for Jaffa carrying profitable shiploads of pious tourists to wonder at the sights of the Holy Land. In the fifteenth century Venetian galleys quartered the seas with high-value goods while cogs carried the bulk merchandise.

Venice's genius was to grasp the laws of supply and demand, based on centuries of mercantile activity, and to obey them with unmatched efficiency. The secret lay in regularity. Venetian merchants lived with an acute sense of time. The clocks in St Mark's Square and in the Rialto fixed the pattern of the working day. On a larger scale the annual pattern of voyaging was dictated by seasonal rhythms far beyond the confines of Europe. The metronomic cycle of monsoon winds over the Indian subcontinent set in motion a series of interconnecting trading cycles, like the meshing cogs in an enormous mechanism, which moved goods and gold all the way from China to the North Sea. Borne west on the autumn winds in the wake of the monsoon (the Arabic *mawsim*, a season), ships from India departed for the Arabian peninsula in September, carrying spices and the goods of the Orient. These would be trans-shipped to reach Alexandria and the marts of Syria in October. The Venetians' merchant convoys would depart for Alexandria in late August or early September, within a time slot rigorously dictated by the senate, reaching their destination a month later to coincide with the arrival of these goods. Beirut was set to the same rhythm. The duration of the stays was firmly fixed – Beirut usually twenty-eight days, Alexandria twenty – and enforced with severity. Return was set for mid-December, variable within a month for the hazards of winter navigation. With the snow on the mountains the great galleys would haul themselves back into Venice to mesh with another set of trading rhythms. German merchants, furred and booted, would jingle their way across the Brenner Pass from Ulm and Nuremberg with pack animals for the winter fair. The departure and arrival of the long-distance Flanders galleys would also be synchronised to interlock with this exchange and with the sturgeon season and the silk caravans at Tana.

What Venice had understood was the need for predictable delivery, so that foreign merchants drawn there could be confident that there would be desirable merchandise, worth the long haul over the Brenner Pass in the grip of winter. Venice made itself the destination of choice, profiting individually by the trades and as a state from the element of tax it extracted from the movement of all goods in and out. 'Our galleys must not lose time' was the axiom.

It was never a perfect system. There could be delays in the arsenal fitting out the vessels for departure, contrary winds, menacing pirates and political turmoil in any of the countries to which the galleys went to trade. The round trips had a reasonable predictability: three months to Beirut, five to Bruges. In exceptional circumstances, however, the time lags were immense. The shortest round trip on the Tana route was 131 days, the longest 284; in 1429 the Flanders galleys sailing on 8 March overwintered and did not tip the lagoon again until 25 February the following year. In cases of late return, the goods were almost always sequestered, so that when merchants arrived at Venice for the regular trade fairs they could be certain of a healthy stock of merchandise to buy. Customer satisfaction was the key.

Each route conformed to its own rhythm, and the Venetians conferred on these cyclical convoys the name of *muda*, a word which conveyed a complex set of meanings. The *muda* was both the season for buying and exchanging spices, and the merchant convoy that carried them. The various different *mude* played an emotional part in the annual round of the city's life. The city stirred into intense activity in the run-up to sailings. The arsenal worked overtime through the hot summer days ready for the Levant sailing; as the departure approached there would be a hubbub along the waterfront. Benches were set up for recruiting crews; merchandise and food, oars and sailing tackle were sorted, parcelled up and ferried out to the galleys anchored off shore. The voyage was blessed in St Mark's or the seafarers' church of St Nicholas on the Lido and the ships set sail watched by an intent crowd, for some of whom the enterprise contained their ready wealth. When the German pilgrim Felix Fabri left on a pilgrim galley in 1498 it was ceremonially decked out with banners;

... after the galley was dressed they began to get ready to start, because we had a fair wind, which was blowing the banners up high. The crew began with a loud noise to weigh up the anchors and take them on board, to hoist the yard aloft with the mainsail furled upon it, and to hoist up the galley's boats out of the sea; all of which was done with exceeding hard toil and loud shouts, till at last the galley was loosed from her moorings, the sails spread and filled with wind, and with great rejoicing we sailed away from the land: for the trumpeters blew their trumpets just as though we were about to join battle, the galley-slaves shouted, and all the pilgrims sang together 'We go in God's name' . . . the ship was driven along so fast by the strength of a fair wind, that within the space of three hours we . . . had only the sky and the waters before our eyes.

The ritual of departure, the crossing of the threshold of the lagoon to the open sea, were pivotal moments in the communal experience of Venetian people, as well as for outsiders. There was both excitement and apprehension. Wills were written. Some on board would not return.

The merchant galleys regularly carried a handful of young noblemen, recruited as crossbowmen, as apprentices learning the skills of trade and the seafaring life. For many of these 'nobles of the poop' this was their first overseas experience. When Andrea Sanudo was preparing for his first voyage to Alexandria in the late fifteenth century, his brother Benedetto gave him copious instructions on how to behave and what to expect and avoid. They ranged widely from behaviour on board ship – treat the captain with reverence, only play backgammon with the chaplain, how to cope with seasickness – to the perils of port life – avoid the prostitutes of Candia: 'they are infected with the French disease' – and eating quails in Alexandria.

There was much to learn, both cultural and commercial, about foreign parts. Andrea was advised to shadow the local Venetian agent: 'Always stay with him, learning to recognise every sort of spice and drug which will be of enormous benefit to you.' Information was as vital as cash to all merchants voyaging to lands where dealings might be conducted through an interpreter in unfamiliar weights, measures and currencies. Practical handbooks were compiled with trading information on all the concerns of the travelling merchants, and these were widely circulated. Local currency conversions, units of measure, the quality of spices, how to avoid fraud were all covered. One of these, the *Zibaldone da Canal*, reveals the difficulties of conducting dealings on a foreign shore. In Tunis, it helpfully explains,

. . . there are many kinds of money. There are two kinds of gold coins, the one is called *dopla* and is worth 5 *bezants*, and the *bezant* is worth 10 *miaresi*, so the *dopla* is worth 50 *miaresi*. And the other kind of gold coins is called the *masamutina*, which is worth half a *dopla*, and 2 *masamutina* are worth one *dopla*, and the *masamutina* is worth 2½ *bezants*. Accordingly, the *masamutina* is worth 25 *miaresi*.

Local weights and measures could be equally tough, with the wily Christian merchants of Lesser Armenia setting the ultimate challenge:

. . . wheat and barley is sold by a measure that is called *marzapane* and by the wish of the Armenians no one can truly tell from one month to another [what this measure might be] because no measure converts with this one, because it increases and decreases at their wish and so the merchants get out of it many times what they give.

An enormous amount of practical information was required: the quantity of fox furs, fish, matting, blocks of wood, lances or walnuts to be loaded in a barrel or bale, the measure for weighing English cloth from Stamford, the Venetian equivalents for olive oil measures in Alexandria or purple dye in Negroponte, the advantages of smuggling gold into Tunis, how to avoid fraud and appraise spices. Frankincense powder might be adulterated with marble dust; nutmegs should be 'big and firm . . . you want to pierce the shell with a needle, and if it yields water, it is good; and any other way is not worth anything . . . The reeds of cassia . . . should not make a sound when a man shakes them.' The merchant needed to be quick-witted, armed with a formidable memory (for which commercial courses were available) and an excellent grasp of practical arithmetic as he stepped blinking and groggy down the gangplank at the end of a long sea voyage.

For all Venetians – novices or old hands – the final destinations, be they Beirut or Tana, Alexandria or Bruges, were territories which they did not control. They traded on the erratic sufferance of foreign powers. Xenophobia, extortion, cheating, political upheavals and commercial rivalry made the merchant's life terribly insecure – even within the Christian lands. A colony could be sacked in London, as it was in the fifteenth century, but nowhere were the merchant venturers so exhaustingly tested as within the Muslim Levant. Dealings across the frontiers of faith were tensioned by mutual suspicion and the long back story of the crusades. Alexandria, which must have looked so fair to Andrea Sanudo on first sight when spied from out at sea, was a decaying place. 'Every day one house falls upon another, and the grand walls enclose miserable ruins,' wrote Felix Fabri in 1498. The cause of much of the devastation was the Christian sack of 1365 – an expedition which Venice had strenuously opposed, but for which it had been apportioned blame by the Mamluk sultan in Cairo. The process of exchange was edgy, fraught with suspicion on both sides, but neither could live without it. On the shores of the Levant in the Middle Ages Venice developed the first efficient operation of a world trade.

European merchants in Alexandria, Aleppo, Damascus or Beirut lived a barricaded life. Apart from their consul and a small group of long-term residents, they were generally forbidden to dwell outside their *fondaco* – a large enclosed complex of residential buildings provided for their security. Each nation had its own *fondaco* which contained sleeping quarters, warehousing, kitchens, bakery, a bath house, a chapel – and frequently quite extensive gardens, where exotic animals might roam. The Aragonese in Alexandria kept ostriches and a chained leopard in theirs in the 1480s. The sultan in Cairo provided these *fondaci* as a service for foreign traders. He wanted to keep his valuable customers safe from the potential hostility of the population, but he also wanted to control them. The key to the outer door was in the care of a Muslim keeper; overnight and during Friday prayers they were locked in from the outside. Within they could live the semblance of an embassy life; wine would be drunk (sometimes in the surreptitious company of visiting Muslims) and worse. When Fabri visited the Venetian *fondaco*, he was surprised to meet a large pig snuffling in the courtyard, which the Venetians kept out of contempt, but for which they paid the Sultan a handsome sum, 'otherwise the Saracens would not have allowed it to live and even worse, would have destroyed the house on account of the pig'. Provocations existed on both sides.

From the *fondaco*, the merchants went forth into the streets of Alexandria in the care of an interpreter to buy and sell. The negotiations were always tough, the abuses numerous. They started and ended with the welcome and farewell of the customs officials who were adept at random deductions, double taxation or confiscation. Scarlet cloth and Cretan cheeses were eyed particularly keenly. The process of spice dealing was fraught. Ascertaining the quality could be tricky, according to a merchant, as the Venetians bought in bulk often 'without sorting and without picking over . . . as they come from India, nor do they let us see beforehand what we are going to buy'. Both sides needed the deal but it was a game of brinkmanship. Knowing the fixed period of the *muda* – and senatorial decrees were peremptory in the matter – Egyptian merchants might wait until the last day to set the price, leaving no time to haggle, or the far worse prospect of returning empty-handed. The transaction could go down to the wire. Fabri watched the final trans-shipment of a spice deal. The giant sacks, five foot wide and fifteen foot long, lay on the quayside, watched by a jostling and intent crowd. The spices had been inspected, weighed and cleared from customs. The galleys were anchored off shore. The sailors rowed across in long boats to load up. At the last moment there was a sudden intervention:

And though all the sacks had just been filled and weighed at the *fondaco* in the presence of the Saracen officers, and examined at the gates, yet even now when they were just about to be taken on board, the whole contents were spilled out upon the ground so that they might see what was being taken away. And round about this place was a great press, and many came scurrying thither, for [when] the sacks . . . are emptied there comes hastening a crowd of poor folk, women and boys, Arabs and Africans, and whatever they can grab they steal, and they search in the sand for ginger and cloves, cinnamon and nutmegs.

On the other side, the Venetians were flinty opponents, well versed in the psychology of the deal. When Fabri and his fellow pilgrims tried to negotiate passage back to Venice with a sick boy, they found the sea captains 'harsher and more unreasonable in the price they asked than Saracens or Arabs, for some demanded from every pilgrim fifty ducats, and when we stuck at paying this, another proud captain said that he would not accept less than a hundred a man'. The boy died in port. The merchant class could be crafty and devious, expert at smuggling gems and gold from the probing officials, capable of embezzlement, tax evasion and

flight from a sealed bargain unless severely constrained by punitive Venetian law.

However, on foreign soil it was usually an unequal contest.
Despite trading agreements, the sultans might insist on arbitrarily fixing the prices. In 1419 a pepper price of 150–160 dinars a
unit was imposed in Alexandria, against the market rate of one
hundred. Sometimes Cairo would enforce purchase – or sale of
the goods the merchants had brought with them. In Syria the
Venetians often fared worse. Landing at Beirut, they travelled to
Damascus to buy. On return they might be attacked or the camel
and donkey drivers might steal part of their loads. Under the
strain of theft, abuse and rapacious extortion patience frequently
gave way. In 1407 all the Europeans in Damascus were imprisoned after a brawl; in 1410 they were bastinadoed. The Venetian
consul travelled repeatedly to Damascus to plead release of a
Venetian subject or to request fulfilment of agreed trading terms.
He might be met with understanding – or insouciance. When
a consul threatened the withdrawal of all Venetian merchants
from Alexandria, the sultan responded that 'as to the power of
you Venetians, and after that of the rest of Christendom, I hold
. . . it not so high as a pair of old shoes'. There was an element of
bluff within this – the Mamluks needed the influx of European
gold – but the abuses continued. Sometimes the consul himself
was beaten and imprisoned.

Driven to distraction, some of the trading nations retaliated.
The Genoese raided the coast of Syria; in 1426 a Catalan squadron attacked Alexandria. The Venetians kept their distance from
armed aggression but paid the price by association. In 1434 they
were all expelled from Syria and Egypt at a loss of a massive
235,000 ducats. Their strategy was patience and endless diplomacy. When their merchants were imprisoned they despatched
their long-suffering consul to Cairo; when goods were purloined
they made a claim; when the spices began to be unacceptably cut
with rubbish they used sieves; when the tension became unbearable they prepared to evacuate the whole community. For short

periods they suspended the galley service altogether. They faced down the avaricious Sultan Baybars in a long and intense arm-wrestle during the 1430s when he imposed a blanket price-fixing monopoly on the export of all spices, and they broke his attempt to impose his own gold currency on the deals: the purity and reliability of the ducat outgunned its rivals. Underneath was a calculation – that the unpopular Mamluk rulers needed the lucrative inflow of taxed gold to prop up their rule just as much as Venice needed the trade. And they never lashed out. When the Genoese sent armed galleys, Venice sent diplomats – again and again and again.

In the endless embassies to the potentates of the Levant the Republic deployed the consummate diplomatic skills that it had learned from the Byzantines and that would serve it well in all its long, entangled dealings with the Muslim world. They set aside bribery funds for the sultan and wooed him with sumptuous gifts and impressive shows of gravitas. No single image captures the exotic ritual of these diplomatic exchanges as vividly as the painting of the reception of the Venetian ambassadors at Damascus in 1508. The consul, wearing a red toga expressing the full majesty of the Most Serene Republic, presents his papers to the Mamluk governor, seated on a low dais, before a vast assemblage of Muslim dignitaries in conical red turbans and gowns of multicoloured silk. The setting, with its mosques, hyperreal sky and vivid trees, its attendant black servants and animals – monkeys, camels and deer – catches the note of rapt fascination the East held for Venice. This was a world of vivid sense impressions: the taste of a banana ('so exquisite it's impossible to describe'); the appearance of a giraffe, the beauty of Mamluk gardens. When the consul in question, Pietro Zen, was later caught in collusion with the Persians, an even more magnificent delegation was despatched to the sultan in Cairo.

The account reads like an extract from the *Arabian Nights*. The Venetians arrived with an entourage of eight trumpeters, dressed in scarlet, who proceeded to announce the ambassador's presence with a magnificent fanfare, but their show of splendour was clearly dwarfed by the audience in the sultan's palace.

We climbed the stairs and went into a room of the greatest magnificence – far more beautiful than the audience chamber of our Illustrious Signoria of Venice. The floor was covered with a mosaic of porphyry, serpentine, marble and other valuable stones, and this mosaic itself was covered by a carpet. The dais and the panelling were carved and gilded; the window grilles were bronze rather than iron. The sultan was in this room seated by a small garden planted with orange trees.

However, the new ambassador, Domenico Trevisan, obtained Zen's release with an impressive array of gifts, carefully chosen for the Mamluk taste: fifty brilliantly coloured robes in silk, satin and cloth of gold, seventy-five sable pelts, four hundred ermine pelts, fifty cheeses 'each one weighing eighty pounds'.

If the gifts were magnificent the underlying diplomatic principles were patience and unbending firmness: insist on the strict upholding of agreements; never give up on a claim, no matter how small; never leave an imprisoned subject unreleased; distance oneself from the wrongdoings of other nations – the piratical Catalans, the aggressive Genoese, the crusading Knights of St John; impose strict discipline on one's own subjects. Merchants were absolutely forbidden to buy in Egypt anywhere but Alexandria, to buy on credit, to enter into trading partnerships with Muslims. Any Venetian who cut and ran with an unpaid debt risked the safety and reputation of the whole trading community. Unlike the individualistic Genoese, the Venetian traders, all drawn from the same tight-knit squares and parishes, had a strong sense of group solidarity. They paid into a common insurance fund, the *cottimo*, by which the costs of extortion by Mamluk officials or fiscal penalties imposed on the colony as a whole were shared between its members. 'Like pigs', as the Florentine preacher had unflatteringly put it, they gathered together. Under the circumstances it was a virtue.

The running of the Levant trade was exhausting and risky – merchants faced ruin on an autocratic whim of the sultans. It required continuous oversight, endless senatorial debate, and it drove men to the edge. It was frequently discouraging, always unstable. When Pietro Diedo was sent on an embassy in 1489 his report was doleful in the extreme. The merchants 'meet with so many obstacles that they are pitiful to behold . . . I maintain that in this country . . . there is a greater abundance of pretence than of good results . . . Unless they find a remedy for the errors and extortions made in Alexandria, this country should be abandoned.' Diedo, like many of his countrymen, never came back. He died in Cairo.

But the diplomacy worked. Self-discipline, straight dealing and an appeal to reason over armed force won the grudging respect of the Cairo court – and a sideways glance from much of Christendom, as the Mamluks' friends. Decade by decade through the fifteenth century they inched ahead of their rivals. The regularity of their galley lines made the wheels of commerce turn. The *muda*'s arrival at Alexandria was as welcome to the Egyptians as was its return to the Germans. By 1417 Venice was the foremost trading nation in the eastern Mediterranean; by the end of the century they had crushed the competition. In 1487 there were only three *fondaci* left in Alexandria, the two Venetian and one Genoese; the other nations had withdrawn from the game. Venice beat Genoa, not so much at Chioggia, but in the long-drawn-out, unspectacular trade wars of the Levant. And the profits were huge: up to eighty per cent on cotton, sixty per cent on spices, when sold on to foreign merchants on the Rialto.

The winter spice fleets returning from the Levant, whose imminent arrival would be heralded by fast cutters, would be seen first from lookouts on the campanile of St Mark and welcomed home by the thunderous peal of church bells. The arrivals of the various *mude* – cotton cogs from Beirut, merchant galleys from Languedoc, Bruges, Alexandria or the Black Sea – slotted between the round of religious processions, feast days and historical remembrances, were great events in the cycle of the year. The Alexandria *muda*, putting in some time between 15 December and

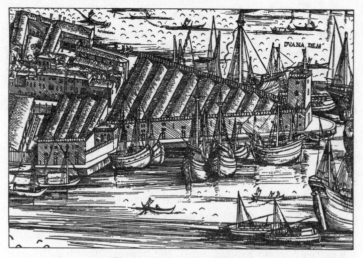

The maritime customs house

15 February, sparked off an intense period of commercial activity. Swarms of small boats put out to welcome the galleys home; everything had to be landed at the maritime customs house – the *dogana da mar* – on the point jutting out into the Basin of St Mark. The word *dogana* (divan) was an exotic Arabic import like the goods it contained. No bales could be landed until they had paid the import tax (between three and five per cent) and been stamped with its seal – though abuses were numerous.

Throughout all the centuries of port life, the Basin of St Mark was a chaotic, colourful theatre of maritime activity. The Venetians treated it as an industrial machine, outsiders were just amazed. The landscape of spars and masts, rigging and oars, barrels and bales dumped on quaysides, the hubbub of ships and merchandise, was celebrated in the great panoramas of Venetian painting, from fifteenth-century woodcuts jammed with detail to the bright seascapes of Canaletto in the eighteenth. Venice was a world of ships. The literal-minded Canon Casola tried to count them, starting with gondolas, but gave up, having already excluded from his count 'the galleys and *navi* for navigating long distances because they are numberless . . . There is no city equal to Venice as regards the number of ships and the grandeur of the port.'

Once taxed and cleared through customs, goods were loaded onto lighters, ferried up the Grand Canal and landed at the Rialto or unloaded into barred ground-floor warehouses, via the water gates of the palaces of the merchant princes. It was the Rialto, situated at the mid-point of the wide S-bend of the Grand Canal, that comprised the centre of the whole commercial system. Its wooden bridge was the only crossing point in the fifteenth century. Here was Venice's second customs house – the *dogana da terra* – where all the goods floated down the rivers of Italy or packhorsed across the Alpine passes arrived by barge. This meeting point became the axis and turntable of world trade. It was, as the diarist Marino Sanudo put it, 'the richest place on earth'.

The abundance dazzled and confounded. It seemed as if everything that the world might contain was unloaded here, bought and sold, or repackaged and re-embarked for sale somewhere else. The Rialto, like a distorted reflection of Aleppo, Damascus or medieval Baghdad, was the souk of the world. There were quays for unloading bulk items: oil, coal, wine, iron; warehouses for flour and timber; bales and barrels and sacks that seemed to contain everything – carpets, silk, ginger, frankincense, furs, fruit, cotton, pepper, glass, fish, flowers – and all the human activity that animated the quarter; the water jammed with lighters and gondolas, the quays thronged by boatmen, merchants, spice garblers (examiners), porters, customs officials, foreign merchants, thieves, pickpockets, prostitutes and pilgrims; on the quaysides a casual spectacle of chaotic unloading, shouting, hefting and petty theft.

This was the bazaar of Europe and the historic location of Venice's founding myth. It was held that Venice was established here on Friday 25 March 421, at noon precisely, by the site of the Church of San Giacomo di Rialto, the merchants' church, said to have been built the same year. An inscription on its walls sternly enjoined probity and fair dealing: 'Around this temple let the merchant's law be just, his weights true and his promises faithful.' The square beside the church was the centre of international commerce, 'where all the business of the city – or rather, of the world – was transacted'. Here the proclamations of the state were read out and the bankers, seated at long tables, entered deposits and payments in their ledgers, and transferred by bills of exchange considerable sums from one client to another without the least movement of actual cash; here the public debt was quoted and the daily price of spices compiled, set forth in lists and distributed to the many merchants – both resident and foreign. Unlike the bawl of the retail markets, everything was conducted demurely in a low voice, as befitted the honour of Venice: 'no voice, no noise . . . no discussion . . . no insults . . . no disputes'. In the loggia opposite, they had a painted map of the world, as if to confirm that all its trade might be imagined here and a clock that 'shows all the moments of time to all the different nations of the world who assemble with their goods in the famous piazza of Rialto'. The Rialto was the centre of international trade: to be banned from it was to be excluded from commercial life.

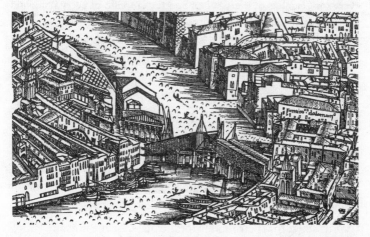

The Rialto to the left of its wooden bridge. The German *fondaco* is the named building on the right.

From this epicentre radiated all the trades, activities and exchanges that made Venice the mart of the world. On the Rialto Bridge were displayed news of *muda* sailings and the announcement of galley auctions, which were conducted by an auctioneer standing on a bench and timed by the burning of a candle. Across the canal the Republic lodged its German merchants in their own *fondaco*, and managed them almost as carefully as they themselves were by the Mamluks; around lay the streets of specialist activities – marine insurance, goldsmithing, jewellery. It was the sheer exuberance of physical stuff, the evidence of plenty that overwhelmed visitors such as the pilgrim Pietro Casola. He found the area around the Rialto Bridge 'inestimable ... It seems as if all the world flocks there.' Casola tried to see it all, rushing from site to site, stunned by the quantities, the colours, the size, the variety, and recording his impressions in dizzying and ever expanding superlatives:

... what is sold elsewhere by the pound and the ounce is sold there by the *canthari* and sacks of a *moggio* each ... so many cloths of every make – tapestry, brocades and hangings of every design, carpets of every sort, camlets of every colour and texture, silks of every kind; and so many warehouses full of spices, groceries and drugs, and so much beautiful white wax! These things stupefy the beholder, and cannot be fully described to those who have not seen them.

The sensuous exuberance of the Rialto hit outsiders like a physical shock.

From here Venice controlled an axis of exchange that ran from the Rhine valley to the Levant and influenced trade from Sweden to China, funnelling goods across the world system: Indian pepper to England and Flanders, Cotswold wool and Russian furs to the Mamluks of Cairo; Syrian cotton to the burghers of Germany; Chinese silk to the mistresses of Medici bankers, Cyprus sugar for their food; Murano glass for the mosque lamps of Aleppo; Slovakian copper; paper, tin and dried fish. In Venice there was a trade for everything, even ground-up mummies from the Valley of the Kings, sold as medicinal cures. Everything spun off the turntable of the Rialto and was despatched again by the *muda* to another port or across the lagoon, up the rivers and roads of central Europe. And on every import and export the Republic levied its share of tax. 'Here wealth flows like water in a fountain,' wrote Casola. All it actually lacked was passable drinking water. 'Although the people are placed in the water up to the mouth they often suffer from thirst.'

In the 1360s Petrarch had marvelled at the ability of the Venetians to exchange goods across the vast expanses of the world. 'Our wines sparkle in the cups of the Britons,' he wrote, 'our honey is carried to delight the taste of the Russians. And hard though it is to believe, the timber from our forests is carried to the Egyptians and Greeks. From here, oil, linen and saffron reach Syria, Armenia, Arabia and Persia in our ships, and in return various goods come back.' The great man had grasped the genius of Venetian trade, even if he was poetically hazy about the details. (The honey was coming from Russia.) A century later, this process had reached its fruition. Its merchants were everywhere – buying, selling, bargaining, negotiating, avid for profit, single-minded and ruthless, exploiting whatever opportunities existed for coining gold. They had even cornered the market in holy relics. The theft of bones – dubious yellowing skulls, hands, whole corpses or dissected pieces (forearms, feet, fingers, locks of hair) – along with material objects attached to the life of Christ added respect to the city and enhanced its potential for the lucrative tourist pilgrim trade. St Mark in 828 was followed by a long list of looted body parts, many of which were acquired during the Fourth Crusade, and which made Venice a stopover of particular attraction for the pious. (So plentiful was this collection of human fragments that the Venetians became hazy about what they had: the head of St George was retrieved from a cupboard in the Church of San Giorgio Maggiore by the American scholar Kenneth Setton in 1971.)

The visual city had become a place of wonder. To float down the Grand Canal past the great palazzos of the merchant princes,

The Ca' d'Oro

such as the Ca' d'Oro shimmering in the sun with its covering of gold leaf, was to be exposed to an astonishing drama of activity, colour and light. 'I saw four-hundred-ton vessels pass close by the houses that border a canal which I hold to be the most beautiful street,' wrote the Frenchman Philippe de Commynes. To attend mass in St Mark's or witness one of the great ceremonial rituals that punctuated the Venetian year – the Sensa or the inauguration of a doge, the appointment of a captain-general of the sea, the blaring of trumpets, the waving of red-and-gold banners, the parading of prisoners and captured war trophies; to witness the guilds, clergy and all the appointed bodies of the Venetian Republic in solemn procession around St Mark's Square – such theatrical displays seemed like the manifestations of a state that was uniquely blessed. 'I have never seen a city so triumphant,' declared Commynes. It all rested on money.

Nothing would have confirmed Petrarch's view of Venetians' material obsessions so much as the journey of Giosafat Barbaro, a merchant and diplomat who set out from Tana with 120 labourers to search a Scythian burial mound on the steppes for treasure. In 1447 he travelled by sledge up the frozen rivers, but 'found the ground so hard we were constrained to forgo our enterprise'. Returning the following year, the workmen dug a deep cutting into the artificial hill. They were disappointed to find only a great depth of millet husks, carp scales and some fragmentary artefacts: 'beads as big as oranges made of brick and covered with glass . . . and half of a handle of a little ewer of silver with an adder's head on top'. They were again defeated by the weather. Barbaro's men had dug into a rubbish tip. They had missed by a few hundred yards the burial chamber of a Scythian princess, adorned with enough jewellery to ignite all their wildest Venetian dreams of oriental gold. It was not discovered until 1988.

16

City of Neptune

In 1500, an exact half-millennium after Doge Orseolo embarked on his voyage of conquest, the Venetian artist Jacopo de' Barbari published an immense and spectacular map, almost three metres long. The angle of vision is giddily tilted to present a bird's-eye view of Venice impossible to human perspective before the invention of flight. From a thousand feet up, Barbari calmly laid out the city in huge and naturalistic detail. The woodcut panorama was based on careful surveys conducted from the city's campaniles. It shows everything: the churches, squares and waterways, the doge's palace, St Mark's and the Rialto, the customs house and the German *fondaco*, and the lazy S-shaped meander of the Grand Canal spanned at its centre by the one wooden bridge.

Despite the level of detail, the map is not quite a factual record. De' Barbari tweaked the perspective to emphasise the marine appearance of the place, so that it looks like an open-mouthed dolphin with its distinctive fish tail at the eastern end. Like the visual propaganda of the city – its buildings and banners, its elaborate rituals, feast days and festivals – the map is a work of profound intention. De' Barbari's Venice is a city of ships, a celebration of maritime prosperity. On the auspicious anniversary it trumpets the glorious ascent from muddy swamp to the richest place on earth. The city appears immortal, as if abstracted from the erosions of time. There are almost no people visible, none of the hubbub and jostle of trade. It displays wealth without human effort.

The lagoon itself is tranquil, just lightly stirred by benign winds blown by the breath of cherubs to speed the fleets on their prosperous way. Tubby sailing ships, fat as jugs, ride at anchor on taut hawsers in all states of readiness: some are fully rigged, some are demasted, others are chocked up in dry dock or tilted on their sides; aerodynamic galleys, raked back and low, lie beside them; on the *Bucintoro*, symbol of the marriage with the sea, the figure of Justice stands, sword in hand, erect in the prow; a merchant ship is being towed up the Grand Canal. Around the ocean-going craft, a host of little vessels skim the woodcut ripples. All the permutations of Venetian rowing styles are on show: a regatta of four-man racing craft; the flat-bottomed lagoon skiffs rowed by two men; gondolas poled by one; small sailing boats like beaked Phoenician traders laden with produce from the vegetable gardens of the lagoon. The mainland has been pushed back, as if irrelevant.

The map is presided over by benign gods. At the top, the tutelary deity of Venice is Mercury, god of trade, proclaiming with a semicircular sweep of his hand the message, 'I, Mercury, shine down favourably on this above all other places of commerce'; underneath the portentous date: 1500. But it is Neptune who really catches the eye at the centre of the map. The powerful muscled figure rides a scaly and snouted dolphin; from his trident, held aloft to the skies, the message proclaims: 'I, Neptune, reside here, watching over seas and this port.' It is a triumphant statement of maritime power. In de' Barbari's image the city is at its peak.

The ships so carefully portrayed, whose number the pilgrim Pietro Casola was unable to count, were Venice's life blood. Everything that the city bought, sold, built, ate or made, came on a ship – the fish and the salt, the marble, the weapons, the oak palings, the looted relics and the old gold; de' Barbari's woodblocks and Bellini's paint; the ore to be forged into anchors and nails, the Istrian stone for the palaces of the Grand Canal, the fruit, the wheat, the meat, the timber for oars and the hemp for rope; visiting merchants, pilgrims, emperors, popes and plagues. No state in the world occupied itself so obsessively with managing the business of the sea. A sizeable proportion of the male

City of Neptune

population earned their living there; all ranks and classes partici-pated, from the noble shipowners down to the humblest oarsman. When the doge Tommaso Mocenigo gave his deathbed oration in 1423 he counted up the Republic's maritime resources, albeit with some element of exaggeration: 'In this city there are three thousand vessels of smaller burden, which carry seventeen thou-sand seamen; three hundred large ships, carrying eight thousand seamen; five-and-forty galleys constantly in commission for the protection of commerce, which employ eleven thousand seamen, three thousand carpenters, three thousand caulkers.'

In de' Barbari's map the single most prominent structure is the immense walled enclosure of the state arsenal at the tail of the

The arsenal

dolphin. It had grown in size continuously over three hundred years with the maritime requirements of the Republic. By 1500 the sixty-acre site, enclosed by blind fifty-foot-high brick walls topped with battlements, comprised the largest industrial complex in the world. It was capable of building, arming, provisioning and launching eighty galleys at a speed and a level of consistency unmatched by any rival. The 'Forge of War' manufactured all the maritime apparatus of the Venetian state. It provided dry and wet docks, hangars for building and storing galleys, carpenters' workshops, rope and sail factories, forges, gunpowder mills, lumber yards, and storehouses for every component of the process and the associated equipment.

By continuous refinement the Venetians had evolved something as close to assembly-line production as was possible given the organisational resources of a medieval state. The key concepts were specialism and quality control. Skill separation was critical, from the woodmen growing and selecting trees in distant forests, through the master shipwrights, sawyers, carpenters, caulkers, smiths, rope weavers and sail makers down to the general labourers who carried and fetched. Each team's work was the subject of rigorous inspection. Venice knew well that the sea was an unforgiving judge, gnawing iron, rotting cables, testing seams, shredding sailcloth and rigging. Strict regulations were in place governing the quality of materials. The bobbin of each hemp spinner was marked so that the work could be individually identified; every rope that emerged from the ropewalk was tagged with a coloured label, indicating the use to which it could reliably be put. The care with which the Signoria oversaw each stage of production was a reflection of its understanding of the marine life. A ship, its crew and thousands of ducats of valuable merchandise could founder on shoddy work. For all the mythological rhetoric, Venice rested on profoundly material facts. It was a republic of wood, iron, rope, sails, rudders and oars. 'The manufacture of cordage', it was declared, 'is the security of our galleys and ships and similarly of our sailors and capital.' The state made unconditional demands; its caulkers should be accountable for split seams, its carpenters for snapped masts. Poor work was punishable with dismissal.

The arsenal was physically and psychologically central to Venice. Everyone was reminded of 'the House of Work' on a daily basis by the ringing of the *marangona*, the carpenter's bell, from the campanile in St Mark's Square to set the start and end of the working day. Its workers, the *arsenalotti*, were aristocrats among working men. They enjoyed special privileges and a direct relationship with the centres of power. They were supervised by a team of elected nobility and had the right to carry each new doge around the piazza on their shoulders; they had their own place in state processions; when the admiral of the arsenal died, his body was borne into St Mark's by the chief foremen and twice raised in the air, once to betoken his acceptance of his responsibilities and again his fulfilling of them. The master shipwrights, whose skills and secret knowledge were often handed down through the generations, were jealously guarded possessions of the Venetian state.

The arsenal lent to the city an image of steely resolve and martial fury. The blank battlements that shut out the world were patrolled at night by watchmen who called to each other every hour; over its intimidating gateway the lion of St Mark never had an open book proclaiming peace. It was firmly closed: the arsenal lion was ready for war. The industry of the place amazed visitors. When Pietro Casola came in 1494 he saw in the munitions store 'covered and uncovered cuirasses, swords, crossbows, large and small arrows, headpieces, arquebuses, and other artillery'; in each of the large sheds used for galley storage there were twenty compartments, holding

. . . one galley only, but a large one, in each compartment; in one part of the arsenal there was a great crowd of masters and workmen who do nothing but build galleys or other ships of every kind . . . there are also masters continually occupied in making crossbows, bows and large and small arrows . . . in one covered place there are twelve masters each one with his workmen and his forge apart; and they labour continually making anchors and every kind of iron-work . . . then there is a large and spacious room where there are many women who do nothing but make sails . . . [and] a beautiful contrivance for lifting any large galley or other ship out of the water.

And he saw the Tana, the rope-making factory, a narrow hall a thousand feet long, 'so long that I could hardly see from one end to the other'.

The arsenal worked on a just-in-time basis; it dry-stored all the components of galley construction in kit form for rapid assembly in times of war. Orderly arrangement was critical. To despatch a fleet of war galleys at short notice, the arsenal might be holding five thousand rowing benches and footbraces, five thousand oars, three hundred sails, a hundred masts and rudders, rigging, pitch, anchors, weapons, gunpowder and everything else required for quick deployment. The Spanish traveller Pero Tafur saw the fitting-out of a squadron of galleys in double-quick time during the summer of 1436: one by one hulls were launched into the basin where teams of carpenters fitted the rudders and masts. Tafur then watched as each galley passed down an assembly line channel:

... on one side are windows opening out of the houses of the arsenal, and the same on the other side, and out came a galley towed by a boat, and from the windows they handed out of them, from one the cordage, from another the bread, from another the arms, and from another the ballistas and mortars, and so from all sides everything which was required, and when the galley had reached the end of the street all the men required were on board, together with the complement of oars, and she was equipped from end to end. In this manner there came out ten galleys, fully armed, between the hours of three and nine.

The arsenal produced not only ships of war but also the state-owned merchant galleys that formed the regular *muda* runs. For Venice, shipping was binary, a deeply understood set of alternatives. There were oared galleys and sailing ships; war galleys and great galleys; private vessels and state-owned ones; armed and disarmed vessels – not so much an opposition between fighting and merchant vessels, because merchant galleys could be used in war, and all ships carried a certain quantity of weapons – more an understanding as to whether a vessel was to sail out with a full complement of men, heavy armour, arquebuses and trained crossbowmen, or not. The state attended closely to their management. A maritime code was first introduced in 1255 and continuously refined. There were laws

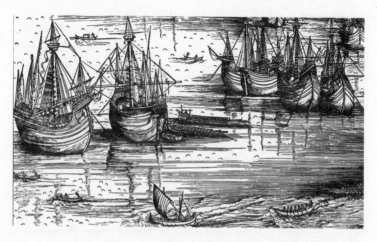

Round ships and galleys in the Basin of St Mark

about loading, crew sizes, the quantity of arms to be carried, the duties and responsibilities of captains and other sea-going officials, taxes to be paid and the managing of disputes.

Every ship had a specified carrying capacity – calculated by mathematical formula in the fifteenth century – and a load line was marked on its side, a forerunner of the Plimsoll line. Before departure, ships were inspected to ensure that they were legally loaded, with a crew adequate to their size and the requisite quantity of weapons. Such regulations could be minutely fine-tuned according to circumstance; when ships were obliged to carry more arms by the law of 1310, they were permitted to load just one inch deeper; from 1291 hats were ordered to replace hoods as protective military headgear; when it became practice on large sailing ships mechanically to compress lightweight bulky loads, such as cotton, with screws or levers, the dangers of damage both to goods and hull became subject to legislation. Maritime law then distinguished between loading by hand and by screw, with the limits on mechanical loading fixed according to the ship's age.

The business of the sea was managed as consistently as the Stato da Mar itself – by regulation, continuous oversight and recourse to law. These hallmarks of the Venetian system, widely admired by outsiders for its good order and sense of justice, ran through all its maritime arrangements. They replicated in miniature all the characteristic workings of the whole state and were closely attended to by the doge and ducal council. Sets of elected officials monitored, inspected, organised and fined both the state and the private sectors: they inspected crews, checked cargoes and collected custom and freight dues, rated loading capacities and handled legal disputes between shippers, masters and crew.

State-controlled voyages were organised at the highest level by elected officials of the Great Council, the central governing body of Venice. The *savii*, as they were called, planned the *mude* for the coming year, based on a continuous stream of intelligence about threats of war, the political stability of destinations, the state of markets and food stocks and the level of piracy. Their remit was wide. They could stipulate fleet sizes, routes, landing stages, durations of stops, freights to be carried and freight rates. Conditions would be most onerous with regard to high-value cargoes – the transportation of cloth, cash, bullion or spices – and the conveying of important state functionaries, ambassadors and foreign dignitaries. No leasing consortium could refuse to load legitimate freight from any merchant. Even after the vessels had been leased, the ships and their crews could be peremptorily requisitioned in the event of war. The state appointed its own official on merchant galleys, the *capitano*, the nautical and military leader of the fleet, tasked with protecting the Republic's property and the lives of its citizens. Everyone on board down to the lowliest oarsman was contracted to the venture by sworn oath.

The regulation, the safety measures, the quality controls in the materials production in the arsenal, the attempts to legislate against human fallibility, fraud, exploitation and greed were founded on long experience of voyaging. The sea was a taskmaster that could turn profit into plunging loss, safety into extreme danger on a shift of the wind. Nothing made the Venetian system shudder more than dramatic cases of failure. In the spring of 1516, the *Magna*, an older merchant galley, was being fitted out for the Alexandria run. From March to July it was in the arsenal undergoing an examination of the hull. There was unanimous agreement that the vessel was dangerous; it needed repairs for which the hiring consortium was reluctant to pay, and they were anxious not to miss the spice fairs. The arsenal authorities finally permitted departure, with the empty assurance that it would be repaired further down the Adriatic at Pola. The *Magna* sailed on past Pola, carrying, amongst other things, a cargo of copper bars that may or may not have overloaded the vessel. It probably had a crew of about two hundred.

On 22 December, 250 miles off Cyprus, the *Magna* hit a storm and started to ship water. As it thrashed in the rolling sea, the copper bars broke loose and tumbled across the hold; at dawn the following day the vessel broke up into three parts. There was an instant rush for the ship's boat, which quickly became over-loaded. Some managed to scramble aboard, others were forcibly prevented with drawn swords. The late arrivals slipped back into the sea and drowned. There were now eighty-three men crammed onto a raft of death. They contrived a rudder and crude sails from sacks, spars and oars, and tried to sail to Cyprus. For a week they tossed violently day and night on a tempestuous sea 'with waves as tall as St Mark's'. They had no food or water. One by one the men started to die of hunger, thirst and cold. They drank their own urine and ate the shirts off their backs; they started to hal-lucinate: they saw saints carrying bright candles across the sky. Civilisation collapsed. 'And perhaps', it was elliptically explained in a letter from Cyprus, 'some went to alleviate the hunger of others, and they had already resolved to kill the little ship's clerk, because he was young, fat and juicy, to drink his blood.' On the eighth day they sighted land but were too weak to choose a safe landing spot. Some drowned in the swell; the rest crawled ashore on their knees. Of the original eighty-three, fifty were still alive. 'A young Soranzo has survived,' it was reported, 'but he is only holding onto life by the skin of his teeth, and the *patrono*, the noble Vicenzo Magno, but he is very sick and likely to die . . . certain of the other survivors will present the boat as an offering of the True Cross, and some will go on a barefoot pilgrimage to one place, others to another. All have made various vows.' The writer of the letter drew sober conclusions:

. . . this is a most wretched event. Sea voyages entail too many grave dangers, and it's all through greed for money. By what passage I shall come home, I can't tell you. Again this morning I had mass said to the Holy Spirit and Our Lady, because my fear of travelling in old galleys is so great, having seen the wreck of the one bound for Alexandria..

Despite de' Barbari's Neptune, Venetians were always ambiv-alent about the sea; it was both the cornerstone of their exist-ence and their fate. They believed they owned it all the way to

Crete and Constantinople, but it was also dangerous, infinite and unappeased – 'a zone that it is boundless and horrifying to behold', wrote Cristoforo da Canal, an experienced captain of the sixteenth century. If the Sensa was a claim to possession, its subtext was fear. Storm, shipwreck, piracy and war remained cardinal facts. The galley life was particularly hard and increasingly unwelcome as the centuries went on. The sense of shared purpose had begun to fragment. The status of the *galeotti* – the oarsmen sitting at the narrow benches in all weathers – declined steadily with a growing specialism of roles on ships and an aggregation of wealth and power among the noble class. They existed on a diet of wine, cheese, coarse bread, ship's biscuit and vegetable soup. With the nautical revolution, the development of winter sailings worsened their lot – Pisani's sailors, frostbitten and underfed, died of cold. Wages were pitiful; they were made up by the opportunity to trade on their own initiative on the merchant galleys: each man was permitted to carry on board a sack or chest.

In the war galleys, the captains who commanded respect, such as Vettor Pisani and the maverick Benedetto Pesaro a century later, understood what a man at the oars needed to live. A tolerable diet, protection from the worst of winter sailings and the chance to seize booty would win enduring loyalty from the men of the bench. For commanders who would share their food and the perils of battle they would go through hell. It was the galley crews who hammered on the door of the council chamber to free Pisani and who demanded his coffin; for more standoffish aristocrats they occasionally went on strike. They wanted comradeship, identity and a shared destiny. Their patriotism to St Mark was unbounded; when Venetian sea power faced its ultimate test in 1499 it would not be the men of the bench who failed.

By the late fifteenth century, they formed a veritable underclass; many on the merchant galleys were debt slaves to the captains, though rarely chained, and as the Black Death thinned the Venetian population they were increasingly drawn from the colonies. The Dalmatian coast and the shores of Greece were a crucial resource of raw manpower. The German pilgrim Felix Fabri observed their lot closely on the galleys to the Holy Land in 1494:

There are a great many of them, and they are all big men; but their labours are only fit for asses, and they are urged to perform them by shouts, blows and curses. I have never seen beasts of burden so cruelly beaten as they are. They are frequently forced to let their tunics and shirts hang from their girdles, and work with bare backs, arms and shoulders, that they may be reached with whips and scourges. These galley slaves are for the most part the bought slaves of the captain, or else they are men of low station, or prisoners, or men who have run away. Whenever there is any fear of their making their escape, they are secured to their benches by chains. They are so accustomed to their misery that they work feebly and to no purpose unless someone stands over them and curses them. They are fed most wretchedly, and always sleep on the boards of their rowing benches, and both by day and night they are always in the open air ready for work, and when there is a storm they stand in the midst of the waves. When they are not at work they sit and play at cards and dice for gold and silver, with execrable oaths and blasphemies . . .

The good friar was most vexed by the swearing. Protection from his crew was one of the contractual obligations that the captain of a merchant galley had to his pilgrim passengers.

Insecurity was built into the seafaring life; any encounter with an unrecognised ship might cause alarm. In situations of uncertainty, galleys would enter a foreign port backwards, crossbowmen covering the shore with cranked bows, the oarsmen ready to pull out at a blast of the whistle. With the decline of the Byzantine Empire, piracy, always endemic to the Mediterranean, had a ratcheting effect on the maritime system. After 1300, freebooting Catalans, ousted Genoese factions, Greeks, Sicilians, Angevins – and increasingly Turks from the coasts of Asia Minor – turned the sea into a free-for-all. In 1301, all vessels were ordered to augment their armed defences; in 1310, state galleys had to enrol twenty per cent of their crew as bowmen. The crew were all expected to fight and were issued with weapons; laws required the provision of specified quantities of plate armour. The *muda* system, where merchant galleys travelled in convoy, was introduced to ensure a level of mutual defence. Their sizeable crews – about two hundred men – were a deterrent to all but a squadron of Genoese war galleys. It was the lone private sailing ship that was more likely to be picked off by pirates lurking in a passing cove. For Venice, piracy was the most detested crime, an affront to business and the rule of law. The Republic preferred its maritime violence organised at state level. The registers minute thousands of instances of robbery or dubious confiscation of cargoes under pretext, followed by demands for restitution from other states held responsible for the actions of its citizens, but at sea it was frequently the survival of the fittest.

Cleansing the waters of pirates was the duty of both war fleets and merchant galleys. The contests were bloody and punishments exemplary. Captured pirates would be chopped up on their own decks or hanged from their masts, their ships burned. Retribution was particularly ferocious against Christian subjects of the Stato da Mar, but the fate of a detested Turkish pirate in 1501 probably made even the tough-minded Venetians pause. The captain-general of the sea, Benedetto Pesaro, wrote to explain his fate.

The Turkish pirate, Erichi, chanced to land on Milos, returning from Barbary. His ship ran aground on the island during a storm. There were 132 Turks on board. He was captured alive with thirty-two of them. The others drowned or were killed by the people of the island, but we kept hold of him. On 9 December we roasted Erichi alive on a long oar. He lived for three hours in this agony. In this way he ended his life. Also we impaled the pilot, mate and a *galeotto* from Corfu, who betrayed his faith. We shot another with arrows and then drowned him ... Erichi the pirate caused considerable damage to our shipping during peacetime.

By way of further explanation, Pesaro went on to recount that Erichi's ghastly end was revenge exacted for similar inflicted on a Venetian nobleman.

For dashing Venetian galley commanders pirate hunting could almost be a sport. In February 1519 Zuan Antonio Taiapiera wrote to his brother about his recent exploits:

It was the feast day of St Paul, which was the 25th of last month. At dawn I spied the *fusta* [small galley] of Moro de la Valona, one mile off Durazzo, and I went towards it. The ship fled back into the lee of Durazzo. As it ran, I discharged two shots from my cannon but failed to hit it. When I saw it had reached the walls, I turned my stern about to follow my route to Corfu. But they [the pirates] wanting to avenge themselves for another ship, destroyed at Cape Cesta, boarded as many brave men as they thought the galley needed, and started to chase me. When I saw their pursuit, I prepared my ship and retreated five miles out to sea, and there the two sides attacked each other so fiercely that the battle lasted seven or eight hours, and I cut them all to pieces. Among the dead was il Moro and four other captains of the *fuste* . . . On my galley there were seven dead, ninety-three wounded, but only three of these critically, among whom was my chief bombardier whom I killed [as an act of mercy]. The others were also badly wounded. They will lose their eyes or be lame, but we hope they will survive. I have only one lance wound on my thigh, which has only slightly wounded me though it was a heavy enough blow. But I was satisfied that in the last attack they leaped on my prow and with my own hands I slaughtered two of them – it was then they struck me with a pike. I have seized the castanets, drums, banners – and the head of il Moro, which I shall rightfully display on my prow.

As a more permanent memorial than the rotting head, Taiapiera asked his brother particularly to 'have a banner made for me with fields of yellow and blue, separated by a third dotted with turbans, and make it big, and send it at the first opportunity to Corfu, so that I will have it for the first of May for the parade'. He was certainly going to advertise this success.

Travelling by ship was everyday life for many Venetians, too familiar to be described in detail. It was outsiders who provided the most vivid accounts of the Venetian experience of seafaring life towards the end of the Middle Ages, particularly landlubber pilgrims on their way to the Holy Land, such as the German monk Felix Fabri and the Florentine Pietro Casola. Fabri, insatiably curious, made the voyage twice and recorded all the alarms and mood swings of the voyage.

Venice ran regular sailings to the Holy Land in adapted merchant galleys, which, keen to preserve its good name and aware of the unscrupulous instincts of noble captains, it regulated with care. It provided a kind of package service with food provided and transport between Jaffa and Jerusalem included. It was backed up by legal contract. All the same, the each-way voyage of five to six weeks was a form of purgatory – and at times a glimpse of hell. The pilgrims were housed in a long unlighted hold beneath the main deck where each slept in a space eighteen inches wide, with the stench of the bilges below and smoke seeping through the deck from the kitchen above. Nights below deck were foetid and foul, 'right evil and smouldering hot and stinking' one English pilgrim called the experience, what with the cries and groans of fellow passengers, the unfamiliar motion of the rolling ship, the smell of vomit and urine from upturned chamber pots, arguments, fights, bedbugs and fleas.

Storms, when they came, were abrupt and shattering. In June 1494, Casola's galley off the coast of Dalmatia was hit by a rising sea and driven seventy miles west to the tip of Italy. Down in their pitch-black hold, the pilgrims were hurled from side to side in the dark; they could feel the ship 'twisted by the fury of the sea', creaking and groaning 'as if she would break up'. Water was forced through the hatches, soaking the wretched travellers. The screaming was terrible: 'as if all the souls tormented in hell were down there'. 'Death was chasing us,' Casola recalled of such an occasion:

the sea so agitated that every hope of life was abandoned by all; I repeat by all . . . During the night such heavy waves struck the ship that they covered the castle in the poop . . . and the whole galley in general with water . . . the water came from the sky and from the sea; on every side there was water. Every man had 'Jesus' and the '*Miserere*' constantly in his mouth, especially when those great waves washed over the galley with such force, that, for the moment, every man was expected to go to the bottom.

The *galeotti*, drenched to the skin, begged to be allowed below. Those left on deck to steady the ship were exposed to mountainous waves; it took three helmsmen wading in water on the poop deck to manage the rudder.

At times Fabri, keen to witness everything that life had to offer, could experience an almost aesthetic delight in watching a violent sea. 'Waves of sea water are more vehement, more noisy, and more wonderful than those of other water. I have had great pleasure in sitting or standing on the upper deck during a storm and watching the marvellous succession of gusts of wind and the frightful rush of the waters.' At night, though, it was a different story. A gale struck Fabri's galley just north of Corfu.

It was yet dark, and no stars could be seen; as we tacked to windward there arose a most frightful storm, and a terrible disturbance of the sea and air. Most furious winds tossed us aloft, lightning flashed, thunder roared dreadfully . . . on either side of us fearful thunderbolts fell, so that in many places the sea seemed to be on fire . . . violent squalls kept striking the galley, covering it with water, and beating upon the sides of it as hard as though great stones from high mountains were sent flying against the planks.

They hit the ship with a noise 'as though millstones were being flung against her . . . so fierce a wind kept tossing the galley up and down, rolling it from side to side and shaking it about, that no man could lie in his berth, much less sit, and least of all stand'. The pilgrim deck was a shambles.

We were obliged to hang on to the pillars which stood in the middle of the cabin supporting the upper works, or else crouch on our bended knees besides our chests, embracing them with our hands and arms, and so holding ourselves still; and while doing so, sometimes big heavy chests would be upset, together with the men who were clinging to them.

In the dark, objects swinging from the bulkheads came crashing through the air; water poured through the hatches, 'so that there was nothing in the whole ship which was not wet; our beds and all our things were sopping, our bread and biscuits all spoiled by sea water'. It was the creaking of the timbers that petrified most of all. 'Nothing ever frightened me in storms so much as the loud groans of the ship, which are so intense that one thinks that the ship must be broken somewhere.' It was now that the arsenal's quality controls were put to their supreme test.

On deck the situation was more dire. The mainsail had been ripped to shreds, the yardarm 'bent like a bow . . . our mast made many dreadful noises, and the yard likewise; and every joint in the whole galley seemed to be coming to pieces'. Ship management was in a state of pandemonium:

. . . the galley-slaves and other sailors ran to and fro with as much noise and shouting as though they were just about to be run through with swords; some climbed up the shrouds on to the yard, and tried to draw the sail down to them; some on deck below ran about trying to catch hold of the sheet again; some rove ropes through blocks and put brails round the sail.

Amid this terror and confusion and the strobic bursts of lightning, a sudden apparition stopped the crew in their tracks. A fixed light – almost certainly a manifestation of St Elmo's fire – was seen hovering above the prow. 'Thence it slowly moved throughout the whole length of the galley as far as the stern, where it vanished. This light was a ray of fire about a cubit in width.' Astonished and awestruck in the middle of the storm, all those on deck 'left off their working, ceased their noise and shouting, and kneeling down with their hands raised to heaven, cried out in a low voice nothing except "Holy, holy, holy!"' It was taken as a sign of divine grace. 'And after this,' with the storm still raging, 'the galley slaves returned to their accustomed labours . . . and worked with joyous shouts.'

Three days after surviving this storm, Fabri's ship found itself risking another disaster. As night fell off the Dalmatian coast and the wind freshened, the vessel was pitching at 'the foot of a precipitous mountain . . . When we were close to the mountain and were trying to turn the galley head to wind, it was struck by the wind and waves so violently that it became unmanageable, and threatened to run its bows ashore on the precipitous rocks.' There was an instant collapse of discipline; the *galeotti* 'began to run hither and thither and prepared to make their escape'; 'My lords, come on deck; the vessel is a wreck and is sinking,' was the cry heard down in the hold. Everyone ran to the stern in great disorder; there was a crush on the companion ladders, the ship's boats had been launched 'in order that the captain himself with his brother, his brother's wife and his own followers might be the first to escape'. Fabri had been fed enough tales of maritime disaster to know that the instance of the *Magna* was not unique: 'those in the boats would have drawn their swords and daggers and kept others from entering them . . . [and] cut off with their swords the fingers and hands of men who are hanging to the oar or to the ship's sides. Howbeit,' Fabri went on, 'this time also God saved us; the disorder was quieted, the ship was moored to the rocks, the sails furled, and anchors laid out.'

When a ship was being dragged onto a lee shore, human life hung on the quality of its cables and anchors. Ships carried a large number of anchors which could be tested to the limit. When the galley taking Domenico Trevisan to the Mamluk sultan was off the Peloponnese in 1516, 'A furious sirocco wind blew up and although the anchors were cast out and we were firmly fixed to the shore by cables – and we increased the number of anchors to eighteen – we were frightened of dragging on our anchors, seeing our cables snapped and our galley hurled on the rocks.'

Ships carried cables of immense length – Casola's had one that was 525 feet long – but nothing was proof against the vagaries of the sea. The sickening slow-motion doom of the anchors dragging on the sea bed and a looming shore could make even the most hardened seaman quail; the sailors dubbed the heaviest anchor the 'anchor of hope': it was the last resort. Fabri watched in dismay their largest anchor failing to catch; with enormous effort it was hauled in and dropped in another spot

... where it again followed the galley just as a plough follows the horse. It was then weighed again, and we dropped it in a third place, where it caught upon a rock; but when the galley stopped, and rode to her cable, sheering from side to side, the fluke of the anchor slipped off this rock, and began to drag again, but of a sudden came upon another rock where it stuck fast. So there we hung throughout the night ... the captain and all the officers and galley slaves were all night without sleep, expecting their own death and ours at every moment.

Sometimes survival depended literally on a fluke.

Hardly less dreadful were patches of complete calm, when the ship sat motionless for days in the hot sun on a sea so flat 'that it appeared like a glass of water'. 'When all the winds are silent and the sea is dumb and calm everywhere,' thought Fabri,

it is more distressing than any peril, except actual shipwreck ... everything becomes putrid and foul and mouldy; the water begins to stink, the wine becomes undrinkable, meat, even when dried and smoked, becomes full of maggots, and all of a sudden there spring into life innumerable flies, gnats, fleas, lice, worms, mice and rats. Moreover all men on board become lazy, sleepy and untidy from the heat, fretful from the evil passions of melancholy, anger and envy, and troubled with other similar distempers. I have seen few men die on board ship during a storm, but many I have seen sicken and die during these calms.

Sailors who had clean water left could sell it for more than wine, 'although it was lukewarm, whitish and discoloured'. No galley could travel many days without putting in for water, and these great calms caused great suffering. Fabri had such thirst that he daydreamed longingly of his native Ulm, and 'I would go up straightway to Blaubeuren and sit down beside the lake which rises out of the depths until I had satisfied my thirst.'

Seasickness, heat, cold, the foul conditions, the poor diet, the lack of sleep, the tumbling motion of the ship, all took their toll. The galley for Fabri became 'a hospital full of wretched invalids'.

Experiences of death were sudden and frequent. Pilgrims, unused to the conditions of nautical life, sickened and died of fevers and dysentery; sailors perished at their benches from the cold or in maritime accidents. Fabri watched one of the noble pilgrims 'die piteously'.

We wound a sheet about him, weighted his body with stones, and with weeping cast him into the sea. On the third day after this another knight, who had gone out of his mind, expired in great pain and with terrible screams. Him we took ashore for burial in our small boat.

Shortly after, 'while the officers of the ship were engaged in managing the sails and tackling the galley, lo! of a sudden a block fell from the masthead which struck and killed our best officer . . . there was exceeding great lamentation in the galley . . . nor was there his like on board to take his place'. When they landed, more than once Fabri came across drowned corpses on the beach. Burial rites at sea were according to status. The *galeotti* were given not even a shroud; after a short prayer, they 'were thrown overboard naked, for the sea beasts to devour'; whereas when Andrea Cabral, Venetian consul in Alexandria, died on the way home, his body was eviscerated, embalmed and packed in the ballast sand beneath the pilgrim deck, where it became a talisman of bad luck on a frightful run home.

In between, the passengers saw all the wonders and perils of the deep pass them by. Casola watched a water spout 'like a great beam' suck a mass of water out of the sea, and the aftermath of an earthquake in Candia, dashing the ships together in the harbour 'as if they would all be broken to pieces', and churning the sea to a strange colour; he passed Santorini, whose bay was thought to be bottomless, where the captain had once witnessed a volcanic explosion and seen a new island 'black as coal' rise spontaneously from the depths. Fabri's ship was all but sucked down by a whirlpool off Corfu, got mistaken for Turkish pirates off the coast of Rhodes and narrowly dodged a Turkish invasion fleet bound for Italy. And in the midst of this, through calm and storm, seasickness and fear of corsairs, there was landfall in the ports of the Stato da Mar, welcome relief from the interminable rocking of the ship, and a promise of food and fresh water.

The pilgrims had full opportunity to glimpse how hard the marine life was. They watched the intense labours of the *galeotti*, working to the whistle, doing everything at a run and with loud shouts, 'for they never work without shouting'. Passengers learned to keep out of their way or risk being knocked overboard as the seamen lugged up anchors, lowered and raised sails, scurried up rigging, swayed from the tops, sweated on the oars to manoeuvre the ship against the wind into a secure harbour. They swore 'Spanish oaths', terrible enough to shock the pious pilgrims, suffered cold and heat and the endless delays of contrary winds and lived for moments of respite – landfall or a barrel of wine. All seamen were prey to superstition; they disliked holy water from the River Jordan on their ships and stolen holy relics and Egyptian mummies; drowned bodies were an ill omen; corpses in the hold were sure to bring disaster – all misfortunes of a voyage could be attributed to such events. They called on a galaxy of special saints to ease their passage and had their prayers said in Italian rather than Latin. When the winter sea became furious off the coast of Greece, it was the archangel Michael beating his wings; in the rough weather of late November and early December they called on St Barbara and St Cecilia, St Clement and St Katherine and St Andrew; St Nicholas was invoked on 6 December, then the Virgin herself two days later; they were wary of mermaids, whose singing was fatal, though these might possibly be distracted with empty bottles thrown into the sea, with which the mermaids liked to play. And in every port they brought out small quantities of merchandise from chests and sacks to try their luck.

Fabri sat on deck by day and night in good weather and bad, following the intricate life of the ship. He compared it to being in a monastery. In Candia he watched underwater repairs to the rudder:

. . . the waterman stripped to his drawers, and then taking with him a hammer, nails and pincers, let himself down into the sea, sank down to where the rudder was broken, and there worked under water, pulling out nails and knocking in others. After a long time, when he had put everything right, he reappeared from the depths, and climbed up the side of the galley where we stood. This we saw; but how that workman could breathe under water, and how he could remain so long in the salt water, I cannot understand.

He had explained to him navigation by portolan maps and observed at close quarters how the pilot read the weather 'in the colour of the sea, in the flocking together and movement of the dolphins and flying fish, in the smoke of the fire, the smell of bilge water, the glittering of ropes and cables at night, and the flashing of oars as they dip into the sea'. In the dark he frequently escaped the foetid pilgrim dormitory to sit upon the woodwork at the sides of the galley, letting his feet hang down towards the sea, and holding on by the shrouds. If there were the perils of storm and calm, there were also times of exhilaration and beauty when the sea would be like rippled silk, the moon bright on the water, the navigator watching the stars and the compass,

. . . and a lamp always burns beside it at night . . . one always gazes at the compass, and chants a kind of sweet song . . . the ship runs along quietly, without faltering . . . and all is still, save only he who watches the compass and he who holds the handle of the rudder, for these by way of returning thanks . . . continually greet the breeze, praise God, the blessed Virgin and the saints, one answering the other, and are never silent as long as the wind is fair.

Fabri and Casola were able to make almost the entire voyage to Jaffa by way of Venetian ports. All down the Dalmatian coast, round Coron and Modon, via Crete and Cyprus they put in at harbours where the flag of St Mark fluttered in the salt wind. They witnessed the majestic operation of the Stato da Mar at first hand. They observed the prowling menace of its war fleets, its state ceremonies, colonial dignitaries, banners and trumpet calls. They saw the tangible fruits of the sea stacked high in Venetian warehouses. To outsiders, the city projected in de' Barbari's map seemed the pinnacle of prosperity. But this was the last generation of pilgrims to sail so freely. Even as Neptune's trident was raised triumphantly aloft, the Stato da Mar was simultaneously in hidden decline. For seventy years shadows had been creeping over a sunlit sea. There were social factors at work – the toughness of the maritime life was one – and the Venetian lion now had his paws firmly planted on dry land; the business of the terra firma was starting increasingly to consume the Republic's resources. But above all it was the inexorable advance of the Ottoman Empire which threatened to dissolve Venice's marriage with the sea at the moment of its supremacy.

PART III

ECLIPSE: THE RISING MOON

1400–1503

PART III

ECLIPSE: THE RISING MOON

1400–1503

17

The Glass Ball

On 1 June 1416, the Venetians engaged an Ottoman fleet at sea for the first time. The captain-general, Pietro Loredan, had been sent to the Ottoman port at Gallipoli to discuss a recent raid on Negroponte. What happened next he related in a letter to the doge and the Signoria.

It was dawn. As he approached the harbour, a signal to parley was misinterpreted as a hostile attack. The lead ships were met with a hail of arrows. In a short time the encounter had turned into a full-scale battle.

As captain I vigorously engaged the first galley, mounting a furious attack. It put up a very stout defence as it was well manned by brave Turks who fought like dragons. But thanks to God I overcame it and cut many of the Turks to pieces. It was a tough and fierce fight, because the other galleys closed on my port bow and they fired many arrows at me. I certainly felt them. I was struck on the left cheek below my eye by one which pierced my cheek and nose. Another hit my left hand and passed clean through it . . . but by fierce combat, I forced these other galleys to withdraw, took the first galley and raised my flag on her. Then turning swiftly about . . . I rammed a galleot with the spur [of my galley], cut down many Turks, defeated her, put some of my men aboard and hoisted my flag.

The Turks put up incredibly fierce resistance because all their [ships] were well manned by the flower of Turkish sailors. But by the grace of God and the intervention of St Mark we put the whole fleet to flight. A great number of men jumped into the sea. The battle lasted from morning to the second hour. We took six of their galleys with all their crews, and nine galleots. All the Turks on board were put to the sword, amongst them their commander . . . all his nephews and many other important captains . . .

After the battle we sailed past Gallipoli and showered those on land with arrows and other missiles, taunting them to come out and fight . . . but none had the courage. Seeing this . . . I drew a mile off Gallipoli so that our wounded could get medical attention and refresh themselves.

The aftermath was similarly brutal. Retiring fifty miles down the coast to Tenedos, Loredan proceeded to put to death all the other nationals aboard the Ottoman ships as an exemplary warning. 'Among the captives', Loredan wrote, 'was Giorgio Callergis, a rebel against the Signoria, and badly wounded. I had the honour to hack him to pieces on my own poop deck. This punishment will be a warning to other bad Christians not to dare to take service with the infidel.' Many others were impaled. 'It was a horrible sight,' wrote the Byzantine historian Ducas, 'all along the shore, like bunches of grapes, sinister stakes from which hung corpses.' Those who had been compelled to the ships were freed.

In this first hostile engagement, Loredan had almost completely destroyed the Ottoman fleet – and the means quickly to recreate it. The Venetians understood exactly where the source of Ottoman naval power lay. Many of the nominal Turks in their

An Ottoman galley

fleet were Christian corsairs, sailors and pilots – maritime experts without whom the sultan's embryonic navy was unable to function. The Republic's policy was to remain unbending in this respect: snuff out the supply of skilled manpower and the Ottomans' naval capability would wither. It was for this reason that they butchered the sailors so mercilessly. 'We can now say that the Turk's power in this part of sea has been destroyed for a very long time,' wrote Loredan. No substantial Ottoman fleet would put to sea again for fifty years.

The accidental battle of Gallipoli bred a certain over-confidence in Venetian sea power. For decades after, galley commanders reckoned that 'four or five of their galleys are needed to match one of ours'. Touchy about their Christian credentials, they also used the victory to point out to the potentates of southern Europe their reputation as 'the only pillar and the hope for Christians against the Infidels'.

The Ottomans had advanced so swiftly and silently across Asia Minor in the chaotic aftermath of the Fourth Crusade that their progress had passed, for a time, almost unnoticed. They had inserted themselves into the Byzantine civil wars and the trade contests of the Venetians and the Genoese. They were alive to the opportunities of confusion, siding with the Genoese in the 1350s, who shipped them across the Dardanelles to Gallipoli, from which they could not be dislodged. Picking up speed, they struck into Bulgaria and Thrace, surrounded Constantinople and reduced the emperors to vassals. By 1410 Ducas claimed that there were more Turks settled in Europe than in Asia Minor. It was as if the column in the Hippodrome had grown a fourth serpent, whose python-like grasp threatened slowly to squeeze all its rivals to death. Christian Europe, torn by conflicting interests and religious schisms, failed to respond. Successive popes, increasingly aware of the danger of 'the Turk', wrung their hands at the enmity between Catholic and Orthodox, and the endless Venetian–Genoese wars; without the naval resources of the maritime republics crusades died at birth in the antechambers of the Vatican.

Venice was watchful of this burgeoning power. By the 1340s they were warning of 'the growing maritime power of the Turks. The Turks have, in effect, ruined the islands of Romania [the Aegean] and as there are hardly any other Christians to combat them, they are creating an important fleet with a view to attacking Crete.' The power vacuum which Venice had helped to create in 1204 was now being filled. It was the Republic's policy never to make military alliances with the Ottomans, as the Genoese did, but neither were they in a position to act against them. Always distracted by other wars and by trading interests, and wary of unstable crusading alliances which could leave them dangerously exposed, they watched and waited. They observed sceptically from the sidelines an ill-fated crusade against the Ottomans by a joint French and Hungarian force in 1396; their sole contribution was a measure of naval support, picking up a pathetically small huddle of survivors from the shores of the Danube after its total defeat at the battle of Nicopolis. Their response to appeals to defend Christendom was stock: they were not prepared to act alone, but whenever they surveyed the idealistic crusading projects of the papacy they politely declined.

By 1400 the Ottomans had reached the edge of their maritime empire and trading zones. For Venice, as for the rest of Europe, the multicultural Ottomans camped in the Balkans were only and ever 'the Turks', their sultan referred to as 'the Great Turk'. Under their respective banners, the lion and the crescent moon, the two imperial powers were polar opposites: the Christian and the Muslim, the sea-going merchant class concerned with trade, the continental warriors whose valuations were counted in land holdings; the impersonal republic that prized liberty, the sultanate that depended on the autocratic whim of a single man. Venice quickly recognised that the Ottomans were different from the sedentary Mamluks: aggressive, restless, expansionist, their empire was built on the premise of continuous growth, whose intertwined and pre-ordained missions, both imperial and religious, were to enlarge Muslim realms and Ottoman lands. The exhausting persistence of the Turks was destined to tax Venice to the limit. 'Things continue very unhappily with the Turks,' one later ambassador to the sultan declared after years of experience, 'because whether they are at war or peace they always wear away at you, rob you, always want justice their way.' No European power spent so much time, energy, money and resources understanding the Ottomans. Venice would develop an intimate knowledge of their language, psychology, religion, technology, rituals and customs; the personality of each successive sultan would be pragmatically analysed for threat and advantage. No one else understood the nuances of diplomatic performance so finely or played the game of ambassadors with such consummate skill. For Venice diplomacy was always worth a squadron of galleys and it cost a fraction of the price.

As early as 1362 the Republic despatched ambassadors to Sultan Murat I to congratulate him on his new capital at Adrianople, which effectively completed the encirclement of Constantinople. They quickly learned that they were dealing with obdurate opponents. When ambassadors went back to Murat in 1387 to protest about raids on Negroponte they took with them presents: basins and jugs of silver, robes, a fur coat with pearl buttons – and two big dogs, called Passalaqua and Falchon. The dogs were immensely popular; Murat immediately asked for a matching female dog to breed from. He did not however release the prisoners requested and the Venetian senate subsequently received a breathtaking letter declaring that the ambassadors had promised that the Republic would send an army at their own expense to support the Ottomans. They had done no such thing.

The rules of the game were complex, and had to be learned anew. As the Ottomans reduced the Balkans and continental Greece to vassal status, Venice needed to play its hand with care; it was dependent on Greek grain. It could neither give up its role as a defender of Christendom nor be seen as 'a constant accomplice of the Turk'. Pragmatic, cynical, ambivalent – keener on trade than causes – it needed to maintain good relations with both sides. Diplomatic skill with the Ottomans was tantamount. 'Negotiations with the Turks were like playing with a glass ball,' it would later be said. 'When the other player forcibly threw it, it was necessary not to hurl it violently back or let it fall to the ground, because in one way or another it would shatter.'

The Venetians would in time train their own corps of Ottoman linguists, the *giovanni di lingua*, but in the fifteenth century they relied on interpreters to conduct negotiations with the Ottomans through the medium of Greek. They worked out who, why and when to bribe. Knowing the attraction of the gold ducat they set aside specified amounts of baksheesh; they professionally valued gifts received from Ottoman emissaries and replied in kind; they matched the splendour of a diplomatic mission to the importance of the occasion. They paid close attention to each sultan's death; uncertain which son might win the race to the throne, they prepared their letters of accreditation and congratulations in multiple copies, each bearing the name of a different candidate – or left blank for the ambassador to complete on the spot. They judged carefully the balance between threat and promise. During Ottoman civil wars they followed the practice of the Byzantines and supported pretenders to the throne to increase confusion. They sought alliances with rival Turkish dynasties in Asia Minor to squeeze the Ottomans from both sides. They shifted continuously with the wind, balancing threats of force with offers of payments.

It was never easy. As the Ottomans strengthened their hold on Greece, the people of Salonica offered their city to Venice in 1423; the port was a valuable prize – both a strategic and a commercial hub. The senate 'received the offer with gladness and promised to protect and nourish and prosper the city and to transform it into a second Venice'. Sultan Murat II, however, was insistent that it was his by right and demanded Salonica back. For seven years Venice poured in food and defensive resources whilst trying to work out a solution with the sultan, but he was not to be dissuaded. When they offered tribute it was turned down. When they sent ambassadors, he threw them in prison. When fleets were sent to block the Dardanelles, he merely shrugged. They increased their tribute offer; it was rejected. They sacked Gallipoli; the investment of Salonica went on. They forged an alliance with the rival Karaman dynasty in Asia Minor; Murat sent corsairs to ravage the coast of Greece.

Year after year Venice shuttled back and forth between war and peace, working on the flanks of the Ottoman Empire, but the sultan was immovable:

. . . the city is my inheritance, and my grandfather Bayezit took it from the Greeks by his own right hand. So, if the Greeks were now its masters, they might reasonably accuse me of injustice. But you, being Latins and from Italy, what have you to do with this part of the world? Go, if you like; if not, I am coming quickly.

In 1430 he did just that. The Venetians fought their way back to the harbour and sailed away, leaving the Greeks to their fate. It would have been better, a chronicler said, if the city had been hit by an earthquake or a tidal wave. The Ottomans had eaten up another piece of Greece.

The following year Venice made peace and paid tribute to Murat. If the Stato da Mar was guaranteed official freedom from attack, the Ottoman advance went on, pushing out to the west coast of Greece and southern Albania, at the door of the Adriatic. Unattributable freelance raiding continued. It was the Ottoman method of softening up frontier provinces for future conquest – to unleash unpaid irregulars across the borders. At sea, Turkish-inspired corsairs continued to be a nuisance, even if Venetian maritime hegemony was unchallenged. Negroponte, the next base down the coast from Salonica, was becoming a cause for concern. The island was only separated by a narrow channel from mainland Greece, to which it was linked by a bridge. The senate forbade people from going to the mainland to harvest corn and ordered a detachment of eighteen men to guard the bridge night and day.

The senatorial registers kept a running record of these subtle depredations. Year after year news of raids and troop movements, pirate infestations and abductions poured in. 'For the past three years,' it was noted of Negroponte in 1449, 'the island has been subjected to continuous plundering by Turks, who steal flocks then claim they are acting in the name of the Sultan's son at war with the Signoria, it's the work of Turkish irregulars, inveterate plunderers' – this despite the fact Venice was officially at peace with the sultan. They sent yet another ambassador to protest. The following year the misery of the islands came under scrutiny: 'Turks and Catalans are plundering the isles; at Tinos, thirty men taken into slavery, fishing boats snatched, cows, asses and mules killed or seized – without boats or animals the Tiniots cannot work, they are reduced to eating their remaining beasts.' Many of these attacks were directed by disaffected subjects of the imperial system. As early as 1400 it was noted that 'a great number of Cretan subjects ... are fleeing towards the land of the Turks and serve voluntarily on Turkish ships; they are well informed of what's going on in ports and Venetian territories, they guide the Turks to places to pillage'. It was men such as Giorgio Callergis that galley commanders impaled on stakes or chopped up on their own decks.

In the 1440s the slow, relentless Ottoman advance led to yet another call to crusade. For Venice this required a finely judged assessment of risks and returns. Taking advantage of a disruption in the Ottoman succession, the Serbs, Hungarians and the papacy made a fresh attempt to push the Ottomans out of Europe. Venice was brutally realistic about its chances. In return for blocking the Dardanelles to stop Ottoman troops crossing from Asia, it wanted cash payment for the ships and outright ownership of Salonica and Gallipoli in the case of success. It was clear-sighted about the strategic imperatives: 'If the money is collected too late, it will be impossible to send the galleys to the Straits at the right moment, the Turks can cross from Asia into Europe and

Christian defeat is certain.' This became the subject of a furious row between the Republic and the papacy that replayed all the old distrusts. The papacy accused Venice of unchristian behaviour; the response was furious: 'The Signoria spares nothing to defend Christian interests . . . one deplores these papal accusations, so unjust . . . Venice considers its honour impugned.' Venice in the end grudgingly prepared the ships but the money was not forthcoming. 'For the pope to pay up is a matter of honour . . . his conduct is pure ingratitude!' they stormed. The relationship deteriorated from there: 'Eugene IV pretends that Venice is the debtor to the Holy See. It's untrue: on the contrary it's the pope who owes the Republic.' The gap between the merchant mentality and the pious and unworldly cardinals remained as wide as ever. The unpaid debt was not forgotten. A decade later it would surface again in even more tragic circumstances.

As it was, Venice was right to be sceptical. The crusade was hopelessly botched and the Republic mounted a blockade of the straits too late to prevent the Ottoman army being ferried across the Bosphorus by Genoese merchants. It was rumoured that private Venetian sea captains had also participated. At Varna, near the Black Sea, the crusaders were wiped out. This time there was no Venetian fleet to pick up survivors. The Turks left behind a pyramid of skulls. It was the last attempt to drive them out of Europe.

The noose continued to tighten on Constantinople. When Murat died in 1451, Venice again played a cautious hand. On 8 July, the senate despatched an ambassador to the new sultan, Mehmet II, offering peace and condolences; the following day the ambassador was ordered to proceed to the embattled emperor in Constantinople, Constantine, his new rival. A day later it instructed yet another ambassador to contact Mehmet's enemy in Asia Minor, the Great Karaman. Galleys were detailed to ensure that the Dardanelles were kept open. Venice played on all sides.

The day after ascending the throne Mehmet had his young half-brother murdered in the bath. The Venetians, sensitive to the times, were quick to grasp the change of tone. Towards the end of his reign Murat had become less aggressive. The new sultan, aged twenty-one, was both ambitious and highly intelligent. He burned for conquests and he had just one objective in mind. By February 1452, the lagoon was receiving ambassadors from the emperor Constantine warning that 'the enormous preparations of Sultan Mehmet II, both by land and sea, leave no doubt of his intention to attack Constantinople. There is no doubt that this time the city will succumb if no one comes to the aid of the Greeks and the courageous help of the Venetians would be a great prize.' In the autumn the ambassadors were back again, their pleas more desperate. They begged for help to save the city. The senators vacillated, hedged their bets and palmed them off. They passed them on to the pope and the Florentines, citing their pressing war in Italy and, as a concession, allowed the export of breastplates and gunpowder. They lobbied continuously for joint action; 'It's necessary for the Holy See and the other Christian powers to be united.'

During the summer of 1452 Mehmet was busy constructing a castle on the Bosphorus with the intention of closing the passage to the Black Sea. The Ottomans named this new structure the Throat Cutter. Venice was well informed about it. Spies sent back detailed sketch maps of its layout; prominent in the foreground was a splay of large bombards, scanning the straits with the intention of blasting out of the water any passing traffic which failed to stop. The day before its completion, the senate reported that 'Constantinople is completely surrounded by the troops and ships of Sultan Mehmet'. The Venetians strengthened their maritime arrangements accordingly but remained uncommitted. The uncertainty was reflected by a senatorial motion, defeated, that Constantinople should be left entirely to its fate.

Venice soon had personal experience of the implications of Mehmet's blockade. On 26 November, a Venetian merchant galley bringing supplies to the city from the Black Sea was sunk at the Throat Cutter by cannon fire. The crew managed to make it to land, where they were captured and marched off to the sultan at Adrianople. By the time an ambassador made it to the court to plead for their lives, the sailors' decapitated bodies were rotting on the ground outside the city walls. The captain, Antonio Rizzo, hung impaled from a stake.

The European diplomatic exchanges continued shrill, self-justifying and ineffectual throughout the early months of 1453. Venice informed the pope and the kings of Hungary and Aragon 'of the great Venetian preparations, and asked them immediately to join their efforts with those of the Signoria; if not, Constantinople is lost'. The Vatican wanted to send five galleys and looked expectantly at the Republic – but Venice had not forgotten the Varna debts and would not give credit. In its response on 10 April the senate 'rejoices at their intention, but one can not fail to remember the painful behaviour of Pope Eugene IV who, in 1444, unceasingly delayed the payment for ships'. All the tensions in the Christian system were on display. In early May, Venice was preparing galleys on its own behalf with contradictory and cautious orders: to proceed to Constantinople 'if the route does not seem too dangerous . . . refusing combat in the Straits . . . but to participate in the defence of Constantinople'. At the same time the ambassador at Mehmet's court was told to emphasise 'the peaceful inclinations of Venice; if the Signoria has sent a few galleys to Constantinople, it's purely to escort the Black Sea galleys and to protect Venetian interests; he will try to lead the sultan to conclude a peace with Constantine'.

It was already far too late. On 6 April Mehmet was camped outside the walls with a vast army and a formidable array of cannon; on the 12th, at one in the afternoon, a sizeable fleet came rowing up the straits from Gallipoli. It was the first time in forty years that the Ottomans had mounted any organised challenge to the naval power of Venice. The Venetians at Constantinople who saw this fleet approaching with 'eager cries and the sound of castanets and tambourines' were stunned. Mehmet was a master at logistics and the co-ordination of war. He had quickly realised that Constantinople could not be taken unless it was blockaded by sea. At Gallipoli he had caused the construction of a substantial naval force, which startled and challenged the easy assumptions of Venetian maritime hegemony. For the first time the Venetians clearly grasped the immense reach and resources of the Turks, their ability to innovate and to harness the technical and military skills of subject peoples.

If the state was tardy and ambivalent, the Venetian residents, under their *bailo* Girolamo Minotto, and the crews of their galleys in the Golden Horn fought bravely for the beleaguered remnants of the Byzantine Empire. The irony of this situation probably escaped them; 250 years after Venice had worked to sack the imperial city, its citizens stood shoulder to shoulder with Greeks to man the walls, guard the chain across the Golden Horn and repel a besieging army coming for conquest – whose advance the crusade of 1204 had done so much to assist. They dug trenches 'with a will for the honour of the world', as the patriotic diarist Nicolo Barbaro put it; paraded the banner of St Mark along the city walls to add heart to the defence 'for the love of God and the Signoria', kept their ships at the chain to repel the enemy fleet, mounted attacks by land and sea, guarded the Blachernae Palace and fought with stout bravery. In the cycles of Venetian history, the emotional attachment to this city, with which their relationship had been so long and contradictory, was deep and heartfelt. In 1453 they fought for the memory of Dandolo's bones and the profit and honour of the Venetian Republic. It was Venetian sailors who disguised themselves as Turks and slipped out in a light sailing ship to look for signs of a rescue fleet. After three weeks of searching the approaches to the Dardanelles they realised that no help would come. By now the implications were clear: to return to Constantinople was to risk death. In typical Venetian fashion the crew took a democratic vote. The majority decision was 'to return to Constantinople, if it is in the hands of the Turks or the Christians, if it is to death or to life'. Constantine thanked them profusely for their return – and wept at the news.

The deep chafing with the Genoese continued to the last. There were Genoese who fought alongside the Venetians, with whom the relationship was always tense, whilst across the water in Galata the Genoese colony maintained a queasy neutrality, secretly helping each side and earning the opprobrium of both. The low point in this relationship came in mid-April. For all its vaunted strength, the Ottoman fleet did not perform well. It failed to capture four Genoese transport ships sent with supplies by the pope; it was unable to break the chain closing the Golden Horn, guarded by Venetian ships. Frustrated, Mehmet had seventy ships hauled overland at night. When they splashed into the Golden Horn on the morning of 21 April the defenders were stunned. It was a further blow for Venetian maritime self-confidence; 'We were perforce compelled to stand to arms at sea, night and day, with great fear of the Turks,' recorded Barbaro. When the Venetians planned a night attack on this enemy fleet now in the Horn it was betrayed, almost certainly by a Genoese signal; the lead galley was sunk by gunfire, the survivors swam to the shore and were captured. The following day Mehmet impaled forty Venetian sailors on stakes in full view of the city walls. Their shipmates watched the last agonised writhings with horror and pointed the finger at their old rivals: 'This betrayal was committed by the cursed Genoese of [Galata], rebels against the Christian faith, to show themselves friendly to the Turkish sultan.'

The resident Venetians supported Byzantium to the bitter end. The lion flag of St Mark and the double-headed Byzantine eagle flew side by side from the Blachernae Palace. On the day before the final assault, 'The *bailo* ordered that everyone who called himself a Venetian should go to the walls on the landward side, for the love of God and for the honour of the Christian faith, and that everyone should be of good heart and ready to die at his post.' They went. On 29 May 1453, after fierce fighting, the walls were finally breached and the city fell. 'When their flag was raised and ours cut down, we saw that the city was taken and that there was no further hope of recovering from this,' recorded

Barbaro. Those who could fled back to their galleys and sailed away past the corpses floating in the sea 'like melons in a canal'. The Venetian survivors proudly listed the roll call of their dead, 'some of whom had been drowned, some dead in the bombardment or killed in the battle in other ways'. Minotto was captured and beheaded; sixty-two members of the nobility died with him; some of the ships were so short-crewed they could hardly set sail – only the ill-discipline of Mehmet's new navy, which had abandoned the sea to participate in the sack, allowed the escape.

A small frigate brought the news to Venice on the evening of 29 June 1453. According to eyewitnesses, it sailed up the Grand Canal to the Rialto Bridge, watched by an expectant crowd:

Everyone was at their windows and balconies waiting, caught between hope and fear as to what news it brought about the city of Constantinople and the galleys of Romania, about their fathers, sons and brothers. And as it came, a voice shouted out that Constantinople was taken and that everyone over six had been butchered. At once there were great and desperate wailings, cries and groans, everyone beating the palms of their hands, beating their breasts with their fists, tearing their hair and their faces, for the death of a father, a son or a brother – or for their property.

The senate heard the news in stunned silence. Despite the warnings to the rest of Europe it seemed that the Venetians were as incredulous as anyone that the Christian city that had stood intact for 1,100 years should be no more. For Barbaro, it was the Venetian complacency that had helped the Turks take the city. 'Our senators could not believe the Turks could bring a fleet to Constantinople.' It was a warning of things to come.

As soon as the furore had died down, the city of merchants, pragmatic as ever, sent ambassadors back to Mehmet, congratulated him on his victory, and got a renewal of their trading privileges on reasonable terms.

18

The Shield of Christendom

A few years after the fall of Constantinople, the physical appearance, character and ambitions of the young sultan with whom the Republic now had to deal were analysed by a Venetian visitor to the city. Giacomo de' Languschi's account was both chilling and acute:

The sovereign, the Grand Turk Mehmet Bey, is a youth of twenty-six, well built, of large rather than medium stature, expert at arms, of aspect more frightening than venerable, laughing seldom, full of circumspection, endowed with great generosity, obstinate in pursuing his plans, bold in all undertakings, as eager for fame as Alexander of Macedonia. Daily he has Roman and other historical works read to him by a companion called Ciriaco of Ancona and another Italian . . . He speaks three languages, Turkish, Greek and Slavic. He is at great pains to learn the geography of Italy and to inform himself . . . where the seat of the pope is and that of the emperor, and how many kingdoms there are in Europe. He possesses a map of Europe with the countries and provinces. He learns of nothing with greater interest and enthusiasm than the geography of the world and military affairs; he burns with desire to dominate; he is a shrewd investigator of conditions. It is with such a man that we Christians have to deal. Today, he says, the times have changed, and declares that he will advance from east to west as in former times the westerners advanced into the Orient. There must, he says, be only one empire, one faith, and one sovereignty in the world.

Languschi's sharply drawn portrait was prescient of all the trouble that lay ahead. It caught exactly the truth about the new sultan's personality: intelligent, cold, quixotic, secretive, ambitious and deeply frightening. Mehmet was a force of nature; relentless and ruthless, unpredictably prone both to bouts of homicidal rage and moments of compassion. His role model was Alexander the Great; his ambition was to reverse the flow of world conquest; his interest in maps and military technology, supplied in large part by Italian advisers, was purely strategic. Knowledge for Mehmet was practical. Its purpose was invasion. His goal was to be crowned as Caesar in Rome.

In the thirty years of his reign he would wage almost unceasing war, during which time he led nineteen campaigns in person; he fought until his exhausted troops refused to fight on; he spent money until he had devalued the coinage and emptied the treasury; he lived a life of personal excess – food, alcohol, sex and war – until gout had swollen and disfigured him. In the process he was estimated to have caused the deaths of some eight hundred thousand people. His life would be bookended by a second Venetian portrait, this time in oils by the painter Gentile Bellini. In the interval between the two, Mehmet would test the military and diplomatic skills of the Venetian Republic to the outer limit.

Despite the peaceful trading conditions it had secured, Venice was undeceived. The Republic was now a front-line state; the Stato da Mar, stretching for thousands of miles around the coasts of Greece and the Aegean islands, was in direct contact with the remnants of the Byzantine Empire, which Mehmet intended to claim by right of conquest. They had enough previous experience of Ottoman methods to understand that the boundaries of hostilities were always blurred. Unattributed mounted raiders nibbled away at frontier zones until territory was softened up for open war; freelance corsairs ransacked islands. The senate's dictum was emphatic: 'One is always at war with the Ottomans and peace is never certain.' Venice promptly started to re-fortify its colonies and islands.

The aftershock of the fall of Constantinople rippled across the whole of Europe. Its effects were felt almost immediately within the Stato da Mar. A wave of Greek émigrés began to flee before the Ottoman advance. 'Greek priests and landowners don't cease flooding into Corfu,' it was noted. The effects were most keenly felt on Crete. The arrival of refugees sparked a fresh revolt, driven by the desire to create a Byzantine heartland beyond the reach of the Turks. The authorities, alert to Greek national sentiment, stamped on it with practised ferocity; torture, execution, exile and the use of informers quickly smothered the flames, but everywhere the Republic was in a heightened state of vigilance. The management of the maritime empire was exhaustive, anxious and unceasing. The records acknowledge continuous trouble: a man is caught sending coded letters to the sultan asking for galleys to be sent to Crete; a double spy requests protection in the aftermath of the pre-empted uprising; new immigrants are expelled from the island; the chancellor of Crete is lost in a shipwreck; Joseph de Mayr, a Jew of Retimo, is accused of insulting remarks against the honour of Venice; 'he will be put to the torture, as the facts aren't yet clear'. Crete continued restless and troubled. The island was always lawless and the Turks upped the stakes. 'Many Cretans, banished for murder or other reasons, live in the mountains,' it was noted in April 1454. 'It's a cause of insecurity, also such men would be very useful in the army; if peace with Sultan Mehmet is not concluded by the time this decree is received, the authorities must proclaim a general amnesty.' The background conditions of Cretan life remained ineradicable: poverty, poor harvests, plague, harsh administration, conscription into the hated galleys. After a century of enforced desertification, in 1463 the Republic finally allowed the cultivation of the Lasithi plateau and Sphakia once more.

The authorities also had to patrol the plague frontier, sifting news of outbreaks and seeking their origins. In September 1458 they warned of the arrival of a ship from Negroponte on which 'the plague has caused the death of the secretary and a quarter of the crew'. In June 1461, it was reported that 'a German merchant had died within three days; others are gravely ill. The risk is great. All landing by passengers from Greece, Albania or

Bosnia is forbidden; elsewhere, it is better to cut off all contact with Ancona. The plague threatens Venice.' But above all, it was the insistent, shrill warnings about the Ottomans that preoccupied the senatorial registers for the Stato da Mar after 1453. Mehmet continued his advance. He snuffed out Serbia and pushed into the Peloponnese, the last stronghold of Byzantium. By 1460 almost all of it was in his hands. Only strategic Venetian ports and harbours, including the prize colonies of Modon, Coron and Negroponte, still clung to the Greek shore.

'The perfidy of the Turk demands one get ready,' became the Venetian watchword. The state busied itself with the distribution of cannonballs, gunpowder and oars to various strategic hubs; the construction of galleys and conscription of men; the supply of ship's biscuit; urgent requisitions of masons and materials for the repair of fortifications; instructions to the captain-general to track the Ottoman fleets 'but only from afar and with discretion'. All the Republic's prized possessions suddenly seemed vulnerable. 'It's necessary to defend Crete, where recent reports make manifest a lack of arms,' it was recorded. 'The masters of the galleys must send five hundred iron breastplates before the end of March [1462].' Bombards were installed at Modon.

Nowhere worried the senate more than Negroponte. After 1453, the long ribbon island off the east coast of Greece was now the Republic's forward position. Negroponte was of vital strategic importance as a military and administrative hub and a commercial centre for galleys and merchants. Within six weeks of the fall of Constantinople, the inhabitants were demanding the services of a military engineer and master masons. By the end of the year it was clear that 'the capture of Constantinople has placed Negroponte in the front line and the Turk wants to take it . . . important measures must be taken to fortify [it] because of its crucial importance'. Outside the walls Turkish freebooters continued to seize the crops. In August 1458, the senate sent 'four bombards, six hundred *schiopetti* [muskets], 150 barrels of gunpowder for the bombards and one hundred for the schiopetti, lances and crossbows'. Everywhere the Turks were increasing their ravage of the Greek countryside. It was reported in January 1461,

The information from the captain of the Gulf and the authorities in Modon–Coron show too plainly that the sultan has the intention of imposing his authority on the whole of the Peloponnese and that he's the enemy of Venice. The Turks are right at the borders of the Venetian territories, which they penetrate quite freely, causing damage and snatching the serfs; they have just taken a castle very close to Modon.

During the late 1450s and early 1460s the Republic remained in a state of strained expectancy about what the sultan might do next. 'Though the Turkish fleet is disarmed,' it was reported in October 1462, 'one can't rest easy about Mehmet's intentions.' Wherever he went, tales of arbitrary cruelty trailed behind him. Men were sawn in half; women and children massacred. Sometimes even a guarantee of safety in the case of negotiated surrender proved worthless; at others Mehmet might be unpredictably forgiving. In 1461 he was outside the walls of Coron and Modon; when some of the inhabitants came out to him with a flag of truce, he had them killed. In early September 1458, having bloodlessly taken possession of Athens and unpredictably spared its population out of respect for the ancient culture of Greece, he paid an impromptu 'friendly' visit to Negroponte with a force of a thousand cavalry. The terrified population thought that their last hour had come. They came out to greet the sultan with rich gifts. He jingled across the bridge connecting the island to mainland Greece and inspected the place. It was a warning. Such visits were never innocent; Mehmet had sat outside the walls of Constantinople for three days in 1452, appraising its defences. Venice went on stockpiling gunpowder, deepening ditches and strengthening the town walls.

While Mehmet restlessly gobbled up territories to the west and east – the southern shores of the Black Sea in 1461, Wallachia, the lands of Vlad the Impaler, in 1462, Bosnia the following year –

Negroponte (on the right) was joined to mainland Greece by a
drawbridge guarded by a fort at its midpoint

the Republic continued to play the diplomatic game. Juggling the
glass ball became increasingly fraught, like playing with an ogre.
The position of *bailo* in Constantinople was the most important,
well-paid and least enviable posting in the whole administration.
The *bailo* was at once consul, commercial agent and ambassador
to the Ottoman court, tasked, above all, with ensuring that commerce in the empire continued as smoothly as possible. It was
fear of losing valuable trade in Mehmet's realms which stayed
Venice's hand. The post called for patience and fine judgement.
Again and again, the *bailo* was requested to make representations
to the sultan for the unofficial depredations, thefts and incur-
sions of his subjects into Venetian realms. The senate exhaustively
charged their man with raising these matters. Approach to the
sultan in his newly adorned palace above the Bosphorus was as
extraordinary as the ceremonial of the Mamluks, but infinitely
more frightening. In the back of the mind of every incumbent
was the fate of Girolamo Minotto, beheaded after the city's fall

in 1453, so it was hardly surprising if a *bailo* should be tempted to say what Mehmet wanted to hear. The senate however could be equally demanding. Bartolomeo Marcello was hauled before it in 1456 for having 'negotiated with the sultan about some Turks who had been justly imprisoned at Negroponte, against the honour of the Republic'. His punishment: a year in prison, a hefty fine, dispossession of all honours and permanent exclusion from public office.

The game was being played in bad faith on both sides. Mehmet cast a keen eye over maps of Venice. He kept in his court a number of Florentine and Genoese agents eager to brief against their rival. They fuelled his ravenous strategic appetite. According to one, 'Mehmet wants to know exactly where and how Venice is sited, how far from dry land and how one might force one's way in by land and sea.' The advice was detailed enough for the sultan to conclude that 'it would be easily possible to construct a long bridge from Marghera [on the mainland] to Venice for troops to pass across'. To the man who had hauled seventy galleys three miles across dry land in 1453 anything was possible. In imagination he held the orb of the world in his hand like a ripe apple. Already Mehmet styled himself the sovereign of two seas – the Black Sea and the Mediterranean – assumptions particularly distasteful to Venice.

Beneath the polite surface of diplomatic discourse there was a shadow war in play which would become a hallmark of Venetian–Ottoman relations down the centuries: coded messages, spies and bribery; the collection of information and its mirror image, the dissemination of disinformation; torture, assassination, acts of sabotage – such methods all played their part in state policy. The Ottomans employed a healthy network of paid informers within Venetian realms; Venice replied in kind. It was the patriotic duty of every merchant to spy for his country. The state bribed heavily and strategically. The Jewish population, disinterested middlemen with no particular national or patriotic ties, were considered particularly promising agents but were correspondingly also badged as potential traitors. The senate sought unofficial routes to influence the sultan – and branching solutions. In 1456 the *bailo* in Constantinople was ordered to offer Mehmet's Jewish doctor, 'Master Giacomo', a hefty one thousand ducats if negotiations with Mehmet over the islands of Imbros and Lemnos proved satisfactory.

The same year they also started plotting to kill him. They accepted a proposal from 'the Jew N' to assassinate Mehmet 'with pleasure . . . considering the benefits that would ensue, not only for the Signoria, but for the whole of Christendom . . . everything must be done secretly . . . it's important to act with the greatest prudence, no witnesses, nothing written down'. Nothing came of it, but the idea was revisited regularly. In 1463 a similar proposal by a Dominican priest, also 'N', was considered 'a laudable project', worthy of ten thousand gold ducats and a further pension of a thousand a year if successful. Between 1456 and 1479 the Council of Ten authorised fourteen attempts to poison Mehmet, via a string of unlikely operatives, including a Dalmatian seaman, a Florentine nobleman, an Albanian barber, a Pole from Cracow. Most promising of all was Mehmet's physician, the aforementioned Giacomo, who may or may not have been a double agent and may indeed have been the first 'N'. These murder projects, apparently unsuccessful (though the actual circumstances of Mehmet's death remain murky), were never abandoned. Eliminating the Mehmet problem with a single phial remained immensely appealing.

The whole of southern Europe had been deeply shaken by Mehmet's continuous advance. Step by step the Ottomans were moving closer, now scouring out Bosnia, now establishing themselves on the Albanian coast, just sixty miles from Italy. The prospect terrified the papacy. Vivid imagination saw turbaned cavalry riding up the Appian Way to Rome. Mehmet, 'son of Satan, perdition and death', was drawing ever nearer. 'Now Mohammed reigns over us. Now the Turk hangs over our very heads,' wrote the future Pope Pius II, breathless with dread. 'The Black Sea is closed to us, the Don has become inaccessible. Now the Vlachs must obey the Turk. Next his word will reach the Hungarians, and then the Germans. In the meantime we are beset by internecine strife and hatred.'

The implications – which Venice never failed to trumpet to the rest of Italy – loomed large in the minds of successive popes after 1453. Immediately after the fall the Venetians fired off a brusque report: 'We fear greatly for the Venetian possessions in Romania . . . if these territories fall, there is nothing to stop the Turk landing in Apulia . . . We invite the pope to preach concord among the Christian princes, so that they unite their forces against the Ottomans.' The papacy responded with ringing calls for new crusades – but the strife and hatred that Pius acknowledged proved insuperable obstacles. Venice was making its case off the back of a bitter war with Milan and Florence and its long and dubious relationships with the Islamic world. Italy was fragmented into a score of commercial and territorial rivalries. Where Venice tried to present itself as the front-line state – the shield of Christendom – others perceived it as proud, rich, and self-seeking – the infidel's friend.

Within Italy the diplomatic atmosphere was poisonous; all parties were guilty of hypocrisy. Venice was only concerned in furthering its trading interests and gaining a firmer hold on the Peloponnese; its Christian credentials were flourished as convenient. Its opponents were equally culpable. Almost all the Italian states were prepared to do deals with the sultan at one time or another. The Florentines hoped to replace Venice as preferred merchants in the Ottoman Empire; the Anconitans sent war supplies to Constantinople; in time the king of Naples would be willing to open his ports to Mehmet. The prospect of Venice exhausting its wealth in a bitter war was immensely pleasing to its rivals.

Pope Pius himself, ardent for crusade, was given to the anachronistic belief that Christianity might be stirred by the force of papal rhetoric to rise up, as in days of old, and take the cross,

Venice, protected by its lagoon, was seen as the last line of defence
for Christian Europe

spontaneously showering money, resources and manpower on
the holy project to retake Constantinople. In moments of pure
fantasy he even drafted letters appealing to Mehmet to convert
to Christianity. The pope was hundreds of years too late. What
had proved difficult in 1201 was impossible in the 1460s. Europe

was too nationalistic, too divided, too materialistic, too secular. In 1461, the Venetians intercepted a ship carrying the painter Matteo de' Pasti, on his way from the court of Rimini to Istanbul to paint the sultan's portrait. They found amongst his possessions a copy of *De Re Militari*, a modern treatise on military tactics and war machines, and a detailed map of the Adriatic. He was travelling at the behest of the lord of Rimini, Sigismondo Malatesta, 'the Wolf of Rimini', the most treacherous and intimidating *condottiere* in Italy. (In the ever switching allegiances of Italian politics the Wolf would be fighting for Venice three years later.)

Venice was determined that it would crusade if, and only if, everyone else did. As long as unity remained uncertain, the senate forbade the preaching of crusade within its territories; there were too many informants ready to report back to Constantinople that Venice had broken the 'peace'. In June 1463, as Bosnia collapsed, the doge warned the detested Florentines that Mehmet would advance 'almost to the gate and entrance of Italy' if no stout resistance was mounted. It all fell on deaf ears. By now the Republic, goaded beyond endurance, saw a stark choice: fight alone, or see the Stato da Mar dismantled piece by piece. In July, by a narrow majority, Venice voted to fight. At once the Venetians rediscovered a healthy interest in Pius's initiative. The following month the crusade was preached enthusiastically in St Mark's Square, in another cyclical repeat of Venetian history. Conscious of its own myths, the senate was determined that the aged doge, Cristoforo Moro, should follow in the footsteps of Dandolo and pin the cross to his *corno*. Apart from age, Moro had little in common with his illustrious predecessor and politely declined. The senate bluntly insisted that 'the honour and welfare of our land are dearer to us than your person'. A doge could be treated as harshly as anyone else.

Elsewhere the crusade remained unpopular. The tithes imposed by the pope were dubbed 'sheer robbery' in Bologna; the venture was widely seen as little more than a Venetian imperial project. The Florentine ambassador briefed furiously against it:

Your holiness, what are you thinking of? Are you going to wage war on the Turks that you may force Italy to be subject to the Venetians? All that is won in Greece by driving out the Turks will become the property of the Venetians who, after Greece is subdued, will lay hands on the rest of Italy.

Venice launched ferocious counterblasts against such lobbyings, setting out the record of its fifty-year resistance to the Ottoman advance point by point, if somewhat creatively:

The accusations being made at Rome are intolerable: the Signoria has always done its duty; [the ambassador] will insist on the victory at Gallipoli in 1416; the Turkish fleet was almost completely destroyed; but the other Christian powers are content to applaud, without ever responding to the exhortations of Venice; in 1423, Salonica . . . was occupied and protected for seven years at the expense of incredible efforts and enormous cost with the help of no one; in 1444–1445 Venice armed its galleys and kept them on action stations all winter, while the pope did not pay what he promised. Rather than listen to these libellers, the pope should consider that the Ottomans are squeezing all Venice's possessions: the situation of Venice is totally different to that of the other Christian states . . . in reality no other state makes comparable efforts.

Pius was aware of Venice's self-seeking interest in empire, but like Innocent III in 1201 he needed the Venetians for his crusade and conceded a measure of pragmatism. 'We admit that the Venetians, as is the way of men, covet more than they have . . . [but] it is enough for us that if Venice conquers, Christ will conquer.' Privately his view of the Venetians was far less flattering. In a passage of his *Commentaries*, tellingly deleted in the printed version, he wrote:

Traders care nothing for religion nor will a miserly people spend money to avenge it. The populace sees no harm in dishonour if their money is safe. It was lust for power and insatiable greed of gain that persuaded the Venetians to equip such forces and undergo such expense . . . They spent money to get more money. They followed their natural instincts. They were out for trade and barter.

Innocent could have written such words himself 250 years earlier.

But strategically Venice was right: if the Stato da Mar were weakened, Mehmet would advance on Italy. It understood the Ottomans better than anyone. However ambivalent it might be about the role, it was the only maritime shield that Christendom had. The Italian peninsula would be reminded of the fact in bitter circumstances sixteen years later.

The crusade never got off the ground. Pius was a hopeless organiser, better at rhetorical prose than the practical planning of wars. Only a rabble turned up at the mustering point of Ancona in the summer of 1464. Pius, who intended to crusade in person, surveyed the scene with growing despair. By the time that twenty-four Venetian galleys hove into view with their reluctant doge on 12 August, he was a dying man. He had to be carried to the window of the episcopal palace to see the lion banners of St Mark sweep into the bright bay. He died three days later. The venture collapsed ignominiously. His dying days stood as a metaphor for the death of crusading dreams. Cristoforo Moro sailed back home, no doubt with some measure of personal relief, but Venice was destined to fight alone – and for a long time. The Florentines, the Milanese, the king of Naples sat back to watch the spectacle from what they thought would be a safe distance.

19

'If Negroponte Is Lost'

⊶∞∞⊷

1464–1489

The war opened brightly enough with a successful invasion of the Peloponnese but quickly became unsustainable. The mercenary troops, commanded by the Wolf of Rimini, proved unreliable, though this was perhaps not surprising given that Venice failed to pay them reliably either. Venice's galleys controlled the seas but could inflict little damage in a land-based war, while the Ottoman fleet, remembering the debacle of 1416, refused to fight. And the war was expensive: by 1465 it was costing seven hundred thousand ducats a year. A decade later that figure would have almost doubled.

Venetians within the Ottoman Empire suffered badly. The *bailo* died in a Constantinople prison; captive soldiers and resident merchants were publicly executed, their bodies left to rot in the streets. Trade in the Ottoman Empire was dying; commercial establishments collapsed. The Venetian advance in the Peloponnese was checked, then reversed. The inspirational captain of the sea, Vettor Capello, was unable to prevent the recapture of Patras on the western coast. The failure cut him deeply: Capello had been leader of the party that had promoted the war. After Patras, he was never seen to smile again; when he died of a heart attack at Negroponte in March 1467, the appetite for war began to wane. By July of that year Mehmet was five miles from the Venetian port of Durazzo on the Albanian coast. Only sixty miles of Adriatic sea separated the Ottomans from Brindisi on the Italian shore; shiploads of destitute refugees started to arrive there. In Naples it was common knowledge that Mehmet 'hated the Signoria of Venice and that if he found a suitable harbour in those parts of Albania, he would carry the war into its territory'. By 1469 raiders had reached the Istrian peninsula, considerably closer to Venice. Mehmet's scheme of bridging the lagoon seemed not impossible.

The Republic shuttled restlessly between spirited defence, peace initiatives and diplomatic alliances with Mehmet's Islamic rivals in Asia Minor, in an attempt to find a solution to a drawn-out fight. The war would lull and reignite, depending on Mehmet's strategic imperatives, and his health. When he crossed the Bosphorus to campaign in Asia or on the Black Sea, Venice breathed a temporary sigh of relief. His returns were always ominous. Intermittently bouts of morbid corpulence would afflict the sultan; unable to haul himself into the saddle, he shut himself away in the Topkapi palace and the campaigns would pause.

And he played the diplomatic game with consummate skill. His knowledge of Italian politics, supplied courtesy of Florentine and Genoese advisers at his court and paid informers, was excellent. He dallied expertly with Venetian hopes, encouraging their ambassadors then dropping them, accepting gifts then reverting to silence, periodically buying time to regroup, or proposing peace on terms he knew they would refuse. From time to time unattributed emissaries would approach Venetian outposts with suggestions that peace negotiations might be possible, then vanish. Mehmet probed their resolve, tested their war-weariness and spread disinformation, leaving the senate to pick painstakingly over one piece of data after another. Strategically he kept his cards close to his chest, making spies second-guess the objective of each new season's campaign. He was famously secretive. When asked about a future campaign he was reported to have replied, 'Be certain that if I knew that one of the hairs of my beard had learned my secret, I would pull it out and consign it to the flames.' The Rialto was a cockpit of rumours.

The Venetians soon grasped his methods. Considering yet another peace initiative in 1470, the senate resolved that we understand very well that this is one of the usual cunning tricks of the Turk, in whom we believe that absolutely no trust should be placed ... considering the present state of affairs. However, it has seemed best to us to play his own game of pretence and to go along with him.

Venice was at the height of its powers; trade with the Mamluks continued to boom but the war was ruinous, its effects doubled by the snuffing out of trade in the Byzantine lands and the Black Sea. 'The present state of affairs' was always the Republic's power deficit against the larger, better resourced Ottoman Empire.

Towards the end of the 1460s the voices of alarm were becoming increasingly shrill in diplomatic circles. Death and hardship fell heavily on the Greeks, Serbs and Hungarians – everyone on the continuously eroding frontiers of the Ottoman advance. Venice begged the pope for material aid, crusading tithes and support, 'for when [the sultan] has occupied the coast of Albania, which God forbid, nothing else remains but for him to cross over into Italy, whenever he wishes, for the destruction of Italy'.

When Vettor Capello died at Negroponte in 1467, Venice appointed a new captain-general of the sea, Jacopo Loredan. Intelligence from Constantinople made it certain that sooner or later Mehmet would strike at Negroponte, 'the shield and base of our estate in the east'. The imperative was to hold the island at all costs. It appointed a new *provveditore* to Negroponte with the self-same instructions. He was Dr Nicolo da Canal, previously ambassador at the Vatican. As a fail-safe, da Canal was given a further set of instructions:

If by chance, which God forbid, the captain-general of the sea should fall ill or suffer some infirmity so that he should be unable to carry on or if he should die, we order you ... at once to embark as captain of the galleys of our fleet ... assuming the responsibility of the said captaincy until ... the captain-general shall regain his former health.

It was a fateful decision. Da Canal was a highly learned lawyer, the best-educated man ever to be entrusted with the command of Venice's fleets, but he was no Pisani or Carlo Zeno. Unfortunately, by the time that Mehmet did strike, it was da Canal at the helm.

In February 1469 a Venetian merchant on the island of Scios, Piero Dolfin, alerted the Republic to significant intelligence. His information was highly specific:

At the start of December we learned from Galata that the Turk has begun to prepare a fleet and has summoned the army; he has come in person to Constantinople, disregarding the danger of plague, to arrange things . . . and he aims to take his army from the mainland to the island via a bridge which will be constructed.

He went on to outline the preparations: so much flour was being diverted for ship's biscuit that there was a shortage and unrest on the streets; large quantities of charcoal were being prepared for the manufacture of gunpowder; sixty ship's caulkers had been despatched to the arsenal at Gallipoli; thousands of men were being called up; artillery was being hauled towards Salonica. He restated what everyone already knew about Negroponte: 'The security of the whole state hangs on it. If Negroponte is lost, all the rest of the Levant will be in danger.'

On 8 March 1469, lawyer-admiral Nicolo da Canal received his commission as captain-general:

. . . because both by letters and by various other means we have word that the Turk, cruellest enemy of Christ's name, is preparing a strong fleet and a powerful army to attack our city of Negroponte . . . we wish and order you, owing to the extreme importance of this matter, to hasten your voyage with all possible speed . . . to Modon and Negroponte in order to meet, with your customary prudence and valour and with the help of God's clemency, the perils which could well be in store for us there.

Dread news continued to gather pace throughout the months of 1469 and into 1470. The sultan's force was wildly estimated at a hundred thousand men and 350 ships – a tidal wave of military might. Venice, already exhausted by seven years of war, made desperate preparations; 'We are squeezing not merely money from every source but even blood, so to speak, from our very veins to aid the aforesaid city, if it is possible, lest such a slaughter and calamity fall upon all the Christians [in Negroponte].' Again and again the Republic pressed the consequences of its loss on the Italian shore and the need for united action – to no avail. By the spring of 1470, Venice was on red alert. Two *patroni* of the arsenal were ordered to reside there permanently, the third sent to procure fleet supplies. Two thousand men were sent out on ten round ships with gunpowder and five hundred hired infantry. On 3 June, an Ottoman fleet set sail from Gallipoli.

It was sighted in the northern Aegean by a squadron of Venetian galleys. The galley commander, Geronimo Longo, was shaken by what he saw:

I have seen the Turkish fleet, which will be the ruin of Christianity, if God does not help us . . . otherwise we will lose in a few days what has taken us a long time to acquire . . . At first I judged it to be three hundred sail, now I think it's nearer four hundred . . . the sea is like a forest; it might seem incredible, but the sight of it was quite extraordinary. They row very well, with a fast stroke, though not as well as us. But the sails and everything else are better than ours. I think they have more men than us.

'We need action now, not words,' he continued breathlessly, assessing their cannon and other equipment.

I promise you that from head to tail the whole fleet is conservatively more than six miles long. To tackle this armada at sea, in my opinion we would need not less than a hundred good galleys, and even then I don't know how it would turn out; to be certain of winning, it's necessary to have seventy light galleys, fifteen heavy galleys, ten sailing vessels each of a thousand *botte* [perhaps about six hundred tons] – all well armed . . . now we need to show our power . . . and send with all possible speed ships, men, food, money; if not, Negroponte is in peril, all our empire in the Levant will be lost as far as Istria.

Longo was predicting the collapse of the whole Stato da Mar. The Adriatic itself would be in terrible danger: Istria lay at the doorstep of Venice, just a night's sail away.

In Venice, public prayers were being ordered. Late in the day, the danger was at last being perceived on the Italian mainland. Everyone now understood what defeat might bring. 'The Turkish navy will soon be at Brindisi, then Naples, then Rome,' wrote Cardinal Bessarion. 'With the Venetians defeated, the Turks will rule the seas as they do the land.' Pope Paul directed prayers be said throughout Italy. On 8 July a penitent procession of cardinals wound its way barefoot from the Vatican to St Peter's; a Turk was baptised as a morale-raiser; everyone was exhorted to pray; indulgences were granted to people who fought or paid another to fight. Despite the vast fleet and Longo's urgent words, the memory of Gallipoli buoyed Venetian confidence. Its naval supremacy had never been challenged in battle.

Negroponte – the Black Bridge – was the name the Venetians had given to both the principal town and the whole of the Greek island of Euboea. The island is a freak in the geological history of the Mediterranean. It lies so hard up against the eastern coast of Greece that it is hardly an island at all: a long ribbon of land, mimicking the rhythm of the mainland into which it interlocks, but separated from it by a drowned valley, the Euripus, which comprises a minor wonder of the marine world. The narrow channel acts like a hydraulic ram, pumping the water through in a series of tidal bores at the rate of fourteen a day, seven in each direction. At its narrowest point, where the island and the mainland are separated by a strait only fifty yards wide, the water surges with the speed of a mill race. It was here that the Venetians had their town, on the site of the ancient Greek settlement of Chalkis. This was the Italian state in miniature, impressively bastioned, with a harbour and a bridge linking it to the mainland that was surmounted, halfway, by a fortified tower and a double drawbridge to seal the island from intruders.

After the fall of Constantinople the strategic importance of the island was inestimable. Its population was never large – probably no more than three thousand – but it was Venice's hub in the

Negroponte, separated from mainland Greece by the Euripus.
The Ottomans built their bridge to the right of the island's black bridge.
Da Canal's fleet came down the strait from the north, to the left of
the bridge.

northern Aegean. 'The place was well stocked with wealthy men
and great merchants . . . so that it was in its greatest splendour
and prosperity,' according to a flattering contemporary account.

Some time around 8 June, the Ottoman fleet reached Negroponte and anchored downstream from the city, disembarking
men and guns on the shore. As intelligence had predicted months
earlier, they immediately started constructing their own bridge of
boats across the straits, south of the Black Bridge, whose drawbridge was now pulled up. What was obscured from the defenders
was that this naval force was just one arm of a pincer movement.
The shouts of defiance died on their lips on 15 June when a large
army was spotted cresting the skyline on the mainland opposite,
led by Mehmet himself. The personal presence of the sultan lent
weight to a campaign; Mehmet only took to the field to win.
Reining in his horse on the ridge, he spent two hours telescopi-
cally appraising the panorama below him: the narrow strait, the
causeway with the fortress at its midpoint, then the moated and
fortified city beyond, with the lion of St Mark carved on its outer

walls and fluttering from its towers; his own fleet rocking at anchor. The immaculately co-ordinated operation was a trademark of Mehmet's style. His aim was to deliver a knockout blow before the Venetian fleet could respond.

His army of perhaps twenty thousand jingled down the slope to the banks of the Euripus, followed by a long train of camels and mules with all the impedimenta of a beseiging army. He crossed the pontoon bridge, erected his tents and started to draw his forces tightly around the city. The stock request to surrender was shouted over the walls: none of the inhabitants would be harmed; they would be free from all taxation for ten years; 'To any nobleman who own a villa, he will give two. And the magnificent *bailo* and captain he will appoint as lords if they want to stay here; if not he will give them great honours in Constantinople.' Mehmet was well aware that no Venetian governor could tamely surrender a city and return home alive.

The response was spirited. The *bailo*, Paolo Erizzo, conscious that da Canal's fleet was on its way, declared that the place was Venetian and would remain so. He promised that within a fortnight he would burn the sultan's fleet and root up his tents, then warming to his theme, invited the sultan 'to go and eat pig's flesh and come and meet us at the ditch'. When this insult was translated, Mehmet narrowed his eyes and resolved that no one would come out alive.

What followed was a miniature re-enactment of the siege of Constantinople, a pitiless spectacle of cruelty and blood. Mehmet had brought a battery of twenty-one large bombards that pounded the high medieval walls of the town without ceasing, day and night, terrifying the population and gradually reducing their bastions to rubble. The Venetian cannon had some success of their own, knocking out guns and killing their crews, but the weight of Ottoman firepower was relentless. Incendiary bombs and mortars, which lobbed missiles into the heart of the city, compelled the terrified population to shelter in the lee of the outer walls, 'since the firing for the most part hit the centre of the city'. 'There was so much artillery and because the firing was so continuous,' wrote Giovan-Maria Angiolello, a survivor of the siege, 'it was impossible to make lasting repairs, since so many of our men were killed by the gunfire which scoured the city both frontally and from the flanks.' The Turks inched their ladders and siege trenches forward into the rubble of the outer walls; on 29 June, accompanied by a wall of noise – the blaring of horns and the deep rhythmic thud of drums – Mehmet ordered a general assault. It was beaten back with much loss of life.

The *bailo* soon had to contend not only with continuous attacks but also the presence of a fifth column within his walls. Critical to the Venetian defence were five hundred mercenary infantry recruited largely from the Dalmatian coast under their commander Tommaso Schiavo. It was discovered that Schiavo had been sending envoys to the Ottoman camp; the administration covertly unpicked the plot, arresting and torturing his associates to expose a web of spying and intrigue that stretched years back and all the way to Venice. Mehmet had agents planted deep within the state. Under torture Schiavo's brother revealed a plan to let the Turks into the city at the next attack. He was quietly killed.

The *bailo* now had to deal with Schiavo himself. It required extreme stealth as the traitor commanded a substantial force. Erizzo summoned him to the loggia – the administrative centre of the town – to discuss details of the defence. Doubtless suspicious, he came to the central square with a large and fully armed retinue. Entering the loggia, his fears were allayed by the *bailo*'s cordial manner. After some lengthy discussion, Schiavo dismissed his men back to their posts. With his back turned, twelve concealed men fell upon the commander and struck him down. He was strung up in the square by the foot.

Mehmet, meanwhile, was unaware of this turn of events. He was awaiting a pre-arranged signal to indicate that a certain bastion would surrender without a fight. The *bailo* prepared a trap. The signal flag was hoisted; when the Ottomans rushed forward, they were slaughtered, according to a chronicler, 'like pigs'.

In the aftermath, the authorities in the town moved to kill many of the other ringleaders but the whole event had a deeply destabilising effect on the citizens' morale. There was uproar in the streets and fighting between the townspeople and some Cretans on one side and the Dalmatian mercenaries on the other. An increasing number of the hired Slavs had to be put to death. With the supply of manpower ebbing away, public criers went round the streets ordering all boys of ten and over to the arsenal. Five hundred were chosen, rapidly trained in the use of handguns and sent to the walls, with the promise of a reward of two aspers for every Turk shot dead. 'Each day in the evening,' according to an eyewitness, 'the *bailo* distributed to these boys three to five hundred aspers.' A further major attack was beaten off.

The Ottomans continued to pound the walls, killing men on a daily basis, but Erizzo knew that if he could just hold out a little longer, da Canal would come. By the same token, Mehmet became increasingly anxious. To shore up his position, he had boats dragged over land and a second bridge constructed on the other side of the Black Bridge, as a defence against a rescue attempt down the channel from the north. He stepped up the bombardment, pulverising the walls and mounting attacks day and night to wear down the defence. He interspersed these with promises of safe conduct for a peaceful surrender. On the morning of 11 July, after three days of heavy gunfire, Mehmet was about to launch what he hoped might prove the final assault when he was stopped dead in his tracks.

Ottoman lookouts suddenly became aware of the Venetian fleet sweeping down the Euripus channel from its northern end. There were seventy-one ships, short of Longo's recommended hundred, but still a sizeable force, including a powerful squadron of fifty-two war galleys and one weighty great galley, much feared by the Turks. They were under sail, making strong headway down the strait with the breeze and the tidal bore behind them. At a stroke Mehmet was horribly vulnerable. The fleet had only to smash the pontoon bridges to sever the Ottoman line of retreat and isolate it on the island. Mehmet was said to have shed tears of impotent rage at the imminent ruin of his plan; he mounted his horse ready to escape from the island. On the walls of the citadel the defenders' spirits rose. Relief seemed certain. Another hour and the bridges would be broken.

Then, quite inexplicably, the fleet stopped and anchored upstream. And waited.

Nicolo da Canal, captain-general of the sea, was a scholar and a lawyer rather than a seaman, more used to carefully weighing legal options than to decisive action. At that moment the lawyer's instinct came into play. He was worried for the safety of his ships against gunfire and unnerved by the strange shifts of the current. He ordered the fleet to pause. His captains urged him forward; he resisted. Two Cretans begged to charge the first pontoon bridge in the great galley with the momentum of the wind and the tidal bore. Some of the sailors had family in the city; the will was there to do or die. Reluctantly permission was granted. The galley raised sail, but just as it was underway, da Canal changed his mind. It was commanded back by cannon shot.

On the walls, the defenders watched all this – first with joy at the prospect of rescue, then with disbelief, finally with horror. They sent increasingly desperate signals to the static fleet – torches were lit and extinguished, then the standard of St Mark was raised and lowered. Finally, according to Angiolello, 'a great crucifix, the size of a man, was constructed and carried along the side of the city facing towards our fleet, so the commanders of the fleet might be moved to have some pity on us in ways that they could well imagine for themselves'. To no avail. Da Canal took his fleet back upstream and anchored. 'Our spirits sank,' remembered Angiolello; 'and [we] were left with almost no hope of salvation.' Others cursed: 'May God forgive the individual who failed to perform his duty!'

Mehmet was quickest to react. Responding to this surprising turn of events, he immediately announced an all-out attack early next day and personally toured the camp on horseback promising the troops everything in the city by way of plunder. He then commanded a large detachment of hand gunners to the upper bridge to protect it from da Canal's fleet. In the dark hours before dawn, to the customary din of drums and trumpets, he ordered forward his least reliable troops – 'the rabble' – to wear down the defence. As they were shot down, the regulars advanced over the trampled corpses and stormed their way in. The whole population, men, women and children, participated in a last-ditch defence, barricading the narrow lanes and hurling scalding water, quicklime and boiling pitch on the enemy as it battled forward, foot by foot, street by street. By mid-morning they had reached the central square; from the fortress on the bridge, the defenders hoisted a black flag as a last despairing plea for help. Da Canal responded too little and too late. A half-hearted assault was mounted on the pontoon, but when the sailors saw the Ottoman flag fluttering from the walls, the captain-general raised his anchor and sailed off, leaving the despairing populace to a ghastly fate. Alvise Calbo, commander of the city, was killed in the Church of St Mark, Andrea Zane, the treasurer, in the Church of St Bastiano. Heaps of bodies were piled up in the streets. Mehmet remembered the jibes about pig meat and issued stern orders: no prisoners. Those who surrendered were slaughtered on the spot. Others were pointedly taken to the Church of the Holy Apostles to be killed. Their heads were piled up outside the patriarch's house. In cold fury, Mehmet ordered any of his men hiding profitable captives to be beheaded along with their victims; he had the galleys searched accordingly.

So many tried to escape over the bridge that it collapsed, hurling them into the sea, but the fort in the middle was unreachable and still holding out. Eventually the defenders surrendered with a promise of safe conduct. When this was reported to Mehmet, he turned furiously on the pasha responsible: 'If you gave your word [to spare their lives], you did not remember my oath.' They were all killed. In some accounts, it was reported that the *bailo* was among those on the bridge and that Mehmet had agreed to spare his head. He complied to the letter: the *bailo* was sandwiched between planks and sawn in half. More likely he had died at the walls. It does appear that the sultan exacted terrible revenge. Particularly enraged by the mere boys who had shot down his men so effectively, he had all the male survivors ten years and above, about eight hundred, brought into his presence. Their hands were tied behind their backs; they were made to kneel in a large circle, then beheaded one by one, creating a pattern of corpses. The bodies were thrown in the sea, the surviving women and children marched off into slavery.

Despite Mehmet's oath, a few did survive, among them Giovan-Maria Angiolello, taken off as a slave, and a monk, Jacopo dalla Castellana, who was probably able to disguise himself. His short account ends autobiographically: 'I, Brother Jacopo dalla Castellana, saw all these events, and escaped from the island because I speak both Turkish and Greek.'

The Venetian fleet ineffectually tracked the enemy convoy back to Gallipoli, then trailed home in disgrace.

The news from Negroponte was, if anything, more devastating than that from Constantinople seventeen years earlier. First there were just rumours. On 31 July a shipwrecked sailor turned up with some damp letters from the rector of Lepanto: fires had been seen along the enemy coast – ominous signs of a victory. It was quickly followed by confirmed reports. The senate was struck dumb with shock.

Those of the Collegio, coming out into St Mark's Square to go home, were accosted by lots of people who wanted to know how things were going. They refused to reply and walked away as if dumbstruck with lowered heads, so that the whole city was filled with dismay, wondering what extraordinary event had occurred; it began to be rumoured that Negroponte was lost; the whole place was abuzz with this news; it's impossible to describe the groans and laments.

Bells rang throughout the city; penitential processions wound through the squares; preachers lamented Christian sin. 'The whole city is so struck with horror that the inhabitants seem dead,' wrote the Milanese ambassador. The fall of Negroponte was the first intimation of imperial decline; it felt like the beginning of the end. 'Now,' wrote the chronicler Domenico Malipiero, 'it seems that the greatness of Venice has been humbled and our pride destroyed.' In that second, far-seeing commentators glimpsed the future decline of the Stato da Mar and its sea power. The shocking news was spread across Italy by new-fangled Venetian printing presses.

The senate attempted to maintain a stiff upper lip. The messages it sent out to the states of Italy were resolute:

. . . we are neither shattered by this loss nor broken in spirit, but rather we have become the more aroused and are determined with the advent of these great dangers, to augment our fleet and to send out fresh garrisons in order to strengthen and maintain our hold on our other possessions in the East as well as to render assistance to the other Christian peoples whose lives are threatened by the implacable foe.

However it was soon transmitting a more desperate appeal for help, unity, money and men. 'All Italy and all Christendom are in the same boat,' wrote the doge to the duke of Milan. 'No coastline, no province, no part of Italy, no matter how remote and hidden it may seem, can be considered safer than the rest.' The pope preached crusade again but it made no difference. There was not one state reluctant to enter into agreement with Mehmet. As for da Canal, he avoided the mandatory death sentence. The senate recognised that the mistake had been in the original commission – he should never have been appointed. He was banished permanently to the dusty town of Portogruaro, thirty miles from Venice. For the educated lawyer, 'born to read books but not to be a sailor', it might have been as distant as the Black Sea. But the lessons of his appointment had not been learned: the mistakes would be repeated a generation later.

Venice fought on alone, losing ground little by little. Most of the fortresses gained early in the war were lost again; Coron, Modon and Lepanto held out because they could be continuously supported by sea. Peace initiatives came and went; alliances within Italy and with Hungary and Poland proved fruitless. After Mehmet crushed Uzun Hassan in 1473, Venice's ally on the Persian frontier, his full attention was turned to the Venetian possessions in Albania. In 1475 he finally snuffed out Genoese and Venetian colonies in the Black Sea. By 1477, the mood had become grim indeed.

There were small victories in an otherwise unhalted decline. In early 1472 the new captain-general of the sea, Pietro Mocenigo, was approached by a Sicilian called Antonello with a proposition. The young man, who had been taken away as a slave after the fall of Negroponte, offered to sabotage the arsenal at Gallipoli. Mocenigo agreed. Antonello was provided with a small boat, six volunteers, barrels of gunpowder, sulphur, turpentine, and a large quantity of oranges. Sailing up the Dardanelles with their materials hidden under the fruit, they approached Gallipoli at night on 20 February. The defences of the arsenal were evidently slack, a fact that Antonello well knew. Creeping ashore, each man carrying a sack of gunpowder on his shoulder, they forced the lock on the arsenal with pliers and made their way into the magazines. They stacked gunpowder amongst the sails, weapons and rigging, laid trails of gunpowder, then set light to them from outside. Nothing happened. The powder had got damp on the voyage. Finally they managed to set fire to a large quantity of pitch and tallow. The night sky erupted in flame; Antonello began firing the galleys as the Turks came running, then took to the boat.

Pulling away, the saboteurs were overtaken by disaster; a sack of powder set fire to their vessel. They managed to row back to shore and scuttle it, but were caught and hauled off to face Mehmet's wrath. Antonello was fearless to the last. He admitted freely to the deed without the need for torture and boldly confronted the 'Terror of the World', declaring

. . . with great spirit, that any one would have done this, because [the sultan] was the plague of the world, he had plundered all his neighbouring princes, kept faith with no one and tried to eradicate the name of Christ, and that's why he had taken it into his head to do what he had done.

Mehmet's response to the bravery of a doomed man was somehow typical. 'The sultan listened to his words with patience and much admiration – then ordered his decapitation.' The fire at Gallipoli burned for ten days. It gutted the arsenal and caused a hundred thousand ducats' worth of damage.

Elsewhere Venice fought resolutely to stem the Ottoman tide. Antonio Loredan, a Venetian commander of the old school, conducted a heroic defence of the Albanian fort of Scutari against overwhelming odds. The same feat was repeated in 1478 when Mehmet came in person to supervise the capture of this irritating but strategic obstacle, but the expense of war was mounting steadily. By the mid-1470s the annual cost had risen to 1,250,000 ducats a year. Venice was war-weary and demoralised; hope would be raised from time to time by the prospect of peace, then dashed again. There were repeated rumours that Mehmet had died, only to be confounded by a new campaign. Year after year the sultan raised fresh armies and set out for unpredictable destinations. And in the Venetian response there was a creeping loss of nerve. They were still superior at sea but failed repeatedly to engage the Ottomans in open battle. Maybe, by now, the consequences of failure were so daunting that no captain of the sea dared take the risk. Like Mocenigo, they preferred saboteurs to sea battles.

The Ottomans kept drawing nearer. In 1477 freelance Ottoman cavalry entered the plains of Friuli, plundering and killing, burning houses, woods, crops and farms. Captives were carried back to the sultan. In the city these strikes induced terror. From the top of the campanile in St Mark's Square the Venetians could see a line of flame marching across the landscape just thirty miles beyond their lagoon. Mehmet's appetite for war seemed inexhaustible. When the Venetians agreed peace with him the following year, he changed his mind, ordered another attack on Friuli and went in person to the siege of Scutari. The king of Naples offered Mehmet his ports for a final assault on the Republic. In Constantinople, the sultan was coining gold ducats in imitation of Venice's unassailable currency. They bore the legend 'Sultan Mehmet, son of Murat Khan, glorious be his victory!' and on the reverse an assertion of imperial power across all terrains: 'The Coiner of Gold, the Lord of Power and Victory, on Land and Sea'.

Venice had reached the limits of endurance. It had fought to the point of despair. Pessimism and plague infected the stagnant backwaters of the city. The sight of burning Friuli terrified the populace. Heretofore Venice had been too proud to negotiate on any but reasonable terms. Now it was prepared to concede almost anything; dignity was abandoned, peace essential. The senate despatched their most capable statesman, the Cretan Giovanni Dario, with almost limitless freedom to negotiate. He was ordered only to protect Venice's commercial interests as best he could; almost anything else could be conceded. Mehmet demanded harsh terms. Scutari, so bravely defended, was given up; Negroponte was gone for ever and all other territories taken in the war returned to the Turks. After 1479, the Republic controlled just twenty-six forts in the Peloponnese; the Ottomans had fifty. In addition they paid the sultan a hundred thousand gold ducats outright and a further ten thousand a year for the right to trade in the Ottoman Empire. The *bailo* was restored to Constantinople. With him went the painter Gentile Bellini as part of the peace settlement, to decorate his palace and to produce an imperial portrait of the conqueror.

Venice was relieved and exhausted. The war had lasted for sixteen years. The Venetians considered it an exceptional event in their history and referred to it as the Long War, but they were mistaken. It was just the overture, an opening skirmish.

They had fought alone and had gained no help or credit from Christian Europe. The following year, Mehmet did what Venice had already predicted he would if unchecked: he sent an invasion force to Italy. Venetian squadrons were ordered to track the fleet but not to interfere in any way; diplomats were to keep silent about all the preparations that they had observed. This armada attacked and sacked the town of Otranto, massacred its population and felled the bishop at his altar. This strike into the heart of Christendom, just three hundred miles from Rome, caused utter consternation. Terror was palpable, blame apportioned. The Venetians, who had assumed intermittently the role of Christendom's shield, were held accountable for watching the Ottomans sail by. In the aftermath it was declared that 'this business arises from the Signoria of Venice'. The Venetians were excoriated by their fellow Christians for their inactivity, or connivance – 'traders in human blood, traitors to the Christian faith', the French howled – but they had fought alone for sixteen years and would take no lectures from anybody, nor would they any longer entertain talk of a Christian league. They had paid a fortune in money and blood for Ottoman peace. In reality the lords of a quarter and half a quarter had been squeezed into neutrality by more powerful forces. No one burned with a fiercer joy when an emissary arrived in Venice on 19 May 1481 with the news of Mehmet's death. The cry 'The great eagle is dead!' rang through the city. Church bells clanged; there were services of deliverance and fires in the streets. The Otranto beachhead was abandoned – and with it the fickle notion of crusades.

Meanwhile the trade with the Mamluks, for all its difficulties, was at its peak. The Venetians were assiduous in their collection of commercial intelligence about trading conditions and political disturbances that might disrupt the spice business, but there were forces at work in world trade that had escaped their gaze. During the *muda* season of 1487, while Venetian spice traders were buying ginger and pepper in Alexandria, elsewhere in the city two Moroccan merchants were dying of fever. The city's governor was so certain of their fate that he had already appropriated their property, according to right. Miraculously the two men survived, demanded the return of their goods and departed for Cairo.

In fact they were not Moroccans nor were they merchants. Their names were Pero da Covilha and Afonso de Paiva and they were Portuguese spies. Fluent Arabic speakers, they had been sent from Lisbon to explore the spice route to India. For seventy years Portuguese navigators had been inching down the west coast of Africa, leaving stone crosses on the headlands to mark the extent of their voyages as an encouragement to their successors. The following year Bartolomeu Dias would round the southern tip of Africa, which he named the Cape of Good Hope, but was unable to go on; his men refused, fearing they might sail off the edge of the world. The two spies were to try to discover all they could about the routes to India across the Indian Ocean and the east coast of Africa. The secrecy of their mission was not just to avoid the Arab gaze – discovery would mean certain death – but also to conceal their interest from Christopher Columbus and the Spanish king, who had competitive interests. The prize was to win the race to cut out the Arab and Venetian middlemen and to buy spices in bulk and at source.

For two years Covilha criss-crossed the Indian ocean disguised as an Arab merchant, passing between the ports of India and the coasts of Africa, learning about the pattern of the monsoon winds, the currents, harbours and spice bazaars, and recording his findings on a secret chart. By the time he returned to Cairo, Paiva was dead, in unknown circumstances. In 1490 Covilha handed over his chart and his report to Jewish agents who had come to Cairo to find him. The master spy never made it home. Addicted to travel, he went to Mecca as a Muslim pilgrim, then to the Christian kingdom of Ethiopia, from where the king of the country refused to let him depart. Thirty years later a Portuguese mission found him still alive, living like an Ethiopian. His information, however, did make it back to Lisbon. It resolved vital blanks in the Portuguese navigators' maps.

20

Pyramid of Fire

—∞∞—

1498–1499

On 31 October 1498 Andrea Gritti wrote from Constantinople to Zacharia di Freschi in Venice: 'I can't tell you more about business and investments than I've told you already; if prices go down I will let you know.' Gritti, forty-one years old, was well established in Constantinople as a Venetian grain trader. He was also a spy, sending back information to the senate *sub enigma* – in coded or concealed messages to a fictional business partner. The meaning in Venice was plainly taken: 'The sultan continues to assemble a fleet.'

For nearly twenty years after Mehmet's death, peace with the Ottomans had held firm. Bayezit II, who inherited the throne in 1481, initially promised more tranquil times for Christian Europe. Bayezit was known as 'the Sufi'; he was devoutly religious, mystical even, with a keen interest in poetry and the contemplative life, and for a long time relations with his Christian neighbours remained temperate. He even released Venice from its annual tribute of ten thousand ducats. In the interim, the Republic felt itself more than compensated for the loss of Negroponte by the acquisition of Cyprus in 1489.

But there were other, strictly worldly reasons for Bayezit's quiescence. Because of his father's appetite for war he had inherited an empty treasury and an exhausted army – and he remained fearful of a counter-crusade in the name of his exiled brother, Cem, who was being conveniently retained in the courts of Europe as a useful hostage. Underlying these restraints, the new sultan was aware of unfinished business in the Aegean: as long as Venice held footholds in Greece, the Ottoman frontier was incomplete. When Cem died in 1495, Bayezit, encouraged by Venice's enemies in Florence and Milan, felt the time right to sweep the Republic from Greece. This could not be achieved without a powerful fleet.

It was impossible to hide the preparations. To Andrea Gritti the evidence was literally in front of his eyes. After its fall, all Europeans were barred from living in Constantinople. Instead they resided on the hills of the old Genoese settlement of Galata, looking across the Golden Horn, the city's deep-water harbour. Gritti could gaze down on the new arsenal below, which was not yet encircled by a high wall, and see the preparations: the arrival of men and materials, the sound of hammers and saws, the boiling of pitch and the endless trundling of ox carts.

Gritti had been supplying a steady stream of subtle gossip back to the Venetian senate since 1494. As 1498 tipped into 1499, the messages were becoming more precise – he was providing guesstimates at timescales and objectives for a Turkish attack – and their despatch more risky. On 9 November 1498, he wrote, 'The

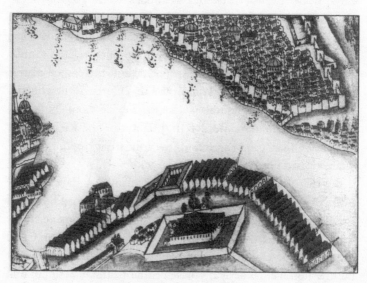

The Ottoman arsenal in Constantinople

corsair has taken a ship with a capacity of two hundred *botte*,' meaning 'The sultan is preparing two hundred ships'; on the 20th he declared himself uncertain of their purpose. On 16 February 1499 he wrote, in cipher, 'It will depart in June . . . a great force by both land and sea, the number is not known, nor where it will go.' This departure date was repeated on 28 March, in an encrypted mention that he was in prison for debt but hoped to depart in June. Sending letters by land was dangerous. Gritti's method was to despatch messengers along the old Roman road to the port of Durazzo, then across to Corfu. Capture for these men meant certain death. In October 1498, the *bailo* in Corfu reported the fate of two messengers sent back to Gritti. The first was discovered buried under a dungheap in a village along the way; the second was taken once he reached the city. He was now despatching a third. In January, Gritti wrote back to say that he 'will write no more by land because of the great danger'.

Both sides claimed peace while preparing for war. In Constantinople it was given out that a fleet was being readied against pirates. The Venetians were not deceived; it was too powerful simply for policing operations. 'They are spending money furiously,' Gritti had pointed out, 'it's being disbursed without even being requested – this is a sure sign.' No one, however, could be certain of the objective. Theories, spying reports, indications poured into Venice from listening posts across the sea – a fuzzy but ominous crescendo of ill-omened noise. Deception was rife. When the latest ambassador arrived from Venice in April, it was reported by the diarist Girolamo Priuli that 'the sultan honoured and banqueted him as an ambassador was never before treated there and that he has sworn peace and will never break the treaty with the Venetians . . . but the Venetians, having taken mature counsel on this, resolved to give no credence to such promises'. But was the operation being prepared against Venice? Rhodes was mooted and the Black Sea. There were even rumours of a strike against the Muslim Mamluk: letters were received from Damascus and Alexandria in May that a large number of Turkish horsemen had

been seen on the Syrian frontier. This sighting proved to be innocent – it was just an escort for the sultan's mother on her way to
Mecca. It was clear however that a sizeable army was also being
assembled. There were fears for Zara; Corfu was guessed; people
in Friuli braced themselves for raids.

The year 1499 was destined to be a cataclysmic one in the annals
of Venetian history. It was tracked month by month in the diaries of two Venetian senators: the banker and merchant Girolamo Priuli, obsessive about the fiscal state of the Republic, and
Marino Sanudo, whose forty-year record provides a vivid description of Venetian life; a third chronicler was the galley commander
Domenico Malipiero, the only one to report from the front line.

They recorded an aggregation of malign events. The year
started badly and went downhill. Venice was deeply entangled
in the affairs of terra firma and money was tight. At the start of
February the banks of the Garzoni family and the Rizo brothers failed. In May the bank of Lipomano went down; the next
day when the bank of Alvise Pisani opened, 'with a huge roar, a
mighty crowd of people came running to the bank to get their
money'. The Rialto was in turmoil. Priuli felt this to be extremely
damaging:

. . . because it was understood throughout the world that Venice was
haemorrhaging money and there was no money in the place, since the
first bank to fail was the most famous of all and it had always had the
greatest credibility, so that there would be a complete lack of confidence
in the city.

In this climate, with rumours of the Turkish menace becoming louder, even the matter-of-fact Venetians were susceptible
to superstition. An extraordinary aerial combat was observed in
Puglia between vultures and crows; fourteen were picked up dead,
'but more vultures than crows', reported Malipiero. 'God willing that this . . . is not an omen of some evil between Christians
and Turks!' More premonitions followed. With news of a Turkish

battle fleet growing by the day, a new captain-general of the sea was elected in March. At the ritual blessing of the battle standard in St Mark's, Antonio Grimani held the admiral's baton the wrong way up. Old men recalled other such instances and the disasters to which they had led.

Grimani was a money man, a fixer with political ambitions. He had made his fortune in the spice markets of Syria and Egypt. His astuteness was legendary. 'Mud and dirt became gold to his touch,' according to Priuli. It was said that on the Rialto men attempted to find out what he was trading in and followed suit, like aping a successful share dealer. Grimani had proved himself to be physically brave in battle but he was not an experienced naval commander and had no knowledge of manoeuvring large fleets. In the banking crisis of the early months of 1499 he got the job, which he undoubtedly saw as a stepping stone to the position of doge, by astutely offering to arm ten galleys at his own expense and advancing a loan of sixteen thousand ducats against the state salt trade. He set up the recruiting benches on the quay in front of the doge's palace, the Molo, with a gaudy display of showmanship – 'with the greatest pomp', according to Priuli. Dressed in scarlet he invited the enlisting of crews before a mound of thirty thousand ducats heaped up in five glittering piles – a mountain of gold – as if to advertise his golden touch. Whatever the techniques, Grimani was highly successful in the organisation of the fleet. Despite shortages of men and money, outbreaks of plague and syphilis among the crews, by July he had assembled off Modon the largest maritime force Venice had ever seen. Grimani was talked up as 'another Caesar and Alexander'.

There were however hairline cracks in these arrangements. The Republic had the right to commandeer the state merchant galleys for war service. In June all these galleys, already auctioned out to consortia for the *mude* to Alexandria and the Levant, were requisitioned and their *patroni* (tenderers) given the title and salary of galley captains. This was not popular; it was indicative of the fraying of group loyalty between the concerns of the state and the commercial interests of sections of a self-serving noble oligarchy. Patriotism to the flag of St Mark was being put under strain. Severe punishments were proclaimed for non-compliance: *patroni* who did not assent would be banished from Venice for five years and fined five hundred ducats. There were still those who did not obey. Priuli believed, perhaps with hindsight, that Venice was being led towards disaster. 'I doubt but that this glorious and worthy city, in which our nobility pervert justice, will through this sin suffer some detriment and loss and that it will be brought to the edge of a precipice.' Over the summer, with all merchant activity suspended, the price of Levantine cargoes – ginger, cotton, pepper – started to rise. The demands of naval defence were starting to stress the city's commercial system.

The news from Constantinople got bleaker. 'With what great and frightening power does Turkish power resound across land and sea,' wrote Priuli. In June all the Venetian merchants in the city were arrested and their goods confiscated. The customary penitential church services were held in the parishes of the lagoon. Meanwhile Gritti's luck had run out. A messenger despatched by land with an unencoded message was intercepted and hanged; another was impaled on the way to Lepanto. Word got back to the city to arrest the merchant; he was soon in a gloomy dungeon on the Bosphorus under threat for his life.

It was reported that the Turkish fleet had passed out of the Dardanelles on 25 June, while a large army had set out for Greece at the same time. Doubtless some kind of pincer movement was intended. As the fleet worked its way round the Peloponnese, many of the impressed Greek crew ran away. Soon Grimani learned that the objective was either Corfu or the small strategic port of Lepanto at the mouth of the Gulf of Corinth. When the Ottoman army showed up outside the walls of Lepanto in early August both the objective and the tactics became clear. The walls of Lepanto were substantial and trundling cannon over the Greek mountains was not an option. The task of the Ottoman fleet was to deliver the guns, that of the Venetians to prevent them. On the same day, the senate learned that Gritti was still alive.

The fleet that had sailed out of the Dardanelles in June had been prepared for battle at a moment of change in naval tactics. Sea warfare was traditionally a contest between oared galleys, but by the late fifteenth century experiments were underway in the use of 'round ships' – sail-powered, high-sided vessels known as carracks, traditionally merchant vessels – for military purposes. The Ottomans had constructed two massive vessels of this type. Like most innovations in their shipyards, these were probably adapted from Venetian models and were the work of a renegade master shipwright, one Gianni, 'who having seen shipbuilding at Venice, had there learned the craft'. These ships, with their high stern and bow castles and steepling crow's nests, were enormous by the standards of the day. According to the Ottoman chronicler Haji Khalifeh, 'the length of each was seventy cubits and the breadth thirty cubits. The masts were several trees joined together ... the maintop was capable of holding forty men in armour, who might thence discharge their arrows and muskets.' These vessels were a hybrid species, snapshots in the evolution of shipping: as well as sails, they had twenty-four immense oars, each pulled by nine men. Because of their enormous size – the estimate is that they displaced 1,800 tons – they could be packed with a thousand fighting men and could, for the first time, carry substantial quantities of cannon able to fire broadsides through gunports. The Ottomans believed their two talismanic vessels would be invulnerable to Venetian galleys.

Bayezit had been thorough in the development of his navy: he had done more than just build the ships. Seeking expertise in naval matters, he had recruited Muslim corsairs from the Aegean to his naval command – privateers who plundered Christian vessels in the name of holy war and were skilled both in practical ship handling and open sea warfare. Two experienced corsair captains, Kemal Reis and Burak Reis, already well known to the Venetians for raids on their shipping, were in the fleet now making its ponderous way round the coast of southern Greece. This injection of expertise gave the sultan the confidence to push his fleet west into the Ionian Sea, the threshold of Venice's home waters.

The Ottoman fleet, though immense, was of variable quality. There were in all around 260 ships – including sixty light galleys, the two mammoth round ships, eighteen smaller round ships, three great galleys, thirty *fuste* (miniature galleys) and a swarm of smaller craft. As well as sailors and oarsmen, the great galleys and round ships carried a large number of janissaries, the sultan's own crack troops. The giant round ships each held a thousand fighting men. This armada probably consisted of thirty-five thousand men in total.

Grimani's fleet was smaller. It numbered ninety-five ships – a mixture of galleys and round ships, including two carracks of their own of more than a thousand tons, carrying both cannon and soldiers. The Venetians had recently employed squadrons of heavy carracks to hunt down pirates, but they had never before brought together such a large mixed fleet of oared and sailing ships. Grimani had about twenty-five thousand men. Despite the discrepancies in fleet size, he was supremely confident. He knew from the Greek sailors that he had more heavy ships, both carracks and great galleys, which could shatter his opponent's line. He wrote to the senate accordingly: 'Your excellencies will know that our fleet, by the Grace of God, will win a glorious victory.'

In late July, off the south-western tip of Greece, Grimani made contact with the Ottoman fleet between Coron and Modon and began tracking its progress, seeking the opportunity to attack. The world's two largest navies – a total of 350 ships and sixty thousand men – moved in parallel up the coast. It quickly became apparent that the Turks had no interest in battle; their mission was to deliver cannon to Lepanto, and they acted accordingly, hugging the coastline so tightly that some of the vessels ran aground and the Greek crews deserted. On 24 July the Ottoman admiral took his fleet into the shelter of Porto Longo on the island of Sapienza. It was a place of misfortune in Venetian history. It was here that Nicolo Pisani, Vettor's father, had been routed by the Genoese 150 years earlier.

In Venice people waited anxiously. Priuli perceived a world in ominous turmoil: 'In all parts of the world now there are upheavals and warlike disturbances and many powers are on the move: the Venetians against the Turks, the French king and Venice against Milan, the Holy Roman Emperor against the Swiss, in Rome the Orsini against the Colonesi, the [Mamluk] sultan against his own people.' On 8 August he noted an unsettling rumour from quite another source, like the dull vibration of an earthquake on the far side of the world. Letters from Cairo, via Alexandria, 'from people coming from India, assert that three caravels belonging to the king of Portugal have arrived at Aden and Calicut in India and that they have been sent to find out about the spice islands and that their captain is Columbus'. Two of these had been shipwrecked, while the third had been unable to return because of the counter-currents and the crew had been forced to journey overland via Cairo. 'This news affects me greatly, if it's true; however I don't give credence to it.'

Grimani, meanwhile, had been waiting for the Turkish fleet to push on from Sapienza. When it did so he hung his ships out to sea and continued tracking it from headland to headland in a game of cat and mouse. In the hot summer days, the breeze dies in the middle of the day off the Greek coast; the captain-general was forced to await the advantage of a steady onshore wind to bear down on his prey. His moment seemed to have come on the morning of 12 August 1499 as the Ottomans pulled clear of the bay the Venetians called Zonchio into a stiff onshore breeze.

Grimani now had the target within his sights; the long line of enemy ships was strung out along miles of open water in front of him and to leeward. He was faced with some unique difficulties in ordering his ships – the combination of sail-powered carracks, heavy merchant galleys and light but faster war galleys was tricky – but he drew up his ships in line with established practice: the heavy vessels – the sailing ships and great galleys – in the vanguard to shatter the enemy line, the lighter racing galleys behind, ready to dart out as their opponents scattered. He had given clear written instructions to the commanders to advance 'at sufficient distance not to get entangled or break oars, but in as good order as possible'. He made it clear that men would be hanged for booty hunting during the battle; any captains who failed to engage the enemy would also be strung up. Such orders were standard before battle but perhaps Grimani had got wind of some dissent from the *patroni* of the requisitioned merchant galleys. The clarity of his orders would later be disputed. Domenico Malipiero considered them to be 'riddled with flaws'; Alvise Marcello, commander of all the round ships and a man with something to hide, declared that the orders had been altered confusedly at the last minute. Whatever the truth, Grimani had just hoisted a crucifix and sounded the trumpets for the attack when his composure was ruffled by the unbidden arrival of an additional detachment of small ships under their commander, Andrea Loredan, an experienced hands-on seaman, popular with crews.

Loredan was in fact guilty of a breach of discipline. He had deserted his post at Corfu to share the glory of the hour. Grimani was irritated at having the attack disrupted; he was also put out at being upstaged. He reproved the newcomer for flouting orders but decided to let him lead the charge in the *Pandora*, one of the Venetian round ships, accompanied by Alban d'Armer in another. These were the largest ships in the fleet, each about 1,200 tons. Loredan had also come with scores to settle. He had spent considerable time hunting the corsair Kemal Reis; he now believed that he had his prey in sight, commanding the largest of the sailing ships built by Gianni; its captain was in fact the other corsair leader, Burak Reis. Excited cries of 'Loredan! Loredan!' rang across the fleet as the seamen watched their trophy ships closing on the invulnerable 1,800-ton floating fortress.

What ensued was a signal moment in the evolution of naval warfare, a foretaste of Trafalgar. As the three super-hulks closed, both sides opened up with broadsides from their heavy cannon in a terrifying display of gunpowder weaponry: the roar of the guns at close range, the smoke and spitting flashes of fire astonished and unnerved those watching from the other ships. Hundreds of fighting troops, protected by shields, massed on the decks and fired a blizzard of bullets and arrows; forty feet higher in the crow's nests, crested by the lion flag of St Mark or the Turkish moon, men fought an aerial battle from top to top, or hurled barrels, javelins and rocks onto the decks below; a swarm of light Turkish galleys worried the stout wooden hulls of the Christian round ships that reared above them. Men struggled to climb the sides and fell back in the sea. Despairing heads bobbed among the wreckage.

In contrast the other Venetian front-line commanders hardly moved. The vanguard of the Christian fleet seems to have been gripped by a terrible indecision at the appalling spectacle before them. Alvise Marcello, the captain of the round ships, captured one light Turkish vessel and withdrew – though Marcello himself would give a much more dramatic account at the end of the day. Only one of the great galleys entered the fray under its heroic captain, Vicenzo Polani. It was set upon by a swarm of Turkish galleys in a battle that lasted two hours. In the smoke and confusion, 'everyone thought it lost; a Turkish flag was hoisted on her, but she was stoutly defended and massacred a large number of Turks . . . and it pleased God to send a breath of wind; she hoisted her sails and escaped from the clutches of the Turkish fleet . . . maimed and burned; and if', Malipiero went on, 'the other great galleys and round ships had followed her in, we would have shattered the Turkish fleet'.

Almost none of the other great galleys and carracks did. There was no response to Grimani's frantic trumpet calls. The command structure collapsed. Orders were given and disobeyed or countermanded, Grimani failed to lead by example, while many of the more experienced captains were locked in the rear. The oarsmen in these galleys behind urged the heavy ships forward with shouts of 'Attack! Attack!' When this failed to provoke a response, howls of 'Hang them!' rang across the water. Only eight ships entered the fray. Most were the lighter vessels from Corfu, vulnerable to gunfire. One was quickly sunk, which further dampened enthusiasm for the fight. When Polani's ship emerged, scorched, battered, but miraculously still afloat, the other great galleys followed her to windward.

Meanwhile the *Pandora* and Alban's ship continued to grapple with the carrack of Burak Reis. The three ships crashed together so that the men were fighting hand to hand, ship to ship. The battle continued for four hours until the Venetians seemed to be gaining the advantage; they clasped their opponent with grappling chains and prepared to board. Exactly what happened next is unclear; the ships were locked together, unable to separate, when fire broke out on the Ottoman vessel. Either by chance or as an act of self-destruction – for Burak Reis was pressed hard and close to despair – the powder supply in the Turkish ship exploded. The flames ran up the rigging, seized the furled sails and roasted the men in the foretops alive. The blackened stumps of the masts crashed to the decks. Those below were either instantly engulfed in flames where they stood or hurled themselves over the side. The watching ships observed this living pyramid of fire in rigid horror. It was maritime catastrophe on a new scale.

But the Turks somehow held their nerve. While their indestructible battleship, carrying a thousand crack troops, ignited in front of them, the light galleys and frigates scuttled about rescuing their own men from the debris and executing their opponents in the water. On the Christian side they just watched, aghast. Loredan and Burak Reis disappeared in the inferno, Loredan, according to legend, still holding the flag of St Mark. More painfully, there was no effort to rescue the survivors. The captain of the other large carrack, d'Armer, escaped from his burning ship in a small boat but was captured and killed. 'The Turks', wrote Malipiero miserably, 'picked up their own men in long boats and brigantines and killed ours, because we on our part showed no such pity . . . and so was done great shame and damage against our Signoria, and against Christianity.'

And so it had been. The battle of Zonchio had not been lost. It had just not been won. Venice had flunked the chance to stem the Ottoman advance. In psychological terms 12 August was an utter catastrophe. Cowardice, indecision, confusion, reluctance to die for the flag of St Mark: the events at Zonchio inflicted deep and long-lasting scars on the maritime psyche. The disaster at Negroponte could be put down to a poor appointment or the inadequacy of a single commander; the debacle at Zonchio was systemic. It revealed fault lines in the whole structure. It is true that the senate had repeated its mistake and appointed an inexperienced man – largely for reasons of cash – but Grimani was not solely responsible. By the end of the day, with the cordite still on their hands and already perceiving hideous disgrace, the major participants were drafting reports.

They all contained conditionals to the effect of 'if someone else had done (or not done) something we would have won a glorious victory'. Grimani's came, by proxy, from his chaplain. It blamed the defeat on the unwillingness of the noble merchant galley captains, and collective funk: 'all the merchant galleys, with the exception of the noble Vicenzo Polani, kept to windward and backed off . . . the whole fleet with one voice cried 'Hang them! Hang them!' . . . God knows they deserved it, but it would have been necessary to hang four fifths of our fleet.' He reserved his special ire for the aristocratic *patroni* of the merchant galleys; 'I'm not going to hide the truth in code . . . the ruin of our land has been the nobles themselves, at odds from first to last.'

Alvise Marcello wrote a highly self-serving account, blaming the confusion of the orders and depicting his own involvement in dramatic terms: he went alone into the melee and had his ship surrounded. 'In the bombardment, I sent a vessel to the bottom with all hands; another came alongside; some of my men jumped aboard and cut many of the Turks to pieces. In the end I set fire to it and burned it.' Finally with huge stone balls smashing into his cabin, wounded in the leg, with his companions being mown down around him, he was forced to withdraw. Others were more scathing of this feat: 'He went in and out, and said he'd taken a ship,' muttered the chaplain. Domenico Malipiero, one of the few to emerge with his reputation unscathed, put much of the blame on Grimani's confusions. The ordinary seamen believed that Grimani had sent Loredan to his death purely out of jealousy.

At the day's end, the Venetian fleet withdrew out to sea; the battered Ottoman fleet inched on round the coast towards Lepanto harbour, protected by a contingent of the army following on land. The running fight continued but Venetian morale was gone and the failure would prove expensive. There were several more ineffectual jabs to prise the enemy out into open water; fireships were driven into the enemy fleet, a few galleys were sunk, but the bulk of the Ottoman armada proceeded intact. At the entrance to the Gulf of Corinth the Ottoman fleet had to risk open water in its final run into Lepanto. The Venetians were presented with a last chance; this time they were accompanied by a French flotilla.

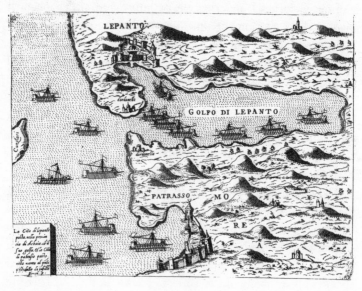

Lepanto

A few brave ships engaged the Turks, sinking eight galleys, but the rest, still apparently traumatised by the fireball at Zonchio, again flunked an encounter with heavy cannon. The French, seeing the confusion, also refused to engage. Their verdict on Venetian arrangements was deeply humiliating: 'seeing that there was no discipline, they said that our fleet was magnificent, but they had no expectation it would do anything useful'. The chance was gone. 'If all our other galleys had attacked, we would have taken the Turkish armada,' bewailed Malipiero once again, 'as sure as God is God.' Instead the bulk of the Ottoman fleet rounded the last point towards Lepanto. Out to sea, the Venetians awaited the inevitable. 'All good men in the fleet – and there were many, broke down in tears,' Malipiero recalled. 'They called the captain a traitor, who had not the spirit to do his duty.'

Within the town, the beleaguered garrison had already beaten off several assaults by the Ottoman troops and expectantly watched the sails pricking the western horizon. They rang the church bells with joy at the approach of a Venetian fleet. As the ships grew on the water, they realised, to their horror, that their flags were not lions but crescent moons. When they learned that they carried siege guns, the town promptly surrendered.

Grimani had hanged no one, reprimanded none of the noble commanders.

21

Hands on the Throat of Venice

1500–1503

In Venice, the loss of Lepanto was the scandal of the age. The inquiry and trials that followed were marked by unprecedented recriminations. Immense animosity was directed against Antonio Grimani and his clan; the Grimani palace was under siege from the mob; all its goods had to be hurriedly moved to a nearby monastery for safe keeping; a faithful Arab slave was attacked and left for dead in the streets; both the palace and the Grimani shops were daubed with graffiti. In the streets urchins took to shouting rhymes: '*Antonio Grimani, Ruina da Christiani* . . . traitor to Venice, may you and your sons be eaten by the dogs'. Other members of the family were too frightened to appear before the senate.

It was nearly four months before Grimani could bring himself to come back to Venice. He was peremptorily told that if he sailed into the Basin of St Mark in his general's galley he would be executed on sight. He returned in a small sailing ship, chained like all disgraced naval commanders, in scenes as dramatic as those that accompanied the failure of Pisani. It was 2 November, the day of the dead.

Unlike Pisani, no sympathetic crowd of well-wishers turned out to watch Grimani struggle down the gangplank after dark. No man had fallen so far or so fast in the public estimation; the common consensus was that the admiral who had appeared to Priuli 'like the Great Alexander, the famous Hannibal, the illustrious Julius Caesar' had turned to jelly at the sight of an enemy. It was an example of the mutability of human fortune that one could see 'this general pass from such fame and fortune to shame, disgrace and infamy . . . and that everything could change in a flash'. Weighted down with fetters and supported just by his sons he clanked his way to the steps of the doge's palace. Four servants had to carry him up to the council chamber. Despite the lateness of the hour, two thousand people watched in dead silence as the proclamation was read out committing him to a damp dungeon.

The proceedings that followed were bitter and long drawn out. With rhetorical fury, the prosecution demanded the ultimate penalty for the man who was declared to be 'the calamity of the nation, rebel of the Republic, enemy of the state, unworthy captain who has lost Lepanto through irresponsibility, a man who is rich and vain'. They contrasted this disgrace with the long and glorious roll call of public offices held by Grimani, now ill from the deprivations of a prison cell, 'commander of galleys, captain of the Alexandria convoy, proviseur of salt, sage of the Terra Firma, governor of Ravenna, leader of the Ten, lawyer of the Commune, admiral in chief' and terminated on a drumbeat of doom: 'On his tomb will be written: here lies he who was executed in St Mark's Square.' The charge of wealth introduced a new note into Venetian public life. To be rich had always been a virtue; now it was a moral stain. The piles of gold flaunted on the recruiting benches returned to haunt him. Behind this lay jealousy and factional spite within the heart of the ruling class. There was a determination to eliminate the Grimani clan from commercial competition.

Grimani's defence was that his orders had not been obeyed; the *patroni* had not engaged; commanders had held back through cowardice and disobedience. Everyone had their own version. Alvise Marcello, despite his own protestations, certainly bore a part of the blame; Malipiero thought that Grimani's fault was not cowardice but inexperience: he had failed to organise the fleet properly and he had caused confusion by raising a crucifix instead of the war standard which he was given in St Mark's – the signal to which captains were accustomed to respond. It was clear that Grimani had not reprimanded the noble commanders for their failures to engage, probably because he had no wish to alienate those on whose support his political future might lie. In the end it was recognised that the blame was collective, not individual. Grimani did not die. He was banished from Venice and forced to pay heavy compensation to the aristocratic families whose members had been killed in battle.

The war went on almost as badly as before. New commanders were appointed but the tide of fortune could not be reversed. At Lepanto the Ottomans now had a secure forward base on the edge of the Ionian Sea from which to conduct naval operations. During this tense time, Leonardo da Vinci arrived in the city to offer his services as a military engineer. He came with a head full of extraordinary schemes for the city's defence – a diving suit of pig's leather with bamboo pipes for air tubes, sketches for submarines. Whatever conversations took place came to nothing. (Two years later he was drawing up proposals to put to Sultan Bayezit for a single-span bridge across the Golden Horn.)

The senate's concerns were more immediate. During the early months of 1500 fears grew for the safety of Coron and Modon. In July, a new commander, Girolamo Contarini, fought a repeat of Zonchio in the same waters, with the same mixture of galleys, round ships and merchant vessels. At they swept in to attack, the wind failed; the round ships were unable to engage; four of the great galleys withdrew; two more were taken. Contarini's vessel, shot to bits and sinking, was forced to withdraw. Again there were recriminations.

Bayezit then proceeded in person with his army to the walls of Modon. He brought with him a large number of cannon, and the standards of the vessels captured from Contarini to demoralise the defence. From the town, the rector despatched short, desperate messages describing their plight: the whole countryside beyond the walls covered with a sea of tents . . . unceasing bombardment day and night . . . a third of the population dead or wounded . . . everyone else expecting to lose their lives . . . the gunpowder almost gone. Off shore, the *patroni* of the merchant galleys, daunted by the Ottoman fleet, again refused to fight. Only one captain, Zuam Malipiero, offered to take four galleys and run the blockade and 'lay down his life for his country'. Such moments of exemplary bravery met their response. 'At once, the galley crews cried out that they would volunteer to die with him, that they would man the galleys. The others,' Priuli recorded bitterly, but from a safe distance, 'lacking spirit and courage remained in the fleet.' Malipiero's galleys heroically pierced the Ottoman blockade and made it into the small encircling harbour of Modon. The exhausted defenders, overjoyed at the prospect of relief, abandoned their posts and started to run for the ships. The result was catastrophic.

On 29 August, at the twentieth hour, the news reached Venice as news always did: a light frigate cutting up fast on the wind to the Basin of St Mark. It was the day of the decapitation of St John, an ill-omened anniversary in the Christian calendar. When the loss of Modon was reported to the Council of Ten in their gilded chamber, the august dignitaries who commanded the Most Serene Republic of Venice burst into tears. Even more than Negroponte, Modon mattered. Its significance was both emotional and commercial. It was not just the six thousand prisoners taken, the loss of 150 cannon and the twelve galleys. Modon was part of the original imperial heritage of the Fourth Crusade; it counted as one of the richest treasures of the Stato da Mar. 'It was', said Priuli, 'as if they had seen the whole ability of shipping to sail taken away, because the city of Modon was the staging post and maritime turntable for all ships on every voyage.' When the sultan turned up at the walls of Coron twenty miles away, the case was judged hopeless; the town surrendered without a fight. The Eyes of the Republic had been extinguished. To Priuli the merchant it was a moment of prescient doom: 'If the Venetians can't make their voyages, their means of living will be gradually taken away, and in a short time they will wither away to nothing.'

On the eve of this gloomy news, the Republic had elected yet another captain-general of the sea. There were no volunteers for the post; all those proposed excused themselves on grounds of age, ill health and so on, so low had fallen the standing of the post, so great was the fear of the Turkish fleet. Eventually they found Benedetto Pesaro, known colloquially as Pesaro of London, who willingly accepted. Pesaro was an experienced commander, stern, resolute, impervious to the politics of the noble class and completely ruthless. At the age of seventy he still apparently kept mistresses. 'Totally reprehensible in such an old man,' yelped Priuli. Pesaro was, in effect, a throwback to the rougher age of Pisani and Zeno – a seaman's seaman, able to command respect and love from his crews, and fear from his captains. In the light of previous failings he was given the widest power to 'kill and execute anyone guilty of disobedience, be they *provveditori*, captains or galley commanders . . . without seeking permission from Venice'. Such phrases had become stock; they were no longer believed, but Pesaro did just that. Like Pisani, the old libertine understood the mentality of the working seamen: he improved their morale enormously by giving them leave to plunder, whilst helping himself as well. He was effective. He rampaged round the coasts of Greece destroying Ottoman shipbuilding efforts, restoring some Ionian islands to Venetian control, preventing the enemy from further consolidating their naval position. He acted without fear or favour. When two noble subordinates, one of whom was a relative of the doge, surrendered their fortresses without a fight he simply killed them. When he captured the Turkish pirate Erichi he roasted him alive. He preserved the integrity of the Adriatic and maintained control over the Ionian Sea so effectively that by the end of 1500 the great galleys were resuming their voyages to Alexandria and Beirut. Ultimately, however, he was unable to reverse the tide of conquest.

In 1503 Venice accepted the inevitable and signed a humiliating peace with Bayezit that confirmed everything he had won. Soon the Venetians would dip their flags to passing Ottoman ships in implicit recognition of a vassal status they were too proud publicly to acknowledge. From now on co-operation with their powerful

Muslim neighbour would become an axiom of Venetian foreign policy and the city would turn its attention increasingly to building a land empire.

On 9 May 1500, as on every Ascension Day for the past five hundred years, the Sensa took place in Venice, the elaborate ceremony that expressed the city's sense of mystical union with the sea. As usual, the doge, decked out in his regalia, set sail in the golden barge and tossed a gold ring into the depths to proclaim the marriage. The same year de' Barbari was running off images of the triumphant maritime city on Venetian presses. These were fine allegories but on the turning of the sixteenth century the reality was different. The sea was no longer quiet and the marriage was tempestuous. The truth had been neatly summed up in Constantinople some time earlier. When a Venetian ambassador presented himself at Bayezit's court to broker a peace deal he was told that there was no point in being there. 'Up till now you have married the sea,' the vizier roundly remarked. 'From now on it's our turn; we've got more sea than you.'

The treaty marked a major shift in naval power. Henceforward no Christian power could compete with the Ottomans single-handed. They had taken just fifty years to neutralise the most experienced naval force in the Mediterranean and to turn around centuries of Christian dominance in its eastern half. Yet during this time they had established no real superiority in nautical matters, had fought few sea battles and conclusively won none. However, both Mehmet and Bayezit had grasped an essential principle of warfare in the closed sea: there was no need for dominion over the waves; it was the land that counted. By working in conjunction with a powerful army and using the fleet for amphibious operations, they had swept up the strategic bases on which galleys, with their need for frequent harbour stops, depended. Now they were established on the edge of the Adriatic, well poised to strike further west and to threaten Venice's other great islands. For fifty years Venice had warned and implored the pope, the other Italian city states, the king of France, anyone who would listen, of the dangers of this possibility: 'When the sultan has occupied the coast of Albania, which God forbid, nothing else remains but for him to cross over into Italy, whenever he wishes, for the destruction of Christendom.' Bayezit added to all the sultan's usual titles a new one: 'Lord of all the sea kingdoms, both of the Romans, and Asia Minor and the Aegean'. Henceforward European merchant ships could hardly sail the eastern seas without permission. Only a few large islands – Corfu, Crete, Cyprus and Rhodes – were left in Christian hands.

The image of the fireball at Zonchio remained seared into the Venetian imagination, crystallised in a brilliant woodcut of the battle just as the flames started to take hold. It was the moment when Venetian naval self-confidence fell guttering to the deck. The Venetians had been overawed by the explosive effects of gunpowder and the apparent strength of their opponent, then betrayed by hairline cracks in their own command structure. In the end it was not so much a question of numbers as a failure of will, a refusal to die for causes. The galley captain Domenico Malipiero was unsparing in his analysis: 'If we had had a larger fleet, there would have been greater confusion. Everything arose from a lack of love for Christianity and our country, a lack of courage, a lack of discipline, a lack of pride.' 'This Turkish engagement', wrote Priuli, summing up in the summer of 1501, 'meant everything; it was not a matter of losing a city or a fort, but of something much more serious' – he meant the Stato da Mar itself, and the wealth that flowed through its channels.

There was another wider legacy of Zonchio. The spectacular destruction of the colossal sailing ships served to discourage both sides from further experiment in this direction. Henceforward battles in the Mediterranean would follow established practice; ever larger fleets of oared galleys would hurtle towards each other, firing their lightweight guns as they closed, then attempt to down each other in hand-to-hand combat. Beyond the gates of

Gibraltar, it would be first the Portuguese, then the Spanish, the English and the Dutch whose wind-powered galleons, packed with heavy cannon, would construct world empires unimaginable in the landlocked sea.

The first inkling of this came hard on the heels of Zonchio. Priuli had been wrong about names, right about the deeds: not Columbus but Vasco da Gama returned from India in September 1499, having rounded the Cape of Good Hope. The Republic despatched an ambassador to the court of Lisbon to investigate; it was not until July 1501 that his report came in. The reality of it fell on the lagoon like a thunderclap. Terrible foreboding gripped the city. For the Venetians, who lived with a particularly intense awareness of physical geography, the implications were obvious. Priuli poured his gloomiest predictions into his diary. It was a marvel, incredible, the most momentous news of the time:

. . . which will take a greater intelligence than mine to comprehend. At the receipt of this news, the whole city . . . was dumbfounded and the wisest thought it was the worst news ever heard. They understood that Venice had ascended to such fame and wealth only through trading by sea, by means of which a large quantity of spices were brought in, which foreigners came from everywhere to buy. From their presence and the trade [Venice] acquired great benefits. Now from this new route the spices of India will be transported to Lisbon, where Hungarians, Germans, the Flemish and the French will look to buy, being able to get them at a better price. Because the spices that come to Venice pass through Syria and the sultan's lands, paying exorbitant taxes at every stage of the way, when they get to Venice the prices have increased so much that something originally worth a ducat costs a ducat seventy or even two. From these obstacles, via the sea route, it will come about that Portugal can give much lower prices.

Cutting out hundreds of small middlemen, snubbing the avaricious, unstable Mamluks, buying in bulk, shipping direct: to Venetian merchants such advantages were self-evident.

There were counter voices; some pointed out the difficulties of the voyage:

. . . the king of Portugal could not continue to use the new route to Calicut, since of the thirteen caravels which he had despatched only six had returned safely; that the losses outweighed the advantages; that few sailors would be prepared to risk their lives on such a long and dangerous voyage.

But Priuli was certain: 'From this news spices of all sorts will decrease enormously in Venice, because the usual buyers, understanding the news, will decline, being reluctant to buy.' He ended with an apology to future readers for having written at such length. 'These new facts are of such importance to our city that I have been carried away with anxiety.'

In a visionary flash, Priuli foresaw, and much of Venice with him, the end of a whole system, a paradigm shift: not just Venice, but a whole network of long-distance commerce doomed to decline. All the old trade routes and their burgeoning cities that had flourished since antiquity were suddenly glimpsed as backwaters – Cairo, the Black Sea, Damascus, Beirut, Baghdad, Smyrna, the ports of the Red Sea and the great cities of the Levant, Constantinople itself – all these threatened to be cut out from the cycles of world trade by ocean-going galleons. The Mediterranean would be bypassed; the Adriatic would no longer be the route to anywhere; important outstations such as Cyprus and Crete would sink into decline.

The Portuguese rubbed this in. The king invited Venetian merchants to buy their spices in Lisbon; they would no longer need to treat with the fickle infidel. Some were tempted but the Republic had too much invested in the Levant easily to withdraw; their merchants there would be soft targets for the sultan's wrath if they bought elsewhere. Nor, from the eastern Mediterranean, was sending their own ships to India readily practical. The whole business model of the Venetian state appeared, at a stroke, obsolete.

The effects were felt almost immediately. In 1502 the Beirut galleys only brought back four bales of pepper; prices in Venice steepled; the Germans reduced their purchases; many decamped to Lisbon. In 1502 the Republic despatched a secret embassy to Cairo to point out the dangers. It was essential to destroy the Portuguese maritime threat now. They offered financial support. They proposed digging a canal from the Mediterranean to the Red Sea. But the Mamluk dynasty, hated by its subjects, was also in decline. It proved powerless to see off the intruders. In 1500, the Mamluk chronicler Ibn Iyas recorded an extraordinary event. The balsam gardens outside Cairo, which had existed since remote antiquity, produced an oil with miraculous properties highly prized by the Venetians. Its trade symbolised the centuries-old commercial relationship between Islam and the West. That year the balsam trees withered away and vanished for ever. Seventeen years later the Ottomans strung up the last Mamluk sultan from a Cairo gate.

Tome Pires, a Portuguese adventurer, gleefully spelled out the implications for Venice. In 1511 the Portuguese conquered Malacca on the Malay peninsula, the market for the produce of the Spice Islands. 'Whoever is lord of Malacca', he wrote, 'has his hand on the throat of Venice.' It would be a slow and uneven pressure, but the Portuguese and their successors would eventually squeeze the life out of the Venetian trade with the Orient. The fears that Priuli expressed would in time prove well-founded; and the Ottomans meanwhile would systematically strip away the Stato da Mar.

The classical allusions of de' Barbari's map already contain a backward-looking note; they hint at nostalgia, a remaking of the tough, energetic realities of the Stato da Mar into something ornamental. They perhaps reflected structural changes within Venetian society. The recurrent bouts of plague meant that the city's population was never self-replenishing; it relied on immigrants, and many of those from mainland Italy came without knowledge of the seafaring life. It was already noticeable during the Chioggia crisis that the volunteer citizens had to be given rowing lessons. In 1201, at the time of the adventure of the Fourth Crusade, the majority of its male population were seafarers; by 1500 they were not. The emotional attachment to the sea, expressed in the Sensa, would last until the death of the Republic, but by 1500 Venice was turning increasingly to the land; within four years it would be engaged in a disastrous Italian war that would again bring enemies to the edge of the lagoon. There was a crisis in ship-building, a greater emphasis on industry. The patriotic solidarity which had been the hallmark of Venetian destiny had been seen to fray: a sizeable part of the ruling elite had demonstrated that, though still keen to recoup the profits of maritime trade, they were not prepared to fight for the bases and sea lanes on which it depended. Others, who had made fortunes in the rich fifteenth century, stopped sending their sons to sea as apprentice bowmen. Increasingly a wealthy man might look to reinvest in estates on the terra firma, to own a country mansion with escutcheons over the door; these were respectable hallmarks of nobility to which all self-made men might aspire.

It was Priuli again, acute and regretful, who caught this impulse and pinpointed the declining glory it seemed to imply. 'The Venetians', he wrote in 1505, 'are much more inclined to the Terra Firma, which has become more attractive and pleasing, than to the sea, the ancient root cause of all their glory, wealth and honour.'

'I do not think there is any city to which Venice, the city founded on the sea, can be compared,' Pietro Casola had written in 1494. Outsiders attempting to grasp the meaning of the place at the end of the fifteenth century found it impossible to match to their known worlds. Everywhere they were confronted by paradox. Venice was sterile but visibly abundant; running with wealth but short of drinking water; immensely powerful yet physically fragile; free from feudalism but fiercely regulated. Its citizens were sober, unromantic and frequently cynical, yet they had conjured a city of fantasy. Gothic arches, Islamic domes and Byzantine mosaics transported the observer simultaneously to Bruges, Cairo and Constantinople. Venice seemed self-generated. The only Italian city not in existence in Roman times, its inhabitants had created their own antiquity out of theft and borrowings; they manufactured their foundation myths and stole their saints from the Greek world.

It was, in a sense, the first virtual city: an offshore bonded warehouse with no visible means of support – almost shockingly modern. As Priuli had put it, the city rested on an abstract. It was an empire of cash. The ducat, a small golden roundel on which a succession of doges knelt before St Mark, was the dollar of its day. It commanded respect all the way to India, where they interpreted the blurred images as a Hindu god and his consort. The Republic's fierce concentration on fiscal management was centuries ahead of its time. It was the only state in the world that had government policies solely geared to economic ends. There was no gap between its political and merchant class. It was a Republic run by and for entrepreneurs and it regulated accordingly. The three great centres of power – the doge's palace, the Rialto and the arsenal, respectively the seats of government, trade and war – were managed by the same ruling group. Venice, before anyone else, understood the essential commercial rules: the principles of supply and demand; the need for consumer choice, a stable currency, on-time delivery, rational laws and taxes; the application of consistent, disciplined and long-term policies. It replaced the chivalrous medieval knight with a new type of hero: the man of business. All these qualities were expressed in the emblem of St Mark. Outsiders had no adequate explanation for the ascent

The ducat

of Venice. Instead they bought into the myth that the city sold: that this greatness was miraculously pre-ordained. Like any long boom, they thought it would last forever.

It was the maritime adventure that had made all this possible. In the process Venice changed the world. Not alone, but as a prime mover, it was an engine in the growth of global trade. With unmatched efficiency the Republic sharpened the sense of material desire and facilitated the long-range exchange of goods that satisfied it. It was the central cog that meshed two economic systems – Europe and the Orient – shunting goods across hemispheres, facilitating new tastes and notions of choice. Venice was the middleman and interpreter of worlds. 'I have seen the world in a two-fold mirror,' wrote Felix Fabri of his voyages. Venice was the first European power to interact seriously and continuously with Islam. It promoted the seepage of oriental tastes, ideas and influences – as well as a certain romantic orientalism – into the European world. Visual ideas, materials, foods, motifs and words passed through its maritime customs post.

This exchange had decisive effects. The merchants of the lagoon also hastened the decline of the economic power of the Islamic Middle East and the rise of the West. Over centuries many of the industries that had made the Levant so wealthy – the manufacture of soap, glass, silk and paper, the production of sugar – were either usurped by the Republic or undermined by its transport systems. Venetian merchants moved from buying Syrian glass to importing the key raw material – soda ash from the Syrian desert – until the superior glass of Murano was being re-exported to Mamluk palaces. Soap and paper-making followed the same trend. Sugar production moved from Syria to Cyprus, where Venetian entrepreneurs employed more efficient production processes to supply western markets. The merchant galleys allowed energetic European industries harnessing new technologies, such as water power and automatic spinning wheels, to undercut Levantine competitors and nudge them into spiralling decline. Every shipload that sailed east from Venice gradually shifted the balance of power. Payment for oriental goods changed from silver bars to barter – on increasingly favourable terms for the westerners.

The function of the Stato da Mar was as much to funnel this trade across the sea as it was to provide wealth in its own right. It was Europe's first full-blown colonial adventure. With exceptions – and the Dalmatians were certainly better treated than the Greeks – it was exploitative and indifferent. It provided something of a model to its successors, notably Holland and Britain, as to the ability of small maritime states to gain global reach. It served as a warning too of the vulnerabilities of far-flung possessions linked by sea power. The Venetian business model became suddenly obsolete and its supply lines vulnerable. Ultimately the Stato da Mar was as hard to defend as the American colonies were for Britain. The collapse of ocean-going empires could be as dramatic as their rise: by 1505 Priuli was already sketching an epitaph.

Epilogue

A few miles west of Heraklion on the coastal highway, there is a prominent rocky outcrop above the sea. If you cross the road and follow the path round its base, you pass by an archway and vaulted tunnel onto an open platform with a wide prospect of the Aegean. The Cretans call this place Paleokastro – the Old Fort. It was built by the Genoese in 1206, then developed by the Venetians to guard the seaward approaches to Candia. It's a lonely spot. At its outer edge the stone bastion falls away steeply down the base of the cliff; there is a smell of thyme on the soft wind; the smack of sea; the ruins of arched magazines; a subterranean chapel. In the distance modern Heraklion sprawls beyond a blue bay.

It was here in the summer of 1669, after the longest siege in world history, that the captain-general Francesco Morosini agreed the surrender of Venetian Crete. For twenty-one years, Venice engaged in a titanic struggle with the Ottomans for its hub of empire, but Priuli had been right. One by one its colonial possessions would be prised away. Cyprus, held for less than a century, was lost in 1570; Tinos, its most northern island in the Aegean, lasted until 1715; by then the rest were gone, and the trade had died. The *muda* system was in decline by the 1520s. The last galleys anchored in the Thames soon after. Pirates started to choke the sea.

Only Venice's home waters held firm. Century after century the Ottomans hammered at Corfu but the door of the Adriatic stayed shut, and when Napoleon finally marched into St Mark's

The siege of Candia 1648–69

Square, burned the *Bucintoro* and trundled the bronze horses off to Paris in wheeled carts, there was something approaching grief along the Dalmatian coast. At Perasto, the governor made an emotional speech in the Venetian dialect and buried the flag of St Mark beneath the altar; the people wept.

The visible remnants of the Stato da Mar lie scattered across the sea; hundreds of crumbling towers and forts; the impressive defences of Candia and Famagusta, with their angled bastions and deep ditches, powerless in the end against Turkish guns; neat harbours at Lepanto, Kyrenia and Hania, drawn tightly around pretty bays; churches, bell towers, arsenals and quays; countless Venetian lions, elongated, squat, tubby, winged and wingless, gruff, fierce, indignant and surprised, guard harbour walls, surmount gateways and spout water from elegant fountains. Far away, at the mouth of the Don, archaeologists still dig breastplates, crossbow bolts and Murano glass from the Ukrainian earth, but overall the traces of Venice's imperial adventure are surprisingly light. There was always something provisional about the Stato da

Mar. Like Venice itself, it lived with the idea of impermanence; harbours and ports came and went and the roots it put down on many foreign shores were not deep. The lintel of more than one collapsed Venetian house on Crete bears the Latin motto 'The world is nothing but smoke and shadows'. As if they knew, deep down, that all the imperial razzmatazz of trumpets, ships and guns was only a mirage.

Over centuries tens of thousands of Venetians engaged in this show – merchants, seamen, colonists, soldiers and administrators. It was mainly a world of men, but there was family life too. Like Dandolo, many never came back; they died of war and plague, were swallowed up by the sea or buried in foreign earth, but Venice was a centrist empire which retained a magnetic hold on its people. The merchant isolated in the *fondaci* of Alexandria, the consul watching the Mongol steppes, the *galeotto* working his oar – for all, the city loomed large. The idea of return was potent – the ship at last passing through the *lidi* again, feeling a different motion to the sea and the familiar skyline rising pale and insubstantial in the shifting light.

People on the quays, watched, idle or intent, for approaching ships. And until a seaman standing in the prow was close enough to shout, those craning to catch his words might wait in trepidation to hear if the news was good or bad – if a husband or son had died at sea, if the deal had been done, if there would be lamentation or joy. Landfall brought all the vicissitudes of life. People returned with gold, spices, plague and grief. Failed admirals came clanking in chains, triumphant ones with trumpets and cannon fire, trailing captured banners in the sea, the gonfalon of St Mark streaming in the wind. Ordelafo Falier stepped down the gangplank with the bones of St Stephen. Pisani's body came packed in salt. Antonio Grimani survived the disgrace of Zonchio and became a doge; so did Gritti the spy. Marco Polo, wild-eyed and anonymous, burst through the door of his house like Ulysses returned – and no one recognised him. Felix Fabri came on the spice fleet of 1480 with the weather so cold that the oars had to break the ice in the canals. He arrived in the dark, just after Christmas. The night was clear and bright; from the deck the snowy tops of the Dolomites glimmered under a large moon. No one could sleep. As dawn rose, the passengers could see the golden roof of the campanile glinting in the sun, topped by the angel Gabriel welcoming them home. All the bells of Venice were ringing for the fleet's return. The ships were dressed with banners and flags; the *galeotti* started to sing and, according to custom, threw their old clothing, rotted by salt and storm, overboard. 'And when we had paid our fare, and the charges,' wrote Fabri,

and tipped the servants who had looked after us, and said goodbye to everyone in our galley, both noblemen and servants, we put all our things into one boat and climbed down into it . . . And although we were glad of our enlargement from that uneasy prison, yet because of the companionship which had grown up between us and the rowers and others, sadness mingled with our joy.

Sources and Bibliography

The bibliography contains all the sources quoted in the book. The sources for the quotations can be found at www.faber.co.uk/work/cityoffortune under the resources section.

ORIGINAL SOURCES

Andrea, Alfred J., *Contemporary Sources for the Fourth Crusade*, Leiden, 2008

Angiolello, Giovan-Maria, *Memoir*, trans. Pierre A. Mackay, at http://angiolello.net, 2006

Barbara, Josafa and Contarini, Ambrogio, *Travels to Tana and Persia*, trans. William Thomas, London, 1873

Barbaro, Nicolo, *Giornale dell'assedio di Costantinopoli 1453*, ed. E. Cornet, Vienna, 1856; (in English) *Diary of the Siege of Constantinople 1453*, trans. J. R. Melville Jones, New York, 1969

Canal, Martino da, *Les Estoires de Venise*, Florence, 1972

Casati, Luigi, *La guerra di Chioggia e la pace di Torino, saggio storico con documenti inediti*, Florence, 1866

Casola, Pietro, *Canon Pietro Casola's Pilgrimage to Jerusalem in the Year 1494*, ed. and trans. M. Margaret Newett, Manchester, 1907

Cassiodorus, *Variaum libri XII*, Letter 24, at www.documentacatholicaomnia.eu, 2006

Chinazzi, Daniele, *Cronaca della guerra di Chioggia*, Milan, 1864

Choniates, Niketas, *Imperii Graeci Historia*, Geneva, 1593; (in English) *O City of Byzantium, Annals of Niketas Choniates*, trans. Harry J. Magoulias, Detroit, 1984

Clari, Robert de, *La Conquête de Constantinople*, trans. Pierre Charlot, Paris, 1939; (in English) *The Conquest of Constantinople*, trans. Edgar Holmes McNeal, New York, 1966

Commynes, Philippe de, *The Memoirs of Philippe de Commines*, trans Andrew Scoble, vol. 1, London, 1855

Comnena, Anna, *The Alexiad of Anna Comnena*, trans. E. R. A. Sewter, London, 1969

Dandolo, Andrea, *Chronica per Extensum Descripta, Rivista Storica Italiana*, vol. 12, part 1, Bologna, 1923

De Caresinis, Raphaynus, *Raphayni de Caresinis Chronica 1343–1388, Rerum Italicarum Scriptores*, vol. 12, part 2, Bologna, 1923

De Monacis, Laurentius (Lorenzo), *Chronicon de Rebus Venetis*, ed. F. Cornelius, Venice, 1758

De' Mussi, Gabriele, 'La peste dell' anno 1348', ed. and trans. A.G. Tononi, *Giornale Ligustico de Archeologia, Storia e Letteratura*, vol. 11, Genoa, 1884

Délibérations des assemblées Vénitiennes concernant la Romanie, 2 vols, ed. and trans. F. Thiriet, Paris, 1971

Die Register Innocenz'III, ed O. Hageneder and A. Haidacher, vol. 1, Graz, 1964

Dotson, John E., *Merchant Culture in Fourteenth Century Venice: the Zibaldone da Canal*, New York, 1994

Fabri, Felix, *The Book of the Wanderings of Brother Felix Fabri*, trans. A. Stewart, vol. 1, London, 1892

Gatari, Galeazzo e Bartolomeo, *Cronaca Carrarese: 1318–1407, Rerum Italicarum Scriptores*, vol. 17, part 1, Bologna, 1909

Gunther of Pairis, *The Capture of Constantinople: The Hystoria Constantinopolitana of Gunther of Paris*, by Alfred J. Andrea, Philadelphia, 1997

Ibn Battuta, *The Travels of Ibn Battuta, AD 1325–54*, trans H. A. R. Gibb, vol. 1, London, 1986

Katip Çelebi, *The History of the Maritime Wars of the Turks*, trans. J. Mitchell, London, 1831 Kinnamos, John, *Deeds of John and Manuel Comnenus*, trans. Charles M. Brand, New York, 1976

Locatelli, Antonio, *Memorie che possono servire alla vita di Vettor Pisani*, Venice, 1767

Machiavelli, Niccolò, *The Prince*, trans. W. K. Marriott, London, 1958

Malipiero, D., 'Annali veneti, 1457–1500', ed. T. Gar and A. Sagredo, *Archivio Storico Italiano*, vol. 7, Florence, 1843

Mehmed II the Conqueror and the Fall of the Franco-Byzantine Levant to the Ottoman Turks: some Western Views and Testimonies, ed. and trans. Marios Philippides, Tempe, 2007

Pagani, Zaccaria, 'La Relation de l'ambassade de Domenico Trevisan auprès du Soudan d'Égypte', in *Le Voyage d'Outre-mer (Égypte, Mont Sinay, Palestine) de Jean Thenaud: Suivi de la relation de l'ambassade de Domenico Trevisan auprès du Soudan d'Égypte*, Paris, 1884

Patrologia Latina, ed. J. P. Migne, vols. 214–215, Paris, 1849–55

Pegolotti, Francesco, *La practica della mercatura*, ed. Allan Evans, New York, 1970

Pertusi, Agostino, *La caduta di Costantinopoli*, 2 vols, Milan, 1976

Petrarca, Francesco, *Epistole di Francesco Petrarca*, ed. Ugo Dotti, Turin, 1978

—, *Lettere senile di Francesco Petrarca*, vol. 1, trans. Giuseppe Francassetti, Florence, 1869

Pokorny, R., ed., 'Zwei unedierte Briefe aus der Frühzeit des Lateinischen Kaiserreichs von Konstantinopel', *Byzantion*, vol. 55, 1985

Polo, Marco, *The Travels*, trans. Ronald Latham, London, 1958

Priuli, G., 'I diarii', ed. A. Segre, *Rerum Italicarum Scriptores*, vol. 24, part 3, 2 vols, Bologna, 1921

Raccolta degli storici italiani dal cinquecento al millecinquecento, in *Rerum Italicarum Scriptores*, new edition, 35 vols, ed. L. A. Muratori, Bologna, 1904–42

Régestes des délibérations du sénat de Venise concernant la Romanie, 3 vols, ed. and trans. F. Thiriet, Paris, 1961

Rizzardo, Giacomo, *La presa di Negroponte fatta dai Turchi ai Veneziani*, Venice, 1844

Sanudo (or Sanuto), Marino, *I diarii di Marino Sanuto*, 58 vols, Venice 1879–1903

—, *Venice, Città Excelentissima: Selections from the Renaissance Diaries of Marin Sanudo*, ed. and trans. Patricia H. Labalme, Laura Sanguineti White and Linda L. Carroll, Baltimore, 2008

Stella, Georgius et Iohannus, 'Annales Genuenses', *Rerum Italicarum Scriptores*, vol. 17, part 2, Bologna, 1975

Tafur, Pero, *Travels and Adventures, 1435–1439*, ed. and trans. Malcolm Letts, London, 1926

Villehardouin, Geoffroi de, *La Conquête de Constantinople*, trans. Émile Bouchet, Paris, 1891; (in English) Geoffrey of Villehardouin, *Chronicles of the Crusades*, trans. Caroline Smith, London, 2008

William, Archbishop of Tyre, *A History of Deeds done beyond the Sea*, vol. 1, trans. Emily Atwater Babcock, New York, 1943

MODERN WORKS

Angold, Michael, *The Fourth Crusade: Event and Context*, Harlow, 2003

Antoniadis, Sophia, 'Le récit du combat naval de Gallipoli chez Zancaruolo en comparison avec le texte d'Antoine Morosini et les historiens grecs du XVe siècle' in *Venezia e l'Oriente fra tardo Medioevo e Rinascimento*, ed . A. Pertusi, Rome, 1966

Arbel, B., 'Colonie d'oltremare', *Storia di Venezia*, vol. 5, Rome, 1996

Ascherson, Neal, *Black Sea*, London, 1995

Ashtor, Eliyahu, 'L'Apogée du commerce Vénitien au Levant: un nouvel essai d'explication', in *Venezia, centro di mediazione tra Oriente e Occidente (secoli XV–XVI): aspetti e problemi*, vol. 1

—, *Levant Trade in the Later Middle Ages*, Princeton, 1983

Babinger, Franz, *Mehmet the Conqueror and his Time*, Princeton, 1978

Balard, M., 'La lotta contro Genova', *Storia di Venezia*, vol. 3, Rome, 1997

Berindei, Mihnea and O'Riordan, Giustiniana Migliardi, 'Venise et la horde d'Or, fin XIIIe–début XIVe siècle', *Cahiers du Monde Russe*, vol. 29, 1988

Borsari, Silvano, 'I Veneziani delle colonie', *Storia di Venezia*, vol. 3, Rome, 1997

Brand, Charles, M., *Byzantium Confronts the West 1180–1204*, Cambridge, 1968

Bratianu, Georges I., *La Mer Noire: des origines à la conquête Ottomane*, Munich, 1969

Brown, Horatio F., 'The Venetians and the Venetian Quarter in Constantinople to the Close of the Twelfth Century', *Journal of Hellenic Studies*, vol. 40, 1920

Brown, Patricia Fortini, *Venetian Narrative Painting in the Age of Carpaccio*, New Haven, 1988

Buonsanti, Michele and Galla, Alberta, *Candia Venezia: Venetian Itineraries Through Crete*, Heraklion, (undated)

Campbell, Caroline and Chong, Alan (eds), *Bellini and the East*, London, 2006

Cessi, R., *La repubblica di Venezia e il problema adriatico*, Naples, 1953

——, *Storia della repubblica di Venezia*, vols 1 and 2, Milan, 1968

Cessi, R. and Alberti, A., *Rialto: l'isola, il ponte, il mercato*, Bologna, 1934

Chareyron, Nicole, *Pilgrims to Jerusalem in the Middle Ages*, trans. W. Donald Wilson, New York, 2005

Ciggaar, Krijnie, *Western Travellers to Constantinople*, London, 1996

Clot, André, *Mehmed II, le conquérant de Byzance*, Paris, 1990

Coco, Carla, *Venezia levantina*, Venice, 1993

Constable, Olivia Remie, *Housing the Stranger in the Mediterranean World: Lodging, Trade, and Travel in Late Antiquity and the Middle Ages*, Cambridge, 2004

Crouzet-Pavan, Elisabeth, *Venice Triumphant: the Horizons of a Myth*, trans. Lydia G. Cochrane, Baltimore, 1999

Crowley, Roger, *Constantinople: The Last Great Siege*, London, 2005

Curatola, Giovanni, 'Venetian Merchants and Travellers', *Alexandria, Real and Imagined*, ed. Anthony Hirst and Michael Silk, Aldershot, 2004

Davis, James C., 'Shipping and Spying in the Early Career of a Venetian Doge, 1496–1502', *Studi veneziani*, vol. 16, 1974

Detorakis, Theocharis E., *History of Crete*, trans. John C. Davis, Heraklion, 1994

Dotson, John, 'Fleet Operations in the First Genoese–Venetian war, 1264–1266', *Viator: Medieval and Renaissance Studies*, vol. 30, 1999

—, 'Foundations of Venetian Naval Strategy from Pietro II Orseolo to the Battle of Zonchio', *Viator: Medieval and Renaissance Studies*, vol. 32, 2001

—, 'Venice, Genoa and Control of the Seas in the Thirteenth and Fourteenth Centuries', in *War at Sea in the Middle Ages and the Renaissance*, ed. John B. Hattendorf and Richard W. Unger, Woodbridge, 2003

Doumerc, B., 'An Exemplary Maritime Republic: Venice at the End of the Middle Ages', in *War at Sea in the Middle Ages and the Renaissance*, ed. John B. Hattendorf and Richard W. Unger, Woodbridge, 2003

—, 'De l'Incompétence à la trahison: les commandants de galères Vénitiens face aux Turcs (1499–1500)', *Felonie, Trahison, Reniements aux Moyen Age*, Montpellier, 1997

—, 'Il dominio del mare', *Storia di Venezia*, vol. 4, Rome, 1996

—, 'La difesa dell'impero', *Storia di Venezia*, vol. 3, Rome, 1997

Duby, Georges and Lobrichon, Guy, *History of Venice in Painting*, New York, 2007

Dursteler, Eric R., 'The Bailo in Constantinople; Crisis and Career in

Venice's Early Modern Diplomatic Corps', *Mediterranean Historical Review*, vol. 16, no. 2, 2001

Epstein, Steven, A., *Genoa and the Genoese, 958–1528*, Chapel Hill, 1996

Fabris, Antonio, 'From Adrianople to Constantinople: Venetian–Ottoman Diplomatic Missions, 1360–1453', *Mediterranean Historical Review*, vol. 7, no. 2, 1992

Fenlon, Iain, *Piazza San Marco*, Boston, 2009

Forbes-Boyd, Eric, *Aegean Quest*, London, 1970

Freedman, Paul, *Out of the East: Spices and the Medieval Imagination*, New Haven, 2008

Freely, John, *The Bosphorus*, Istanbul, 1993

Freeman, Charles, *The Horses of St Mark's*, London, 2004

Geary, Patrick J., *Furta Sacra: Theft of Relics in the Central Middle Ages*, Princeton, 1978

Georgopoulou, Maria, *Venice's Mediterranean Colonies: Architecture and Urbanism*, Cambridge, 2001

Gertwagen, Ruthy, 'The Contribution of Venice's colonies to its Naval Warfare in the Eastern Mediterranean in the Fifteenth Century', at www.storiamediterranea.it (undated)

Gill, Joseph, 'Franks, Venetians and Pope Innocent III 1201–1203', *Studi veneziani*, vol. 12, Florence, 1971

Goy, Richard, *Chioggia and the Villages of the Lagoon*, Cambridge, 1985

Gullino, G., 'Le frontiere navali', *Storia di Venezia*, vol. 4, Rome, 1996

Hale, J. R., ed., *Renaissance Venice*, London, 1973

Hall, Richard, *Empires of the Monsoon: a History of the Indian Ocean and its Invaders*, London, 1996

Harris, Jonathan, *Byzantium and the Crusades*, London, 2003

Hazlitt, William Carew, *The History of the Origin and Rise of the Republic of Venice*, 2 vols, London, 1858

Heyd, W., *Histoire du commerce du Levant au Moyen-Age*, 2 vols, Leipzig, 1936

Hodgkinson, Harry, *The Adriatic Sea*, London, 1955

Hodgson, F. C., *The Early History of Venice: from the Foundation to the Conquest of Constantinople*, London, 1901

—, *Venice in the Thirteenth and Fourteenth centuries, 1204–1400*, London, 1910

Horrox, R., *The Black Death*, Manchester, 1994

Howard, Deborah, *The Architectural History of Venice*, New Haven, 2002

—, *Venice and the East*, London, 2000

—, 'Venice as a Dolphin: Further Investigation into Jacopo de' Barbari's View', *Artibus et Historiae*, vol. 35, 1997

Imber, Colin, *The Ottoman Empire 1300–1600: the Structure of Power*, Basingstoke, 2002

Karpov, Sergei P., 'Génois et Byzantins face à la crise de Tana 1343, d'après les documents d'archives inédits', *Byzantinische Forschungen*, vol. 22, 1996

—, *La navigazione veneziana nel Mar Nero XIII–XV secoli*, Ravenna, 2000

—, 'Venezia e Genova: rivalita e collaborazione a Trebisonda e Tana. Secoli XIII–XV', *Genova, Venezia, il Levante nei secoli XII–XIV*, ed. Gherardo Ortali and Dino Puncuk, Venice, 2001

Katele, Irene B., 'Piracy and the Venetian State: the Dilemma of Maritime Defense in the Fourteenth Century', *Speculum*, vol. 63, no. 4, 1988

Keay, John, *The Spice Trade*, London, 2006

Kedar, Benjamin, *Merchants in Crisis: Genoese and Venetian Men of Affairs and the Fourteenth-century Depression*, New Haven, 1976

King, Charles, *The Black Sea: A History*, Oxford, 2005

Krekic, B., 'Venezia e l'Adriatico', in *Storia di Venezia*, vol. 3, Rome, 1997

Lamma, P., 'Venezia nel giudizio delle fonti Bizantine dal X al XII secolo', *Rivista Storica Italiana*, vol. 74, 1960

Lane, Frederic C., *Andrea Barbarigo, Merchant of Venice 1418–1449*, Baltimore, 1944

—, 'Naval Actions and Fleet Organization, 1499–1502', *Renaissance Venice*, ed. J. R. Hale, London, 1973

—, *Venetian Ships and Shipbuilders of the Renaissance*, Baltimore, 1934

—, *Venice and History*, Baltimore, 1966

—, *Venice: A Maritime Republic*, Baltimore, 1973

Lazzarini, Vittorio, 'Aneddoti della vita di Vettor Pisani', *Archivio Veneto*, series 5, 1945

Lock, Peter, *The Franks in the Aegean: 1204–1500*, London, 1995

Lunde, Paul, 'The Coming of the Portuguese', *Saudi Aramco World*, vol. 56, no. 4

—, 'Monsoons, Mude and Gold', *Saudi Aramco World*, vol. 56, no. 4

Luzzatto, G., *Storia economica di Venezia dall'XI al XVI secolo*, Venice, 1961

MacKay, Pierre A., 'Notes on the sources. The Manuscript, Contemporary Sources, Maps and Views of Negroponte', at http://angiolello.net, 2006

Mackintosh-Smith, Tim, *Travels with a Tangerine*, London, 2002

Madden, T., *Enrico Dandolo and the Rise of Venice*, Baltimore, 2003

—, 'The Fires of the Fourth Crusade in Constantinople, 1203–1204: a Damage Assessment', *Byzantinische Zeitschrift* 84/85, 1992

—, 'Venice and Constantinople in 1171 and 1172: Enrico Dandolo's Attitude towards Byzantium', *Mediterranean Historical Review*, vol. 8, 1993

Madden, T. and Queller, Donald E., 'Some Further Arguments in Defense of the Venetians on the Fourth Crusade', *Byzantion*, vol. 62, 1992

Martin, Lillian Ray, *The Art and Archaeology of Venetian Ships and Boats*, London, 2001

Martin, Michael Edward, *The Venetians in the Black Sea 1204–1453*, PhD thesis, University of Birmingham, 1989

McKee, Sally, 'The Revolt of St Tito in Fourteenth-century Venetian Crete: a Reassessment', *Mediterranean Historical Review*, vol. 9, no. 2, Dec. 1994

—, *Uncommon Dominion: Venetian Crete and the Myth of Ethnic Purity*, Philadelphia, 2000

McNeill, William H., *Venice: the Hinge of Europe, 1081–1797*, Chicago, 1974

Meserve, Margaret, 'News from Negroponte: Politics, Popular Opinion, and Information Exchange in the First Decade of the Italian Press', *Renaissance Quarterly*, vol. 59, no. 2, Summer 2006

Miller, William, *Essays on the Latin Orient*, Cambridge, 1921

——, *Latins in the Levant: a History of Frankish Greece: 1204–1566*, Cambridge, 1908

Mollat, Michel, Braunstein, Philippe and Hocquet, Jean Claude, 'Reflexions sur l'expansion Vénitienne en Méditerranée', *Venezia e il Levante fino al secolo XV*, vol. 1, Florence, 1974

Morris, Jan, *The Venetian Empire: A Sea Voyage*, London, 1990

Muir, Edward, *Civic Ritual in Renaissance Venice*, Princeton, 1981

Nicol, Donald M., *Byzantium and Venice: A Study in Diplomatic and Cultural Relations*, Cambridge, 1992

Norwich, John Julius, *Byzantium*, vols 2 and 3, London, 1991 and 1995

—, *A History of Venice*, London, 1982

Nystazupoulou Pelekidis, Marie, 'Venise et la Mer Noire du XIe au XVe siècle', *Venezia e il Levante fino al secolo XV*, Florence, 1974

O'Connell, Monique, *Men of Empire: Power and Negotiation in Venice's Maritime State*, Baltimore, 2009

Papacostea, Şerban, 'Quod non iretur ad Tanam: un aspect fondamental de la politique génoise dans la Mer Noire au XIVe siècle', *Revue des études Sud-est Européennes*, vol. 17, no. 2, 1979

Phillips, Jonathan, *The Fourth Crusade and the Sack of Constantinople*, London, 2004

Prawer, Joshua, *The Latin Kingdom of Jerusalem: European Colonialism in the Middle Ages*, London, 1972

Prescott, H. F. M., *Jerusalem Journey: Pilgrimage to the Holy Land in the Fifteenth Century*, London, 1954

—, *Once to Sinai: the Further Pilgrimage of Friar Felix Fabri*, London, 1957

Quarta Crociata: Venezia, Bisanzio, Impero Latino, ed. Gherardo Ortalli, Giorgio Ravegnani and Peter Schreiner, Venice, 2004

Queller, Donald E., and Madden, Thomas F., *The Fourth Crusade: the Conquest of Constantinople*, Philadelphia, 1997

Romanin, S., *Storia documentata di Venezia*, 10 vols, Venice, 1912–21

Rose, Susan, 'Venetians, Genoese and Turks: the Mediterranean 1300–1500', at http://ottomanmilitary.devhub.com, 2010

Runciman, Steven, *A History of the Crusades*, 3 vols, London, 1990

Schlumberger, Gustave, *La Prise de Saint-Jean-D'Acre en l'an 1291 par l'armée du Soudan d'Égypte*, Paris, 1914

Setton, Kenneth M., *The Papacy and the Levant (1204–1571)*, vol. 2, Philadelphia, 1978

—, 'Saint George's Head,' *Speculum*, vol. 48, no. 1, 1973

Sorbelli, Albano, 'La lotta tra Genova e Venezia per il dominio del Mediterraneo 1350–1355', *Memorie delle Reale Accademia della Scienza dell'Instituto di Bologna*, series 1, vol. 5, Bologna, 1910–11

Spufford, Peter, *Power and Profit: the Merchant in Medieval Europe*, London, 2003

Stöckly, Doris, *La Système de l'incanto des galéés du marché à Venise*, Leiden, 1995

Storia di Venezia, 12 vols, Rome, 1991–7

Tadic, J., 'Venezia e la costa orientale dell'Adriatico fino al secolo XV', *Venezia e il Levante fino al secolo XV*, vol. 1

Tenenti, Alberto, 'Il senso del mare', *Storia di Venezia*, vol. 12, Rome, 1991

—, 'Le temporali calamità', in *Storia di Venezia*, vol. 3, Rome, 1997

—, 'The Sense of Space and Time in the Venetian World of the Fifteenth and Sixteenth Centuries', *Renaissance Venice*, ed. J. R. Hale, London, 1973

—, 'Venezia e la pirateria nel Levante: 1300–1460', *Venezia e il Levante fino al secolo XV*, vol. 1

Thiriet, F., *La Romanie vénitienne au moyen age*, Paris, 1959

—, 'Venise et l'occupation de Ténédos au XIVe siècle', *Mélanges d'archéologie et d'histoire*, vol. 65, no. 1, 1953

Thubron, Colin, *The Seafarers: Venetians*, London, 2004

Tucci, Ugo, 'La spedizione marittima', *Venezia, Bisanzio, Impero Latino*, ed. Gherardo Ortalli, Giorgio Ravegnani and Peter Schreiner, Venice, 2006

—, 'Tra Venezia e mondo turco: i mercanti', *Venezia e i Turchi, Scontri e confronti di due civiltà*, ed. Anna Della Valle, Milan, 1985

Venezia, centro di mediazione tra Oriente e Occidente, secoli XV–XVI: aspetti e problemi, 2 vols, ed. Hans-Georg Beck, Manoussos Manoussacas and Agostino Pertusi, Florence, 1977

Venezia e il Levante fino al secolo XV, 2 vols, ed. Agostino Pertusi, Florence, 1973–4

Venezia e I Turchi: Scontri e Confronti di Due Civilita, ed. A. Tenenti, Milan, 1985

Venice and the Islam World, 828–1797, ed. Stefano Carboni, New York, 2007

Verlinden, Charles, 'Venezia e il commercio degli schiavi provenienti dalle coste orientali del Mediterraneo', *Venezia e il Levante fino al secolo XV*, vol. 1

Wolff, Anne, 'Merchants, Pilgrims, Naturalists: Alexandria through European Eyes from the Fourteenth to the Sixteenth Century', *Alexandria, Real and Imagined*, ed. Anthony Hirst and Michael Silk, Aldershot, 2004

Zanon, Luigi Gigio, *La galea veneziana*, Venice, 2004

Acknowledgements

Many thanks to Julian Loose and the team at Faber, particularly Kate Ward, for taking so much trouble over this book and for ensuring such a handsome finished result, and to my agent, Andrew Lownie. I also had invaluable help along the way from Ron Morton and Jim Green who took the time to read and comment on the manuscript, whilst Stephen Scoffham handily pointed out that Malacca once had its hands on Venice's throat. To Ron and Rita Morton a second thank you is due for having me to stay in Athens during a tour of the Stato da Mar – and to Jan, as ever, for assisting the book writing in so many different ways and with such good humour.

I am grateful to the following authors and publishers for permission to reproduce material included here: Dr Pierre A. MacKay for extracts from his translation of *The Memoir of Giovan-Maria Angiolello* which is published at www.angiolello.net; Brill for extracts from *Contemporary Sources for the Fourth Crusade* by Alfred J. Andrea, 2008.

Index

Also by Roger Crowley

ff

Empires of the Sea: The Final Battle for the
Mediterranean, 1521–1580

When Suleiman the Magnificent's invasion fleet set sail for
Rhodes in 1521, it was the start of a sixty-year epic struggle for
control of the Mediterranean. This is a breathtaking story of mil-
itary crusading, Barbary pirates, white slavery and the Ottoman
Empire – as well as the contest between Islam and Christianity,
East and West. In this sweeping narrative history, Roger Crowley
takes us from Istanbul to the Gates of Gibraltar, introduces us to
extraordinary warriors including the pirate Barbarossa and the
Knights of St John, and brings vividly to life the bloody siege of
Malta and the shattering final sea battle at Lepanto.

Sunday Times History Book of the Year 2008

'Riveting . . . narrative history at its best.'
Andrew Taylor, *Spectator* Books of the Year

'Nothing less than thrilling. His descriptions of the great set
pieces – the siege of Malta and the battle of Lepanto – left me
holding my breath.'
Michael Prodger, *Sunday Telegraph* Books of the Year

ff

Constantinople: The Last Great Siege, 1453

In the spring of 1453, the Ottoman Turks advanced on Constantinople in pursuit of an ancient Islamic dream: capturing the thousand-year-old capital of Christian Byzantium. During the siege that followed, a small band of defenders, outnumbered ten to one, confronted the might of the Ottoman army in an epic contest fought on land, sea and underground.

'One of the most exciting, cliff-hanging stories in world history, and in Roger Crowley's book it is told extremely well.'
Noel Malcolm, *Sunday Telegraph*

'In this account of the 1453 siege, written in crackling prose . . . we are treated to narrative history at its most enthralling.'
Christopher Silvester, *Daily Express*

'A vivid and readable account of the siege . . . [And] an excellent traveller's guide to how and why Istanbul became a Muslim city.'
Philip Mansel, *Guardian*

ff

Faber and Faber is one of the great independent publishing houses. We were established in 1929 by Geoffrey Faber with T. S. Eliot as one of our first editors. We are proud to publish award-winning fiction and non-fiction, as well as an unrivalled list of poets and playwrights. Among our list of writers we have five Booker Prize winners and twelve Nobel Laureates, and we continue to seek out the most exciting and innovative writers at work today.

Find out more about our authors and books
faber.co.uk

Read our blog for insight and opinion on books and the arts
thethoughtfox.co.uk

Follow news and conversation
twitter.com/faberbooks

Watch readings and interviews
youtube.com/faberandfaber

Connect with other readers
facebook.com/faberandfaber

Explore our archive
flickr.com/faberandfaber